VIZ GRAPHIC NOVEL

MOBILE SUIT
GUNDAM
0079

VOL. 1

By KAZUHISA KONDO

MOBILE SUIT
GUNDAM 0079

The official adaptation of the anime series Mobile Suit Gundam

A 43-episode animated series that began airing in Japan in 1979, **Mobile Suit Gundam** was unusual for a Japanese "giant robot" show in its grim war story and its then-revolutionary concept of using the robots (or "mobile suits," in this case) as mass-produced war machines, like tanks or planes, rather than more colorful, super-hero-like, transforming robots. Edited together into three two-hour movies (**Gundam I, II** and **III**), the **Gundam** saga was released in theaters in 1981 and 1982 to enthusiastic crowds. The resulting boom in toy model kits from the series elevated **Gundam** to legendary status, and animated sequels, comics, and merchandise have been continuously produced for over 20 years to this day.

In condensing the series into six hours, the movie editions removed many of the nuances of the TV series version, as well as several of the more colorful machines. **Gundam 0079**, by using the TV series continuity for much of its story, gives readers who may have only seen the movie editions a look at the whole story with which Japanese viewers are familar. The **Mobile Suit Gundam** TV series is still often rerun on Japanese TV.

STORY

In the not-so-far-off future, Earth's increasing population forces mankind to emigrate into space. Gigantic, orbiting space colonies are built around the Earth to house humanity's billions, and within half a century, entire nations of human beings call these space colonies their homeland.

In the calendar year of the Universal Century 0079, the furthest group of colonies from Earth, Side 3, took the new name "Duchy of Zeon" and began a war of inde-pendence against the Earth Federation government. In slightly over a month of battle, both the Duchy of Zeon and the Federation saw half their populations die. The Zeon forces' use of a new weapon, a humanoid-shaped fighting unit called a "mobile suit," gave it the advantage in battle.

A temporary truce was called, a treaty was signed to prevent the use of nuclear weapons and poison gas, and the war came to a stalemate for a little more than eight months.

Now, the war in space is advancing once again, and on the colony outpost of Side 7, the Federation has been developing its own mobile suits....

CHARACTERS

AMURO RAY

A 15-year-old civilian on the Side 7 colony, Amuro is very intelligent and skilled with machines. Due to his father's frequent business trips, he spends much of his time alone.

TEM RAY

Amuro's father, a Federation engineer and the designer of the Gundam mobile suit.

CAPTAIN PAOLO CASSIUS

Captain of the Federation ship *White Base*.

BRIGHT NOAH

A cadet in training on the Federation mobile suit carrier *White Base*.

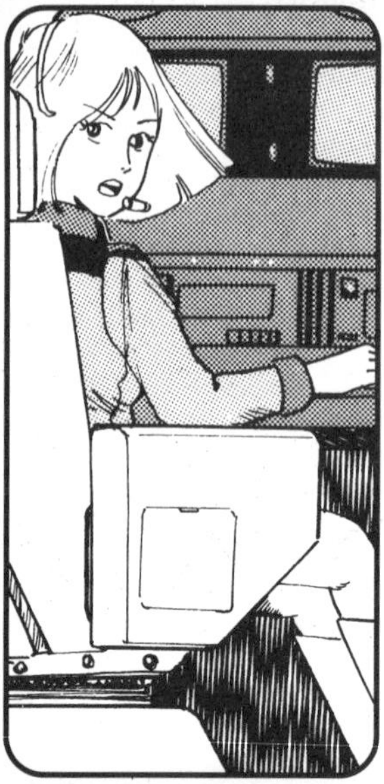

SAYLA MASS

An aloof medical student at Side 7. Her past is something of a mystery.

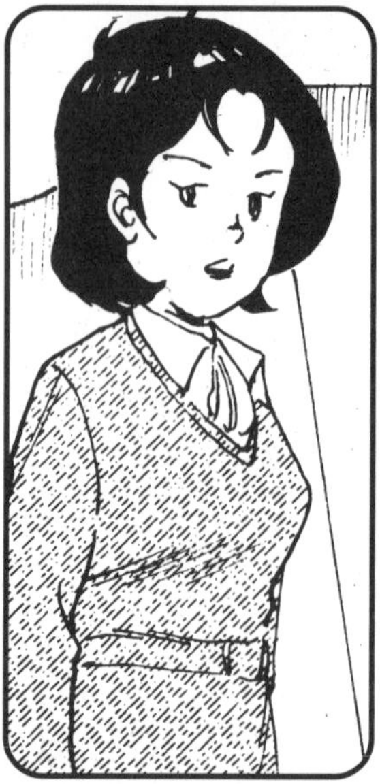

MIRAI YASHIMA

An 18-year-old civilian who carries a space-glider license, Mirai hails from an influential family.

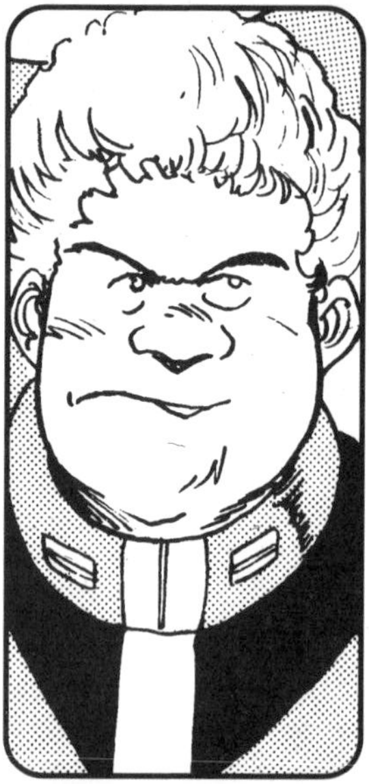

RYU JOSÉ

An 18-year-old pilot-cadet on the *White Base*.

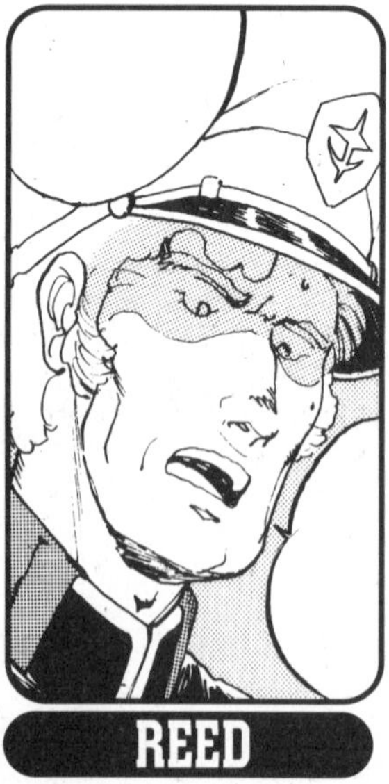

REED

Brash and bullying commander of a Salamis-class cruiser.

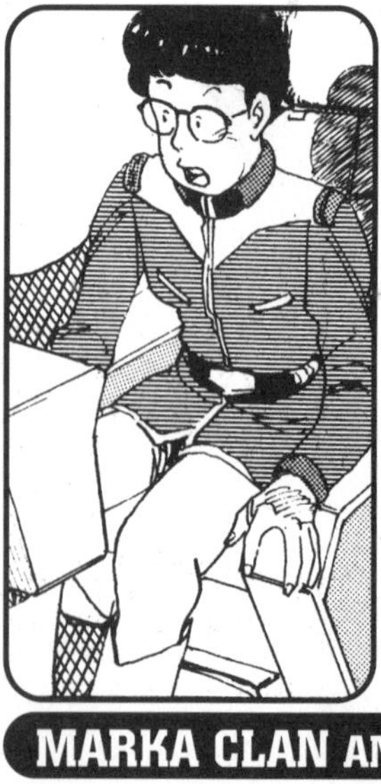

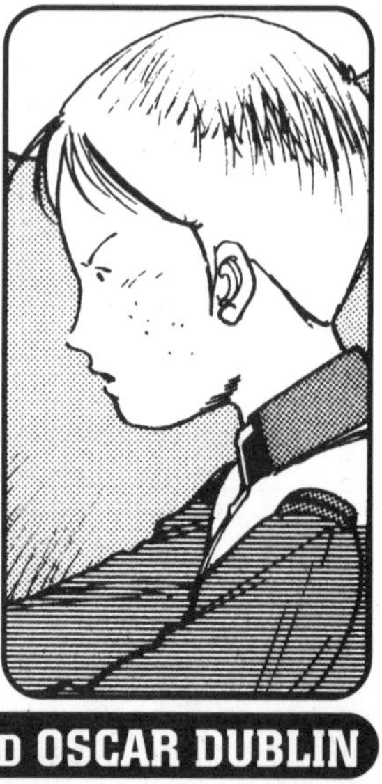

MARKA CLAN AND OSCAR DUBLIN

The *White Base*'s replacement bridge operators, Marka and Oscar sit above the captain's seat. Their specialty is announcing incoming enemy attacks.

CHARACTERS

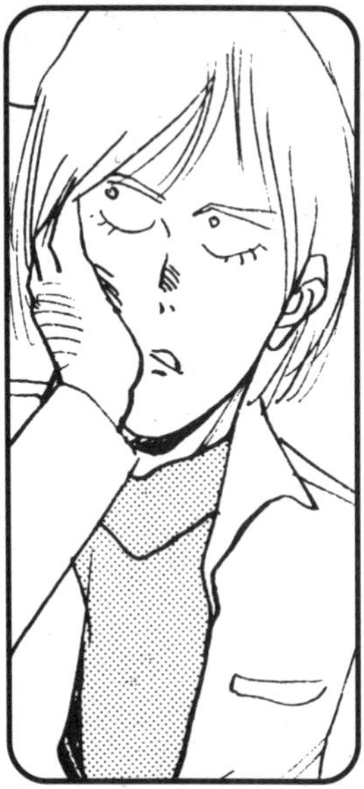

KAI SHIDEN

A 17-year-old civilian and Side 7 citizen, Kai is a confirmed cynic, coward, and complainer.

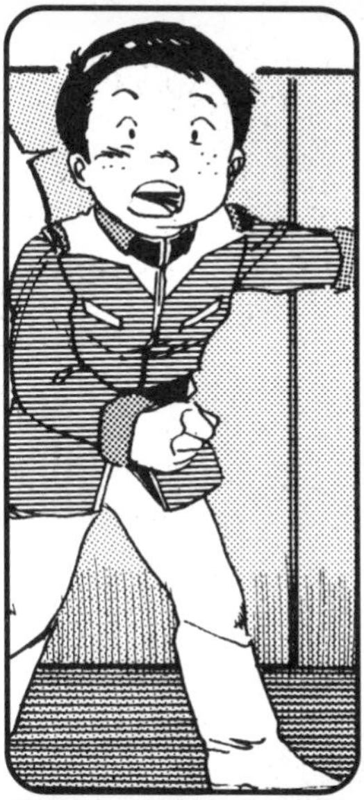

HAYATO KOBAYASHI

Amuro's neighbor on Side 7, Hayato is shy but courageous and practices judo.

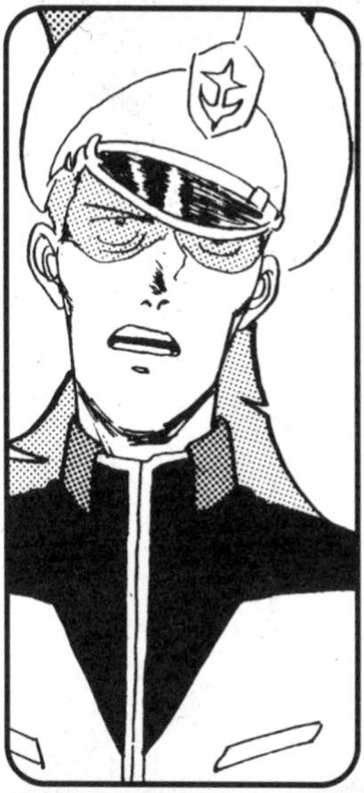

WAKKEIN

The acting commander of the Federation asteroid base Luna 2, Wakkein is overly obsessed with following military procedeure.

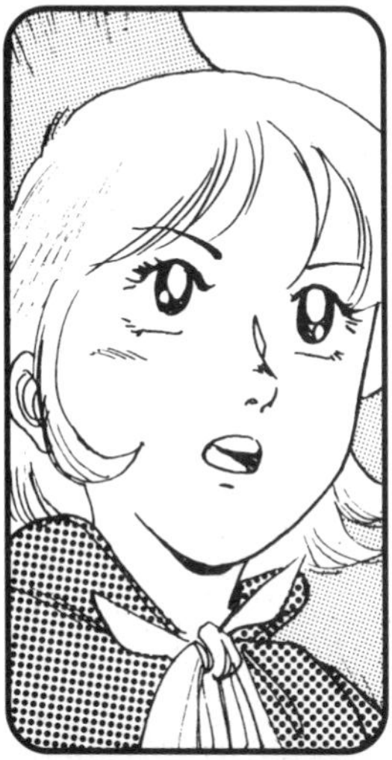

FRAU BOW

Amuro's friend and neighbor who looks after him while his father is away.

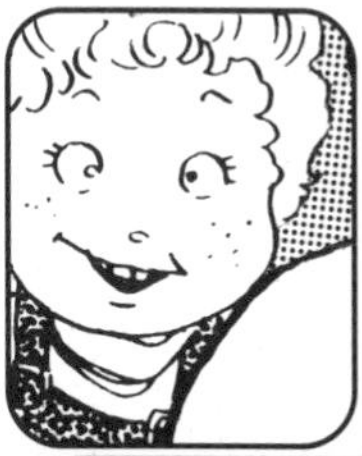
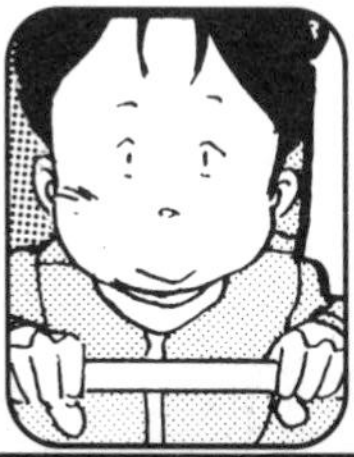
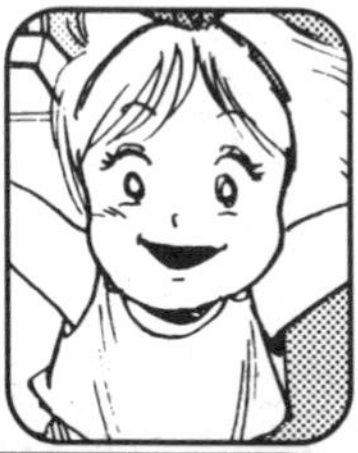

KATSU HAWIN, RETSU COFAN, AND KIKKA KIKAMOTO

A noisy trio of war orphans from Side 7.

HARO

A 16-inch spherical robot, built by Amuro. Haro can briefly take to the air by flapping its access-panel "ears," and is equipped with retractable arms and legs.

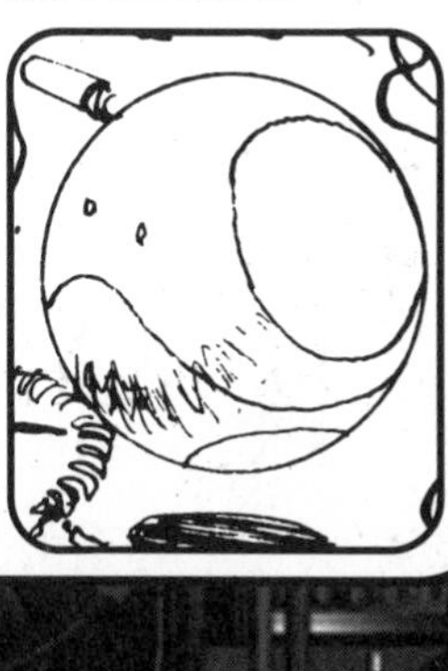

CHAR AZNABLE

Commander of a Zeon Musai-class cruiser, Lt. Commander Char Aznable is one of Zeon's most celebrated aces and his nickname, the "Red Comet," inspires terror among the Federal forces. Char's curious face mask is a hint that there are more than a few mysteries to his background....

GARMA ZABI

The youngest of the Zabi family, Garma is his father's choice as successor to one day take over the Duchy. Although inexperienced and somewhat naïve, Garma's charisma and boyish good looks have made him immensely popular with the Zeon people. He commands the Earth Attack Force, and reports to his older sister Kishiria.

GADEM

A veteran soldier who commands a Papua-class supply ship. He also pilots an antique model of Zaku, which is now used only for mundane labor.

DOREN

Char's trusted aide. On those frequent occasions when his superior is engaged in mobile suit combat, Doren serves as acting captain of Char's cruiser.

GENE

A member of Denim's mobile suit squad. Gene's aggression and ambition inspire him to launch an unauthorized attack inside the Side 7 colony.

DENIM

One of Char's underlings, cautious Denim commands the mobile suit squad that infiltrates the Side 7 research colony.

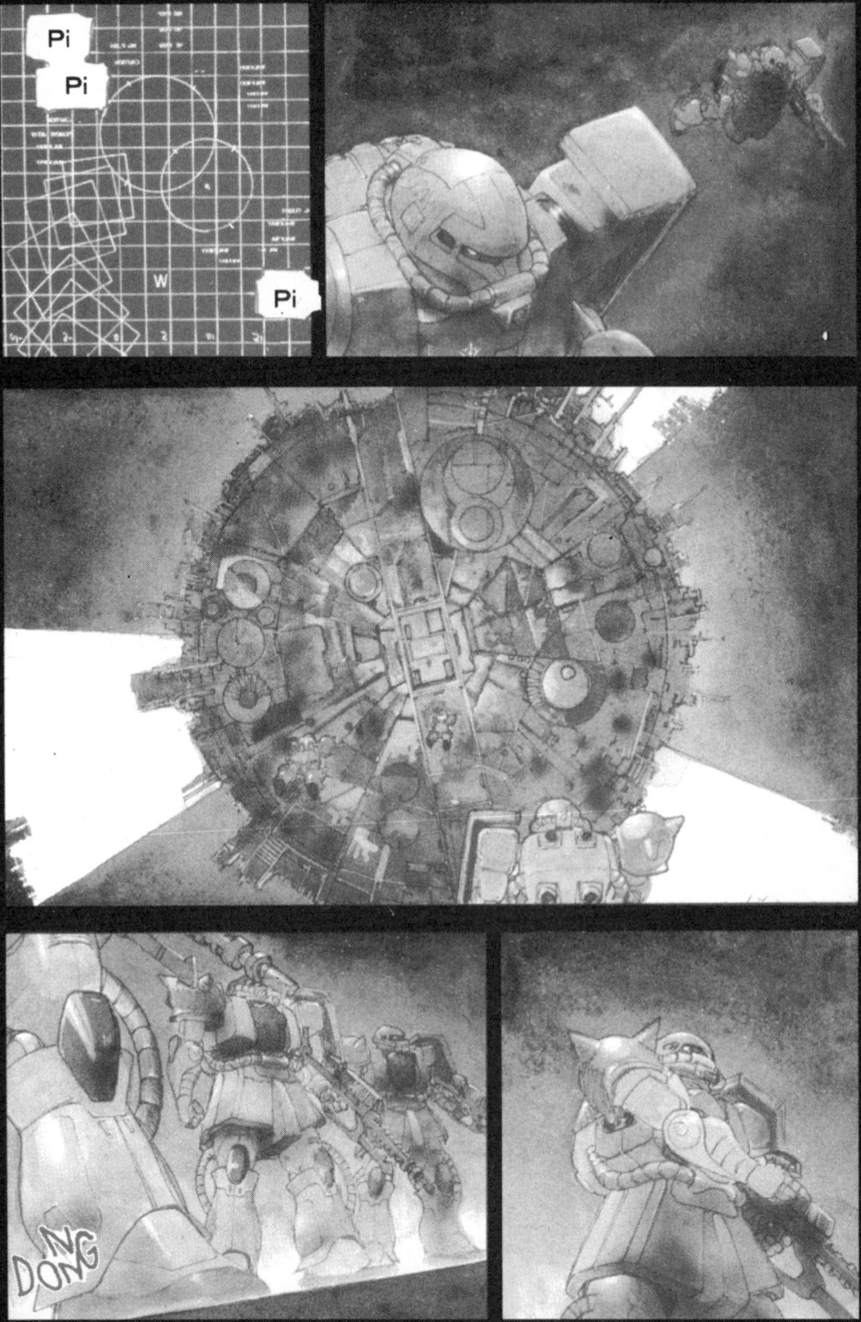
Pi
Pi
Pi
NG
DONG

MOBILE SUIT GUNDAM 0079

THE YEAR OF WAR

Original Story by
HAJIME YADATE
YOSHIYUKI TOMINO

Artwork by
KAZUHISA KONDO

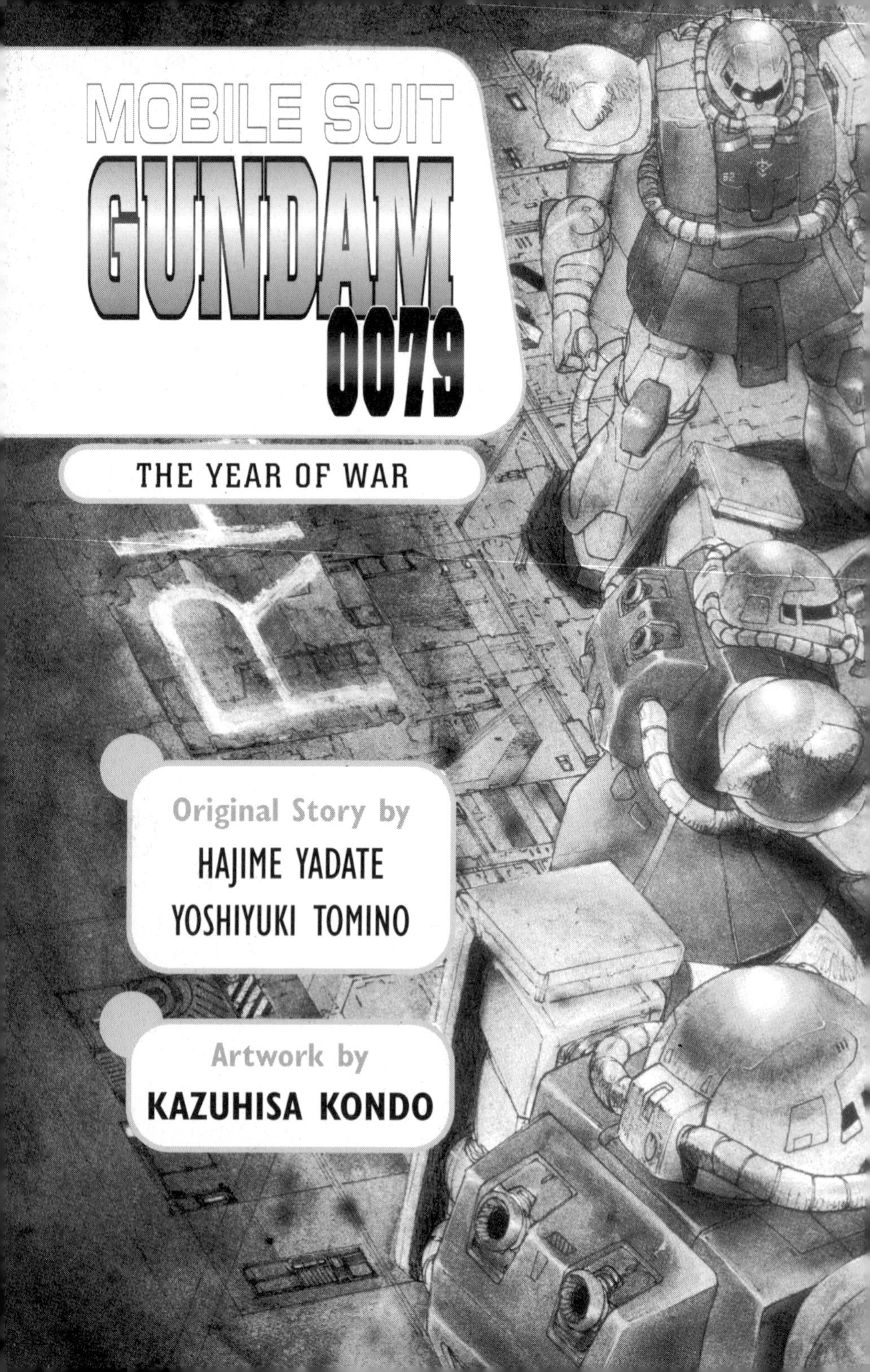

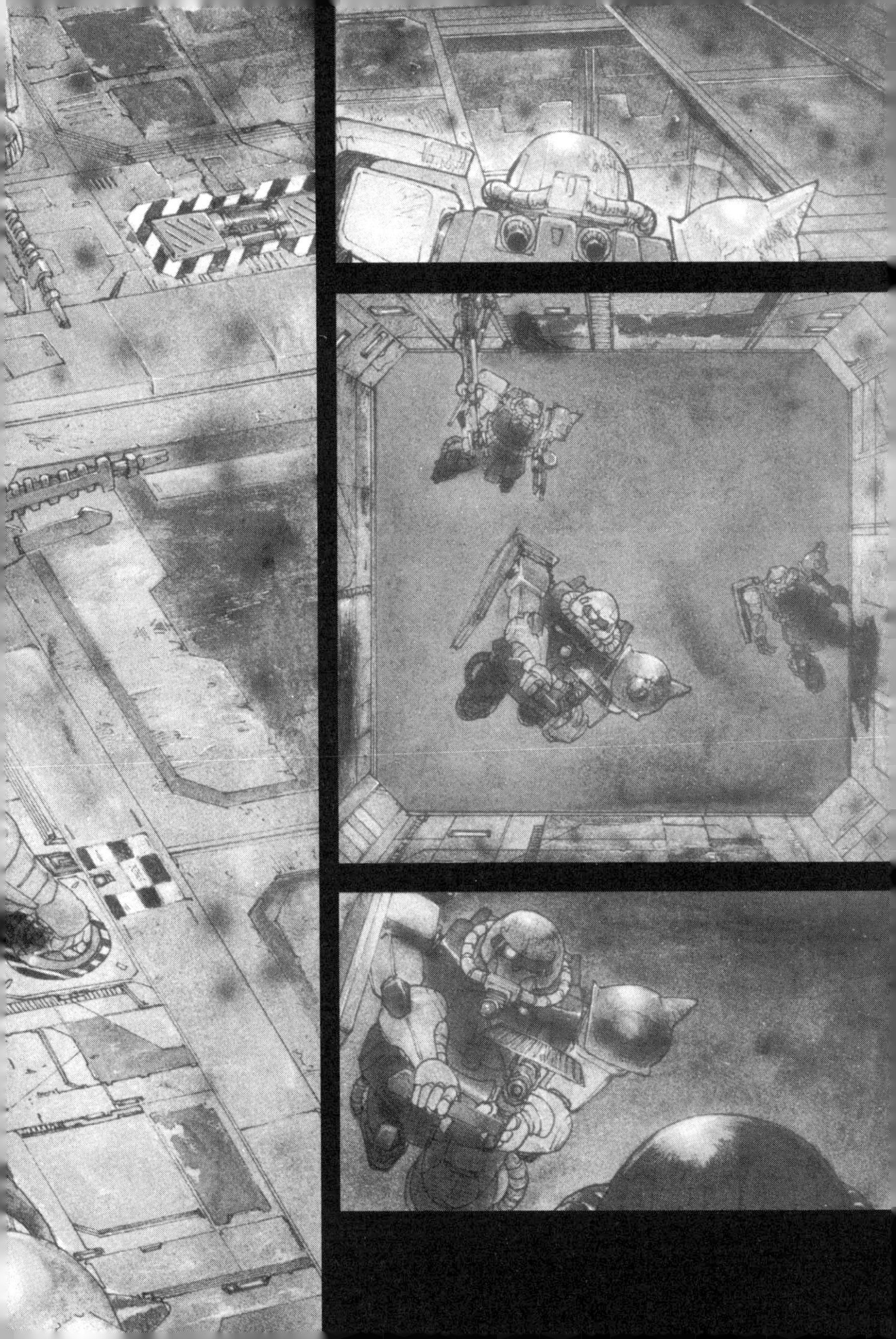

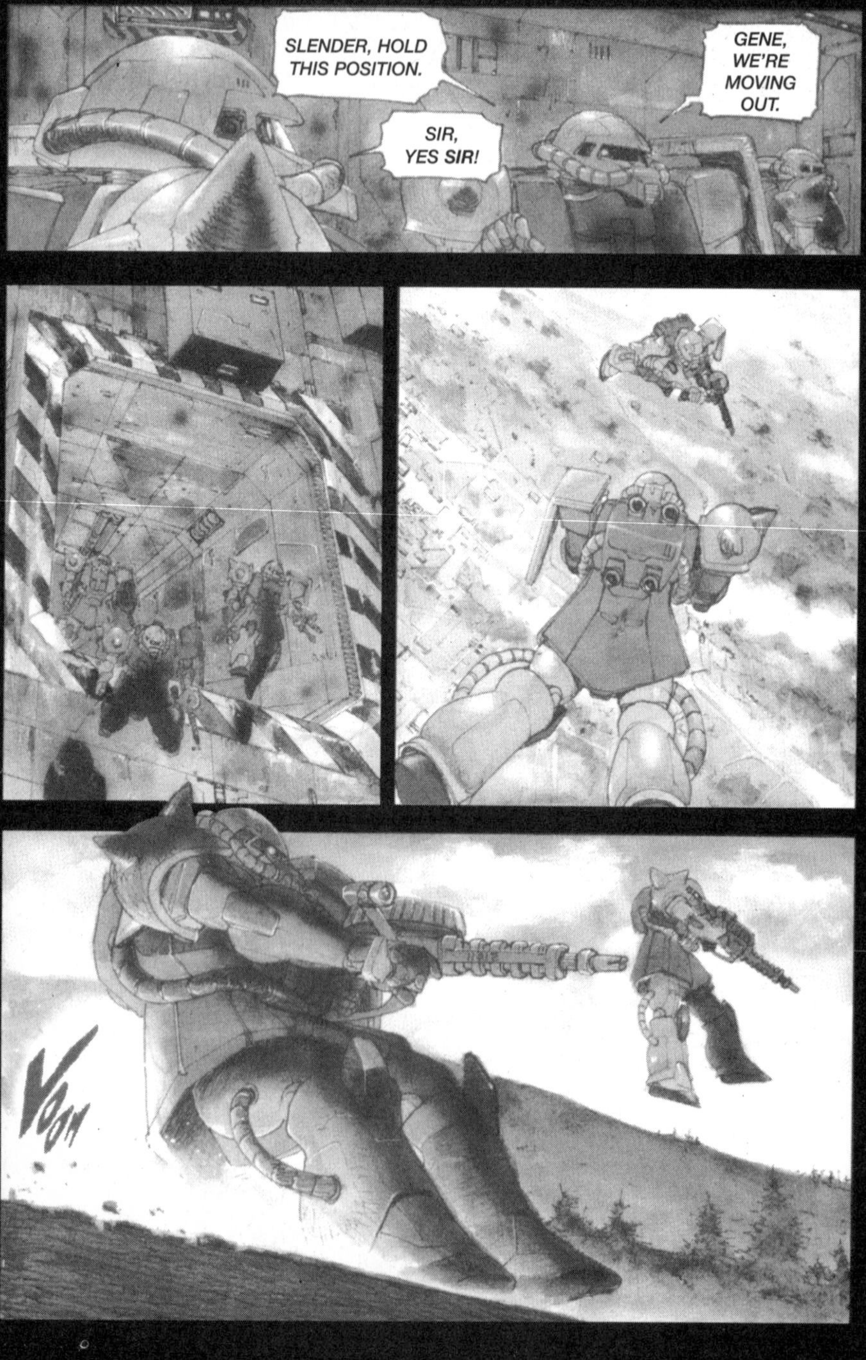
SLENDER, HOLD THIS POSITION.
SIR, YES SIR!
GENE, WE'RE MOVING OUT.
VOOM

WITH THE POPULATION EXPLOSION, MANKIND WAS FORCED TO EMIGRATE INTO SPACE. WITHIN HALF A CENTURY, ENTIRE NATIONS OF HUMAN BEINGS BEGAN TO CALL THE GIANT SPACE COLONIES THEIR HOMELAND.

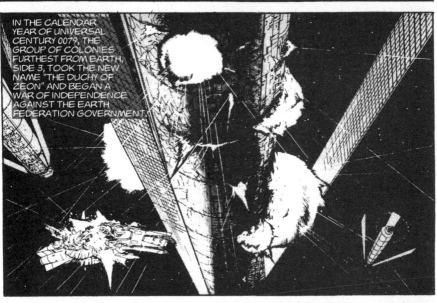

IN THE CALENDAR YEAR OF UNIVERSAL CENTURY 0079, THE GROUP OF COLONIES FURTHEST FROM EARTH, SIDE 3, TOOK THE NEW NAME "THE DUCHY OF ZEON" AND BEGAN A WAR OF INDEPENDENCE AGAINST THE EARTH FEDERATION GOVERNMENT.

IN SLIGHTLY OVER A MONTH OF BATTLE BOTH THE DUCHY OF ZEON AND THE FEDERATION SAW HALF THEIR POP- ULATIONS DIE.

MANKIND WAS HORRIFIED AT ITS OWN ATROCITIES, AND THE WAR CAME TO A STALEMATE FOR A LITTLE MORE THAN EIGHT MONTHS.

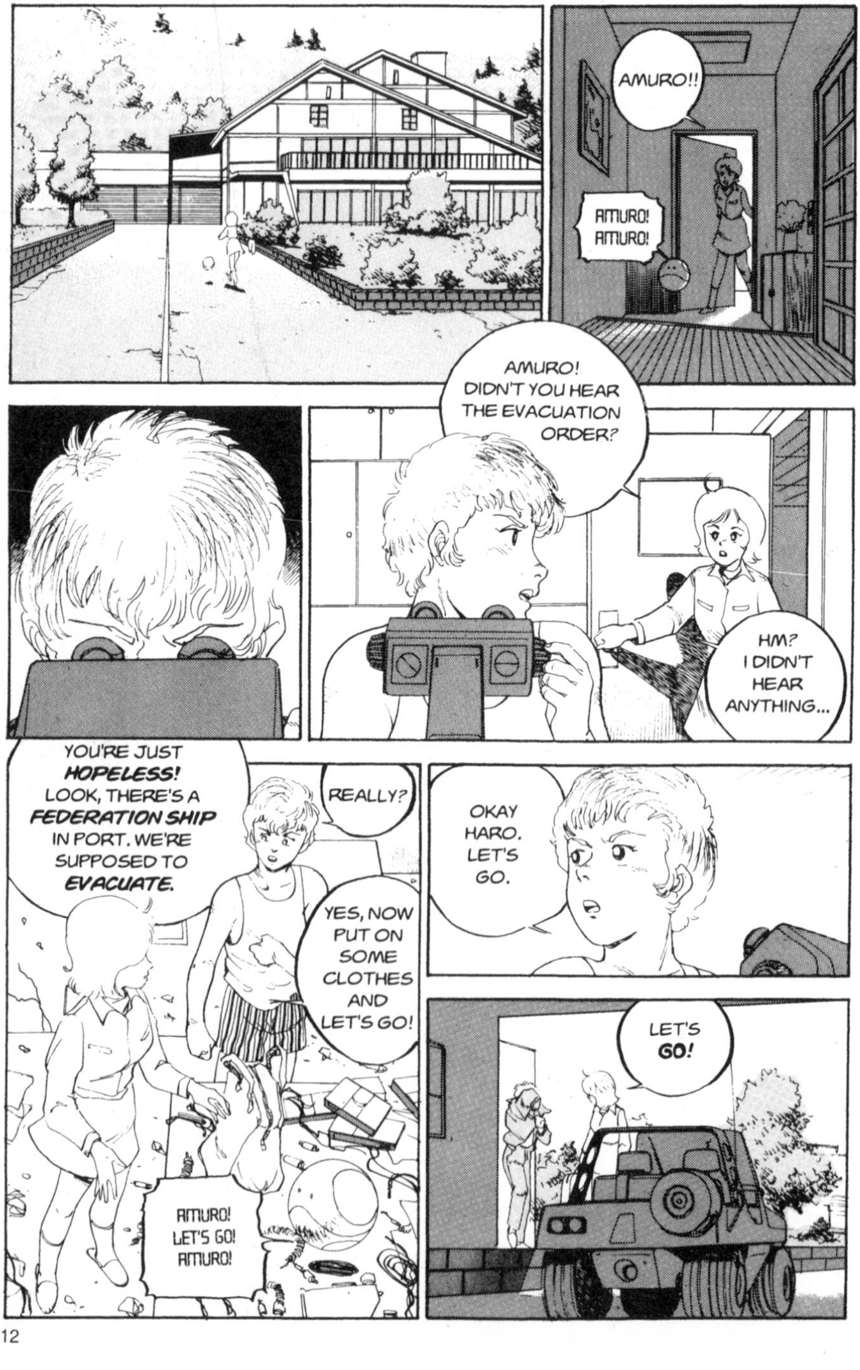
AMURO!!
AMURO! AMURO!
AMURO! DIDN'T YOU HEAR THE EVACUATION ORDER?
HM? I DIDN'T HEAR ANYTHING...
YOU'RE JUST **HOPELESS!** LOOK, THERE'S A **FEDERATION SHIP** IN PORT. WE'RE SUPPOSED TO **EVACUATE.**
REALLY?
YES, NOW PUT ON SOME CLOTHES AND LET'S GO!
AMURO! LET'S GO! AMURO!
OKAY HARO. LET'S GO.
LET'S **GO!**

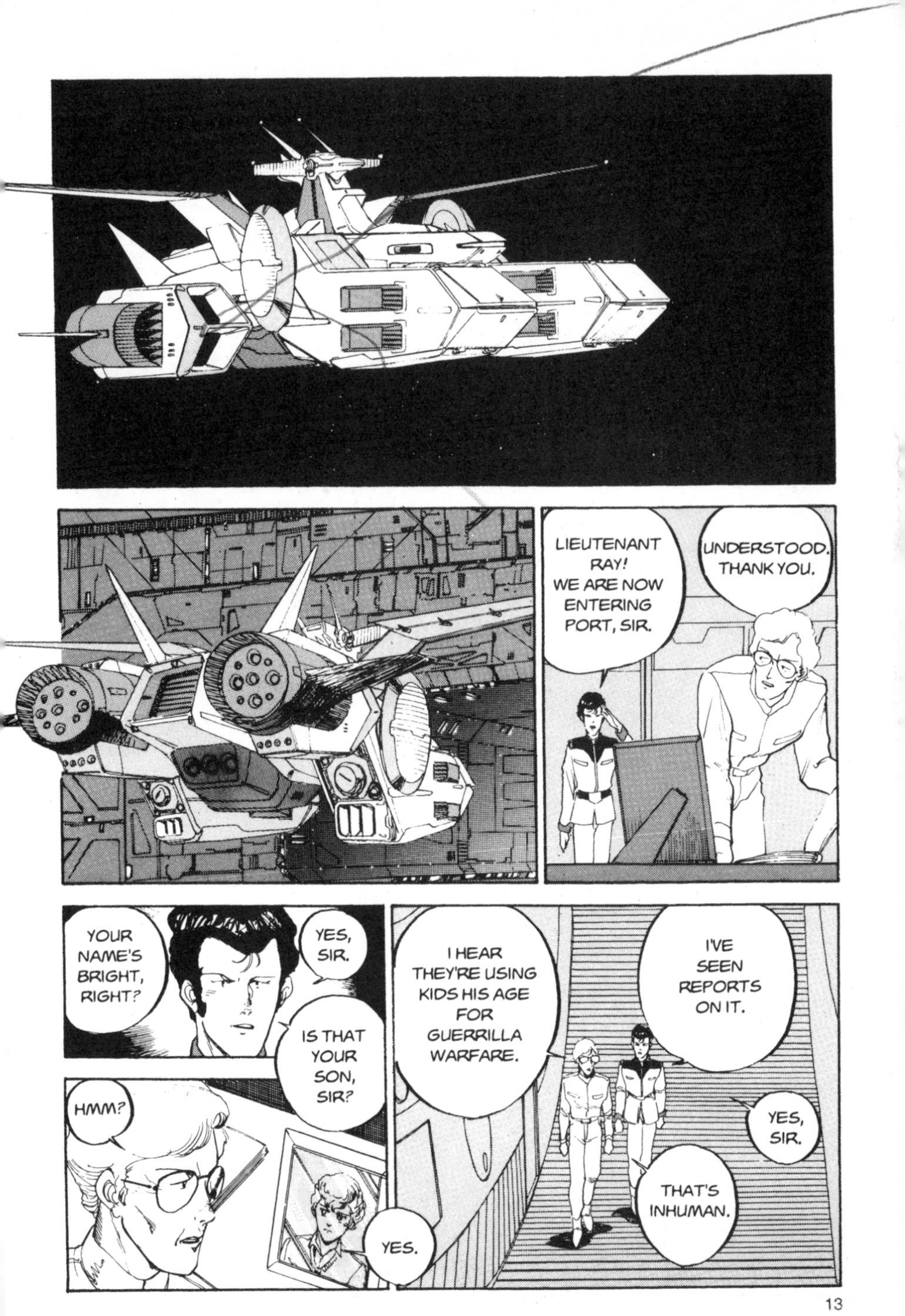
LIEUTENANT RAY! WE ARE NOW ENTERING PORT, SIR.
UNDERSTOOD. THANK YOU.
YOUR NAME'S BRIGHT, RIGHT?
YES, SIR.
IS THAT YOUR SON, SIR?
HMM?
YES.
I HEAR THEY'RE USING KIDS HIS AGE FOR GUERRILLA WARFARE.
I'VE SEEN REPORTS ON IT.
YES, SIR.
THAT'S INHUMAN.

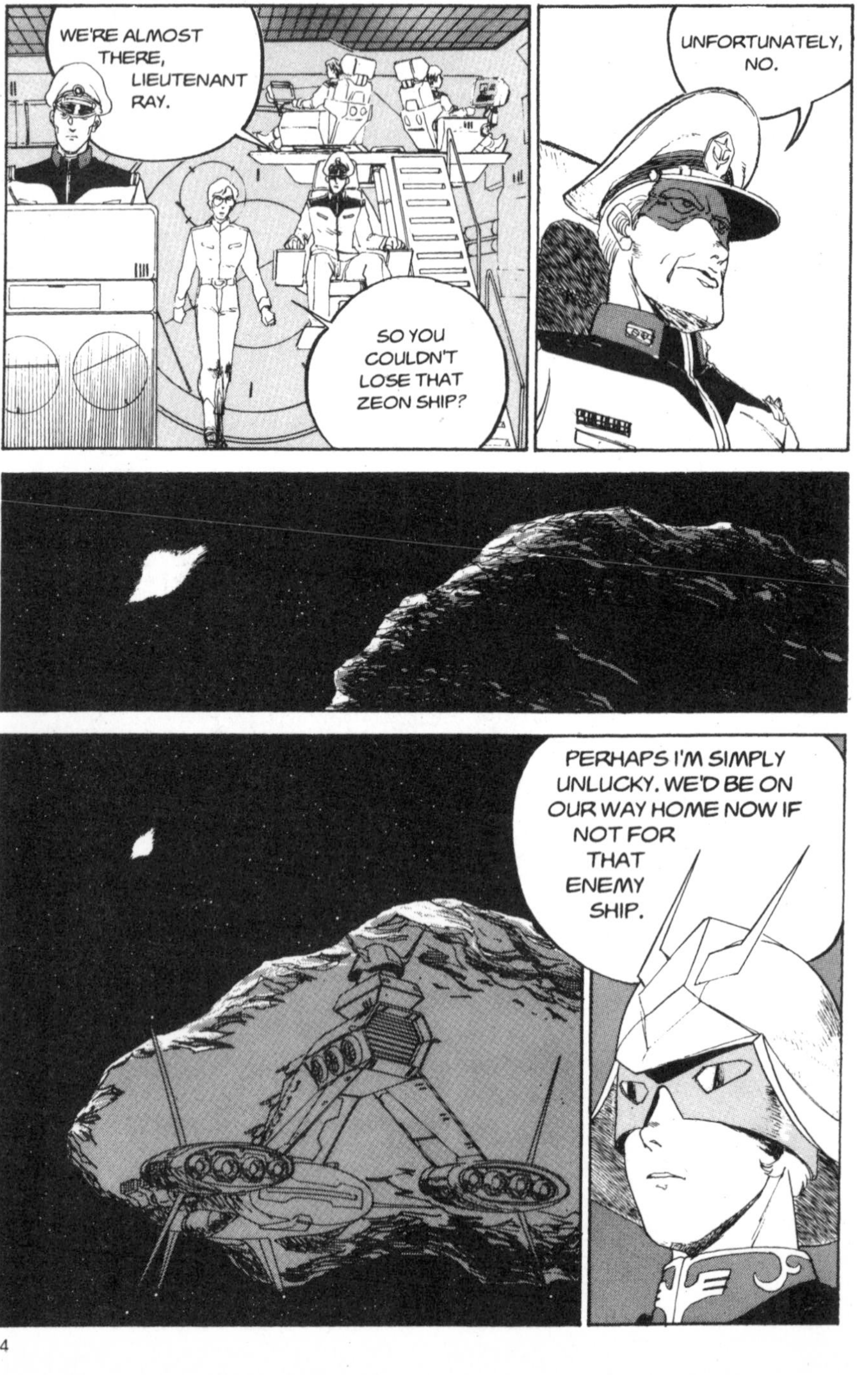
WE'RE ALMOST THERE, LIEUTENANT RAY.
SO YOU COULDN'T LOSE THAT ZEON SHIP?
UNFORTUNATELY, NO.
PERHAPS I'M SIMPLY UNLUCKY. WE'D BE ON OUR WAY HOME NOW IF NOT FOR THAT ENEMY SHIP.

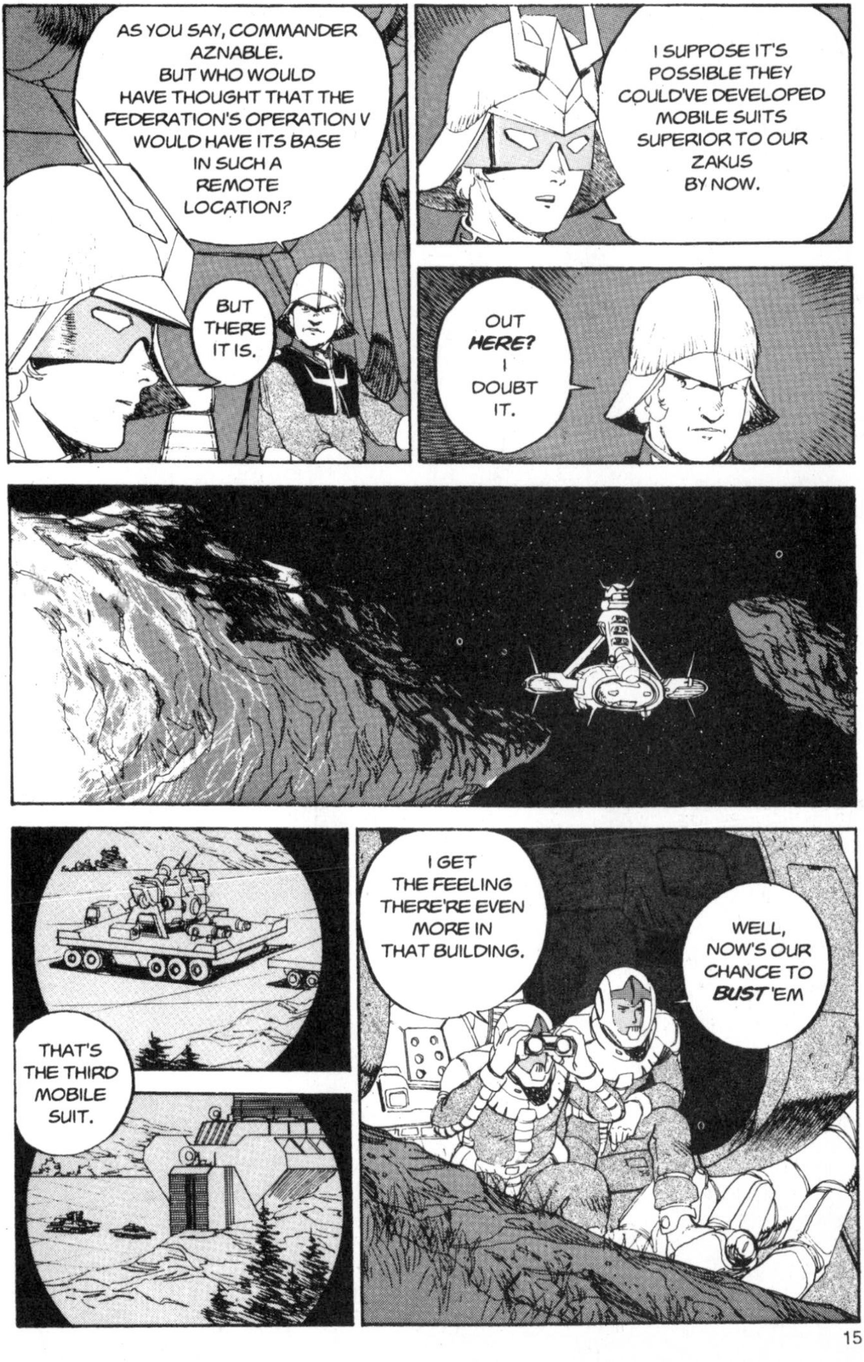
AS YOU SAY, COMMANDER AZNABLE. BUT WHO WOULD HAVE THOUGHT THAT THE FEDERATION'S OPERATION V WOULD HAVE ITS BASE IN SUCH A REMOTE LOCATION?
BUT THERE IT IS.
I SUPPOSE IT'S POSSIBLE THEY COULD'VE DEVELOPED MOBILE SUITS SUPERIOR TO OUR ZAKUS BY NOW.
OUT HERE? I DOUBT IT.
THAT'S THE THIRD MOBILE SUIT.
I GET THE FEELING THERE'RE EVEN MORE IN THAT BUILDING.
WELL, NOW'S OUR CHANCE TO BUST 'EM

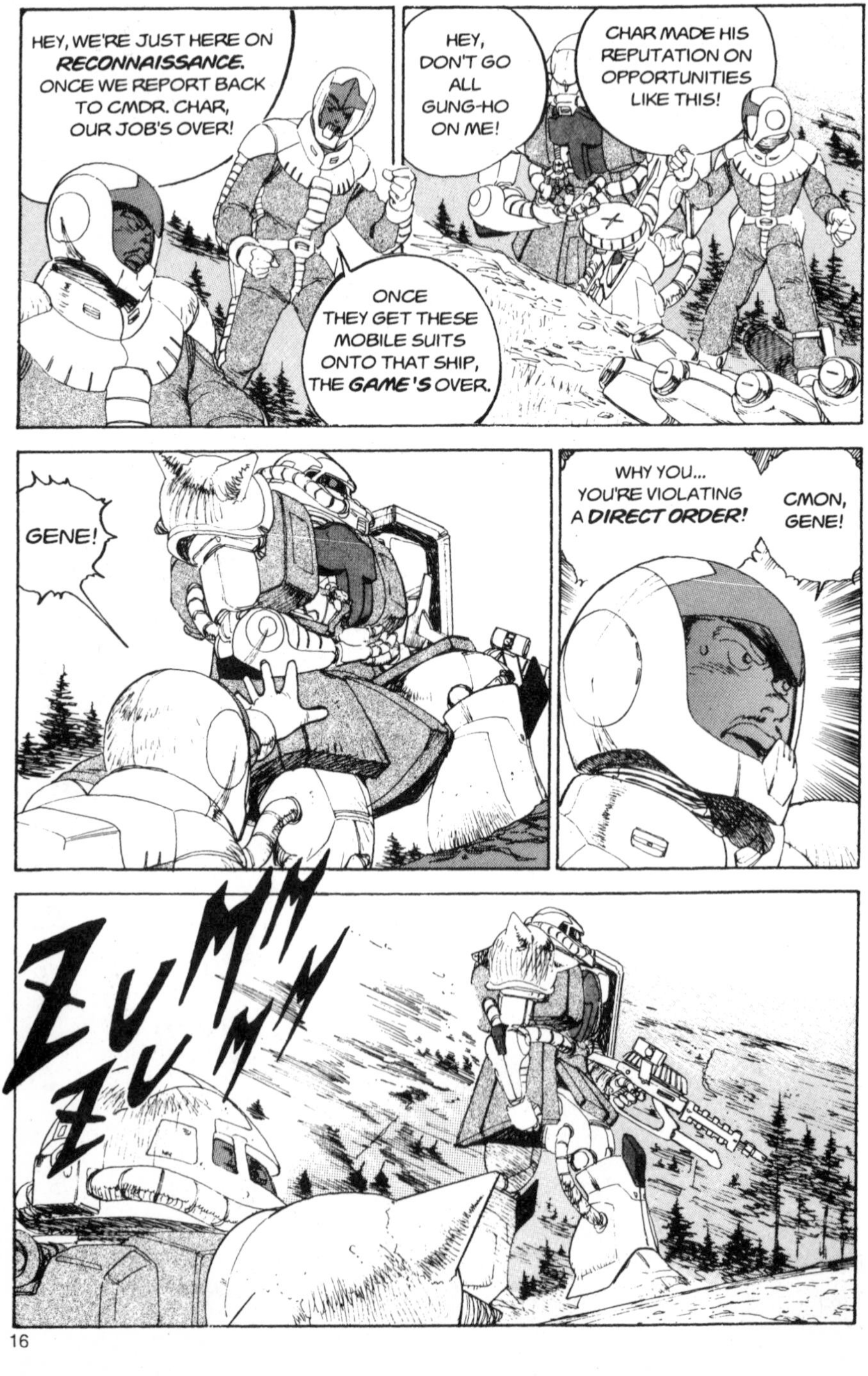
HEY, WE'RE JUST HERE ON **RECONNAISSANCE.** ONCE WE REPORT BACK TO CMDR. CHAR, OUR JOB'S OVER!
ONCE THEY GET THESE MOBILE SUITS ONTO THAT SHIP, THE **GAME'S** OVER.
HEY, DON'T GO ALL GUNG-HO ON ME!
CHAR MADE HIS REPUTATION ON OPPORTUNITIES LIKE THIS!
GENE!
WHY YOU... YOU'RE VIOLATING A **DIRECT ORDER!**
CMON, GENE!
ZUMMM
ZUMMM

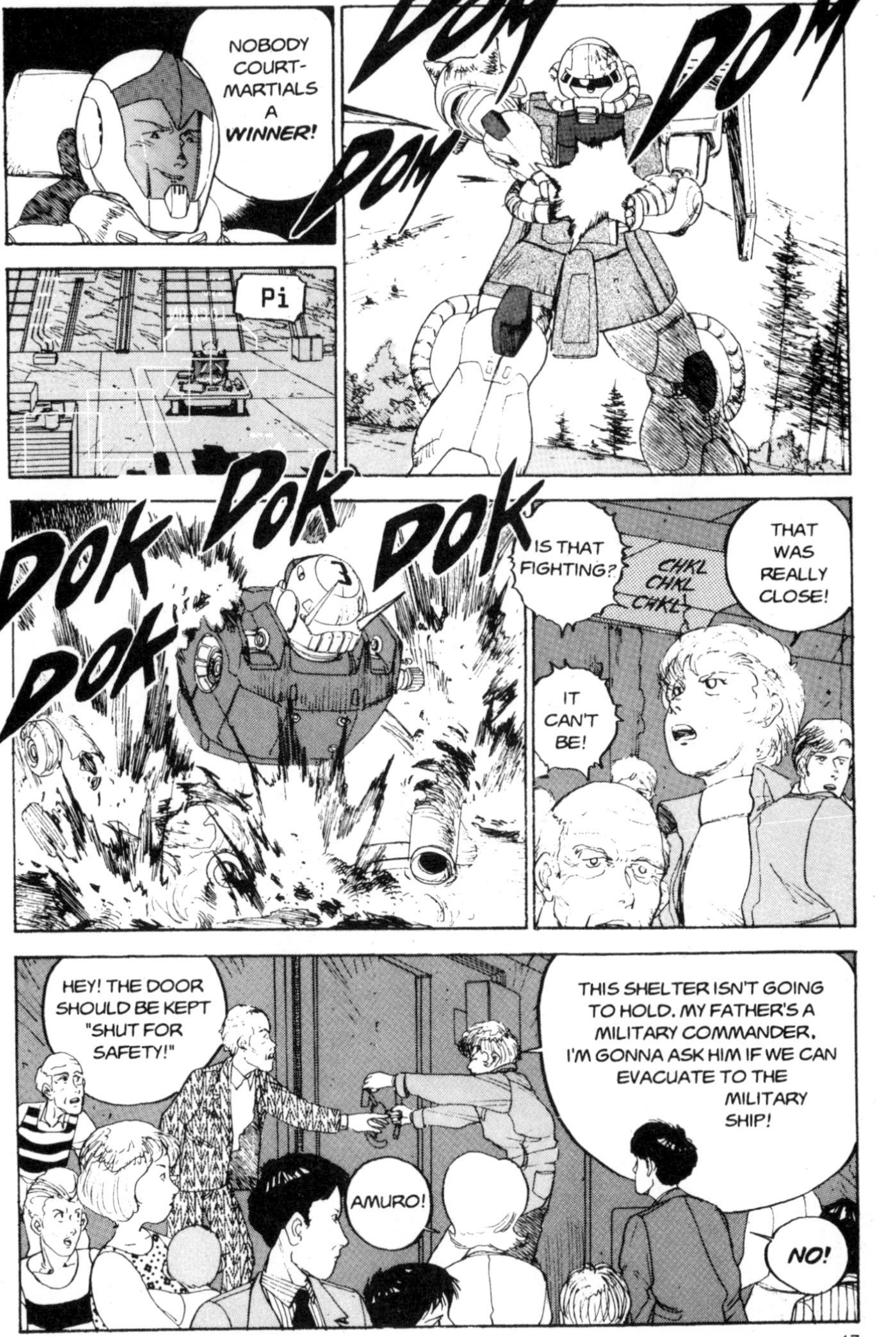
NOBODY COURT-MARTIALS A WINNER!
Pi
DOM
DOM
DOM
DOK
DOK
DOK
DOK
IS THAT FIGHTING?
CHKL CHKL CHKL
THAT WAS REALLY CLOSE!
IT CAN'T BE!
HEY! THE DOOR SHOULD BE KEPT "SHUT FOR SAFETY!"
THIS SHELTER ISN'T GOING TO HOLD. MY FATHER'S A MILITARY COMMANDER. I'M GONNA ASK HIM IF WE CAN EVACUATE TO THE MILITARY SHIP!
AMURO!
NO!

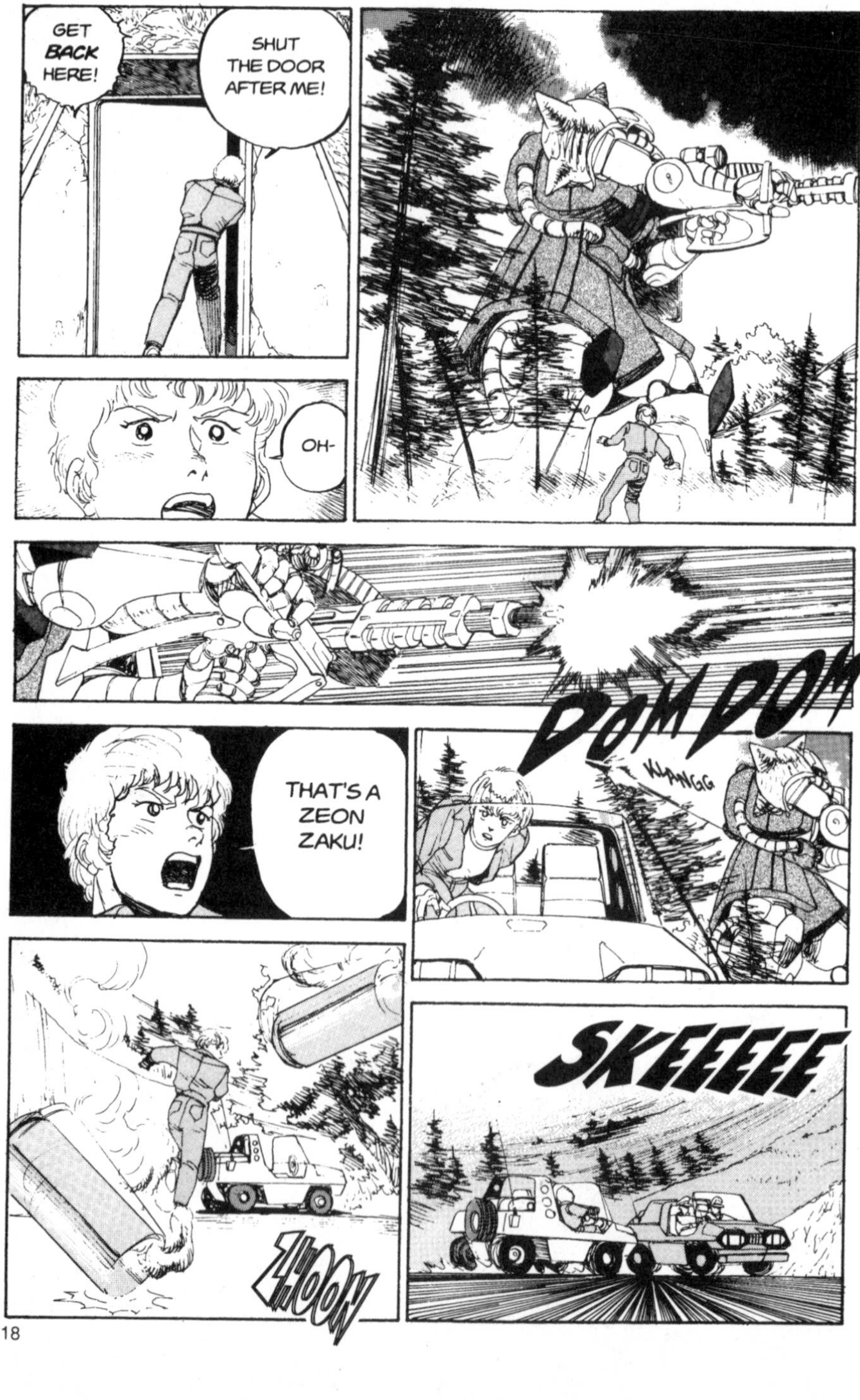
GET BACK HERE!
SHUT THE DOOR AFTER ME!
OH-
DOM DOM
THAT'S A ZEON ZAKU!
KWANGG
ZHOOM
SKEEEEE

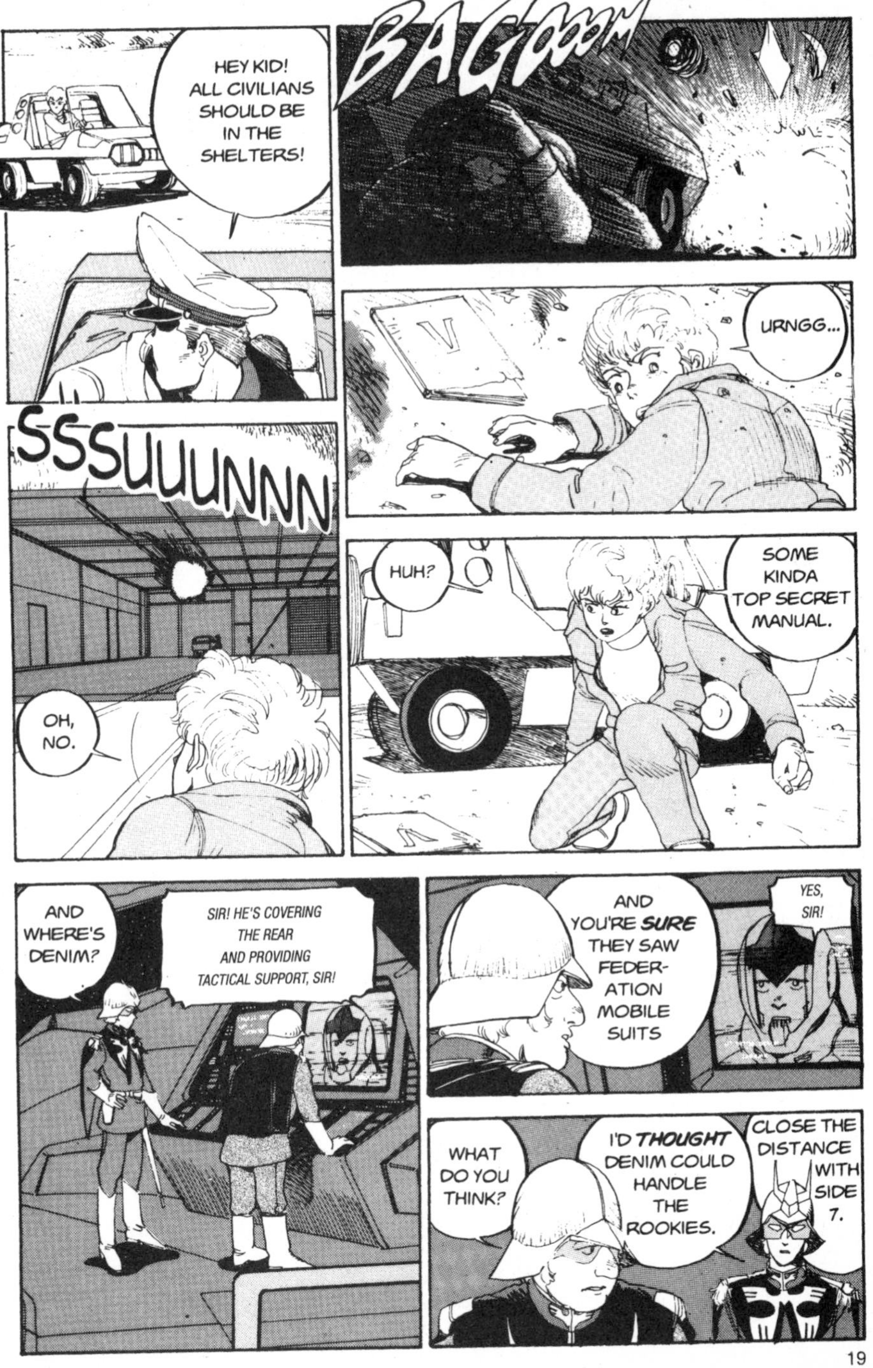
HEY KID! ALL CIVILIANS SHOULD BE IN THE SHELTERS!
BAGOOOM
URNGG...
SSSUUUNNN
OH, NO.
HUH?
SOME KINDA TOP SECRET MANUAL.
AND WHERE'S DENIM?
SIR! HE'S COVERING THE REAR AND PROVIDING TACTICAL SUPPORT, SIR!
AND YOU'RE **SURE** THEY SAW FEDER-ATION MOBILE SUITS
YES, SIR!
WHAT DO YOU THINK?
I'D **THOUGHT** DENIM COULD HANDLE THE ROOKIES.
CLOSE THE DISTANCE WITH SIDE 7.

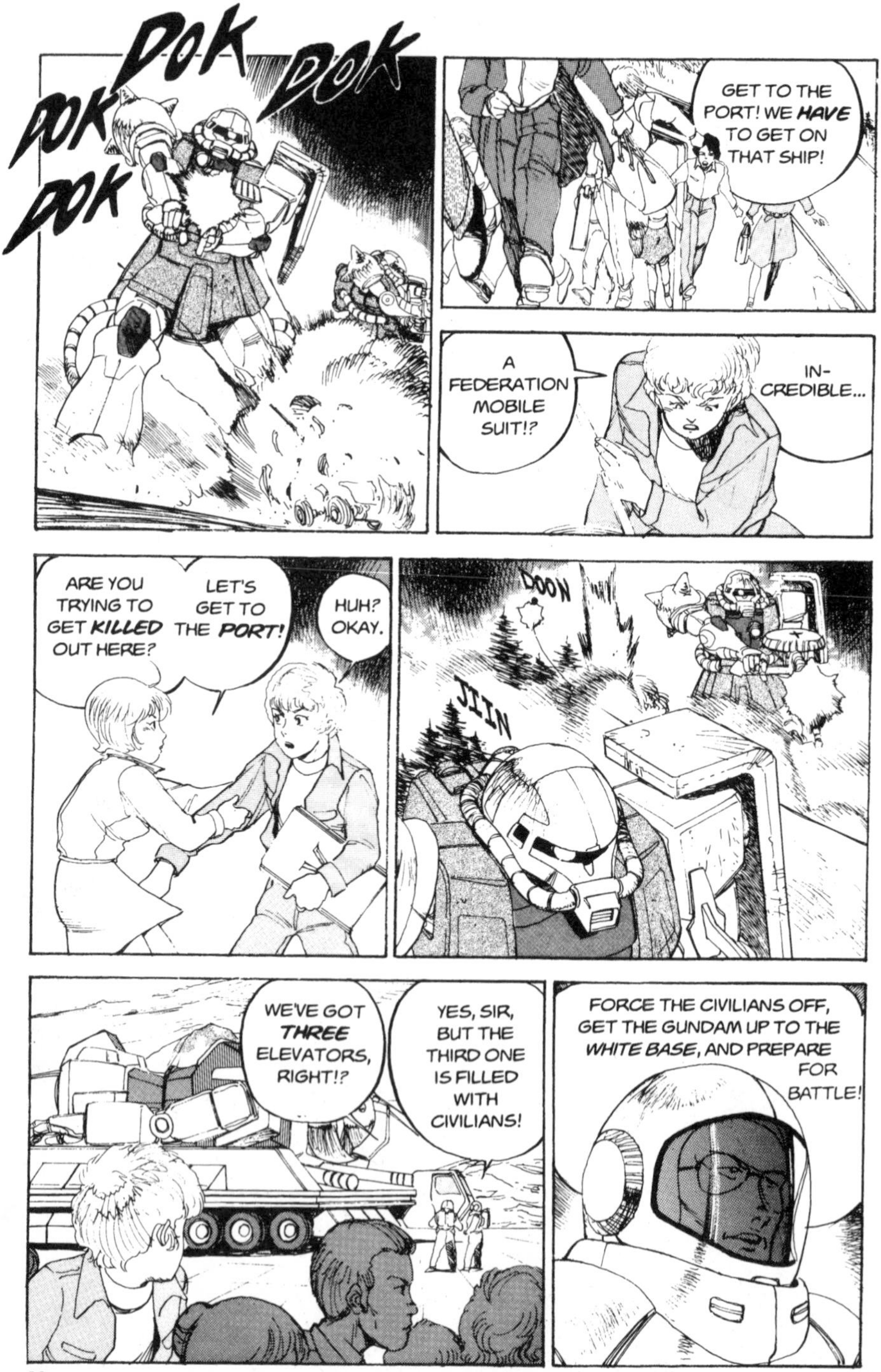
DOK DOK DOK DOK
GET TO THE PORT! WE HAVE TO GET ON THAT SHIP!
A FEDERATION MOBILE SUIT!?
IN-CREDIBLE...
ARE YOU TRYING TO GET KILLED OUT HERE?
LET'S GET TO THE PORT!
HUH? OKAY.
DOON
JIIN
WE'VE GOT THREE ELEVATORS, RIGHT!?
YES, SIR, BUT THE THIRD ONE IS FILLED WITH CIVILIANS!
FORCE THE CIVILIANS OFF, GET THE GUNDAM UP TO THE WHITE BASE, AND PREPARE FOR BATTLE!

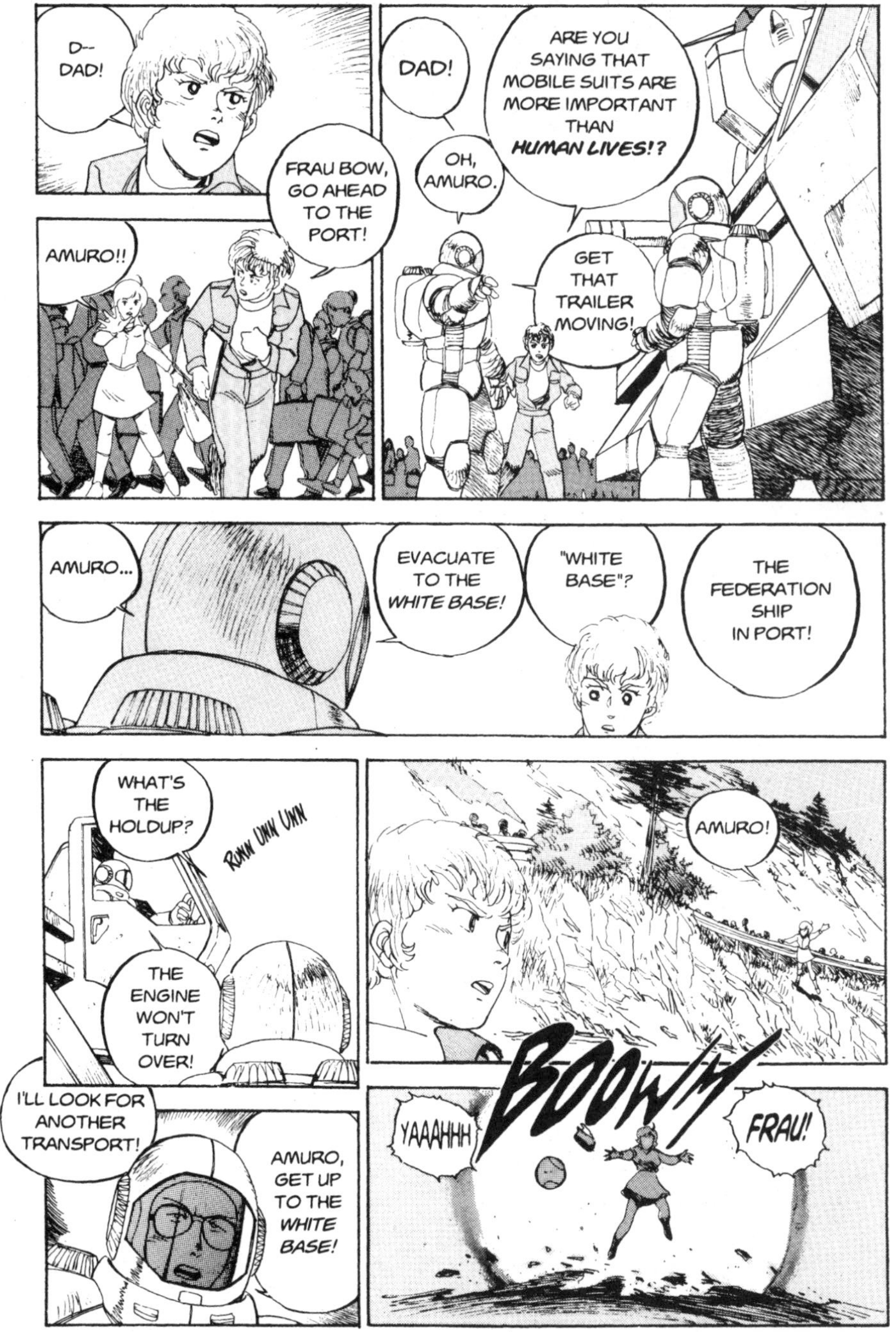
D-- DAD!
AMURO!!
FRAU BOW, GO AHEAD TO THE PORT!
DAD!
ARE YOU SAYING THAT MOBILE SUITS ARE MORE IMPORTANT THAN HUMAN LIVES!?
OH, AMURO.
GET THAT TRAILER MOVING!
AMURO...
EVACUATE TO THE WHITE BASE!
"WHITE BASE"?
THE FEDERATION SHIP IN PORT!
WHAT'S THE HOLDUP?
RUNN UNN UNN
THE ENGINE WON'T TURN OVER!
I'LL LOOK FOR ANOTHER TRANSPORT!
AMURO, GET UP TO THE WHITE BASE!
AMURO!
BOOWM
YAAAHHH
FRAU!

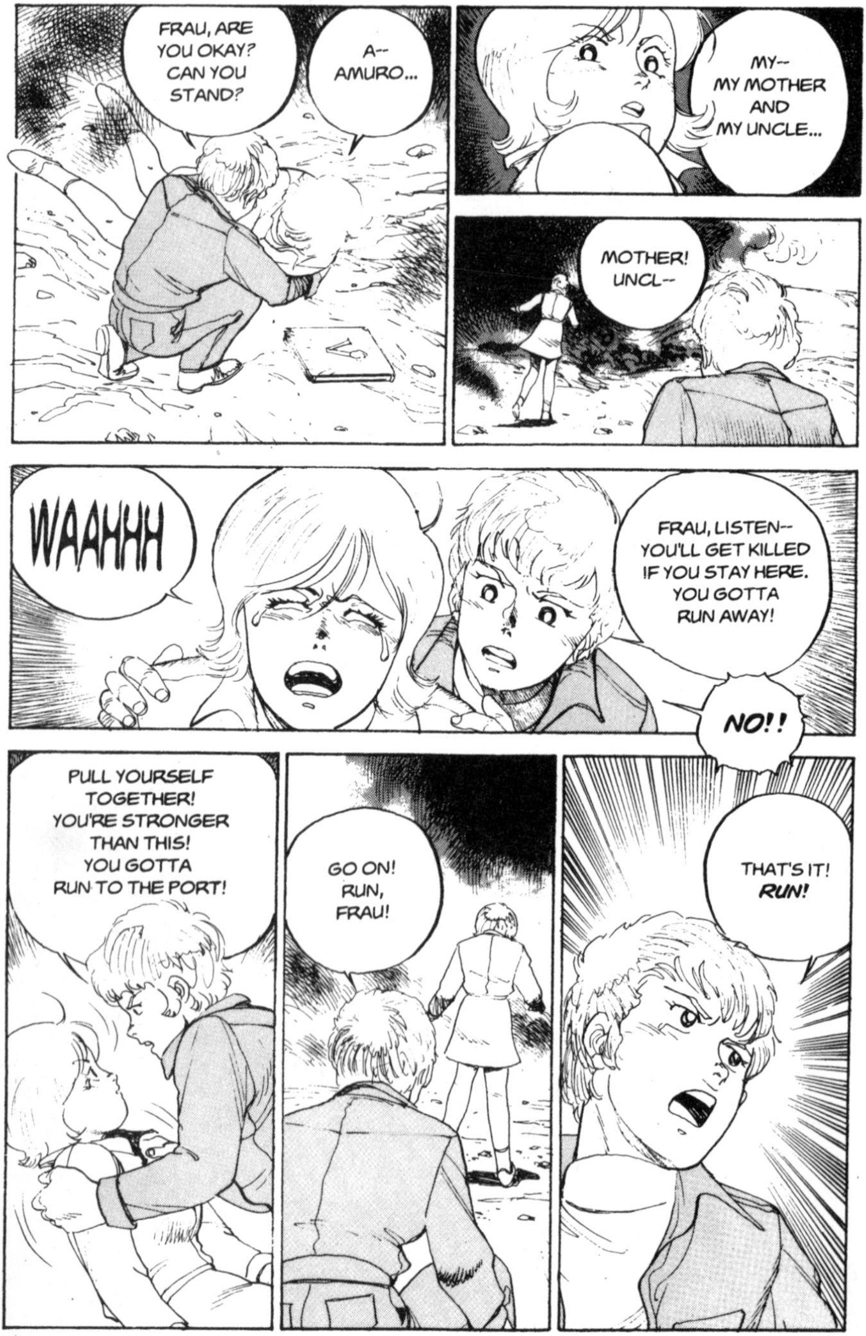
FRAU, ARE YOU OKAY? CAN YOU STAND?
A-- AMURO...
MY-- MY MOTHER AND MY UNCLE...
MOTHER! UNCL--
WAAHHH
FRAU, LISTEN-- YOU'LL GET KILLED IF YOU STAY HERE. YOU GOTTA RUN AWAY!
NO!!
PULL YOURSELF TOGETHER! YOU'RE STRONGER THAN THIS! YOU GOTTA RUN TO THE PORT!
GO ON! RUN, FRAU!
THAT'S IT! *RUN!*

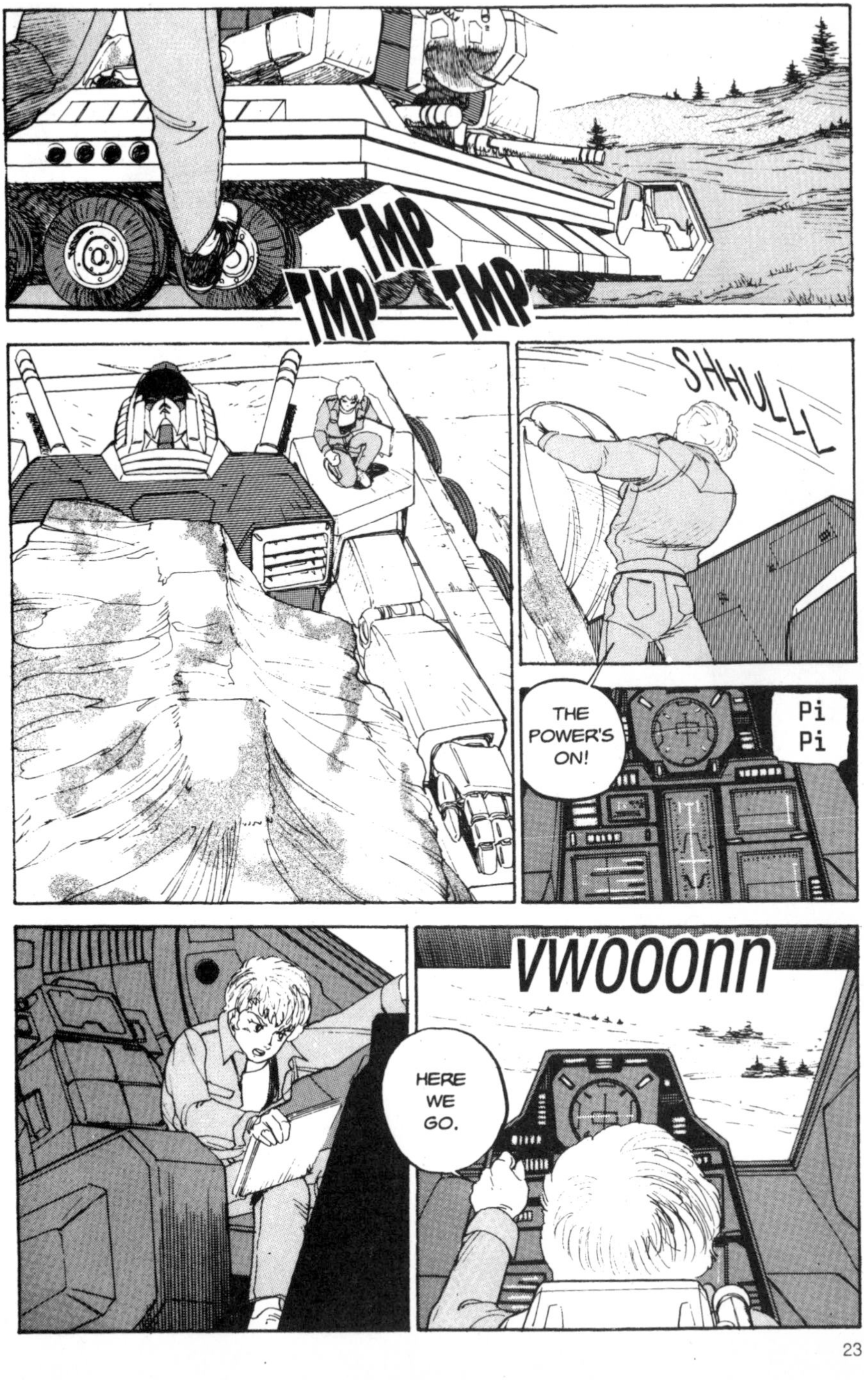
TMP TMP TMP TMP
SHHULLL
THE POWER'S ON!
Pi Pi
VWOOONN
HERE WE GO.

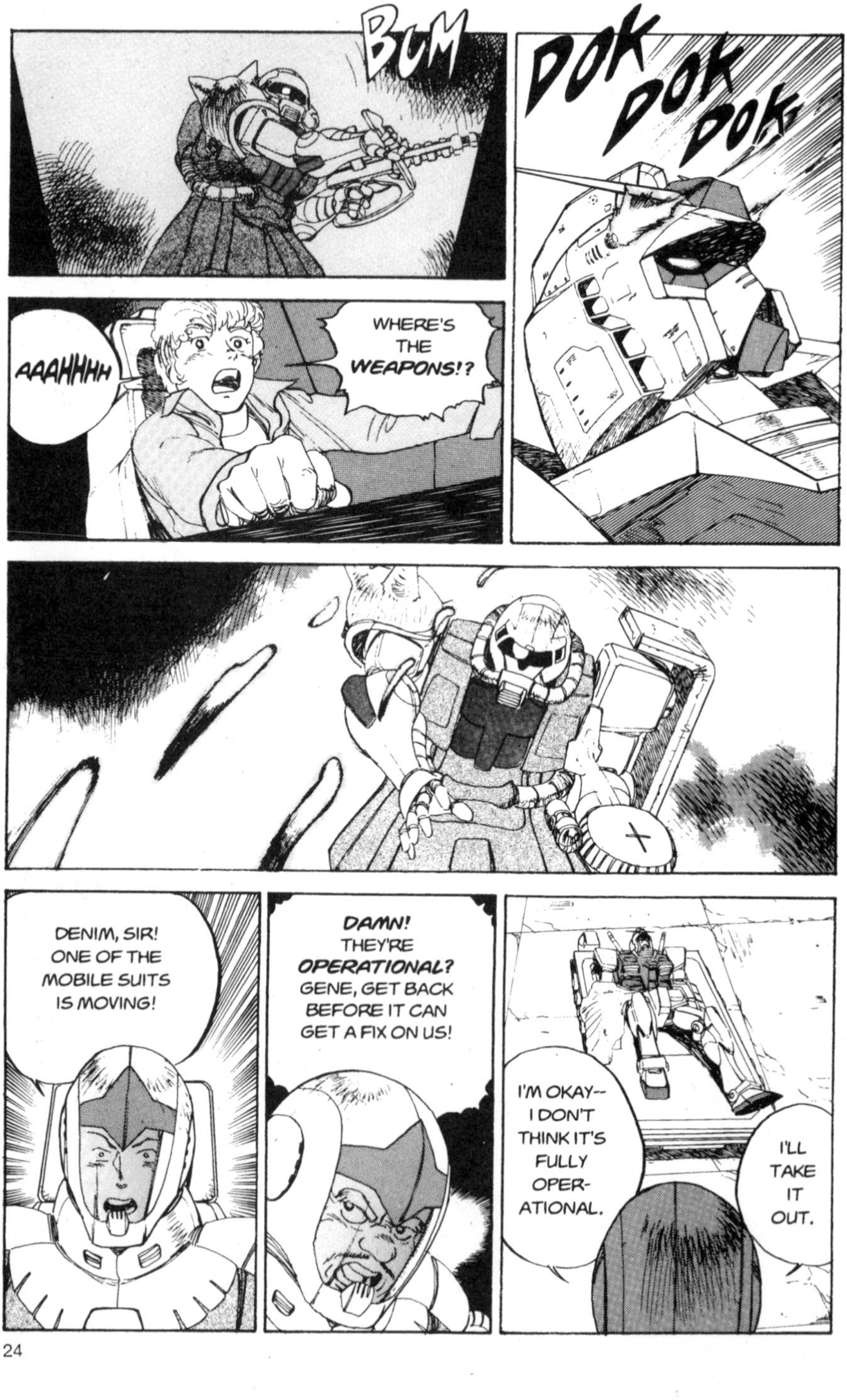
BUM
DOK DOK DOK
AAAHHHH
WHERE'S THE WEAPONS!?
DENIM, SIR! ONE OF THE MOBILE SUITS IS MOVING!
DAMN! THEY'RE OPERATIONAL? GENE, GET BACK BEFORE IT CAN GET A FIX ON US!
I'M OKAY-- I DON'T THINK IT'S FULLY OPER-ATIONAL.
I'LL TAKE IT OUT.

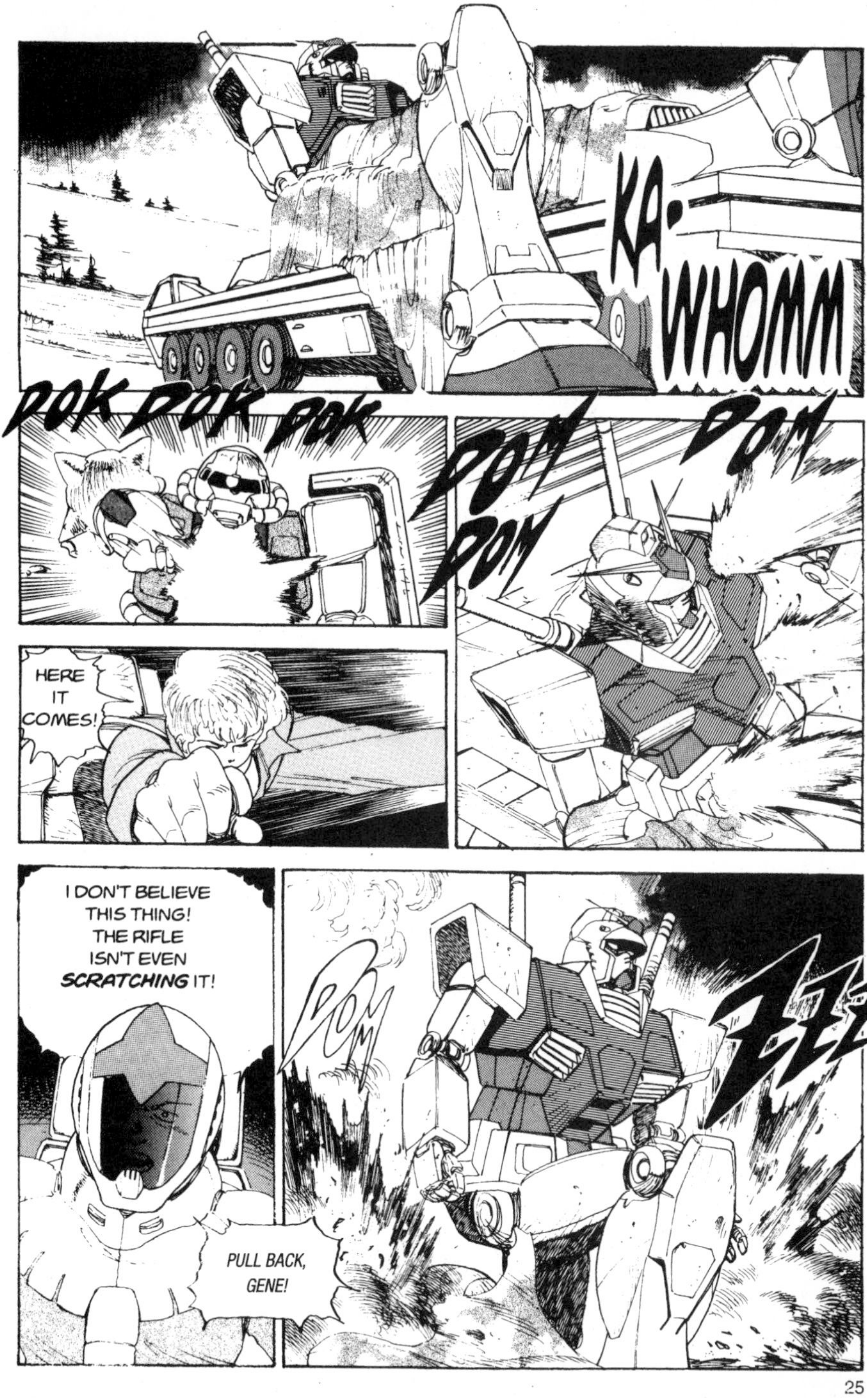
KA-
WHOMM
DOK DOK DOK
HERE IT COMES!
DOM DOM
DOM DOM
I DON'T BELIEVE THIS THING! THE RIFLE ISN'T EVEN **SCRATCHING** IT!
PULL BACK, GENE!
DOM

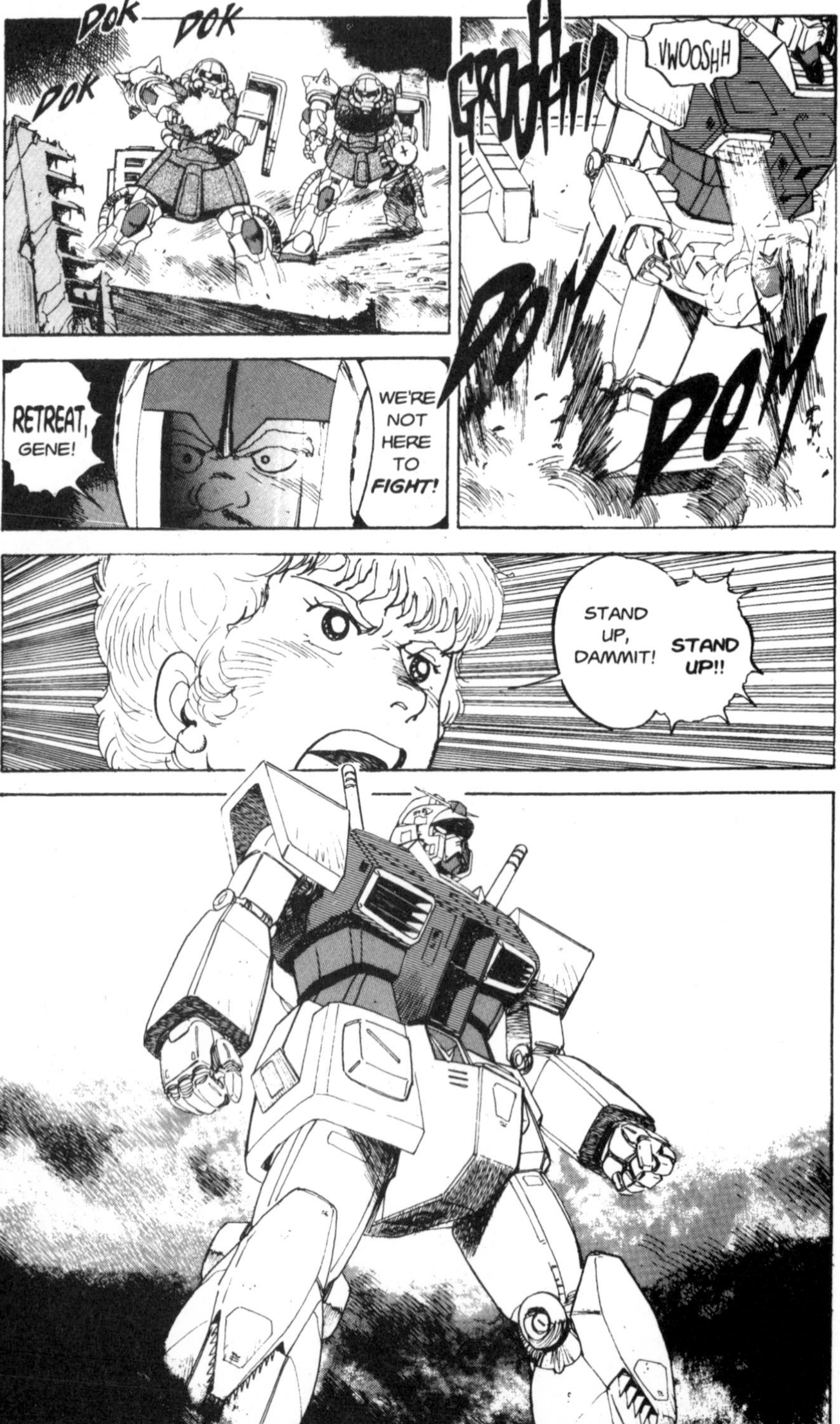
DOK
DOK
DOK
RETREAT, GENE!
WE'RE NOT HERE TO FIGHT!
GROOHH
VWOOSHH
DOM
DOM
STAND UP, DAMMIT!
STAND UP!!

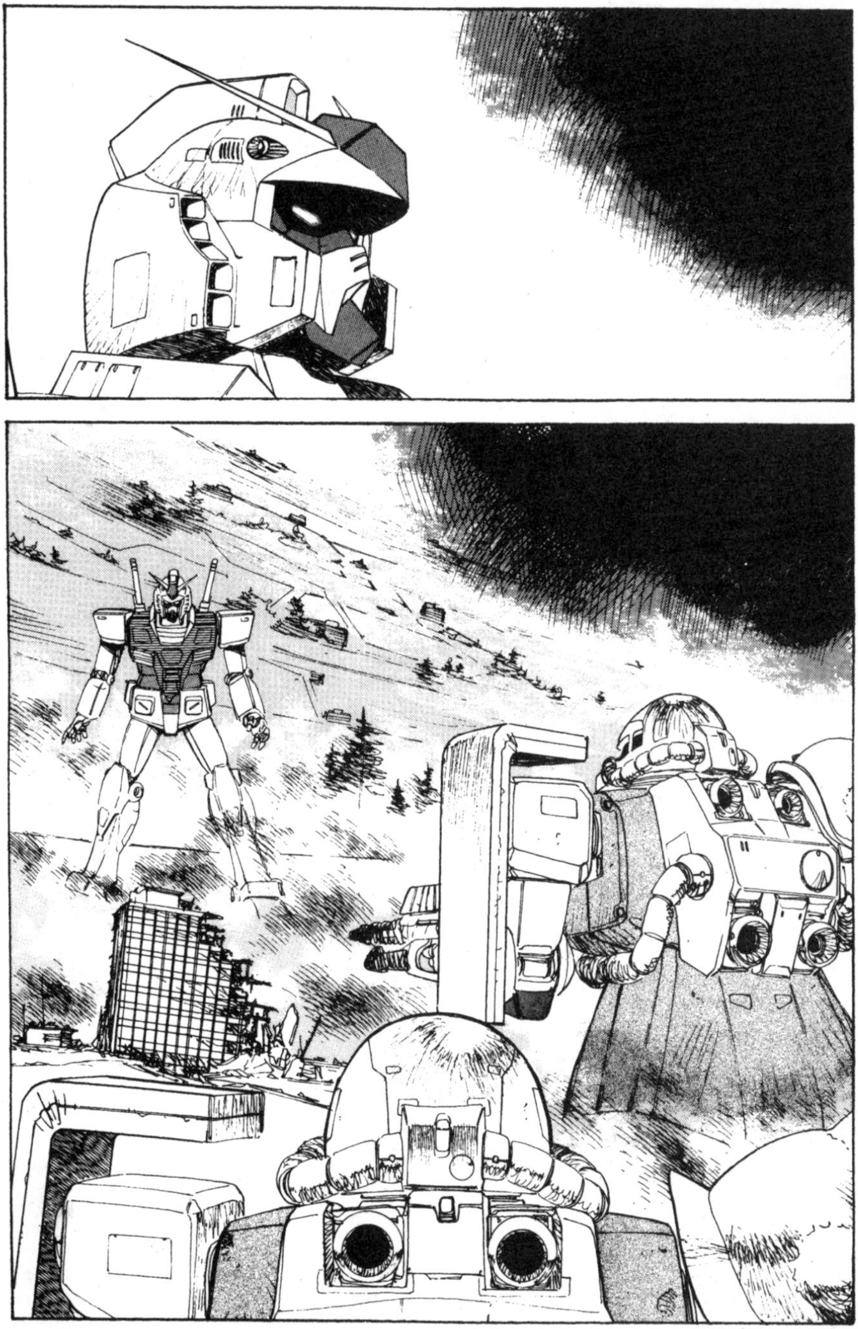

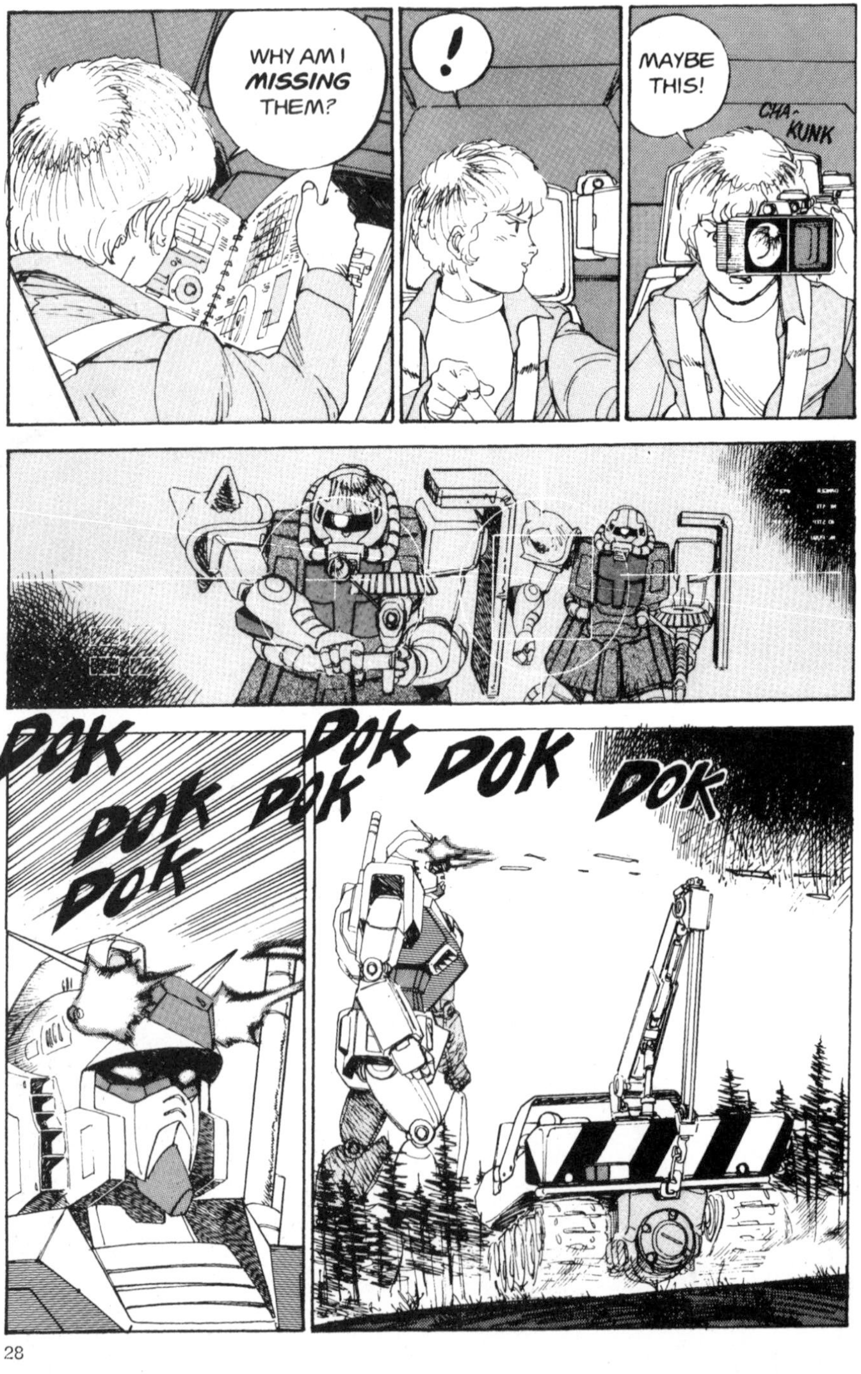
WHY AM I MISSING THEM?
!
MAYBE THIS!
CHA-KUNK
DOK DOK DOK
DOK DOK DOK DOK DOK

LIEUTENANT RAY! ONE OF OUR SUITS HAS MOBILIZED!

THOSE ARE THE WORST TACTICS I'VE EVER SEEN! WHAT *IDIOT* IS PILOTING THAT THING!?

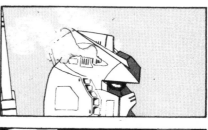

WHAT HAPPENED!?

I'M OUT OF AMMO!

CLIK CLIK

NOW'S MY CHANCE! YOU'RE DEAD!

KEEP YOUR DISTANCE FROM THAT THING, GENE!

BUM

HERE IT COMES!

HEH HEH HEH I DON'T CARE HOW THICK YOUR ARMOR IS! YOU CAN'T SURVIVE A *POINT-BLANK* SHOT!

EAT **THIS!**

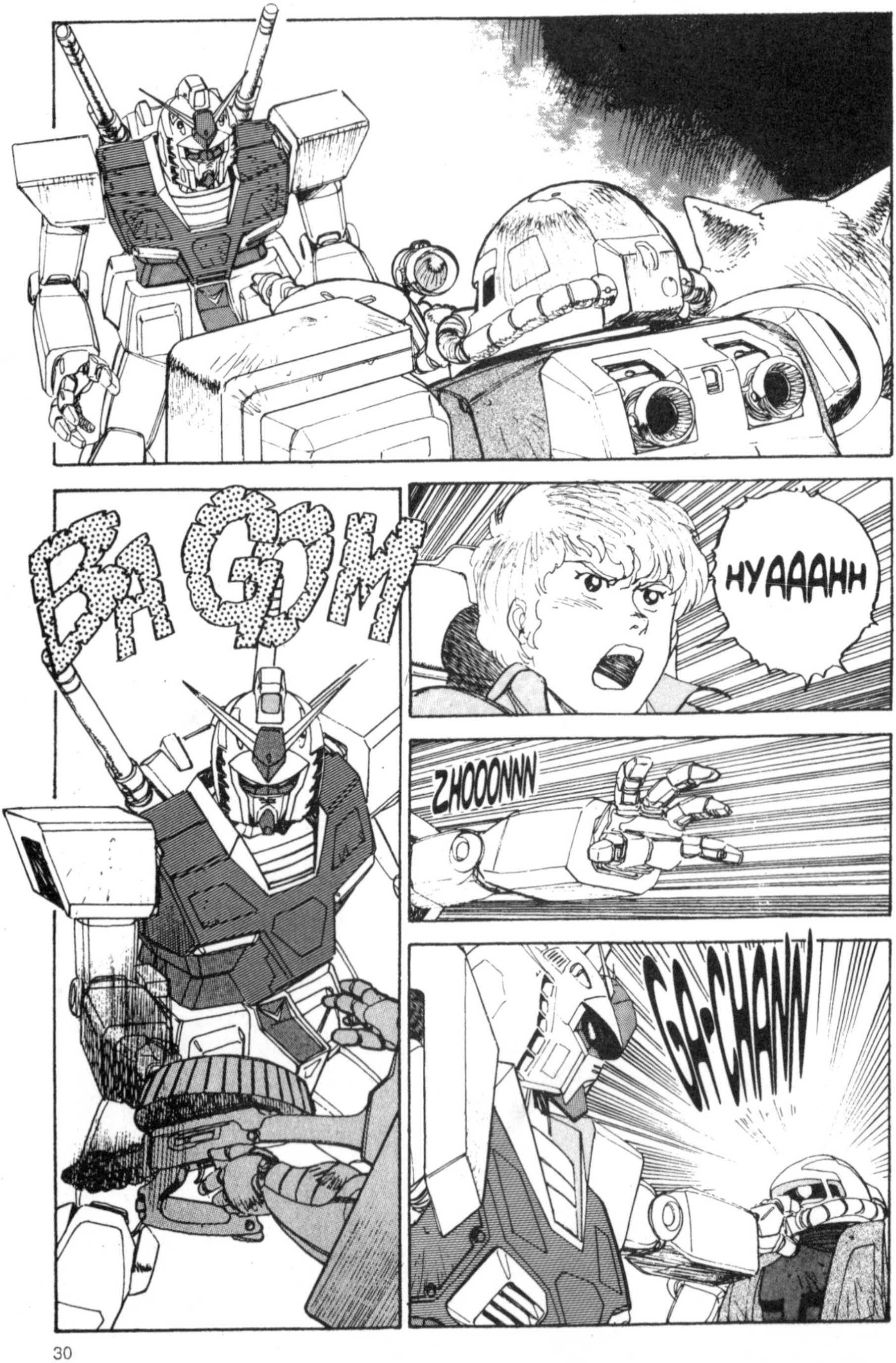
BAGOOM
HYAAAHH
ZHOOONNN
GA-CHANN

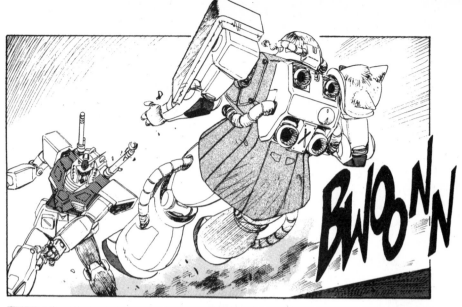

GENE!

THAT MOBILE SUIT'S A MONSTER! IT TOOK DOWN A ZAKU LIKE IT WAS NOTHING!

M-- MY GOD!

D-- DENIM, SIR!

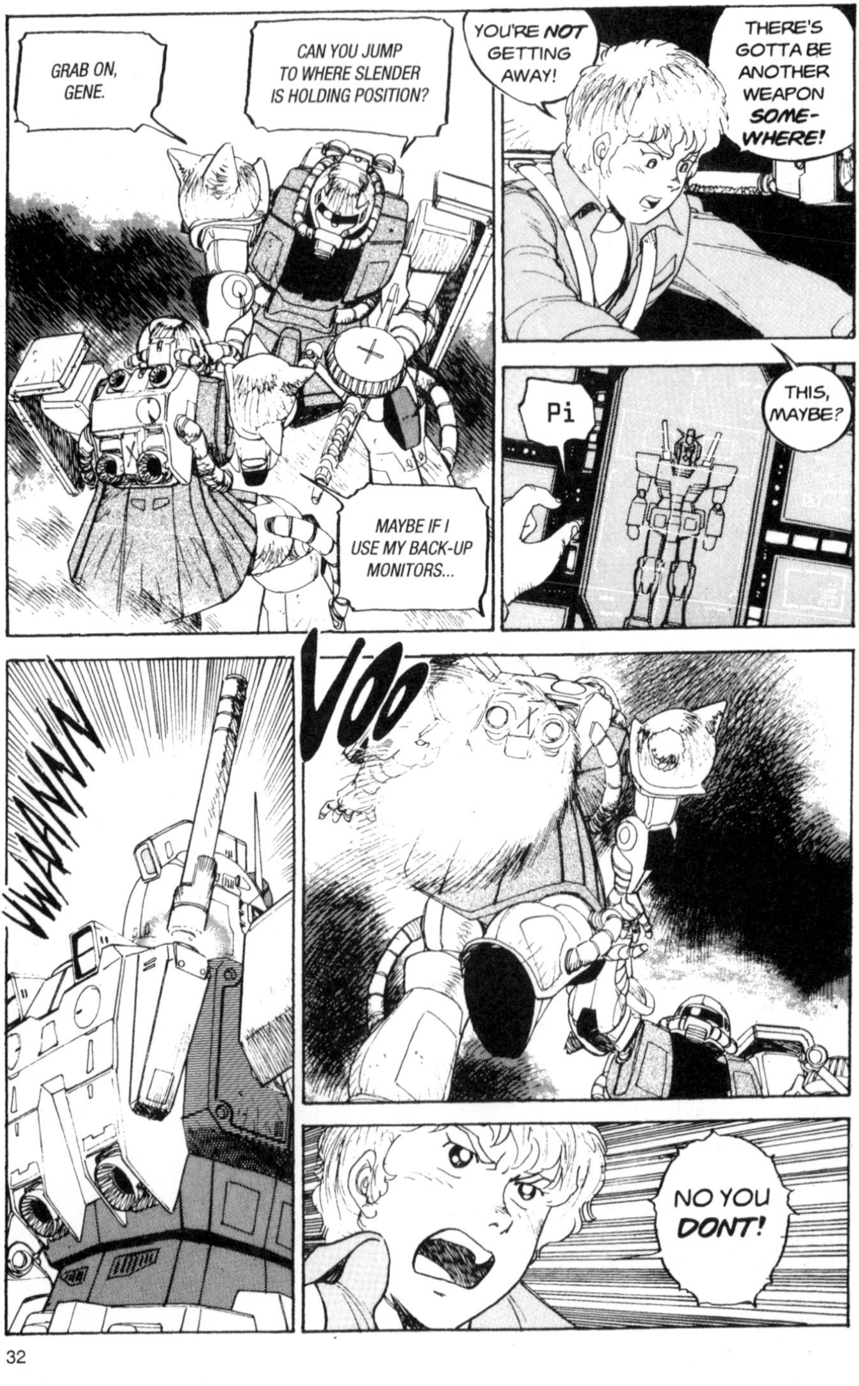
GRAB ON, GENE.
CAN YOU JUMP TO WHERE SLENDER IS HOLDING POSITION?
MAYBE IF I USE MY BACK-UP MONITORS...
YOU'RE **NOT** GETTING AWAY!
THERE'S GOTTA BE ANOTHER WEAPON **SOME-WHERE!**
Pi
THIS, MAYBE?
VWAANNN
VOO
NO YOU **DONT!**

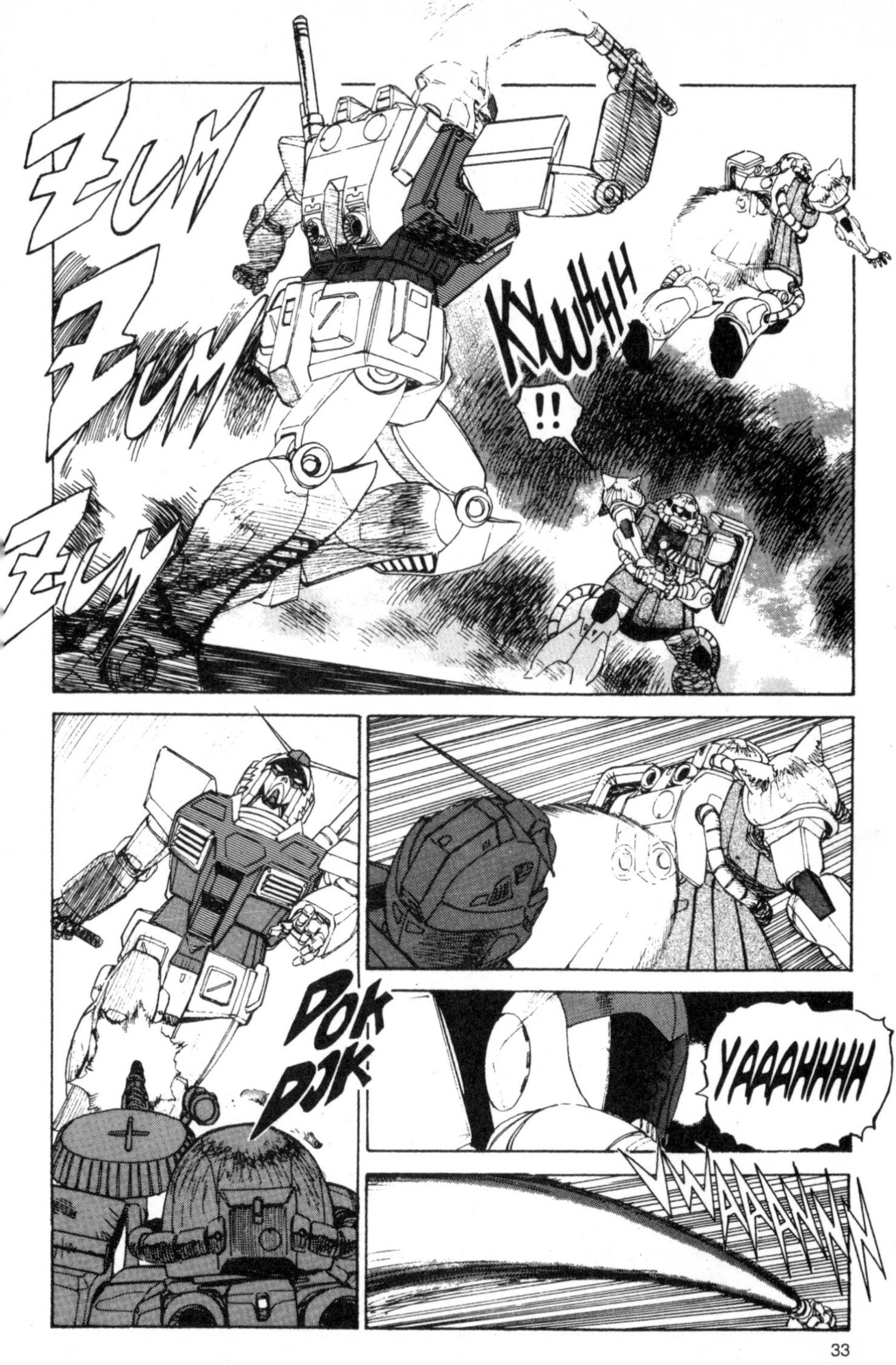
ZUM
ZUM
ZUM
KYUHHHH
!!
DOK DOK
YAAAHHHH
VWAAANNNN

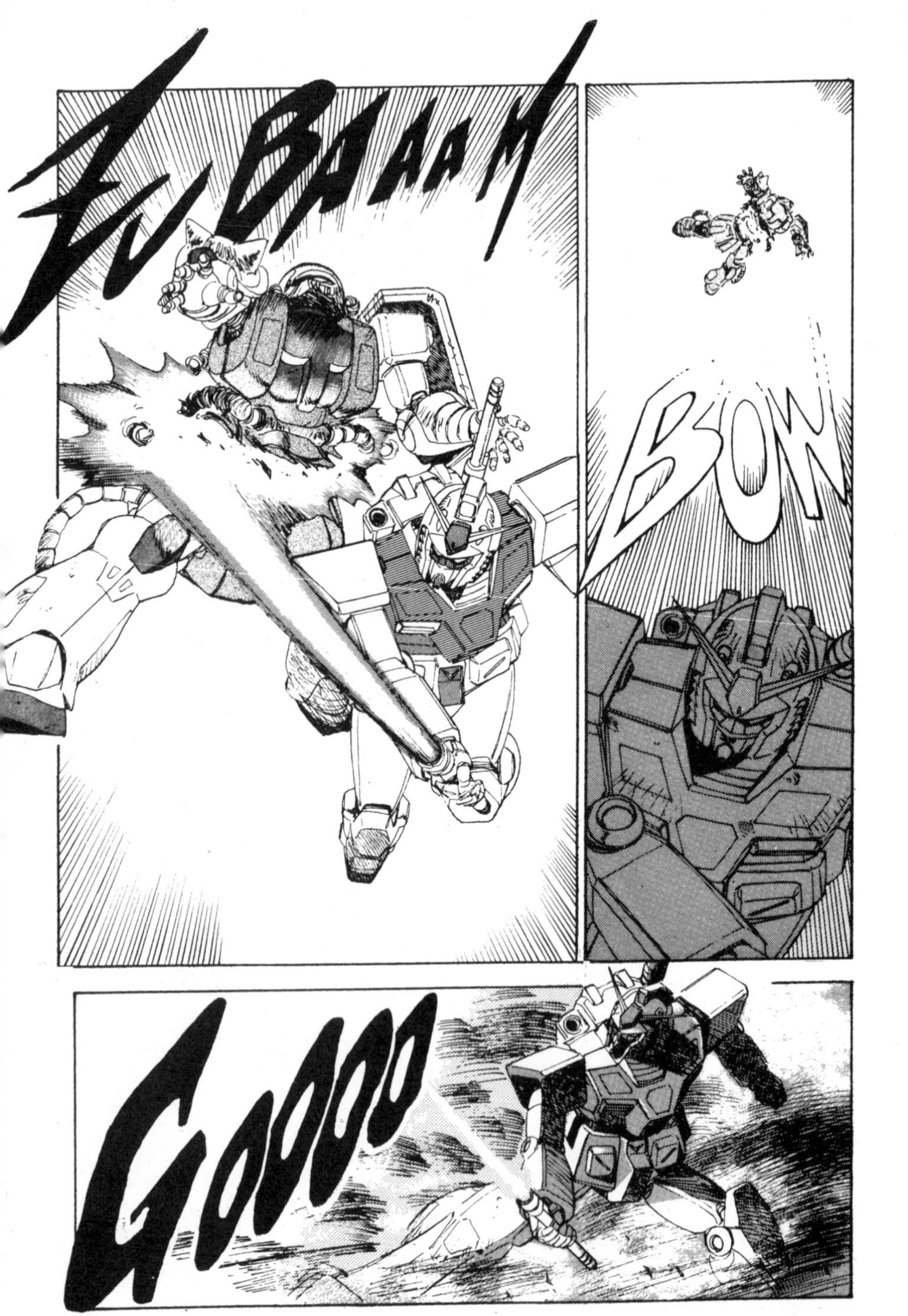
ZUBAAAM
BOW
GOOOO

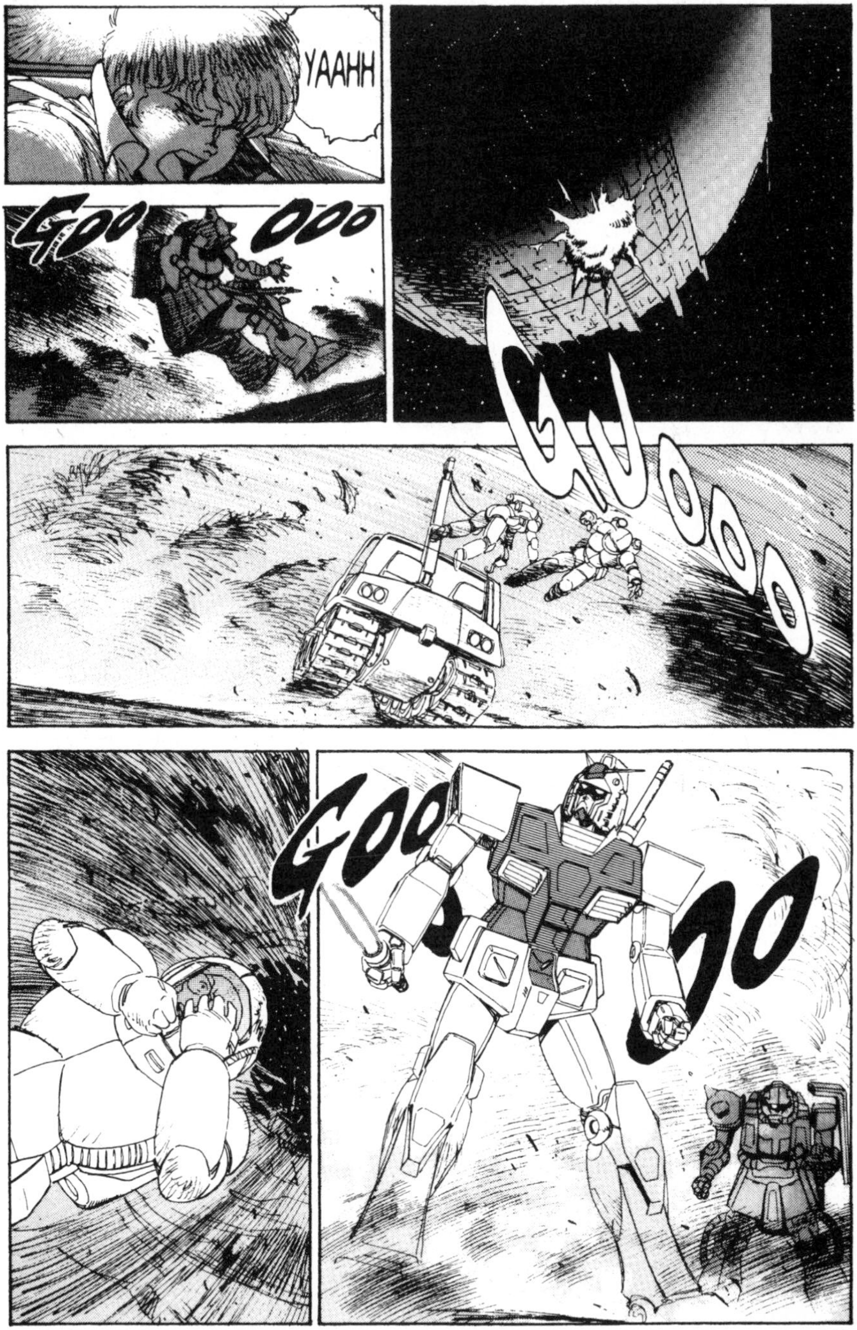
YAAHH
GOO OOO
GUOOOO
GOO OO

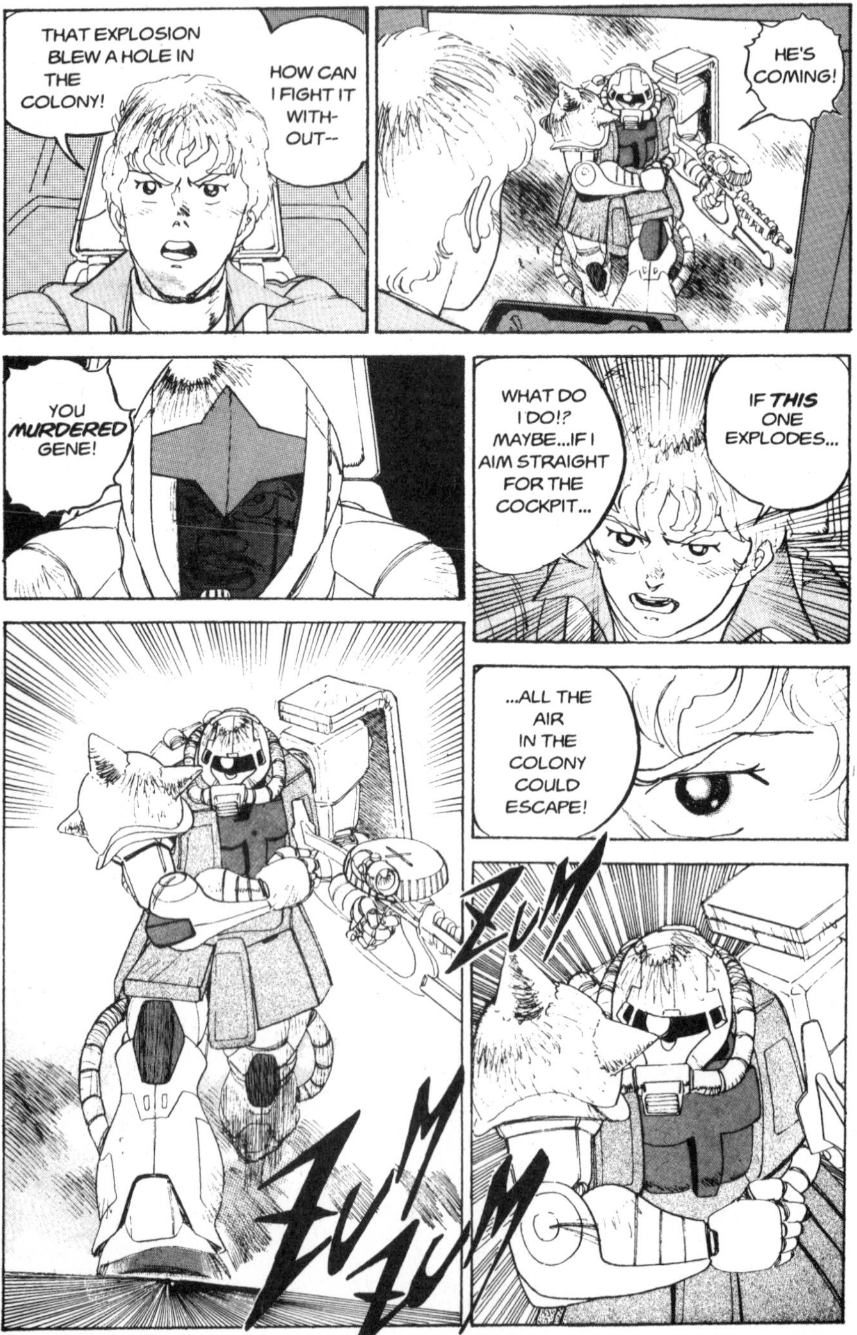
THAT EXPLOSION BLEW A HOLE IN THE COLONY!
HOW CAN I FIGHT IT WITH-OUT--
HE'S COMING!
YOU **MURDERED** GENE!
WHAT DO I DO!? MAYBE...IF I AIM STRAIGHT FOR THE COCKPIT...
IF **THIS** ONE EXPLODES...
ZUM ZUM
...ALL THE AIR IN THE COLONY COULD ESCAPE!
ZUM

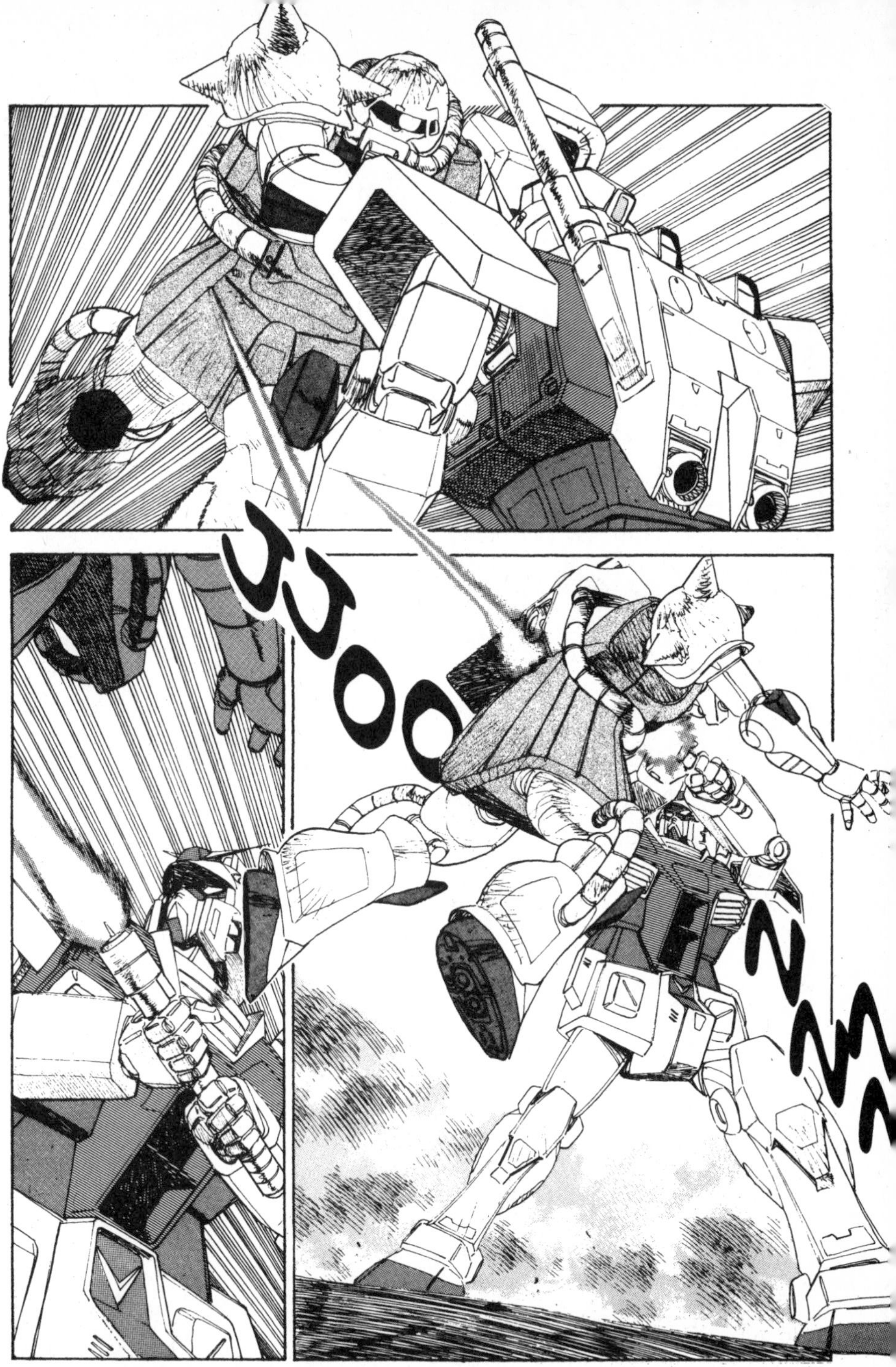

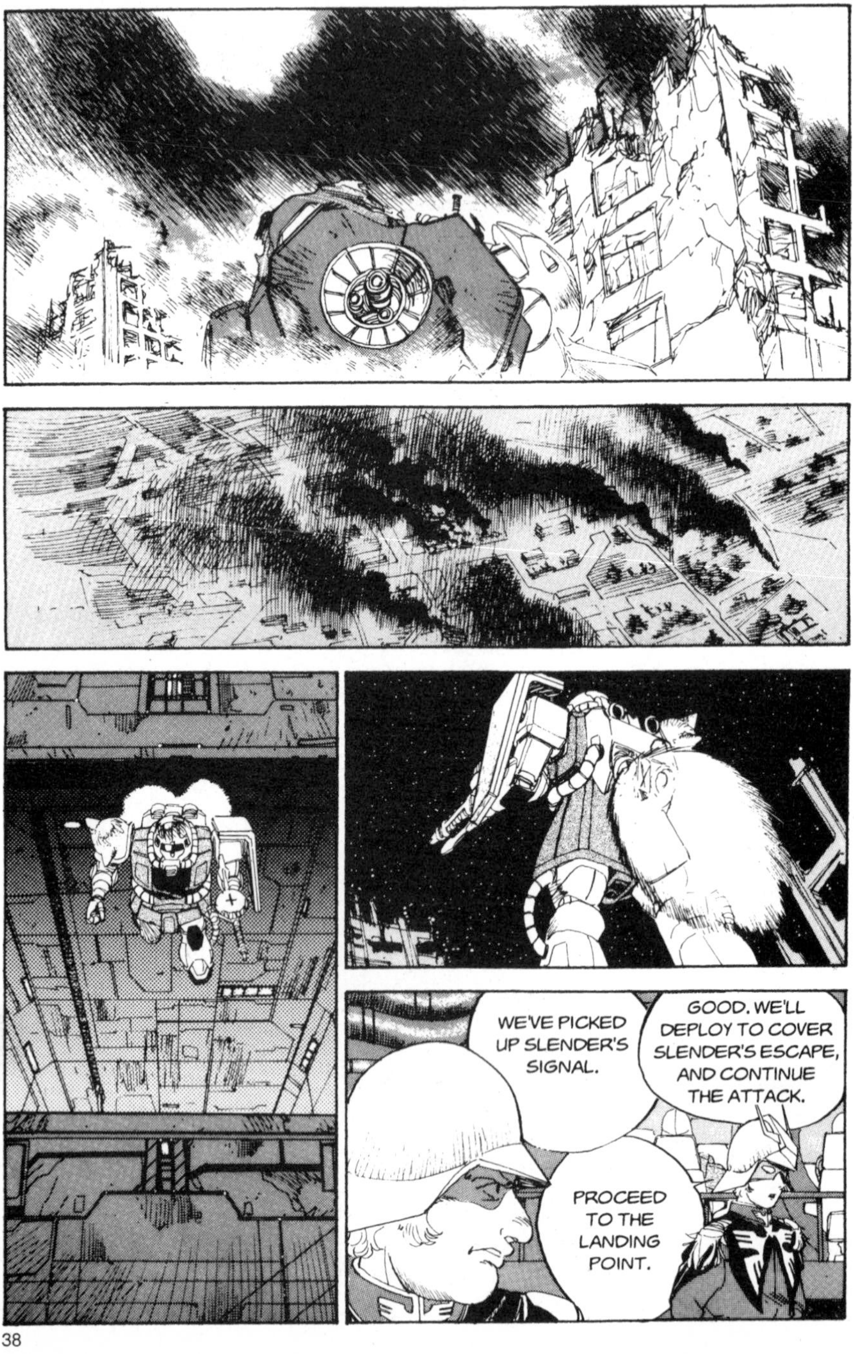
WE'VE PICKED UP SLENDER'S SIGNAL.
GOOD. WE'LL DEPLOY TO COVER SLENDER'S ESCAPE, AND CONTINUE THE ATTACK.
PROCEED TO THE LANDING POINT.

HAHH

HAHH

HAHH

HAHH

VWAAHHH

IT LOOKS LIKE THE LEAK IN THE ATMOSPHERE'S BEEN STOPPED. GET THOSE CIVILIANS EVACUATED TO THE *WHITE BASE.*

YES, SIR.

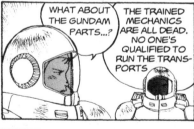

WHAT ABOUT THE GUNDAM PARTS...?

THE TRAINED MECHANICS ARE ALL DEAD. NO ONE'S QUALIFIED TO RUN THE TRANSPORTS

I DON'T KNOW IF *HE'S* A TRAINED PILOT OR NOT, BUT HE'S GOING TO HELP US.

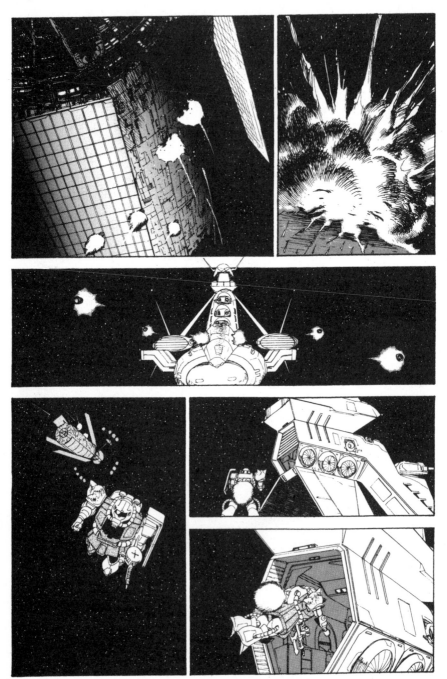

OH!!

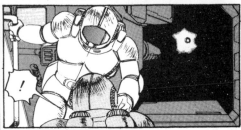

CAPTAIN!
I'LL TAKE OVER
THE GUN.
PLEASE RETURN
TO THE BRIDGE!

ALL
RIGHT.

ARRGHH!

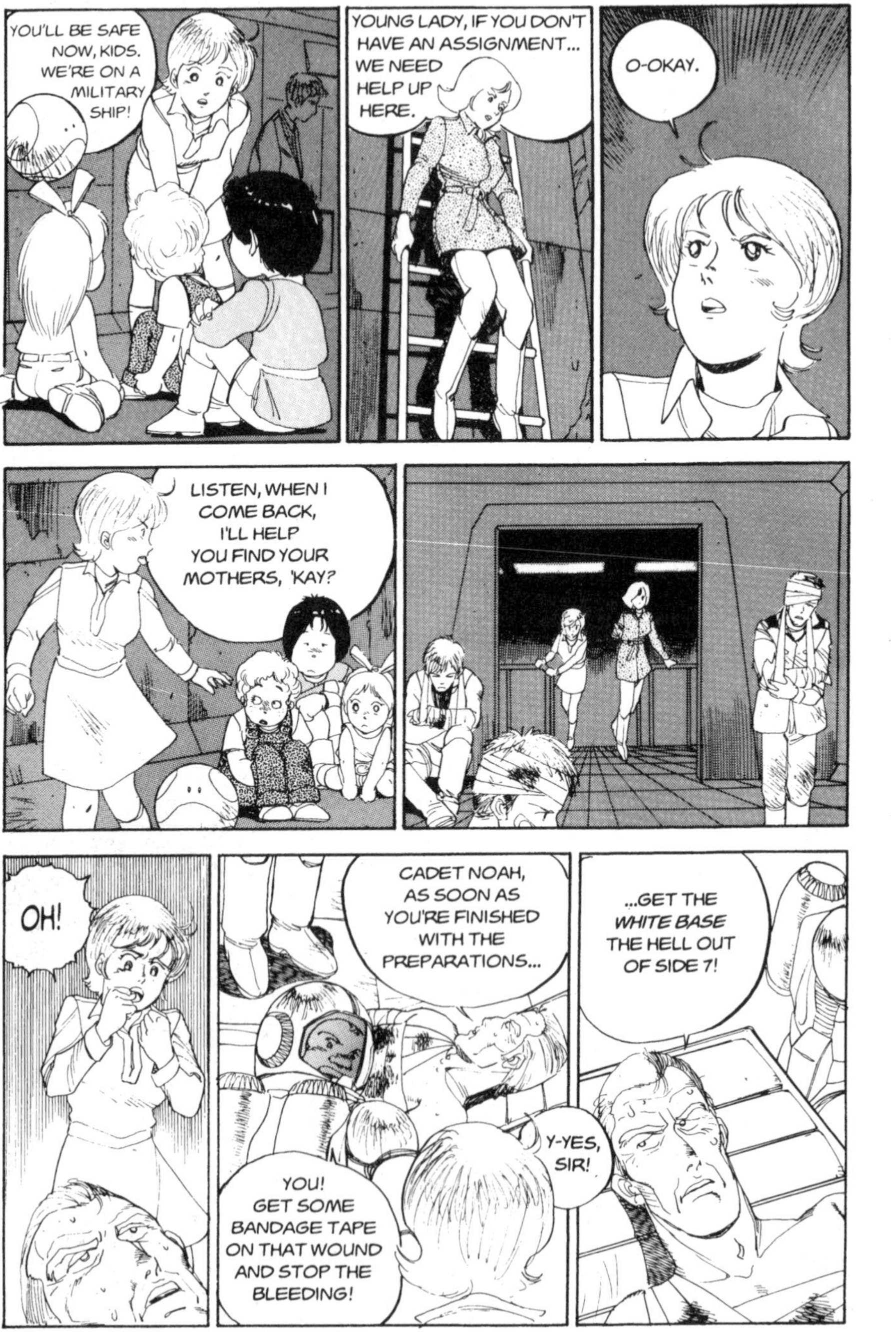

YOU'LL BE SAFE NOW, KIDS. WE'RE ON A MILITARY SHIP!
YOUNG LADY, IF YOU DON'T HAVE AN ASSIGNMENT... WE NEED HELP UP HERE.
O-OKAY.
LISTEN, WHEN I COME BACK, I'LL HELP YOU FIND YOUR MOTHERS, 'KAY?
OH!
CADET NOAH, AS SOON AS YOU'RE FINISHED WITH THE PREPARATIONS...
YOU! GET SOME BANDAGE TAPE ON THAT WOUND AND STOP THE BLEEDING!
Y-YES, SIR!
...GET THE *WHITE BASE* THE HELL OUT OF SIDE 7!

YES, SIR.

BUT WE STILL DON'T HAVE A QUALIFIED PILOT--

=COUGH COUGH=

EXCUSE ME, BUT... I MAY BE ABLE TO HELP.

WHO ARE YOU?

MIRAI YASHIMA. I'M ONLY LICENSED TO PILOT A CRUISER-CLASS SPACE GLIDER, BUT...

YASHIMA? OF *THE* YASHIMA FAMILY?

SEE WHAT YOU CAN DO.

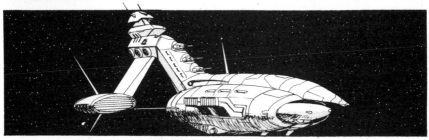

YOU THINK IT'S THE FEDERAL FORCES' V-OPERATION?

Z-Z Z

YES, SIR.

THE ENEMY'S ALREADY COMPLETED THEIR OWN MOBILE SUITS.

43

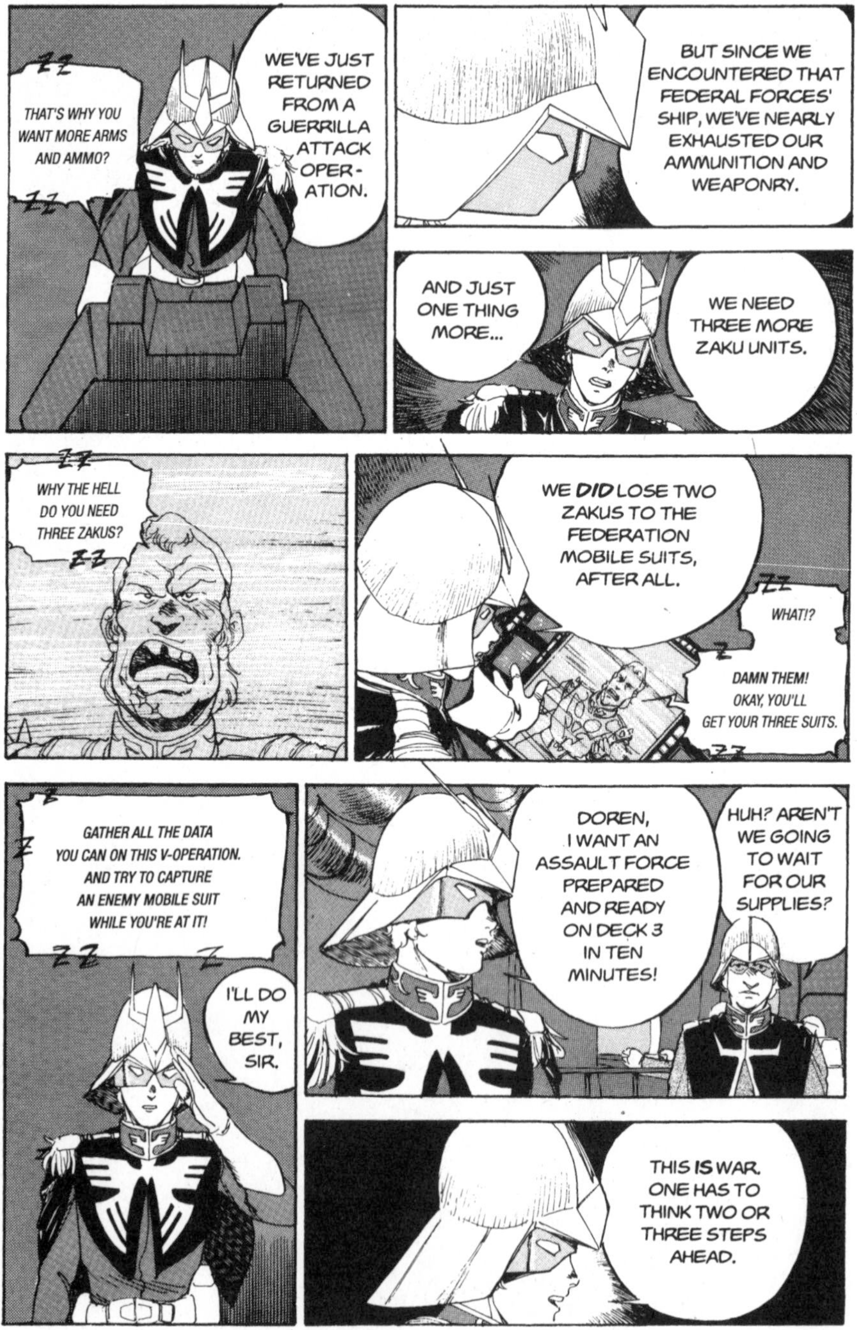
THAT'S WHY YOU WANT MORE ARMS AND AMMO?
WE'VE JUST RETURNED FROM A GUERRILLA ATTACK OPER-ATION.
BUT SINCE WE ENCOUNTERED THAT FEDERAL FORCES' SHIP, WE'VE NEARLY EXHAUSTED OUR AMMUNITION AND WEAPONRY.
AND JUST ONE THING MORE...
WE NEED THREE MORE ZAKU UNITS.
WHY THE HELL DO YOU NEED THREE ZAKUS?
WE DID LOSE TWO ZAKUS TO THE FEDERATION MOBILE SUITS, AFTER ALL.
WHAT!?
DAMN THEM! OKAY, YOU'LL GET YOUR THREE SUITS.
GATHER ALL THE DATA YOU CAN ON THIS V-OPERATION. AND TRY TO CAPTURE AN ENEMY MOBILE SUIT WHILE YOU'RE AT IT!
I'LL DO MY BEST, SIR.
DOREN, I WANT AN ASSAULT FORCE PREPARED AND READY ON DECK 3 IN TEN MINUTES!
HUH? AREN'T WE GOING TO WAIT FOR OUR SUPPLIES?
THIS IS WAR. ONE HAS TO THINK TWO OR THREE STEPS AHEAD.

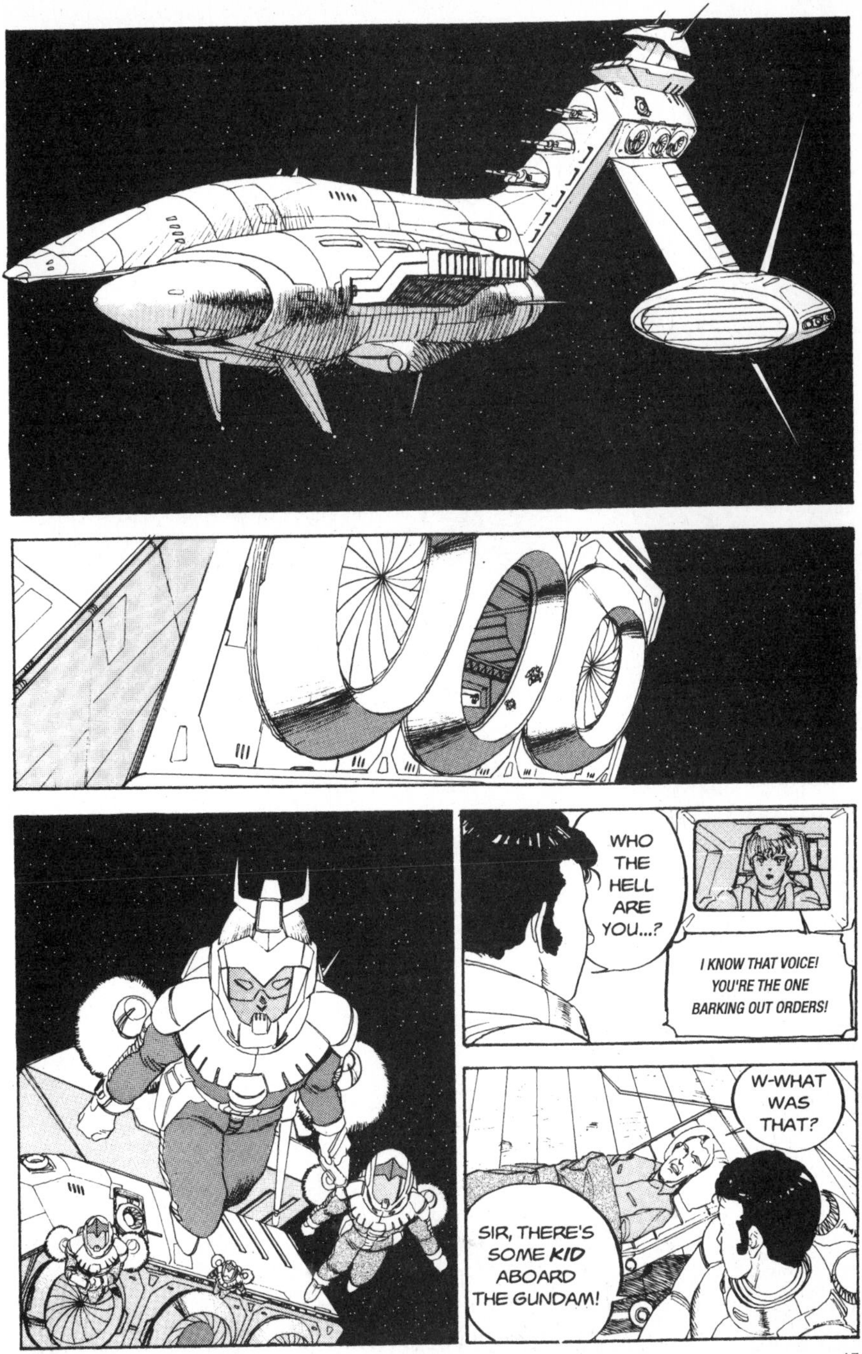

WHO THE HELL ARE YOU...?
I KNOW THAT VOICE! YOU'RE THE ONE BARKING OUT ORDERS!
W-WHAT WAS THAT?
SIR, THERE'S SOME KID ABOARD THE GUNDAM!

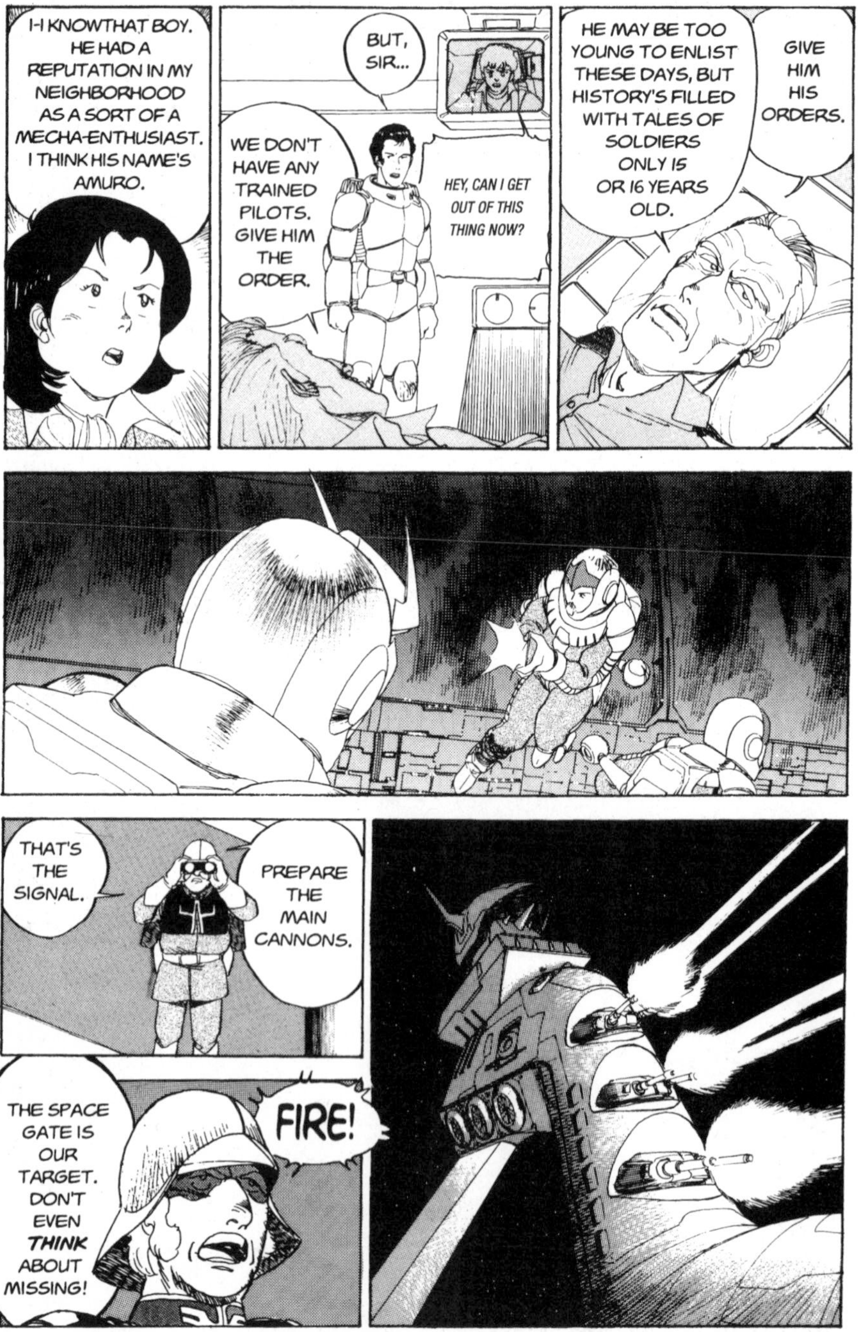
I-I KNOW THAT BOY. HE HAD A REPUTATION IN MY NEIGHBORHOOD AS A SORT OF A MECHA-ENTHUSIAST. I THINK HIS NAME'S AMURO.
BUT, SIR...
WE DON'T HAVE ANY TRAINED PILOTS. GIVE HIM THE ORDER.
HEY, CAN I GET OUT OF THIS THING NOW?
HE MAY BE TOO YOUNG TO ENLIST THESE DAYS, BUT HISTORY'S FILLED WITH TALES OF SOLDIERS ONLY 15 OR 16 YEARS OLD.
GIVE HIM HIS ORDERS.
THAT'S THE SIGNAL.
PREPARE THE MAIN CANNONS.
THE SPACE GATE IS OUR TARGET. DON'T EVEN THINK ABOUT MISSING!
FIRE!

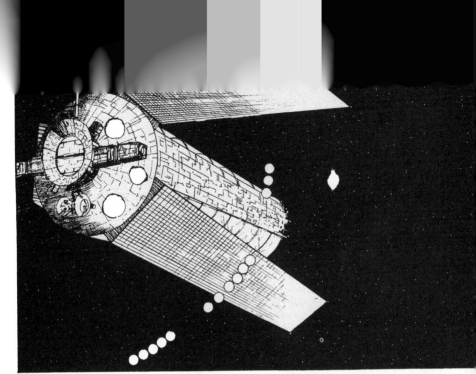

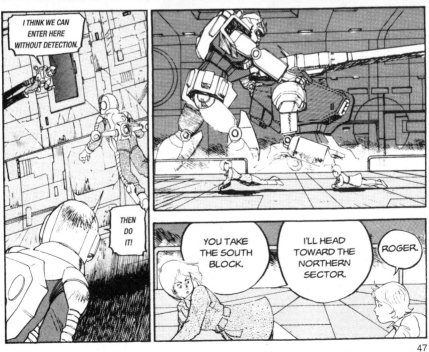

I THINK WE CAN ENTER HERE WITHOUT DETECTION.

THEN DO IT!

YOU TAKE THE SOUTH BLOCK.

I'LL HEAD TOWARD THE NORTHERN SECTOR.

ROGER.

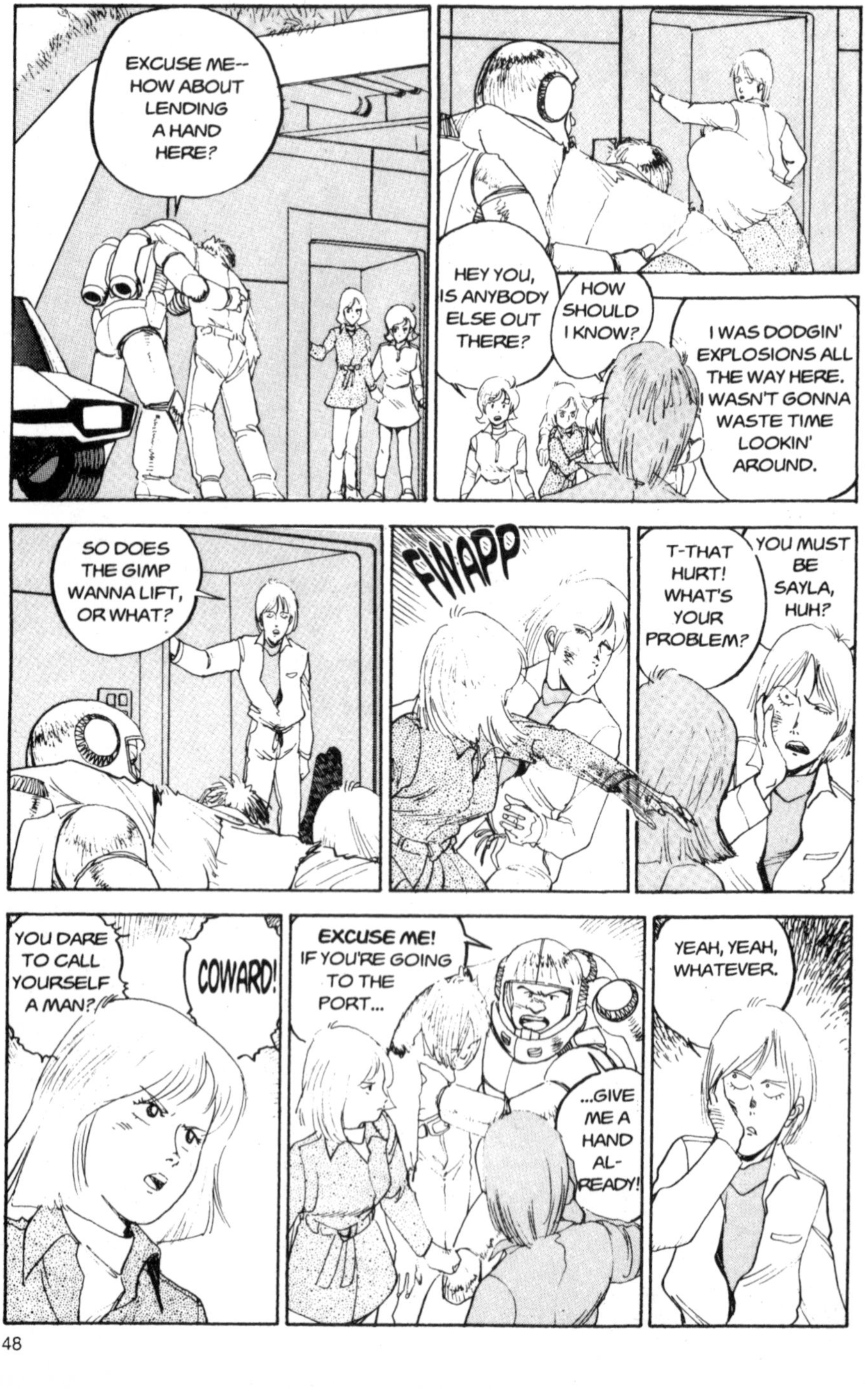
EXCUSE ME-- HOW ABOUT LENDING A HAND HERE?
HEY YOU, IS ANYBODY ELSE OUT THERE?
HOW SHOULD I KNOW?
I WAS DODGIN' EXPLOSIONS ALL THE WAY HERE. I WASN'T GONNA WASTE TIME LOOKIN' AROUND.
SO DOES THE GIMP WANNA LIFT, OR WHAT?
FWAPP
T-THAT HURT! WHAT'S YOUR PROBLEM?
YOU MUST BE SAYLA, HUH?
YOU DARE TO CALL YOURSELF A MAN?
COWARD!
EXCUSE ME! IF YOU'RE GOING TO THE PORT...
...GIVE ME A HAND AL-READY!
YEAH, YEAH, WHATEVER.

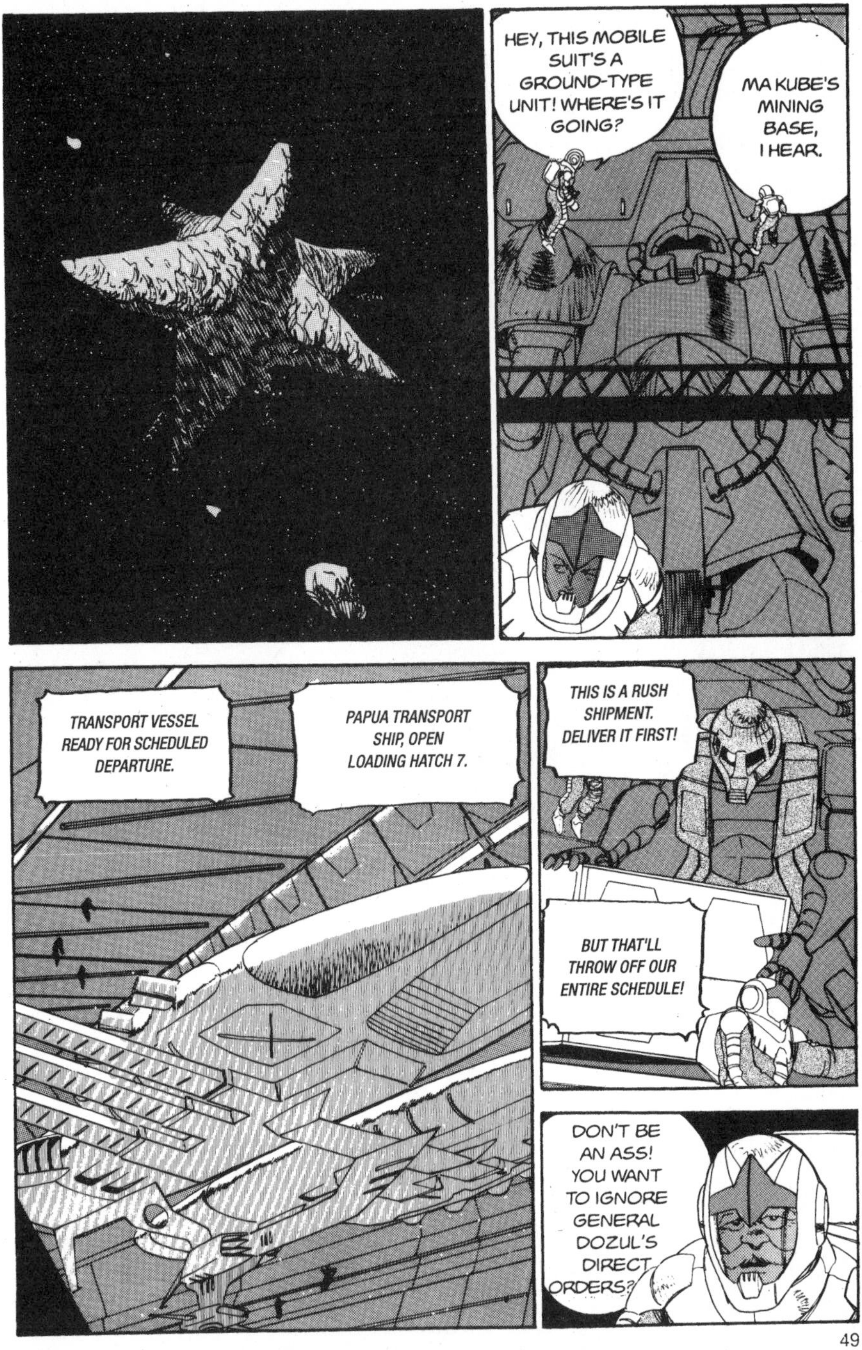
HEY, THIS MOBILE SUIT'S A GROUND-TYPE UNIT! WHERE'S IT GOING?
MA KUBE'S MINING BASE, I HEAR.
TRANSPORT VESSEL READY FOR SCHEDULED DEPARTURE.
PAPUA TRANSPORT SHIP, OPEN LOADING HATCH 7.
THIS IS A RUSH SHIPMENT. DELIVER IT FIRST!
BUT THAT'LL THROW OFF OUR ENTIRE SCHEDULE!
DON'T BE AN ASS! YOU WANT TO IGNORE GENERAL DOZUL'S DIRECT ORDERS?

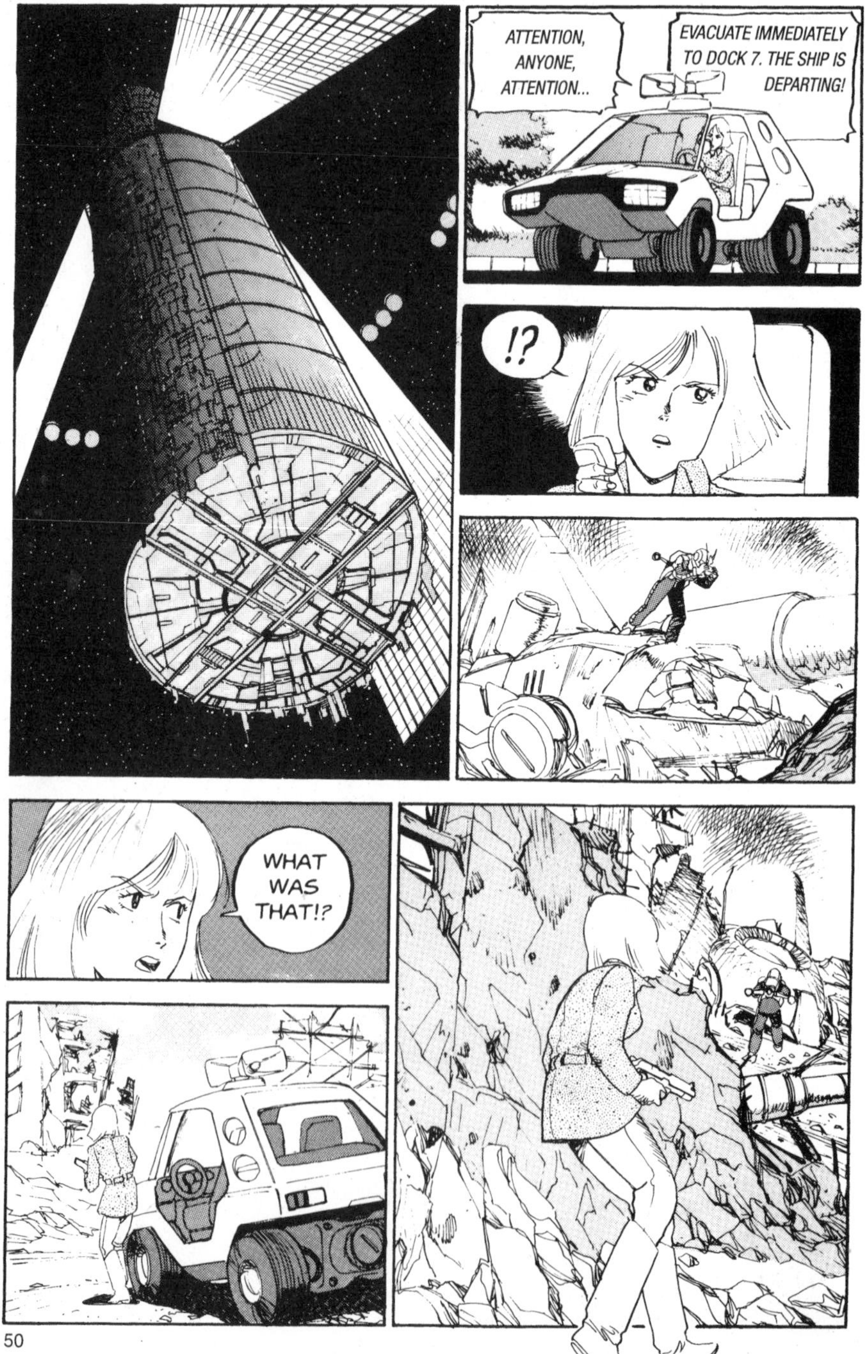
ATTENTION, ANYONE, ATTENTION...
EVACUATE IMMEDIATELY TO DOCK 7. THE SHIP IS DEPARTING!
!?
WHAT WAS THAT!?

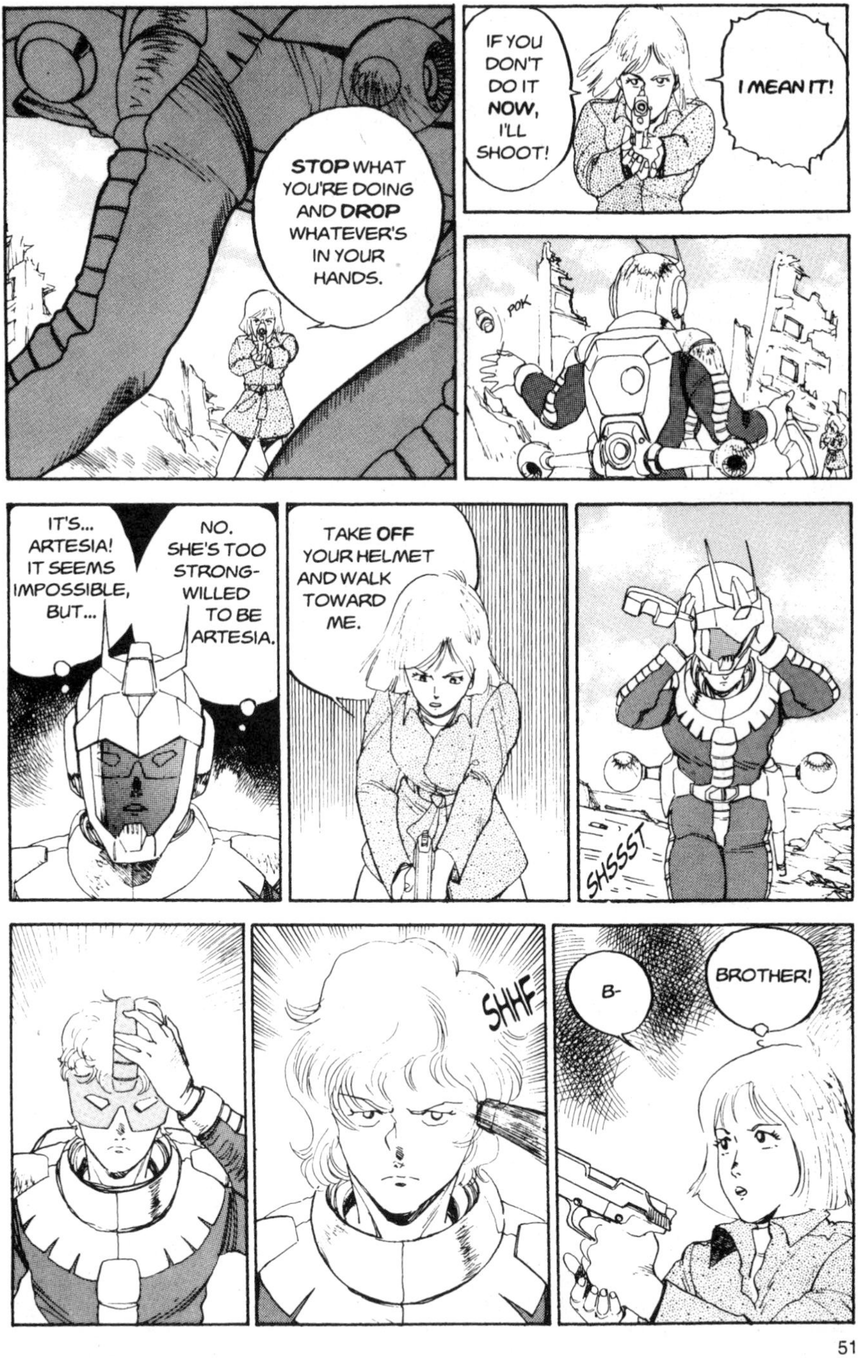
STOP WHAT YOU'RE DOING AND DROP WHATEVER'S IN YOUR HANDS.
IF YOU DON'T DO IT NOW, I'LL SHOOT!
I MEAN IT!
POK
IT'S... ARTESIA! IT SEEMS IMPOSSIBLE, BUT...
NO. SHE'S TOO STRONG-WILLED TO BE ARTESIA.
TAKE OFF YOUR HELMET AND WALK TOWARD ME.
SHSSST
SHHF
B-
BROTHER!

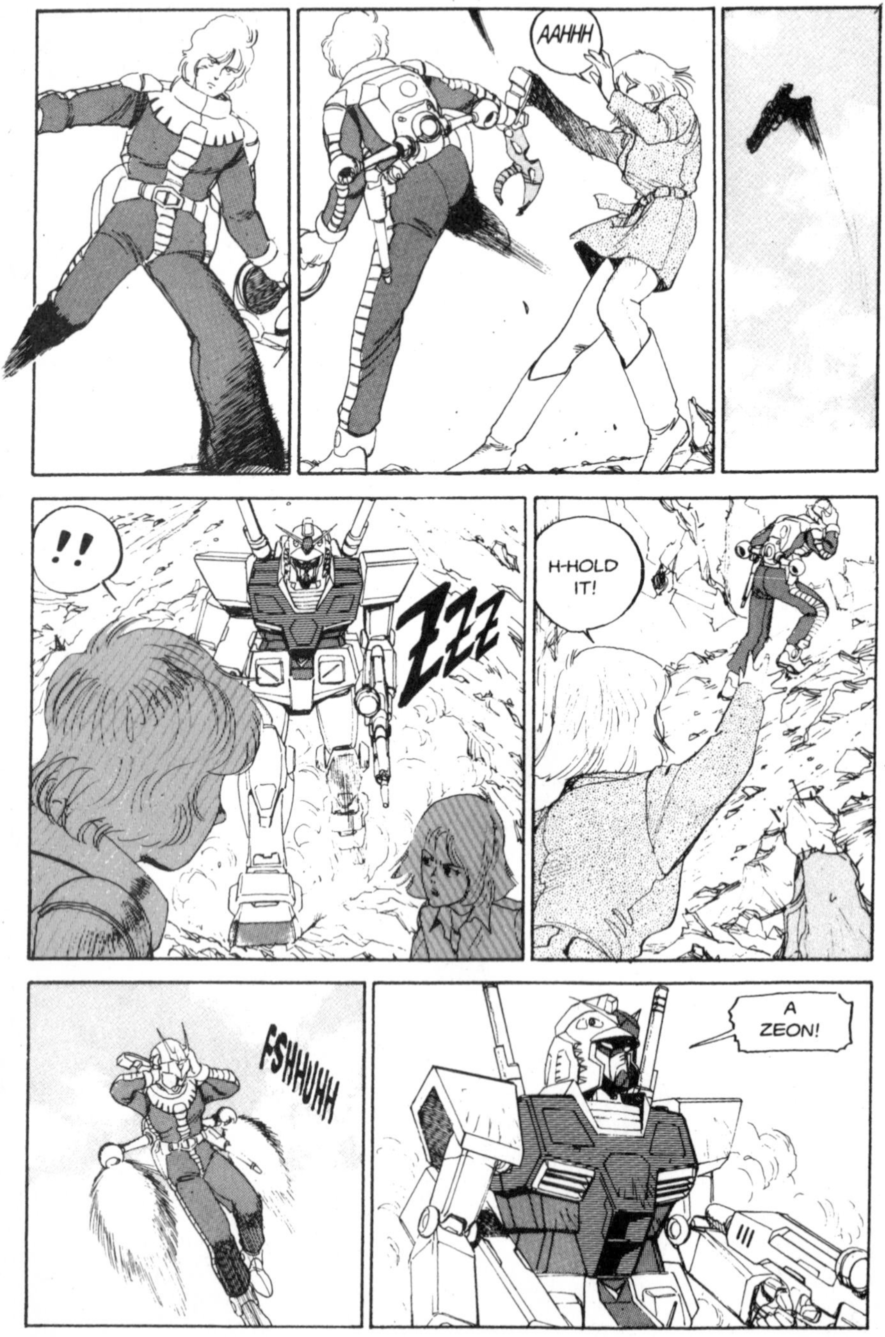
AAHHH
!!
ZZZ
H-HOLD IT!
FSHHUHH
A ZEON!

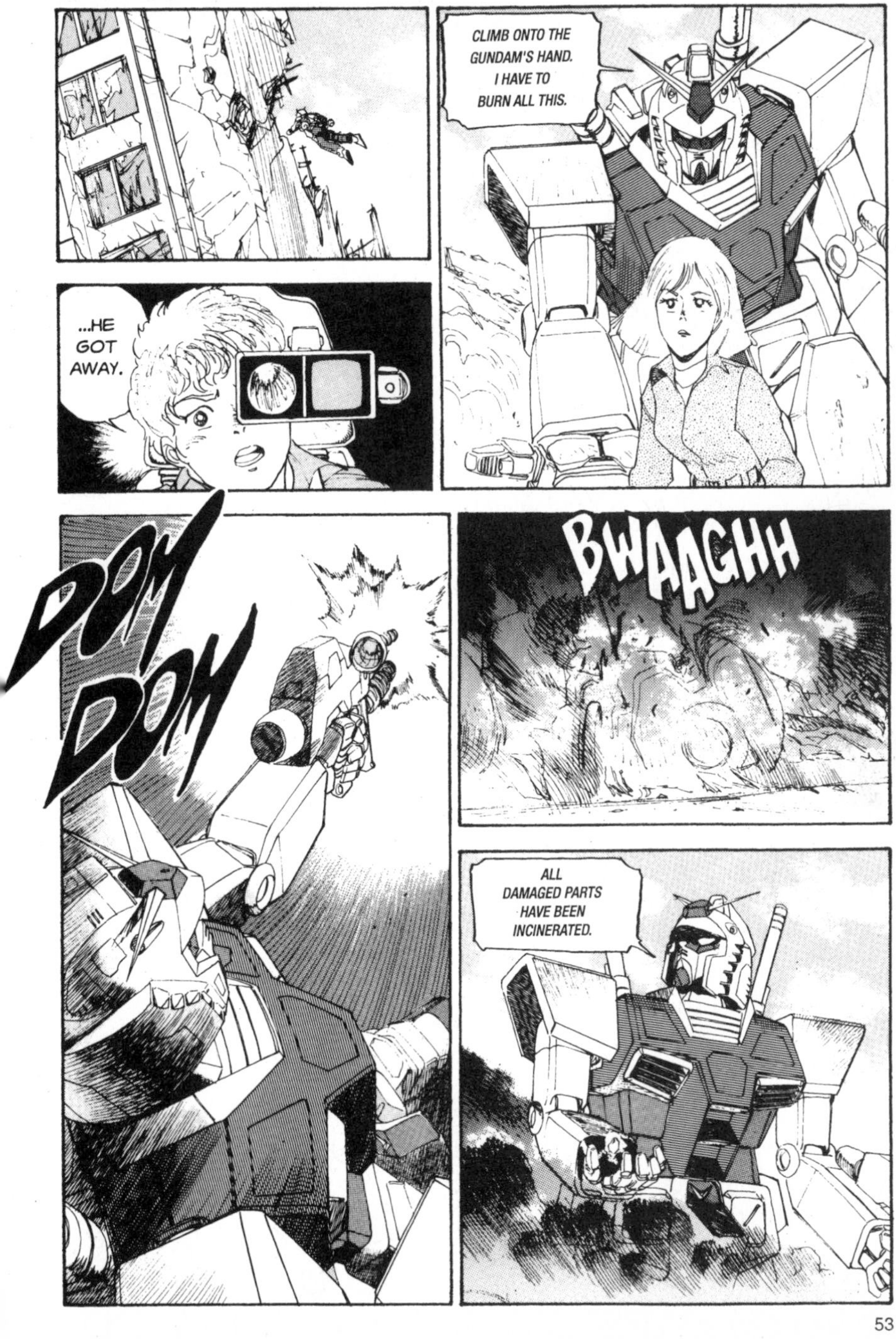
...HE GOT AWAY.
CLIMB ONTO THE GUNDAM'S HAND. I HAVE TO BURN ALL THIS.
DOM DOM
BWAAGHH
ALL DAMAGED PARTS HAVE BEEN INCINERATED.

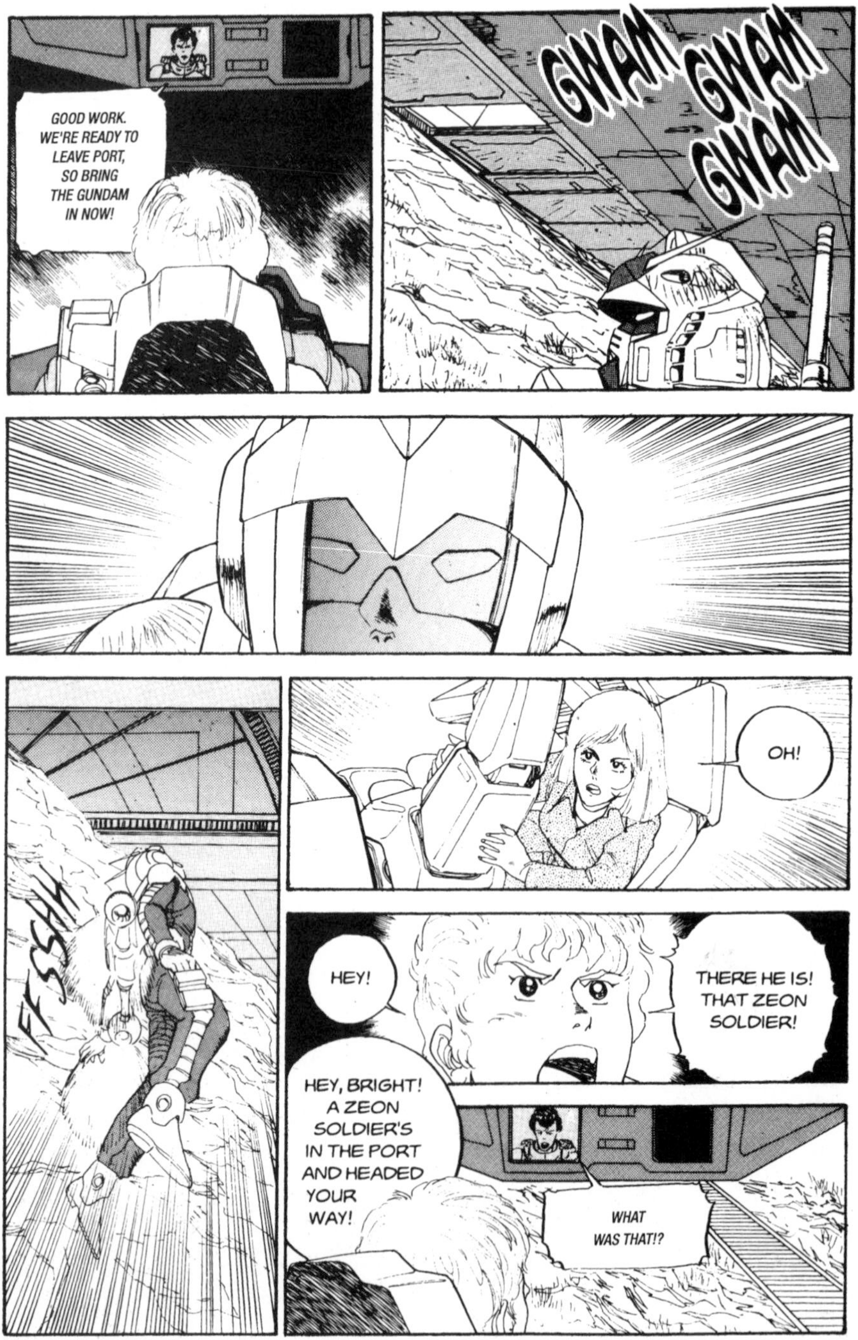
GOOD WORK. WE'RE READY TO LEAVE PORT, SO BRING THE GUNDAM IN NOW!
GWAM GWAM GWAM
FSSSH
OH!
HEY!
THERE HE IS! THAT ZEON SOLDIER!
HEY, BRIGHT! A ZEON SOLDIER'S IN THE PORT AND HEADED YOUR WAY!
WHAT WAS THAT!?

LISTEN UP!

ARM YOURSELVES, NOW! STOP THAT ZEON SOLDIER FROM GAINING ACCESS AT ALL COSTS!

THAT'S IT-- THE NEW FEDERATION SHIP!

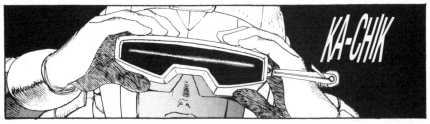

KA-CHIK

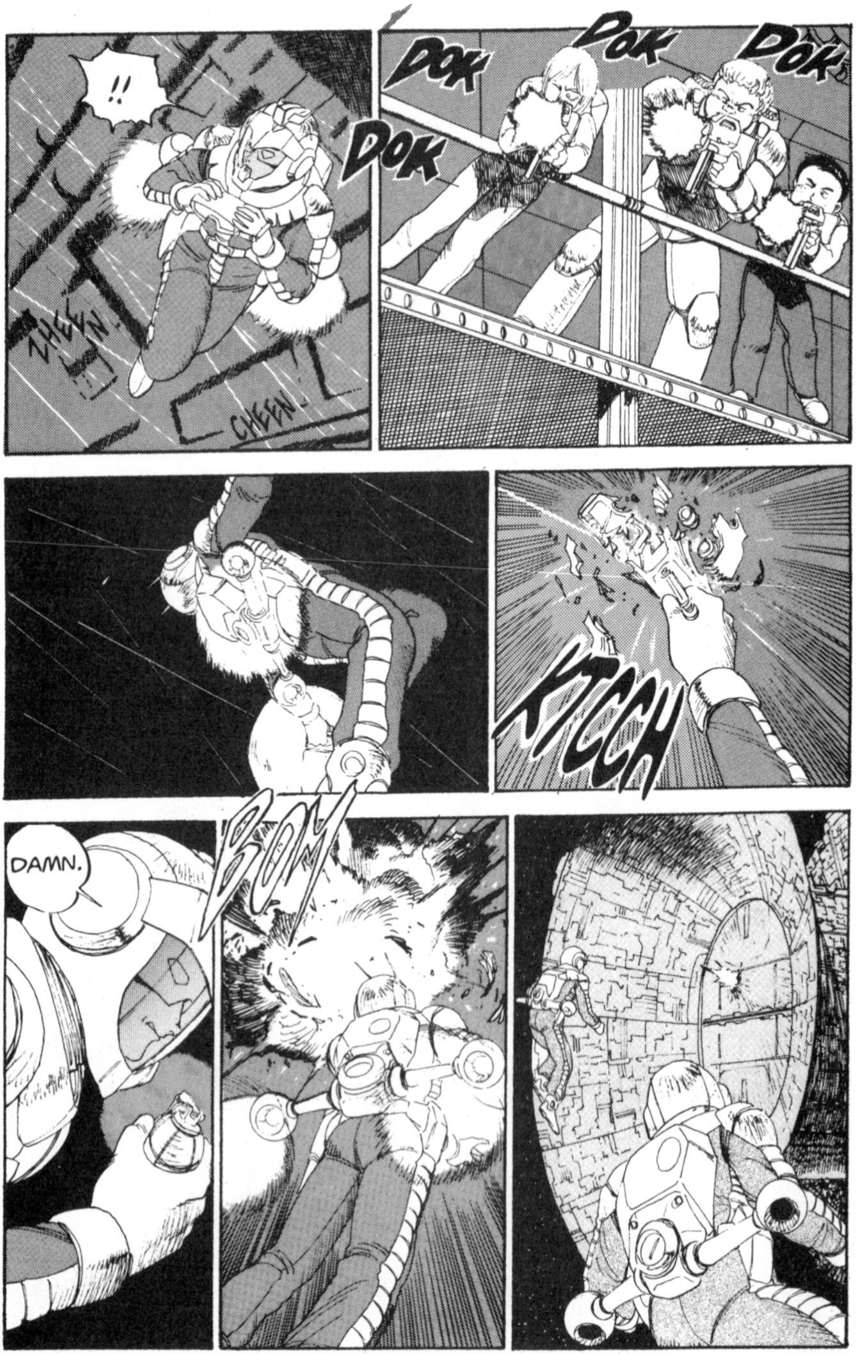
!!
ZHEEN.
CHEEN.
DOK
DOK
DOK
DOK
KITCH
DAMN.
BOM

RETREAT TO THE SHIP! THEY'RE RIGHT BEHIND ME!

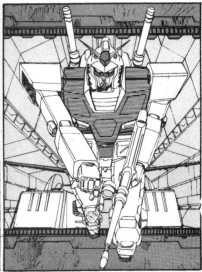

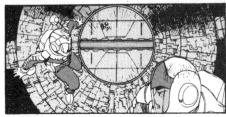

HAHH
HAHH
HAHH

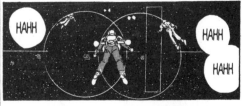

HAHH
HAHH
HAHH

I'LL SHOOT! I'LL SHOOT!

I'M GONNA SHOOT YOU!

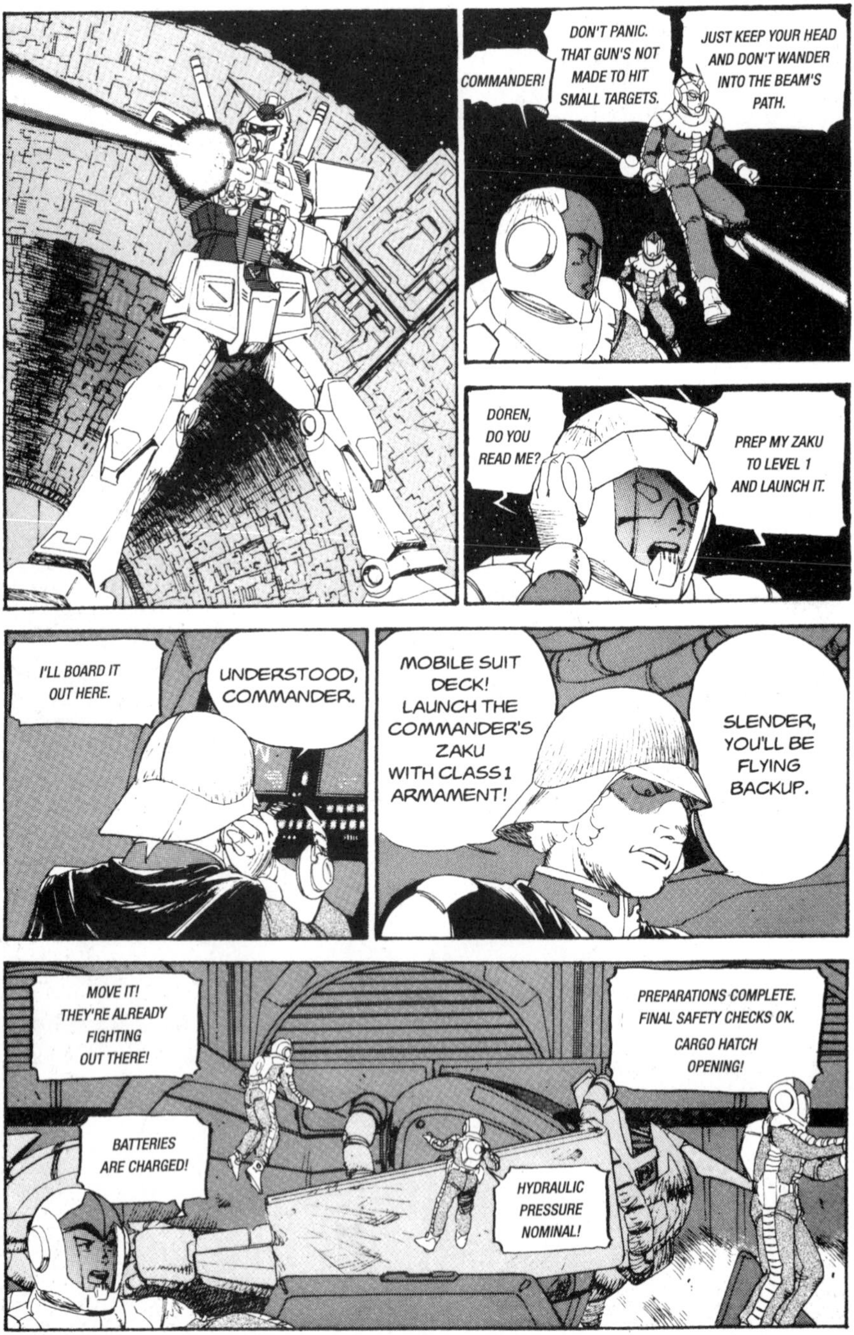
COMMANDER!
DON'T PANIC. THAT GUN'S NOT MADE TO HIT SMALL TARGETS.
JUST KEEP YOUR HEAD AND DON'T WANDER INTO THE BEAM'S PATH.
DOREN, DO YOU READ ME?
PREP MY ZAKU TO LEVEL 1 AND LAUNCH IT.
I'LL BOARD IT OUT HERE.
UNDERSTOOD, COMMANDER.
MOBILE SUIT DECK! LAUNCH THE COMMANDER'S ZAKU WITH CLASS 1 ARMAMENT!
SLENDER, YOU'LL BE FLYING BACKUP.
MOVE IT! THEY'RE ALREADY FIGHTING OUT THERE!
PREPARATIONS COMPLETE. FINAL SAFETY CHECKS OK.
CARGO HATCH OPENING!
BATTERIES ARE CHARGED!
HYDRAULIC PRESSURE NOMINAL!

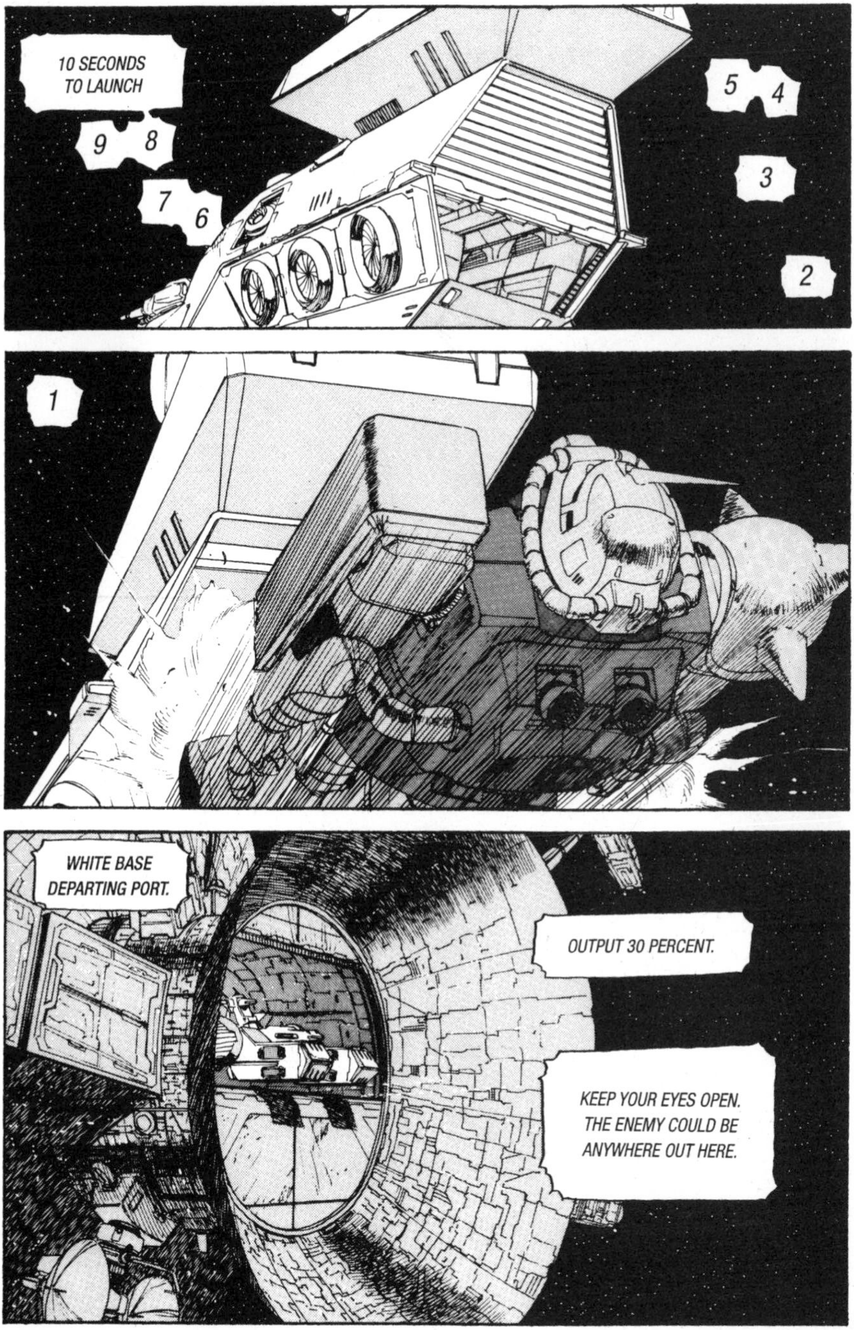
10 SECONDS
TO LAUNCH
9 8
7 6
5 4
3
2
1
WHITE BASE
DEPARTING PORT.
OUTPUT 30 PERCENT.
KEEP YOUR EYES OPEN.
THE ENEMY COULD BE
ANYWHERE OUT HERE.

THE LEFT DISPLAY IS FOR BROADCAST, THE RIGHT IS RECEIVE. WHEN THE RED LIGHT'S ON, YOU HAVE A CLEAR CHANNEL.

I SEE.

KEEP YOUR EYES ON THAT LEFT PANEL.

THE COMPUTER WILL DO MOST OF THE WORK FOR YOU.

YOU'RE LOOKING A LITTLE TENSE.

THE COMPUTER CAN DO MOST OF IT AFTER ALL.

I KNOW.

SAY BRIGHT, CAN YA OPEN THE PORT BAY HATCH?

I WANNA TAKE OUT THE CORE FIGHTER.

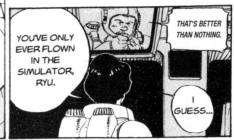

YOU'VE ONLY EVER FLOWN IN THE SIMULATOR, RYU.

THAT'S BETTER THAN NOTHING.

I GUESS...

I'VE GOT OBJECTS ON SCREEN! HEADING IN AT 10 O'CLOCK!

T-THEY'RE MISSILES!

WHAT!?

FIRE COUNTER-MISSILES!

HARD ABOUT!

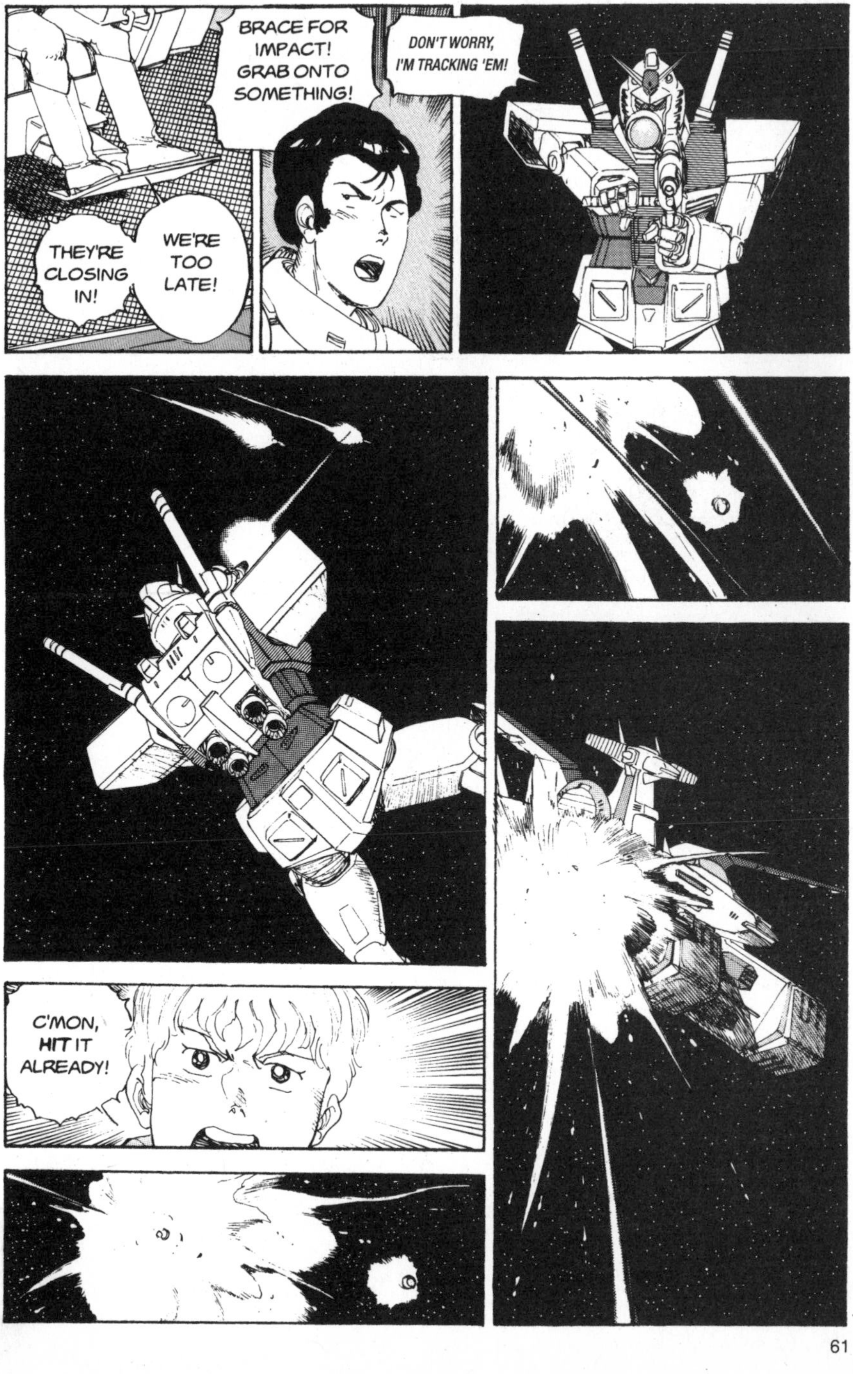
THEY'RE CLOSING IN!
WE'RE TOO LATE!
BRACE FOR IMPACT! GRAB ONTO SOMETHING!
DON'T WORRY, I'M TRACKING 'EM!
C'MON, **HIT** IT ALREADY!

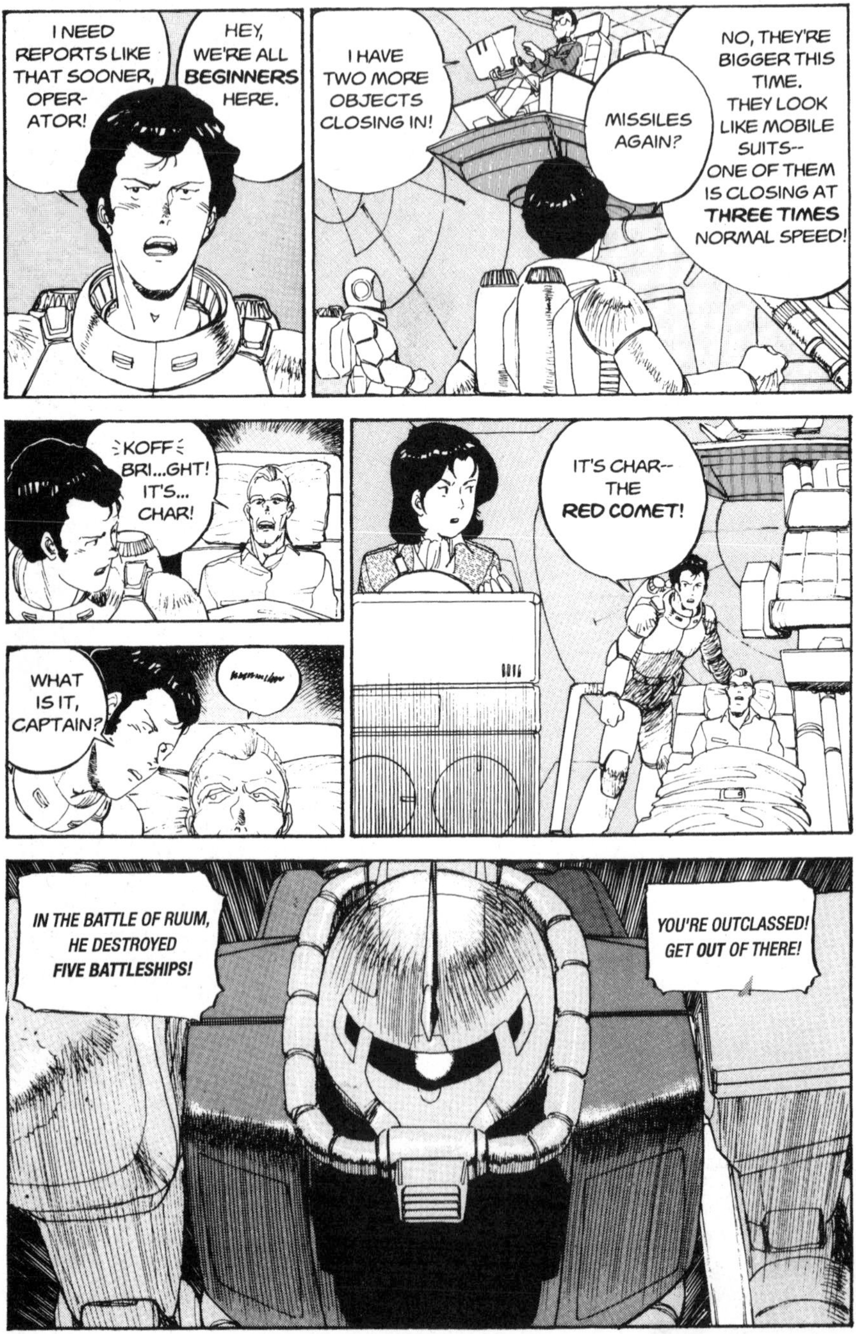
I NEED REPORTS LIKE THAT SOONER, OPERATOR!
HEY, WE'RE ALL BEGINNERS HERE.
I HAVE TWO MORE OBJECTS CLOSING IN!
MISSILES AGAIN?
NO, THEY'RE BIGGER THIS TIME. THEY LOOK LIKE MOBILE SUITS-- ONE OF THEM IS CLOSING AT THREE TIMES NORMAL SPEED!
KOFF
BRI...GHT! IT'S... CHAR!
WHAT IS IT, CAPTAIN?
IT'S CHAR-- THE RED COMET!
IN THE BATTLE OF RUUM, HE DESTROYED FIVE BATTLESHIPS!
YOU'RE OUTCLASSED! GET OUT OF THERE!

NOW SHOW ME...

...JUST WHAT A FEDERATION MOBILE SUIT CAN DO!

I CAN DO THIS! THIS TIME, I'LL BE JUST FIGHTING A ZAKU-- NOT THE HUMAN INSIDE!

NO, AMURO! YOU'RE NOT READY!

I CAN DO IT!

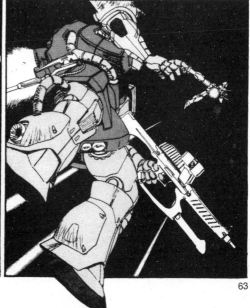

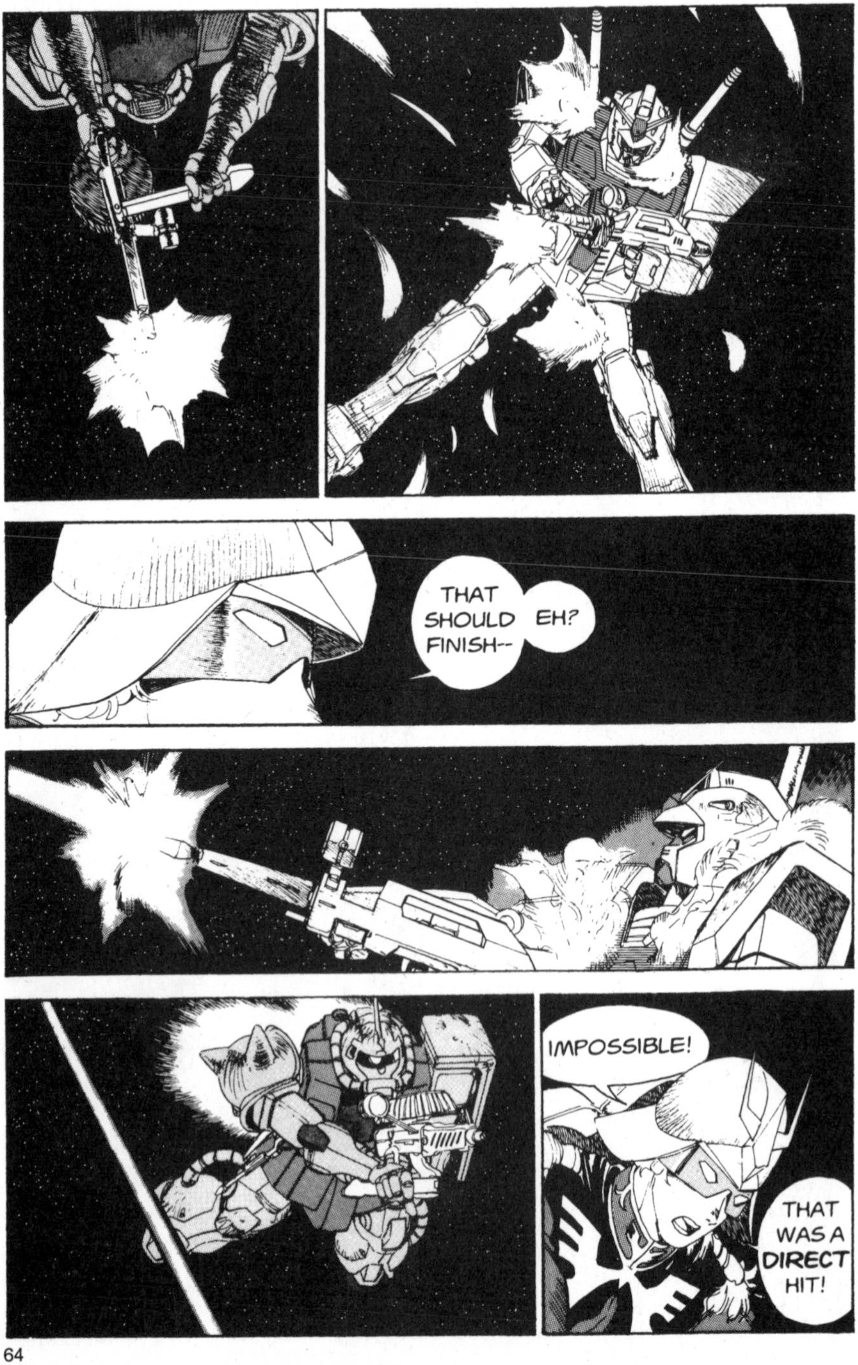
THAT SHOULD FINISH--
EH?
IMPOSSIBLE!
THAT WAS A DIRECT HIT!

HE'S TOO FAST!

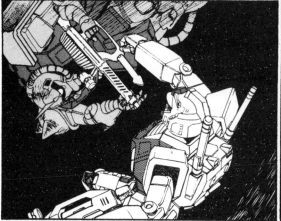

HOW CAN IT *MOVE* LIKE THAT?!

YOU'RE DRAINING THE BEAM RIFLE'S POWER TOO FAST!

I DON'T NEED YOUR *ADVICE*, DAMMIT!

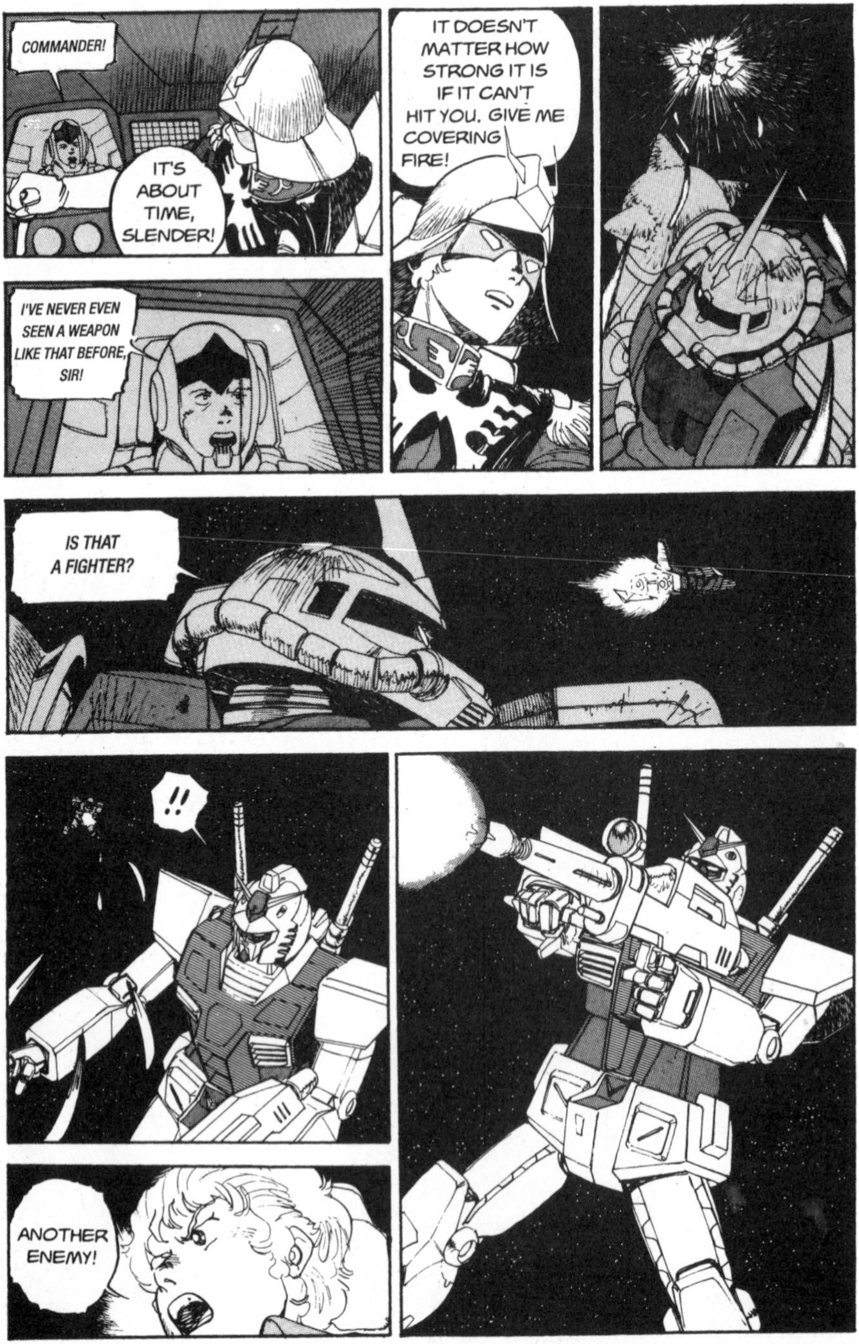
COMMANDER!
IT'S ABOUT TIME, SLENDER!
I'VE NEVER EVEN SEEN A WEAPON LIKE THAT BEFORE, SIR!
IT DOESN'T MATTER HOW STRONG IT IS IF IT CAN'T HIT YOU. GIVE ME COVERING FIRE!
IS THAT A FIGHTER?
!!
ANOTHER ENEMY!

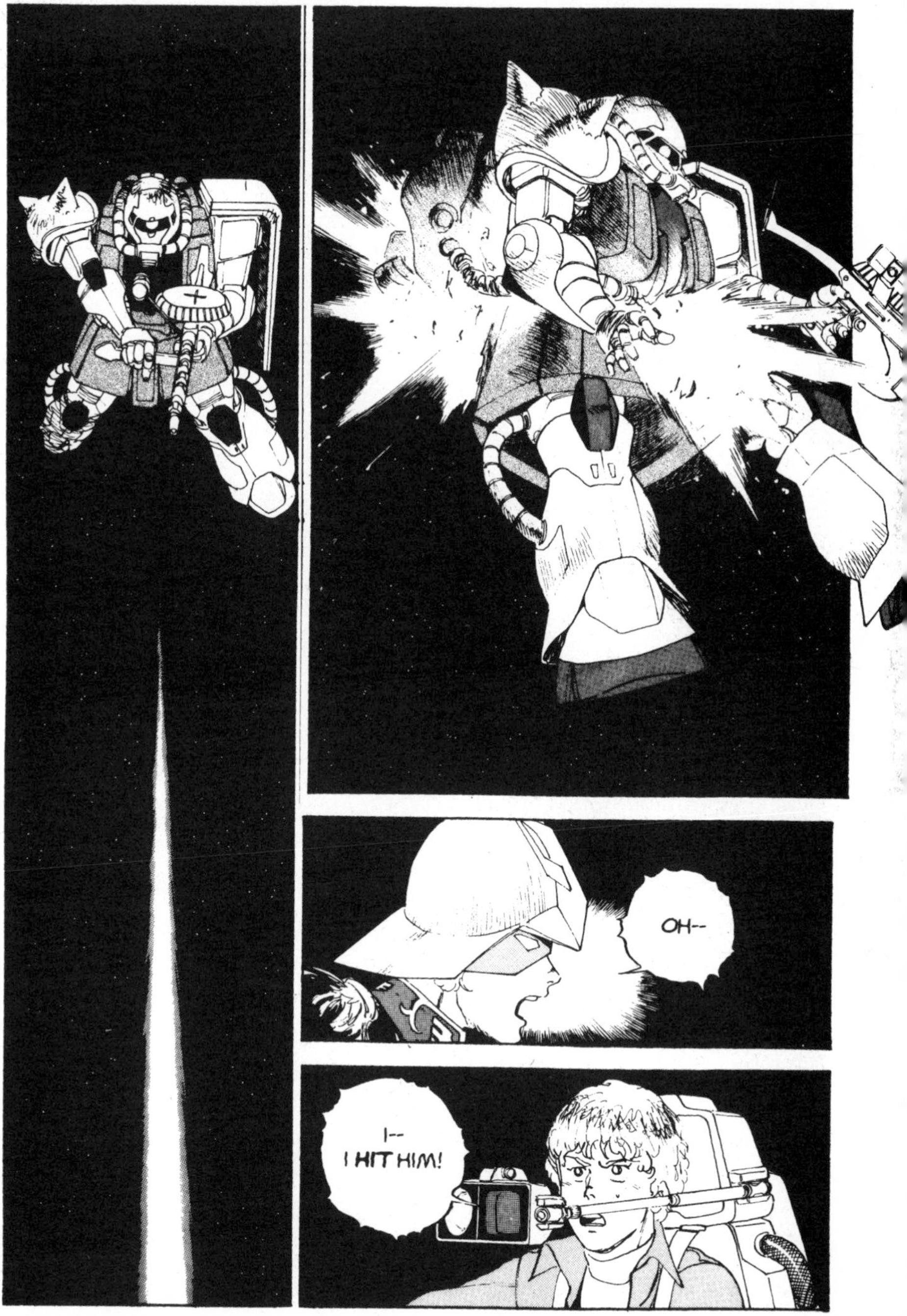
OH--
I--
I HIT HIM!

SLENDER!

NOTHING CAN DESTROY A ZAKU IN ONE SHOT!

DAMNED MOSQUITO!

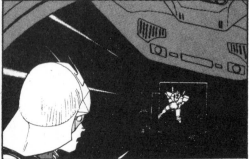

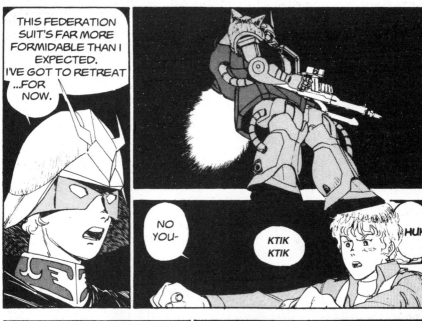

THIS FEDERATION SUIT'S FAR MORE FORMIDABLE THAN I EXPECTED. I'VE GOT TO RETREAT ...FOR NOW.

NO YOU-

KTIK KTIK

HUH?

PI PI

...OUT OF ENERGY.

I GUESS I OVERDID IT.

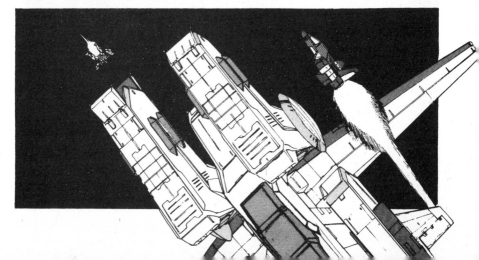

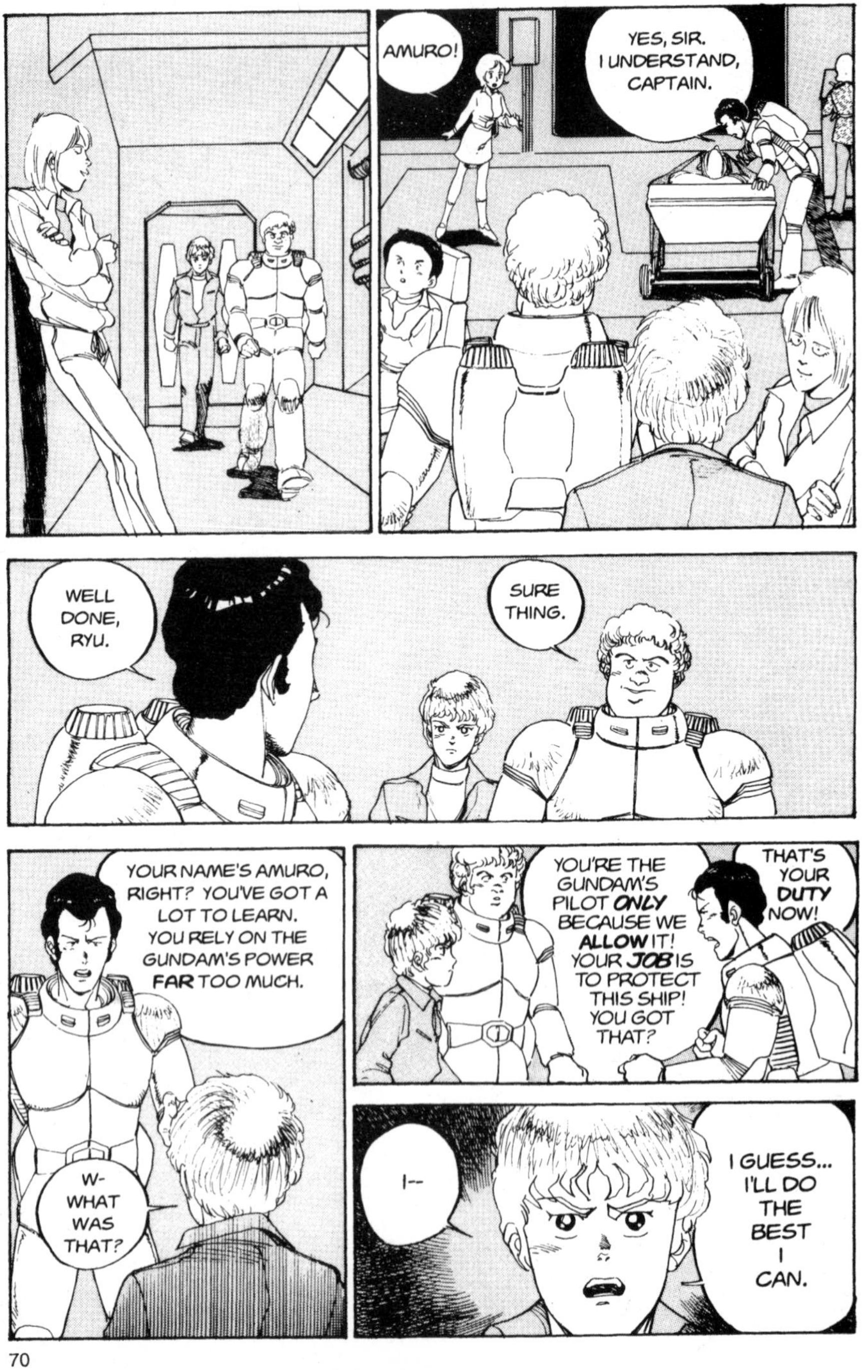
AMURO!
YES, SIR. I UNDERSTAND, CAPTAIN.
WELL DONE, RYU.
SURE THING.
YOUR NAME'S AMURO, RIGHT? YOU'VE GOT A LOT TO LEARN. YOU RELY ON THE GUNDAM'S POWER FAR TOO MUCH.
W-WHAT WAS THAT?
YOU'RE THE GUNDAM'S PILOT ONLY BECAUSE WE ALLOW IT! YOUR JOB IS TO PROTECT THIS SHIP! YOU GOT THAT?
THAT'S YOUR DUTY NOW!
I--
I GUESS... I'LL DO THE BEST I CAN.

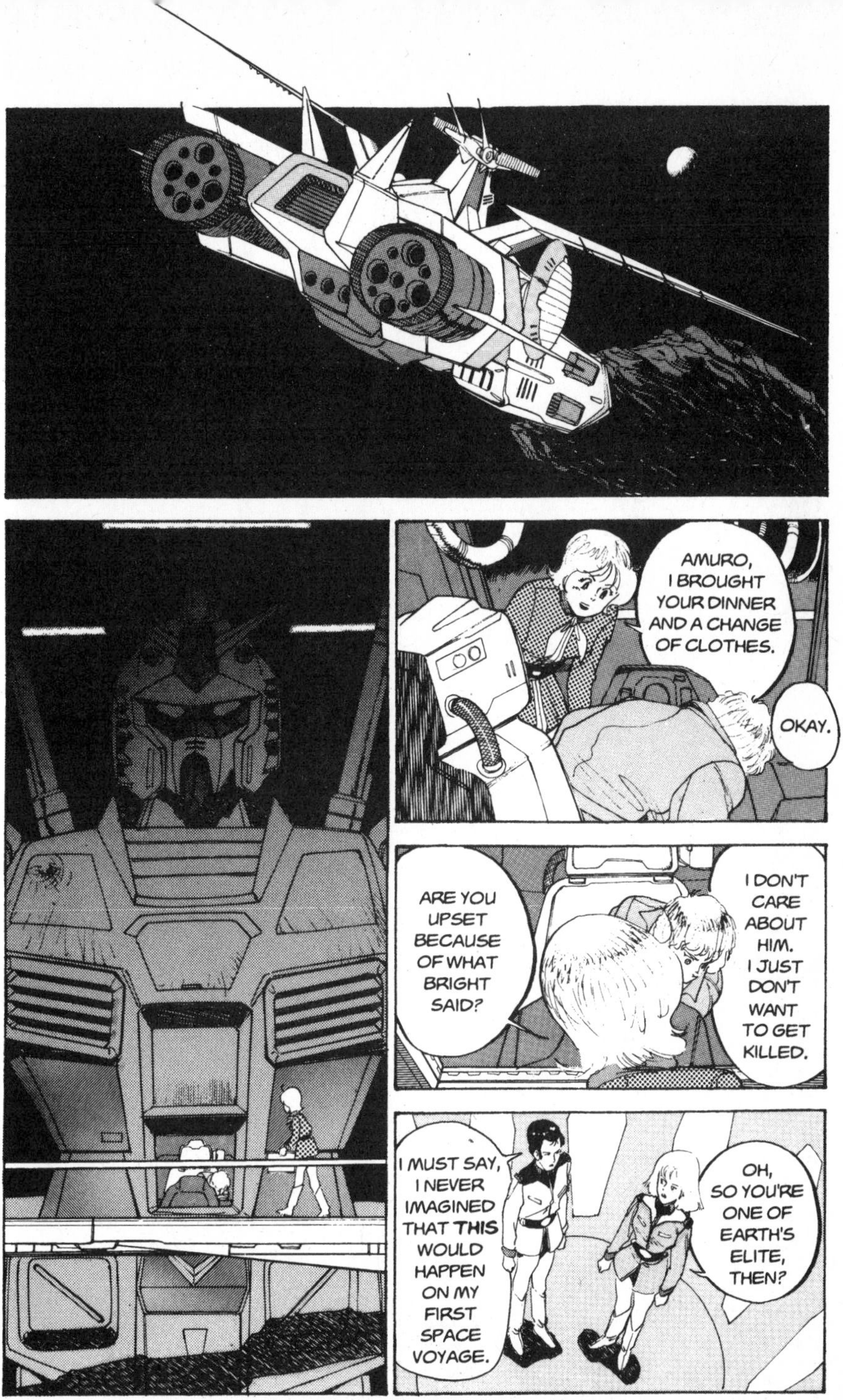
AMURO, I BROUGHT YOUR DINNER AND A CHANGE OF CLOTHES.
OKAY.
ARE YOU UPSET BECAUSE OF WHAT BRIGHT SAID?
I DON'T CARE ABOUT HIM. I JUST DON'T WANT TO GET KILLED.
I MUST SAY, I NEVER IMAGINED THAT **THIS** WOULD HAPPEN ON MY FIRST SPACE VOYAGE.
OH, SO YOU'RE ONE OF EARTH'S ELITE, THEN?

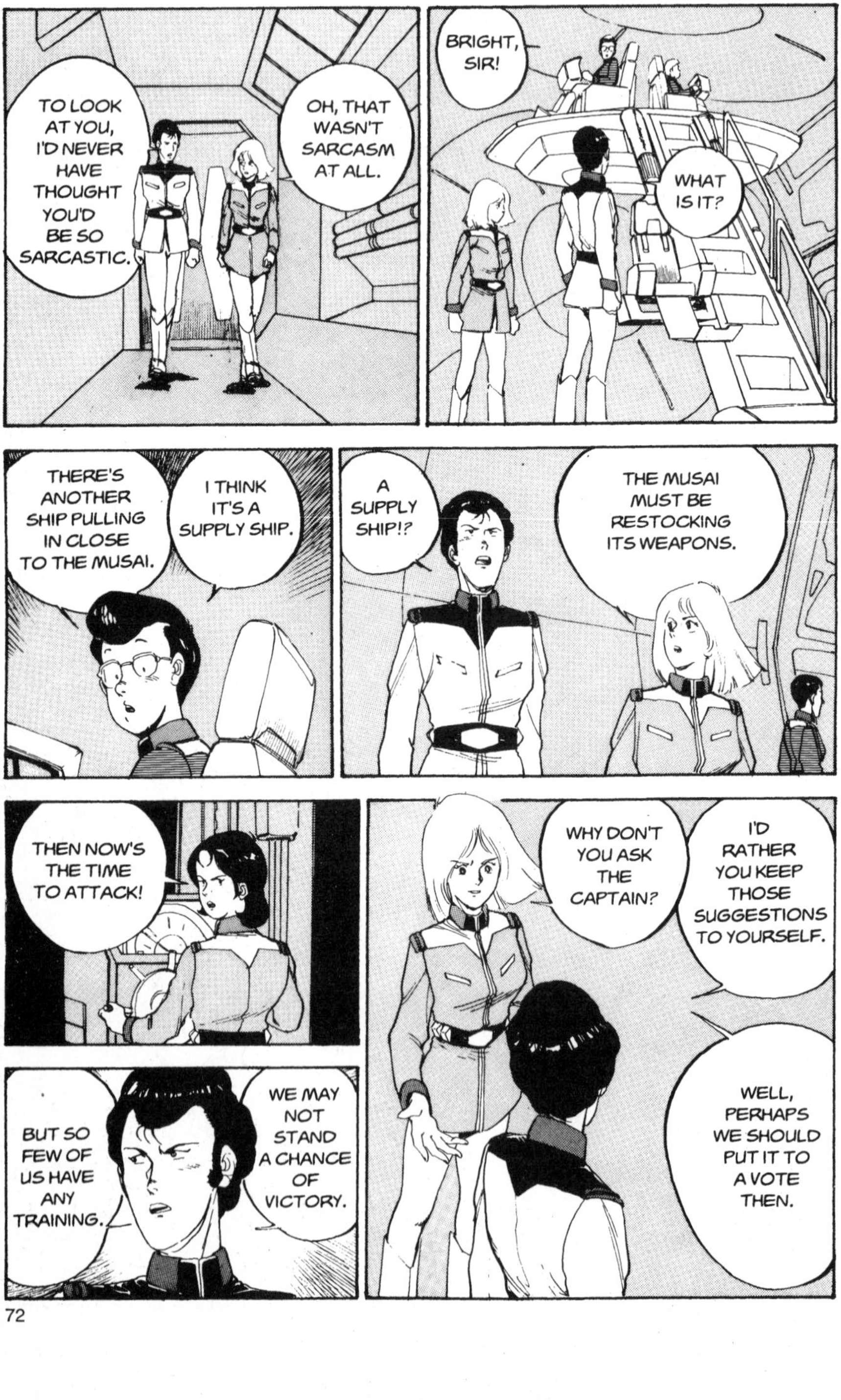
TO LOOK AT YOU, I'D NEVER HAVE THOUGHT YOU'D BE SO SARCASTIC.
OH, THAT WASN'T SARCASM AT ALL.
BRIGHT, SIR!
WHAT IS IT?
THERE'S ANOTHER SHIP PULLING IN CLOSE TO THE MUSAI.
I THINK IT'S A SUPPLY SHIP.
A SUPPLY SHIP!?
THE MUSAI MUST BE RESTOCKING ITS WEAPONS.
THEN NOW'S THE TIME TO ATTACK!
BUT SO FEW OF US HAVE ANY TRAINING.
WE MAY NOT STAND A CHANCE OF VICTORY.
WHY DON'T YOU ASK THE CAPTAIN?
I'D RATHER YOU KEEP THOSE SUGGESTIONS TO YOURSELF.
WELL, PERHAPS WE SHOULD PUT IT TO A VOTE THEN.

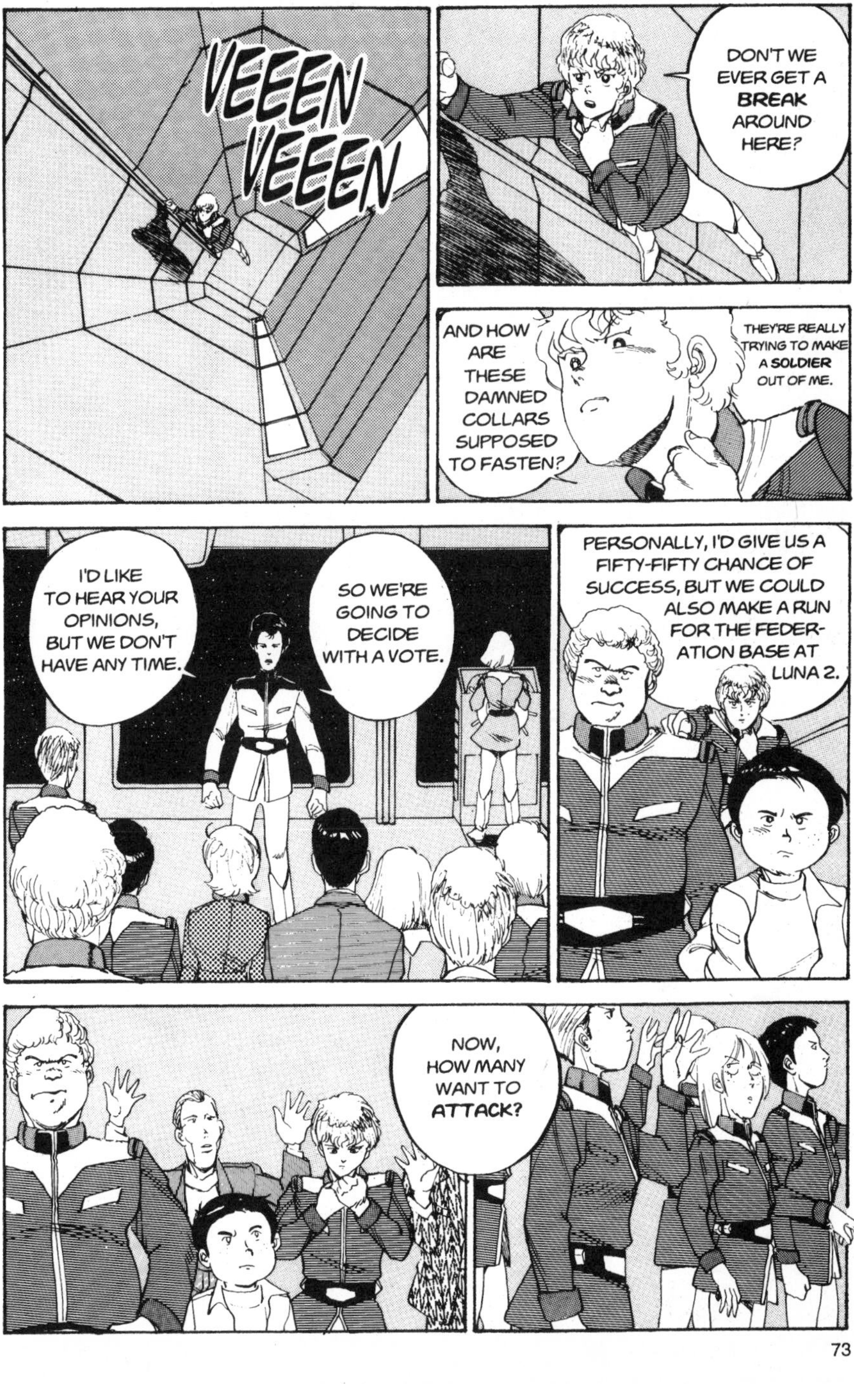
VEEEN VEEEN
DON'T WE EVER GET A BREAK AROUND HERE?
AND HOW ARE THESE DAMNED COLLARS SUPPOSED TO FASTEN?
THEY'RE REALLY TRYING TO MAKE A SOLDIER OUT OF ME.
I'D LIKE TO HEAR YOUR OPINIONS, BUT WE DON'T HAVE ANY TIME.
SO WE'RE GOING TO DECIDE WITH A VOTE.
PERSONALLY, I'D GIVE US A FIFTY-FIFTY CHANCE OF SUCCESS, BUT WE COULD ALSO MAKE A RUN FOR THE FEDER-ATION BASE AT LUNA 2.
NOW, HOW MANY WANT TO ATTACK?

LET'S KICK BUTT!!

THEN IT'S DECIDED. AMURO, YOU'RE TO PILOT THE GUNDAM. RYU, YOU'RE IN THE CORE FIGHTER.

BRING THE *WHITE BASE* ABOUT 180 DEGREES. PREPARE FOR *BATTLE!*

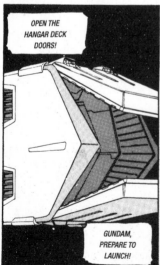

OPEN THE HANGAR DECK DOORS!

GUNDAM, PREPARE TO LAUNCH!

AMURO, TAKE UP YOUR POSITION ON THE CATAPULT. YOU KNOW HOW TO DO THAT?

I CAN TAKE A GOOD STAB AT IT.

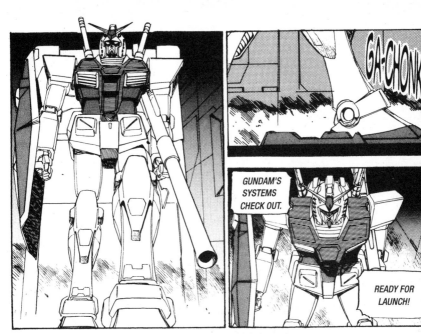

GA-CHONK

GUNDAM'S SYSTEMS CHECK OUT.

READY FOR LAUNCH!

AAHHH!

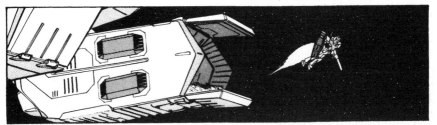

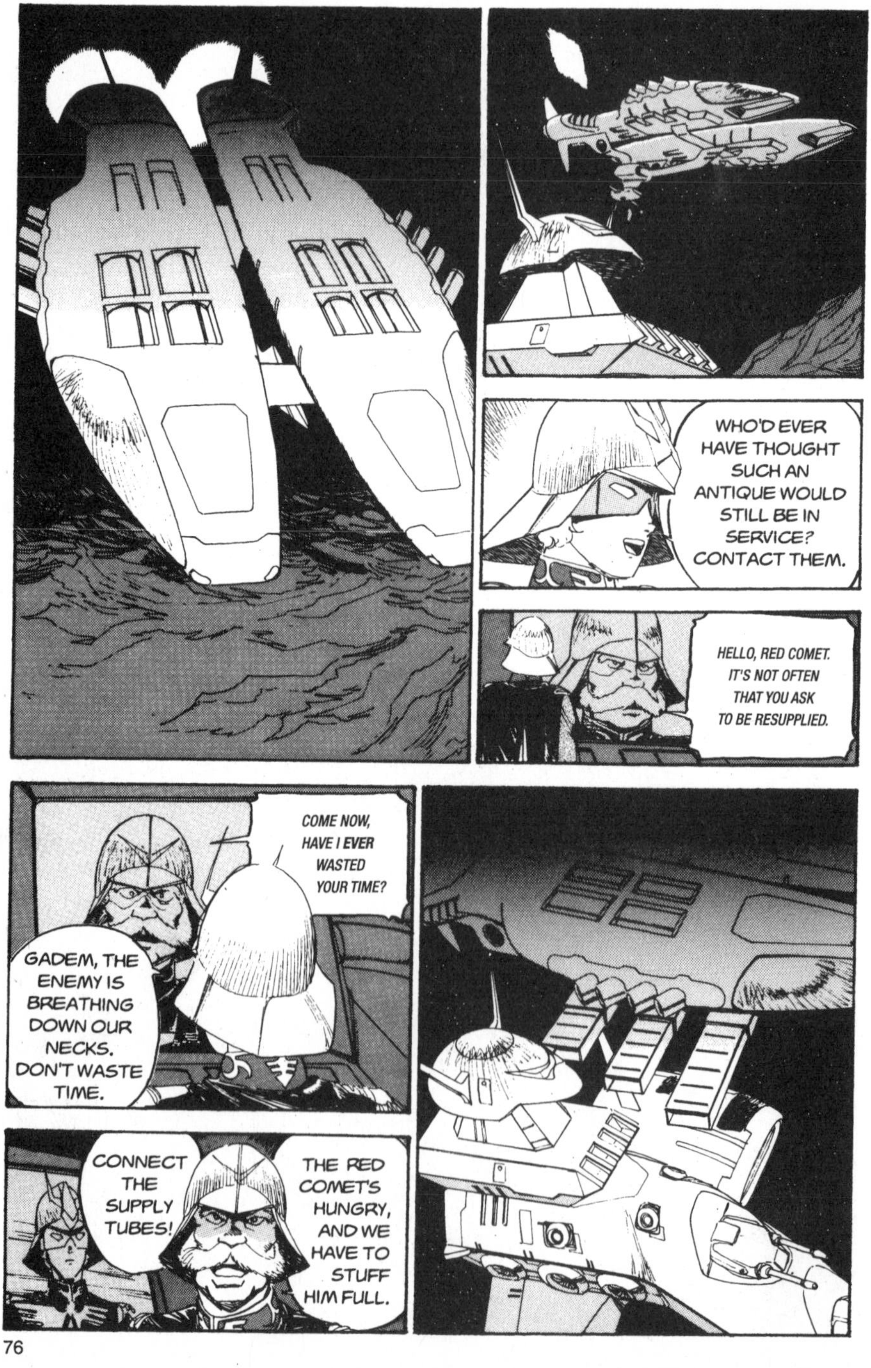
WHO'D EVER HAVE THOUGHT SUCH AN ANTIQUE WOULD STILL BE IN SERVICE? CONTACT THEM.
HELLO, RED COMET. IT'S NOT OFTEN THAT YOU ASK TO BE RESUPPLIED.
COME NOW, HAVE I EVER WASTED YOUR TIME?
GADEM, THE ENEMY IS BREATHING DOWN OUR NECKS. DON'T WASTE TIME.
CONNECT THE SUPPLY TUBES!
THE RED COMET'S HUNGRY, AND WE HAVE TO STUFF HIM FULL.

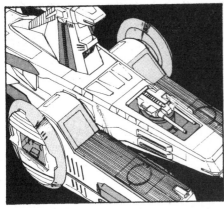

WE HAVE EIGHT MINUTES BEFORE THE ENEMY CAN DETECT US. I WANT EVERY TECH MANUAL READ BY THEN!

JUST GIVE US A COVER FOR OUR APPROACH. THE REST DOESN'T MATTER!

COME ON, RYU! I THOUGH YOU WERE A **PRO**!

GO **HIGHER**?

!?

BUT THE ENEMY'S RIGHT IN **FRONT** OF US!

DOESN'T HE GET IT? IF WE APPROACH THIS WAY, WE'LL BE FLYING STRAIGHT INTO THE SUN. WE NEED A BETTER ANGLE!

I DON'T GET IT. HOW'D A ROOKIE LIKE AMURO KNOW WE WERE FLYING STRAIGHT INTO AN ENEMY HIDING IN THE SUN?

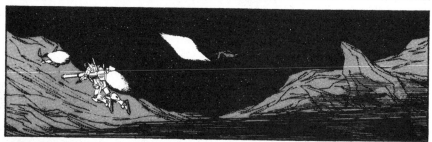

ALL RIGHT... GOT YOU NOW!

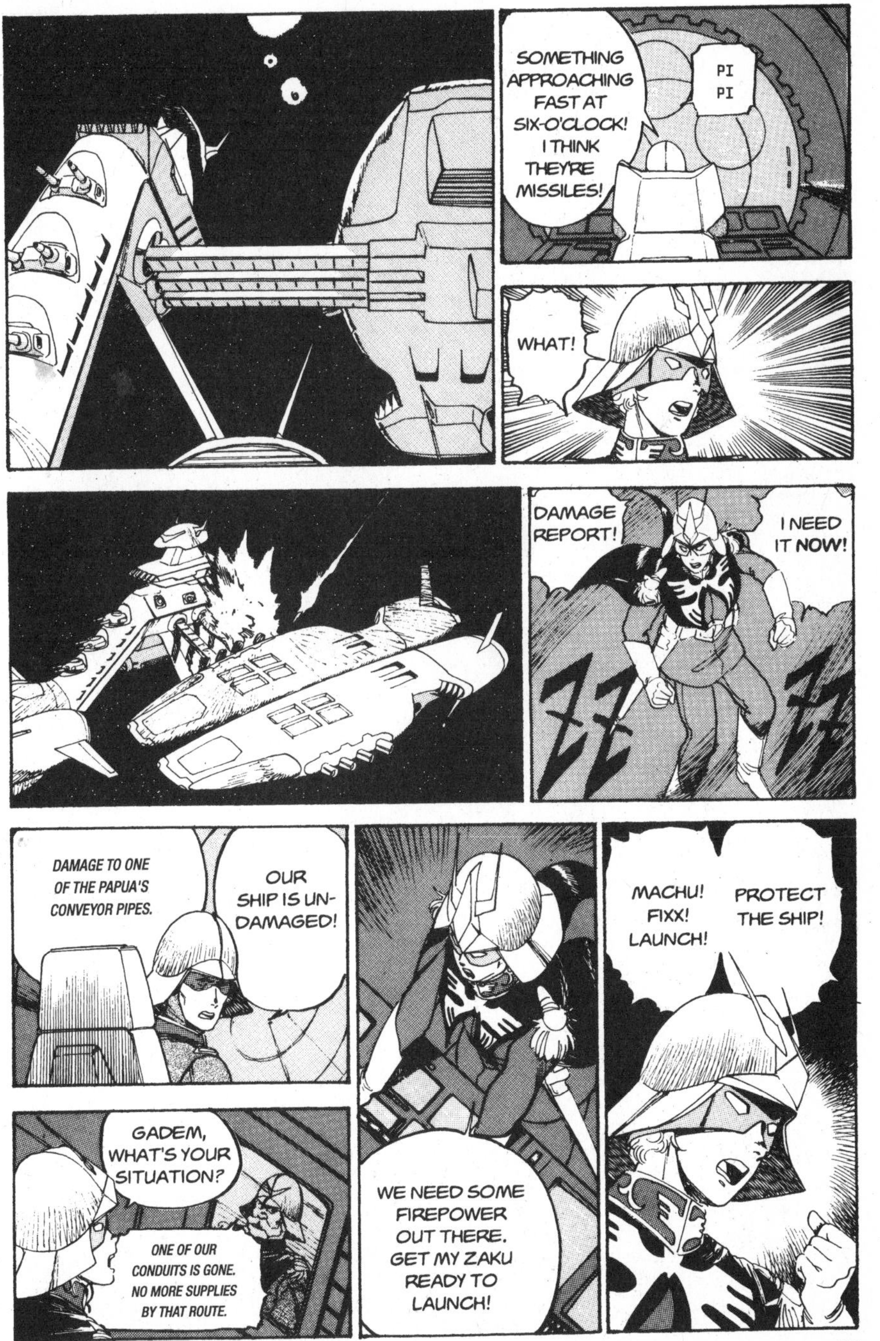
SOMETHING APPROACHING FAST AT SIX-O'CLOCK! I THINK THEY'RE MISSILES!
PI PI
WHAT!
DAMAGE REPORT!
I NEED IT NOW!
DAMAGE TO ONE OF THE PAPUA'S CONVEYOR PIPES.
OUR SHIP IS UN-DAMAGED!
GADEM, WHAT'S YOUR SITUATION?
ONE OF OUR CONDUITS IS GONE. NO MORE SUPPLIES BY THAT ROUTE.
WE NEED SOME FIREPOWER OUT THERE. GET MY ZAKU READY TO LAUNCH!
MACHU! FIXX! LAUNCH!
PROTECT THE SHIP!

DOREN, GIVE THE PAPUA SOME COVER!

WE'RE BEING ATTACKED BY MOBILE SUITS.

BUT WHERE ARE THEY?

THERE!

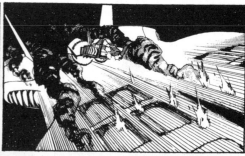

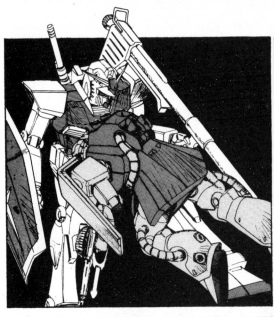

HYURRG

IT'S TIME FOR YOU TO LEARN THAT SHEER POWER DOESN'T MAKE **ALL** THE DIFFERENCE IN BATTLE!

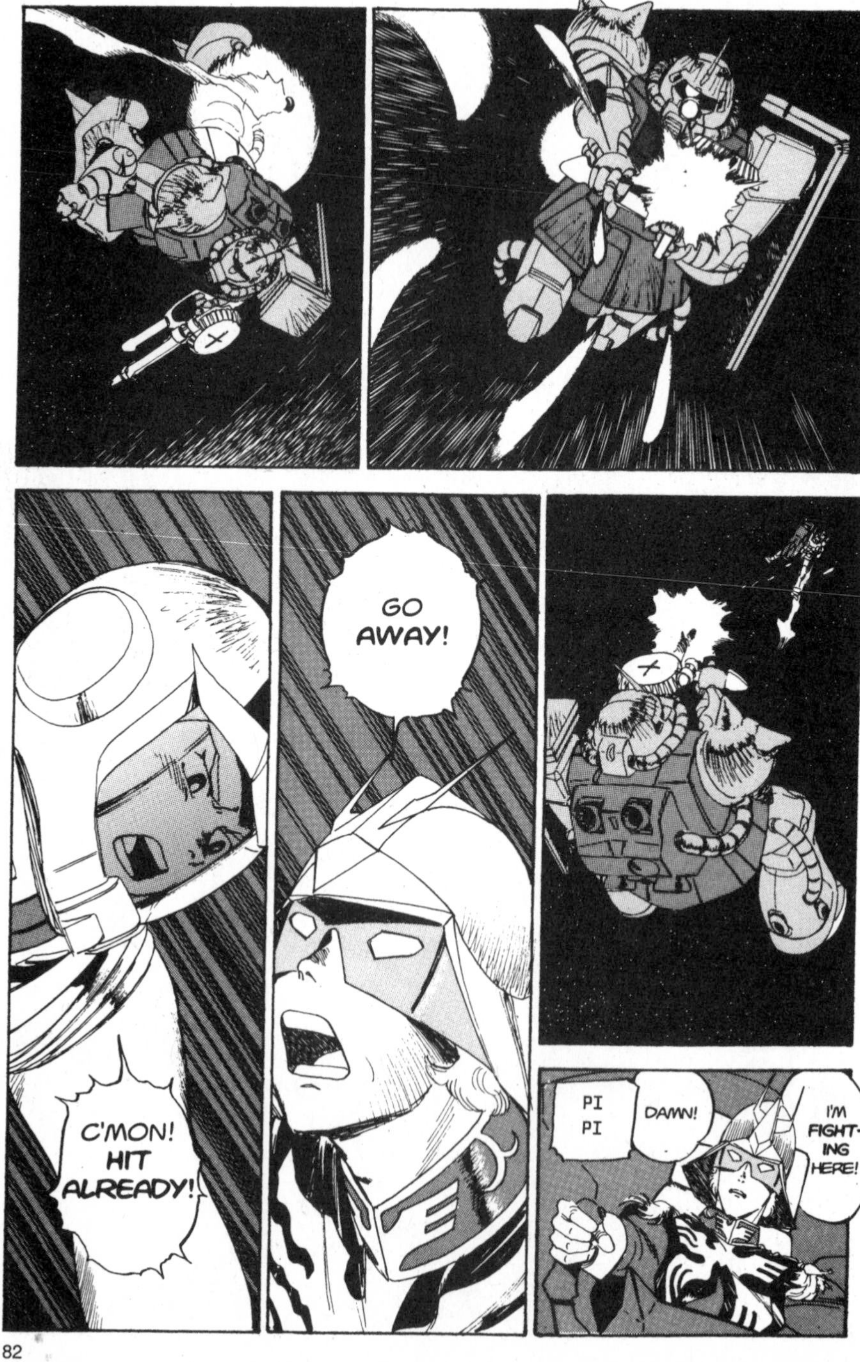
C'MON! HIT ALREADY!
GO AWAY!
PI PI
DAMN!
I'M FIGHT- ING HERE!

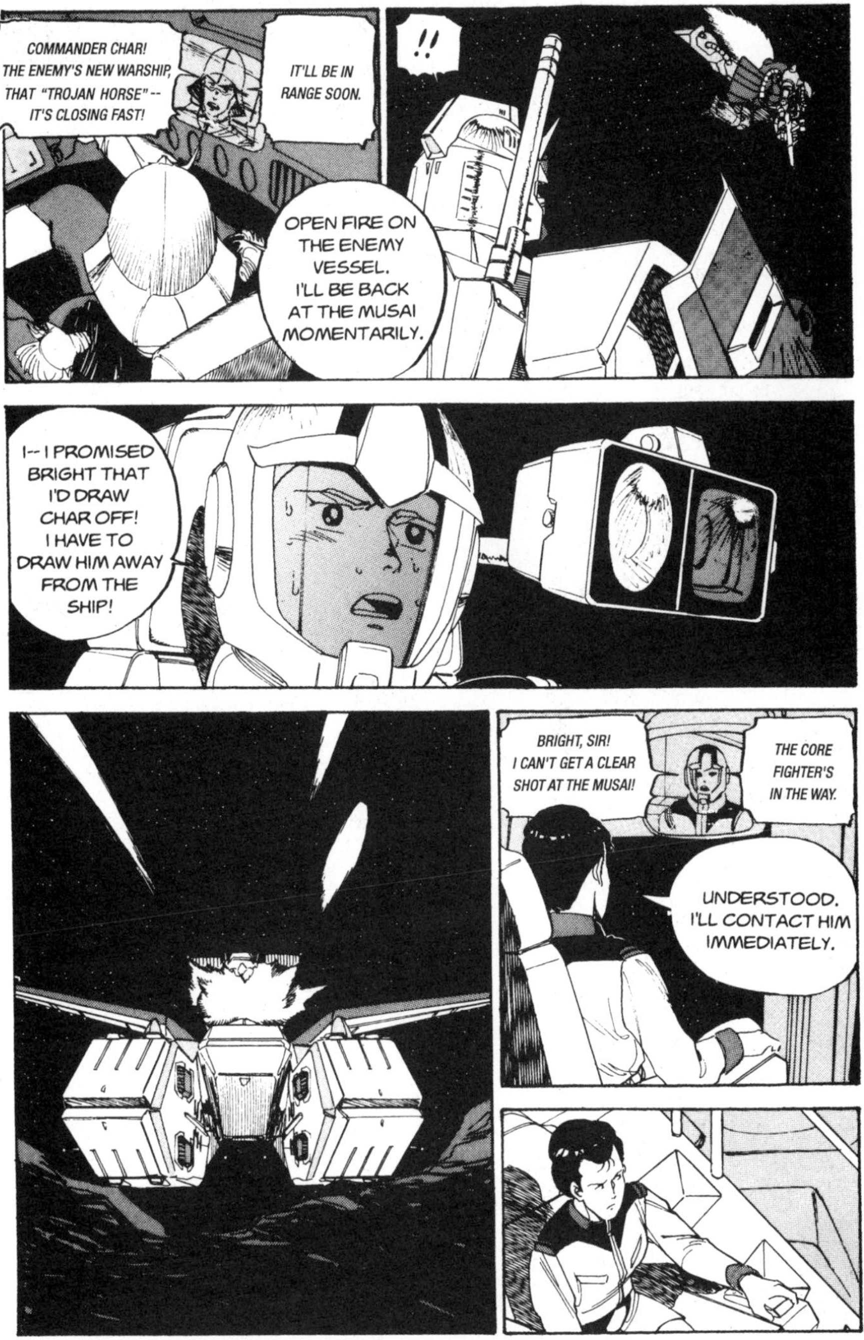
COMMANDER CHAR! THE ENEMY'S NEW WARSHIP, THAT "TROJAN HORSE" -- IT'S CLOSING FAST!
IT'LL BE IN RANGE SOON.
OPEN FIRE ON THE ENEMY VESSEL. I'LL BE BACK AT THE MUSAI MOMENTARILY.
!!
I-- I PROMISED BRIGHT THAT I'D DRAW CHAR OFF! I HAVE TO DRAW HIM AWAY FROM THE SHIP!
BRIGHT, SIR! I CAN'T GET A CLEAR SHOT AT THE MUSAI!
THE CORE FIGHTER'S IN THE WAY.
UNDERSTOOD. I'LL CONTACT HIM IMMEDIATELY.

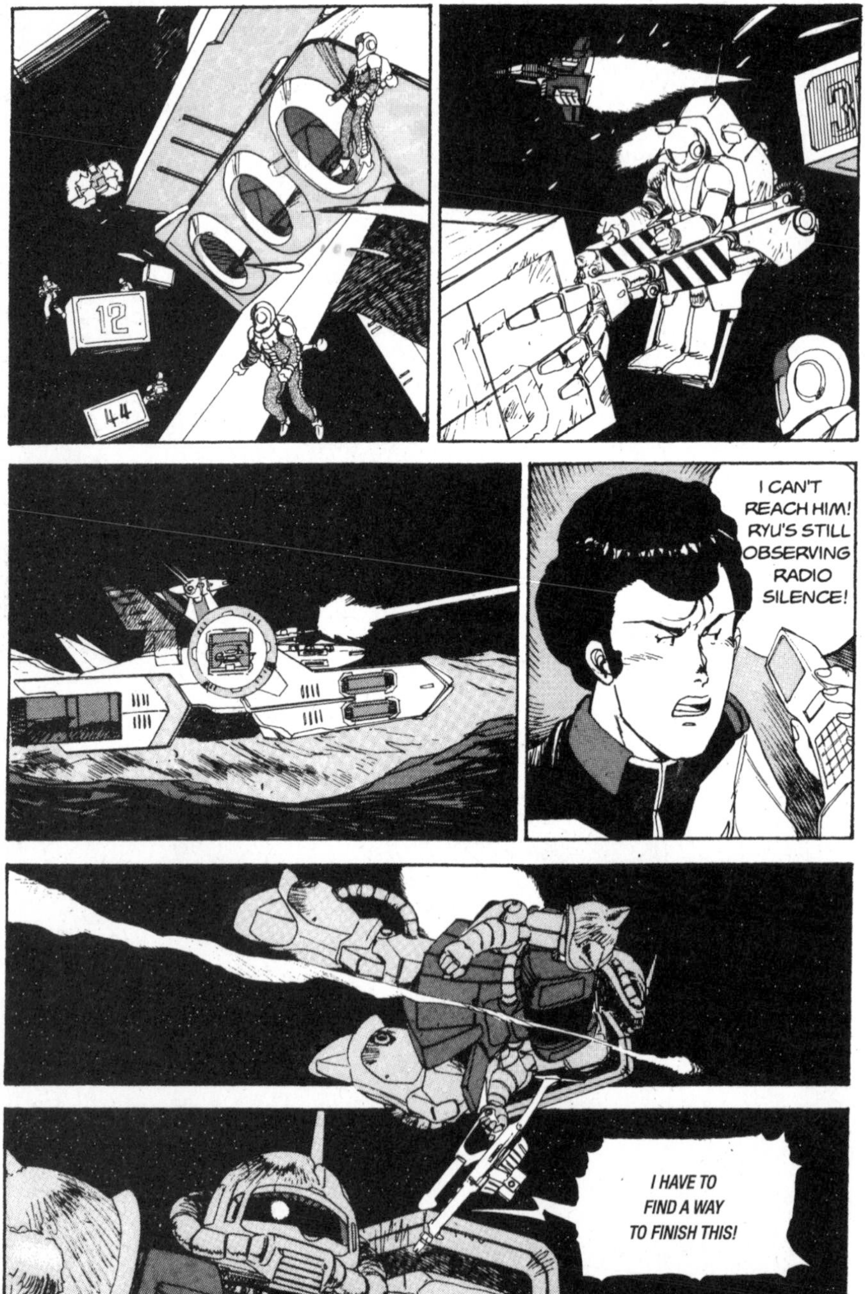
I CAN'T REACH HIM! RYU'S STILL OBSERVING RADIO SILENCE!
I HAVE TO FIND A WAY TO FINISH THIS!

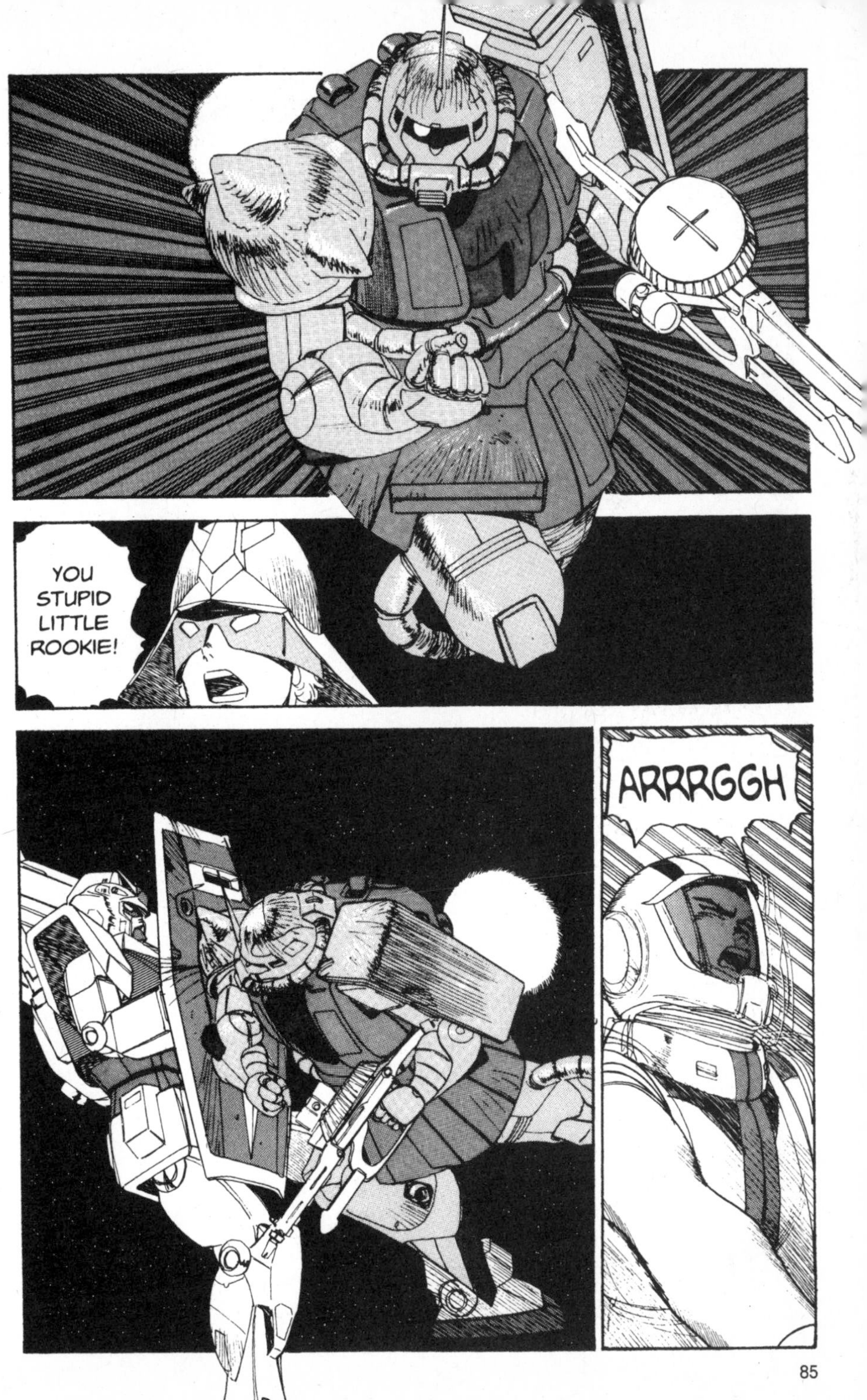
YOU STUPID LITTLE ROOKIE!
ARRRGGH

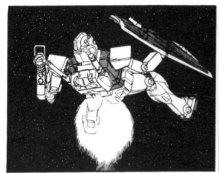

B~
BRAKE!!

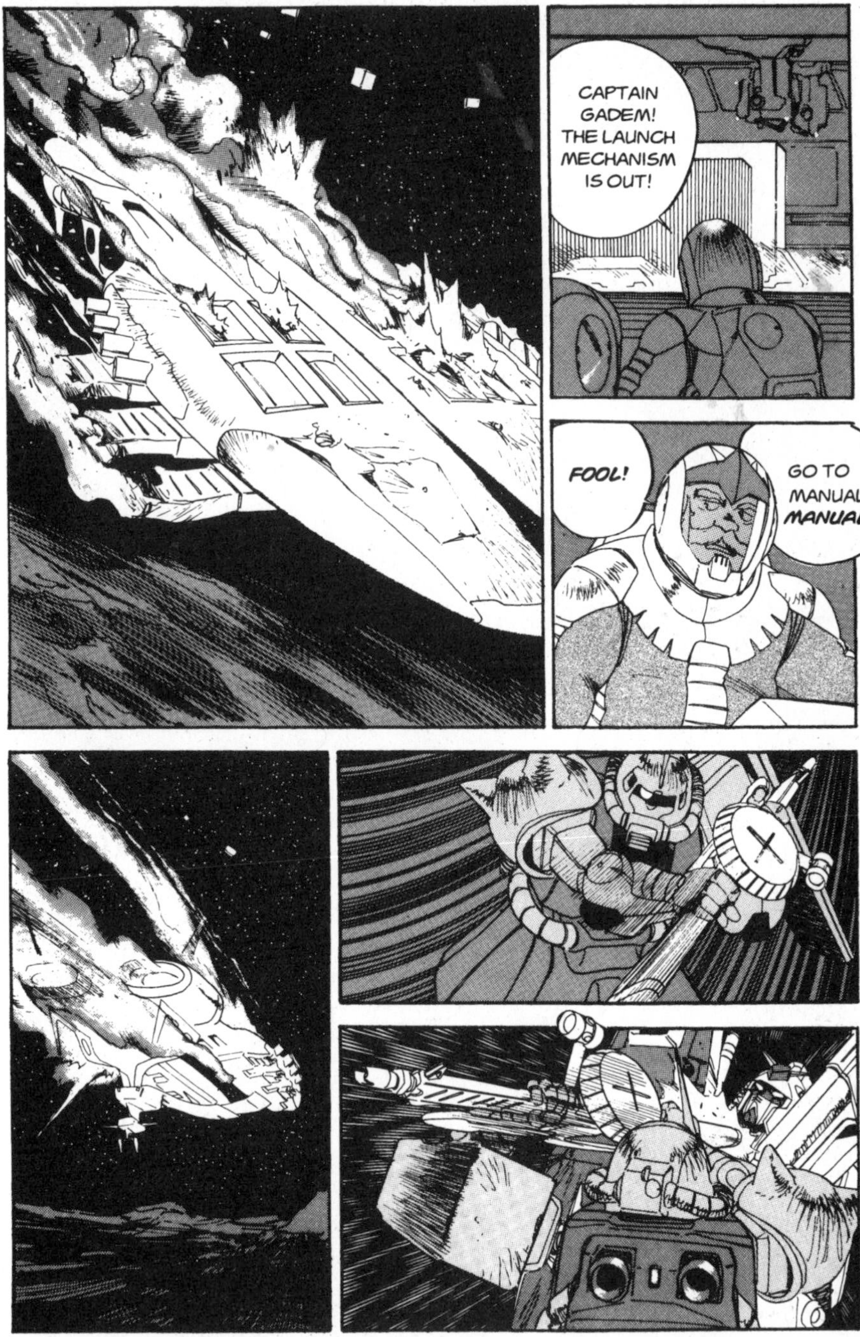
CAPTAIN GADEM! THE LAUNCH MECHANISM IS OUT!
FOOL!
GO TO MANUAL! MANUAL!

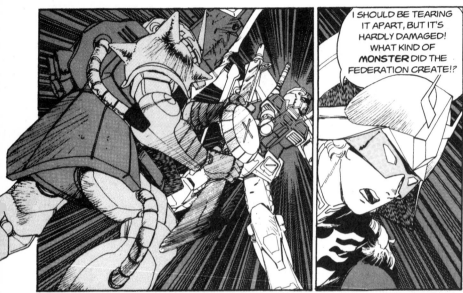

I SHOULD BE TEARING IT APART, BUT IT'S HARDLY DAMAGED! WHAT KIND OF **MONSTER** DID THE FEDERATION CREATE!?

WE'LL HAVE TO PICK THIS ONE UP LATER.

JUST LOOK WHAT THEY DID TO MY SHIP!

DAMNED FEDERATION MOBILE SUIT!

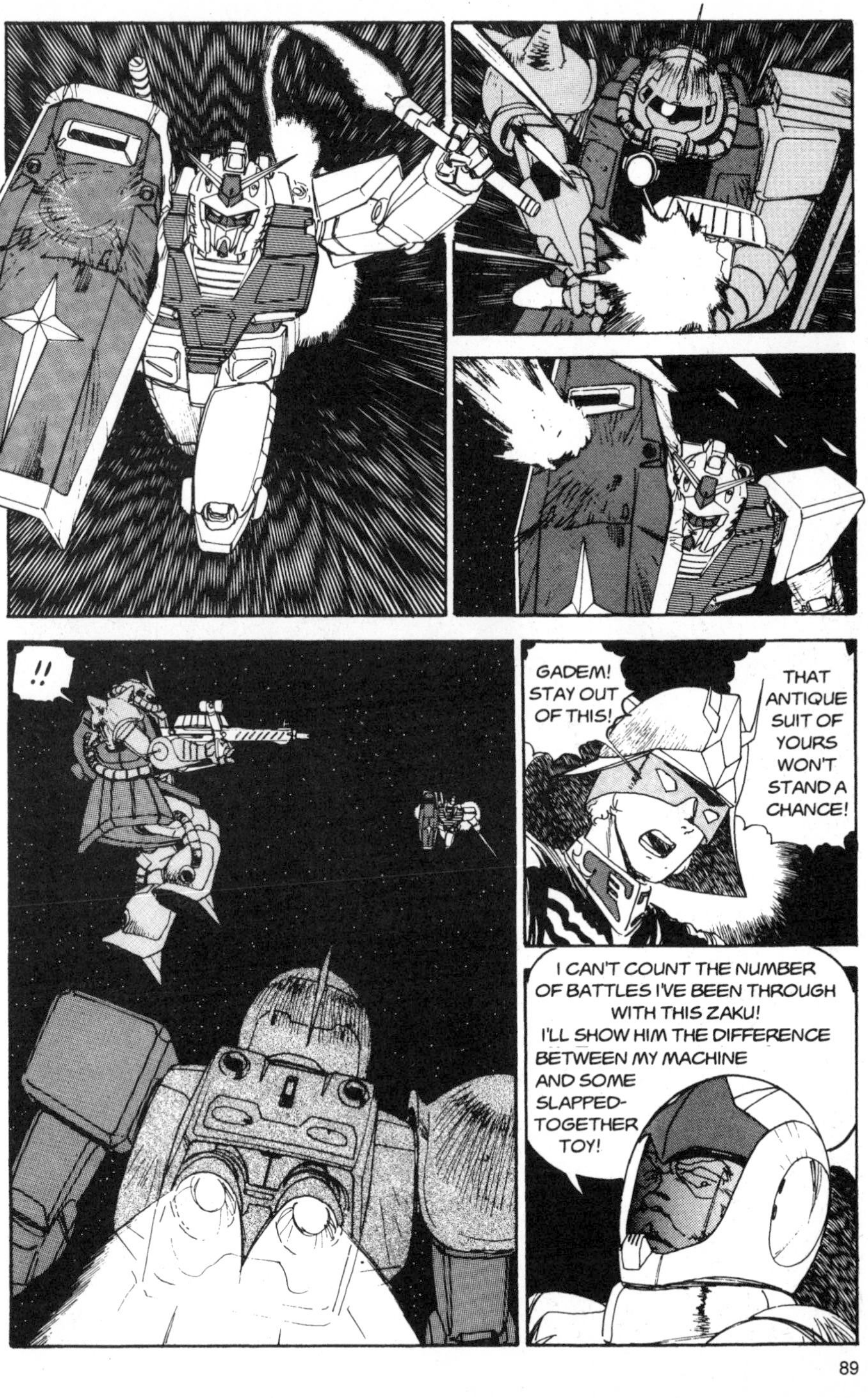
!!
GADEM! STAY OUT OF THIS!
THAT ANTIQUE SUIT OF YOURS WON'T STAND A CHANCE!
I CAN'T COUNT THE NUMBER OF BATTLES I'VE BEEN THROUGH WITH THIS ZAKU! I'LL SHOW HIM THE DIFFERENCE BETWEEN MY MACHINE AND SOME SLAPPED-TOGETHER TOY!

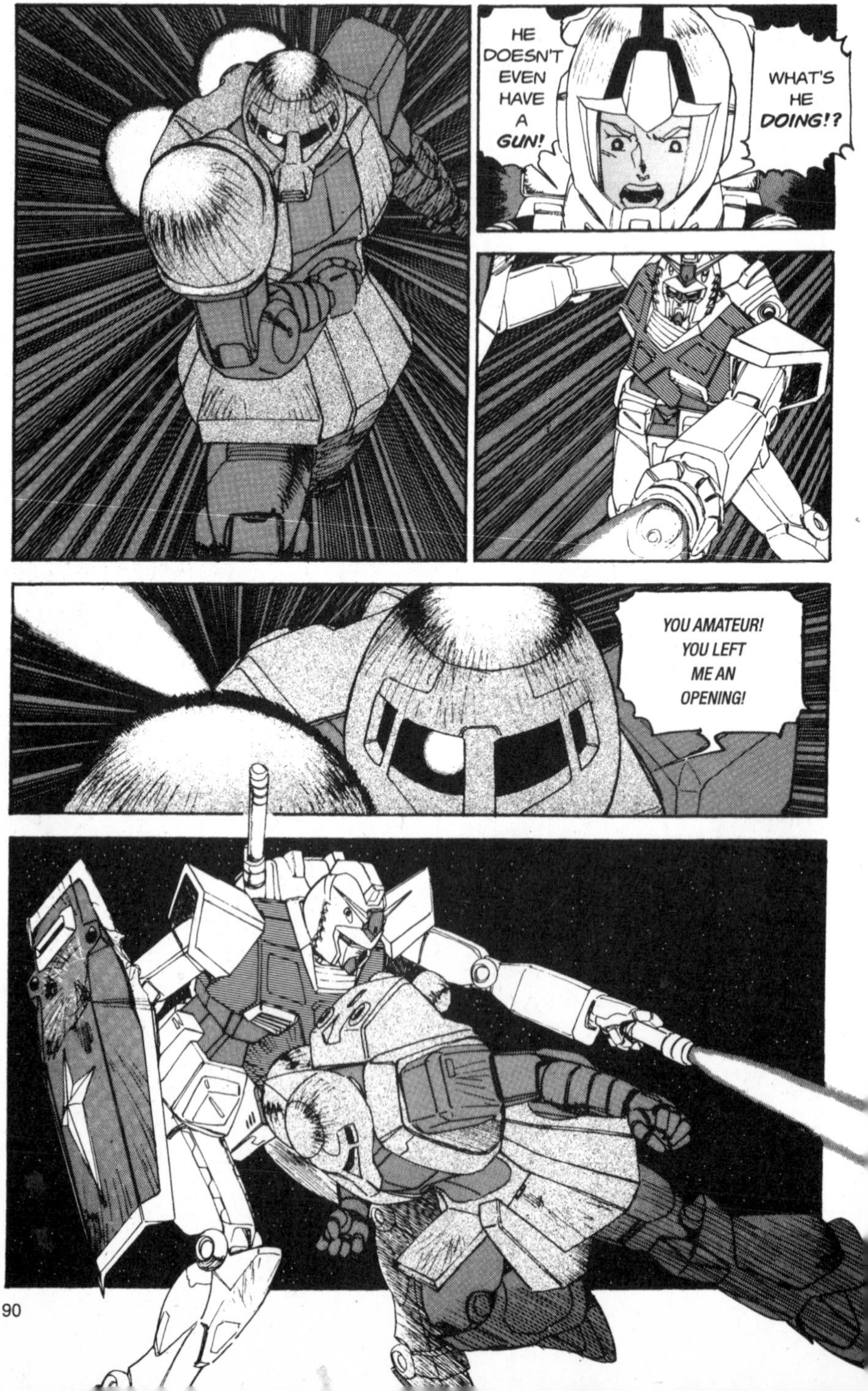
HE DOESN'T EVEN HAVE A GUN!
WHAT'S HE DOING!?
YOU AMATEUR! YOU LEFT ME AN OPENING!

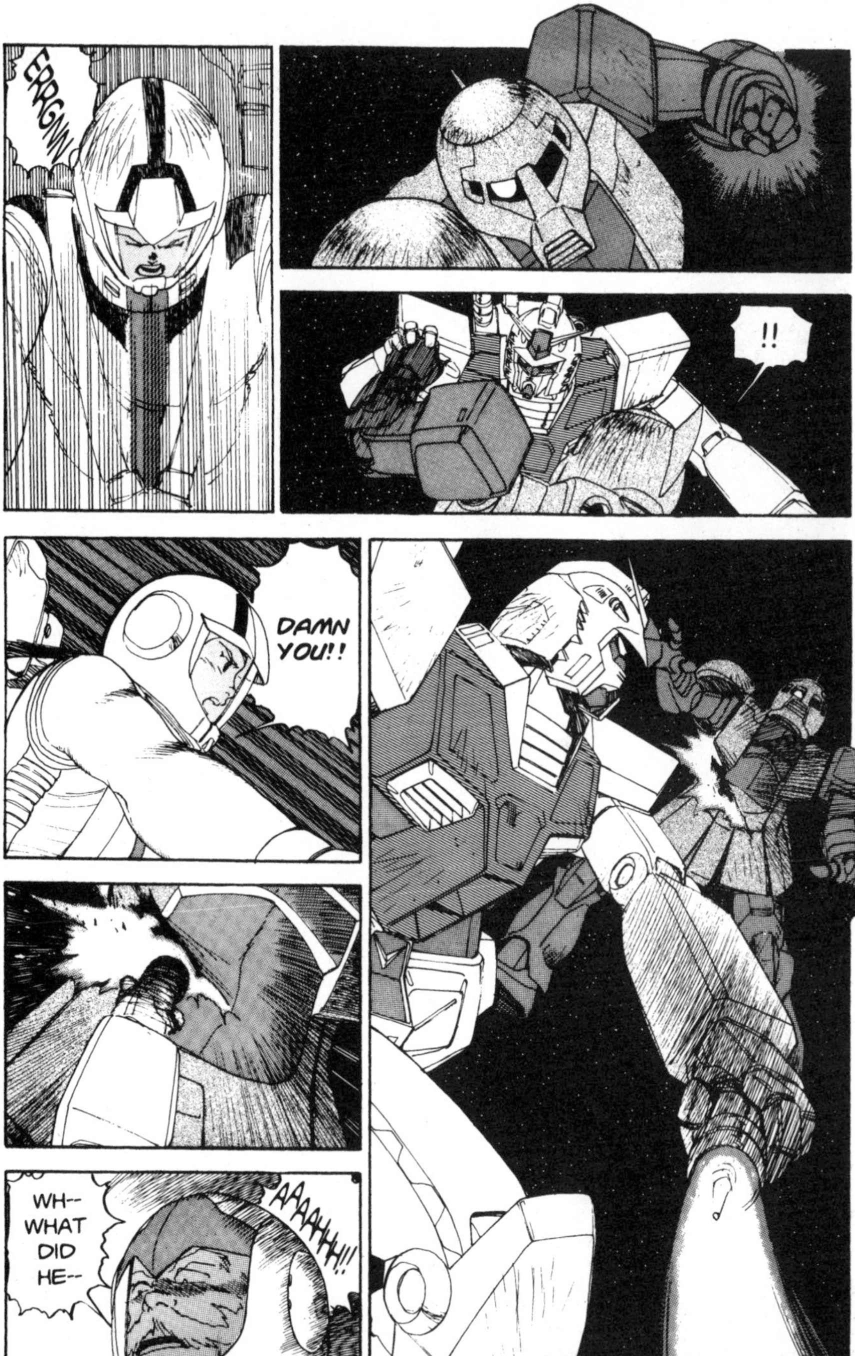
ERRGNN
!!
DAMN YOU!!
WH-- WHAT DID HE--
AAAAHHH!!

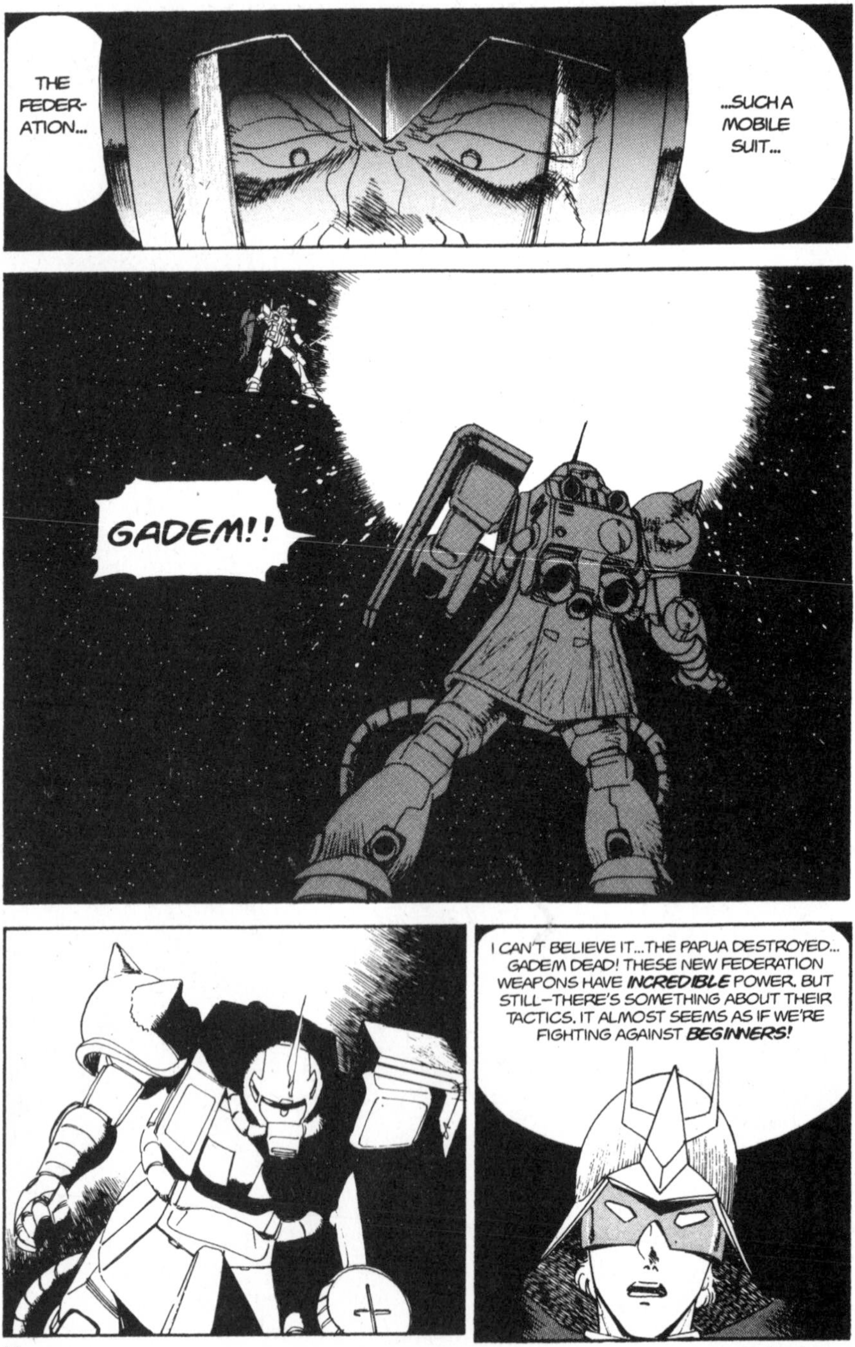
THE FEDER-ATION...
...SUCH A MOBILE SUIT...
GADEM!!
I CAN'T BELIEVE IT...THE PAPUA DESTROYED... GADEM DEAD! THESE NEW FEDERATION WEAPONS HAVE INCREDIBLE POWER. BUT STILL—THERE'S SOMETHING ABOUT THEIR TACTICS. IT ALMOST SEEMS AS IF WE'RE FIGHTING AGAINST BEGINNERS!

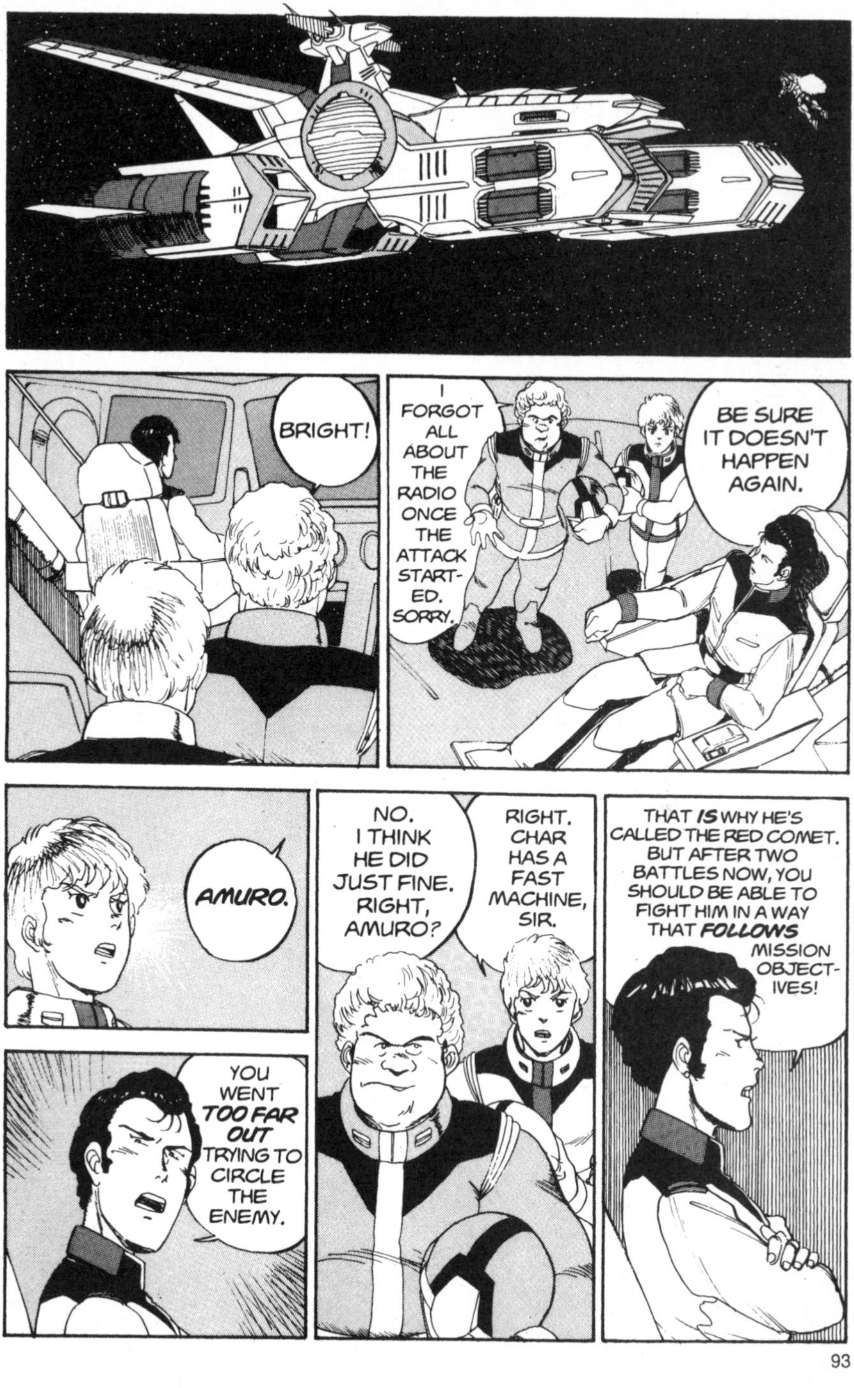
BRIGHT!
I FORGOT ALL ABOUT THE RADIO ONCE THE ATTACK START-ED. SORRY.
BE SURE IT DOESN'T HAPPEN AGAIN.
AMURO.
YOU WENT TOO FAR OUT TRYING TO CIRCLE THE ENEMY.
NO. I THINK HE DID JUST FINE. RIGHT, AMURO?
RIGHT. CHAR HAS A FAST MACHINE, SIR.
THAT IS WHY HE'S CALLED THE RED COMET. BUT AFTER TWO BATTLES NOW, YOU SHOULD BE ABLE TO FIGHT HIM IN A WAY THAT FOLLOWS MISSION OBJECT-IVES!

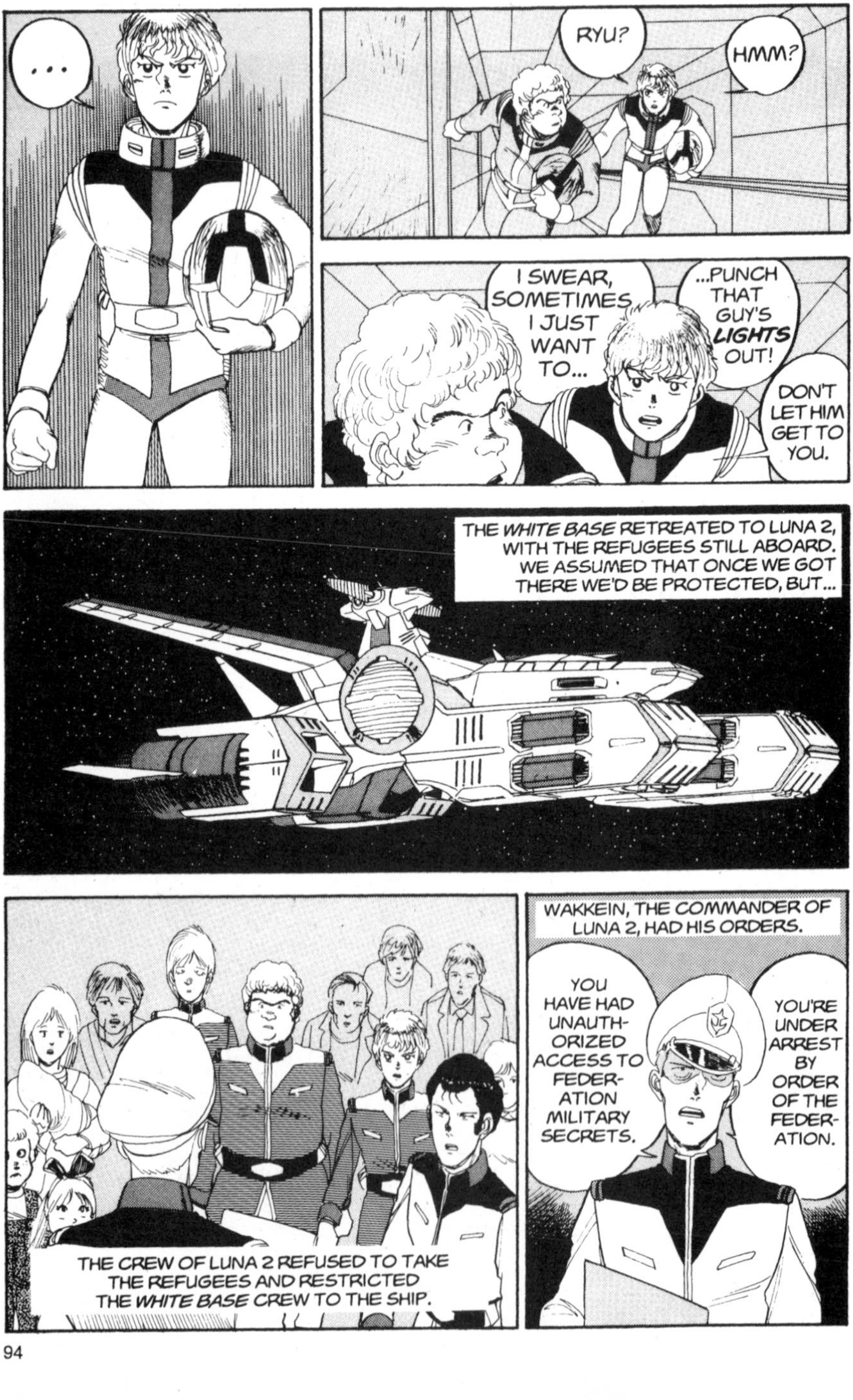
...
RYU?
HMM?
I SWEAR, SOMETIMES I JUST WANT TO...
...PUNCH THAT GUY'S LIGHTS OUT!
DON'T LET HIM GET TO YOU.
THE WHITE BASE RETREATED TO LUNA 2, WITH THE REFUGEES STILL ABOARD. WE ASSUMED THAT ONCE WE GOT THERE WE'D BE PROTECTED, BUT...
THE CREW OF LUNA 2 REFUSED TO TAKE THE REFUGEES AND RESTRICTED THE WHITE BASE CREW TO THE SHIP.
WAKKEIN, THE COMMANDER OF LUNA 2, HAD HIS ORDERS.
YOU HAVE HAD UNAUTH-ORIZED ACCESS TO FEDER-ATION MILITARY SECRETS.
YOU'RE UNDER ARREST BY ORDER OF THE FEDER-ATION.

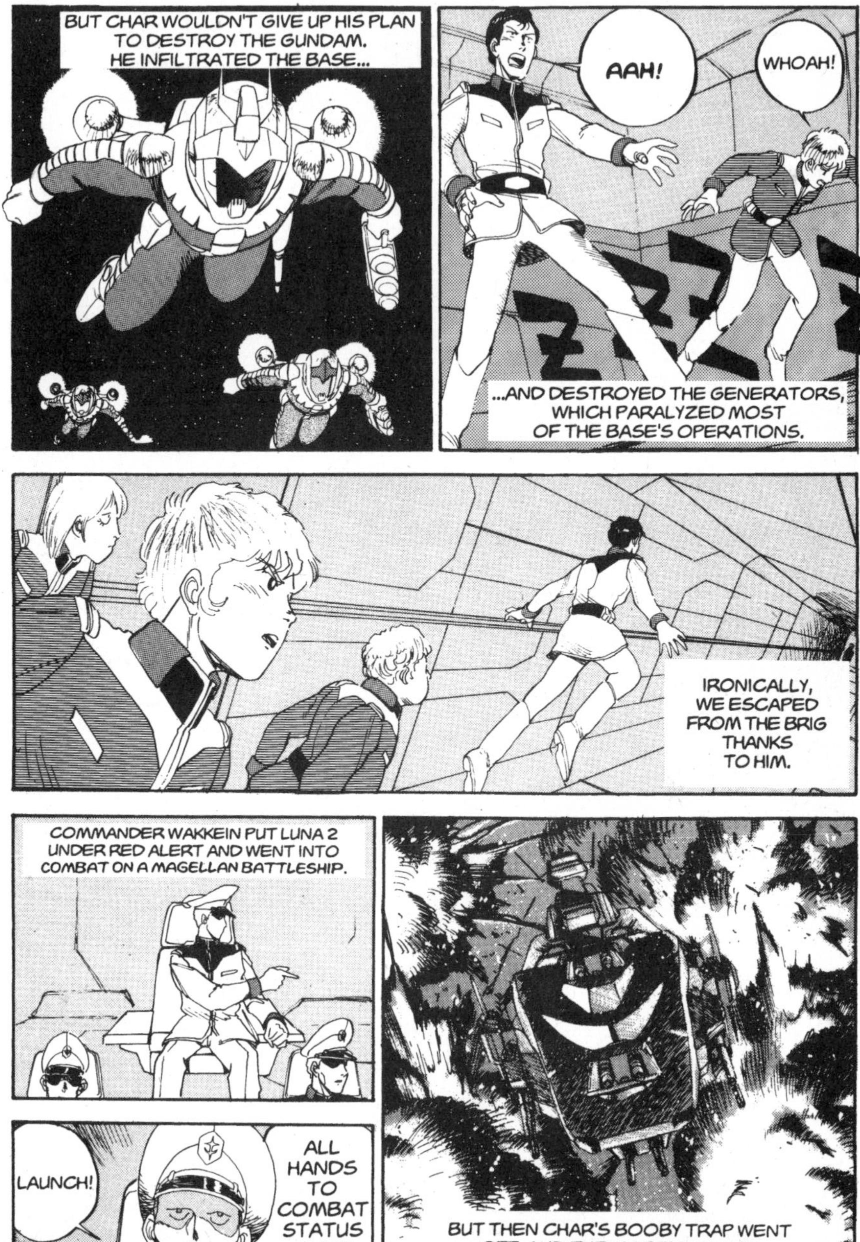
BUT CHAR WOULDN'T GIVE UP HIS PLAN TO DESTROY THE GUNDAM. HE INFILTRATED THE BASE...
AAH!
WHOAH!
...AND DESTROYED THE GENERATORS, WHICH PARALYZED MOST OF THE BASE'S OPERATIONS.
IRONICALLY, WE ESCAPED FROM THE BRIG THANKS TO HIM.
COMMANDER WAKKEIN PUT LUNA 2 UNDER RED ALERT AND WENT INTO COMBAT ON A MAGELLAN BATTLESHIP.
LAUNCH!
ALL HANDS TO COMBAT STATUS ONCE WE'RE CLEAR!
BUT THEN CHAR'S BOOBY TRAP WENT OFF, AND THE MAGELLAN WAS CRIPPLED, BLOCKING THE ENTRANCE TO THE DOCK.

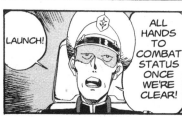

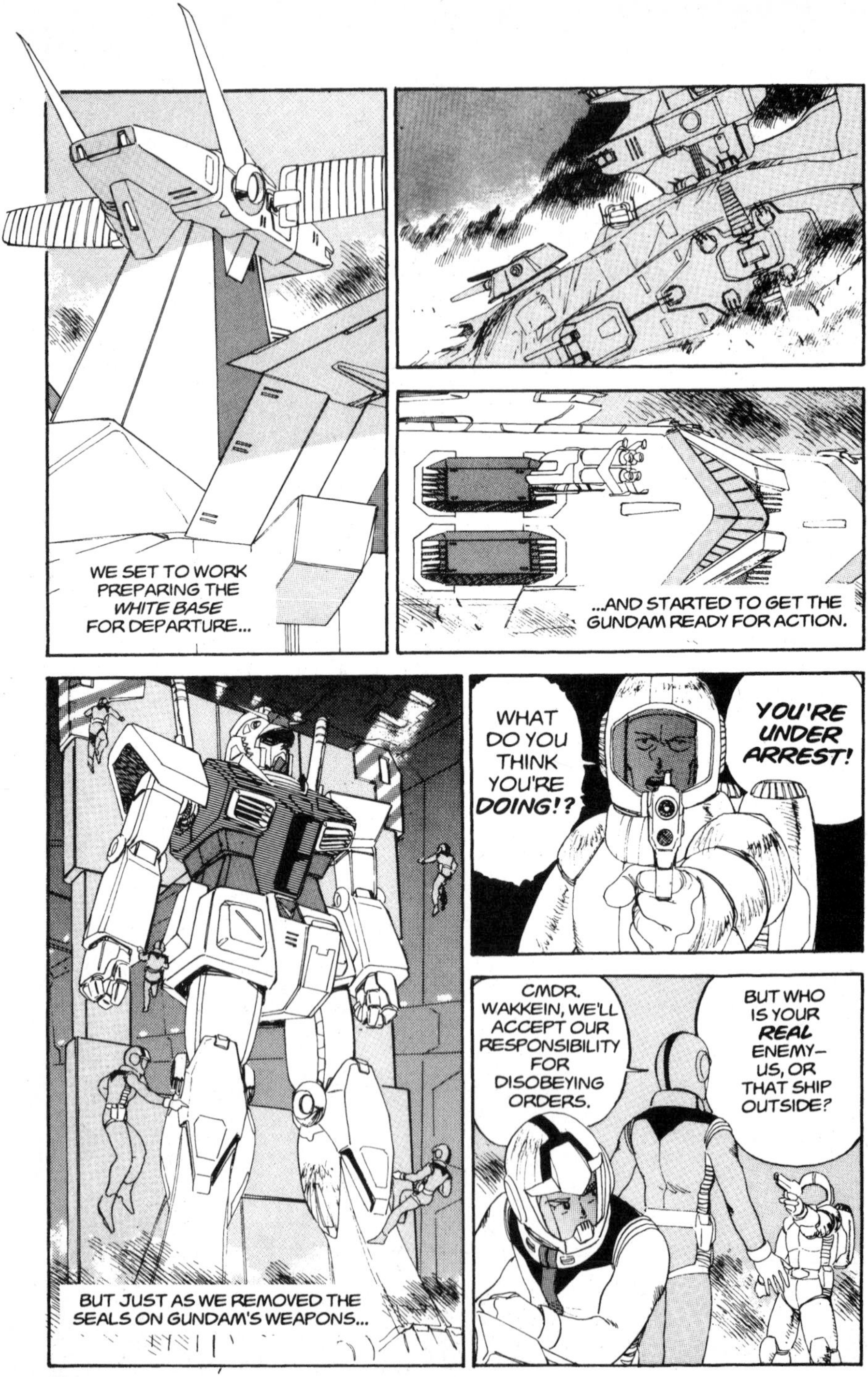
WE SET TO WORK PREPARING THE *WHITE BASE* FOR DEPARTURE...
...AND STARTED TO GET THE GUNDAM READY FOR ACTION.
BUT JUST AS WE REMOVED THE SEALS ON GUNDAM'S WEAPONS...
WHAT DO YOU THINK YOU'RE *DOING!?*
YOU'RE UNDER ARREST!
CMDR. WAKKEIN, WE'LL ACCEPT OUR RESPONSIBILITY FOR DISOBEYING ORDERS.
BUT WHO IS YOUR *REAL* ENEMY— US, OR THAT SHIP OUTSIDE?

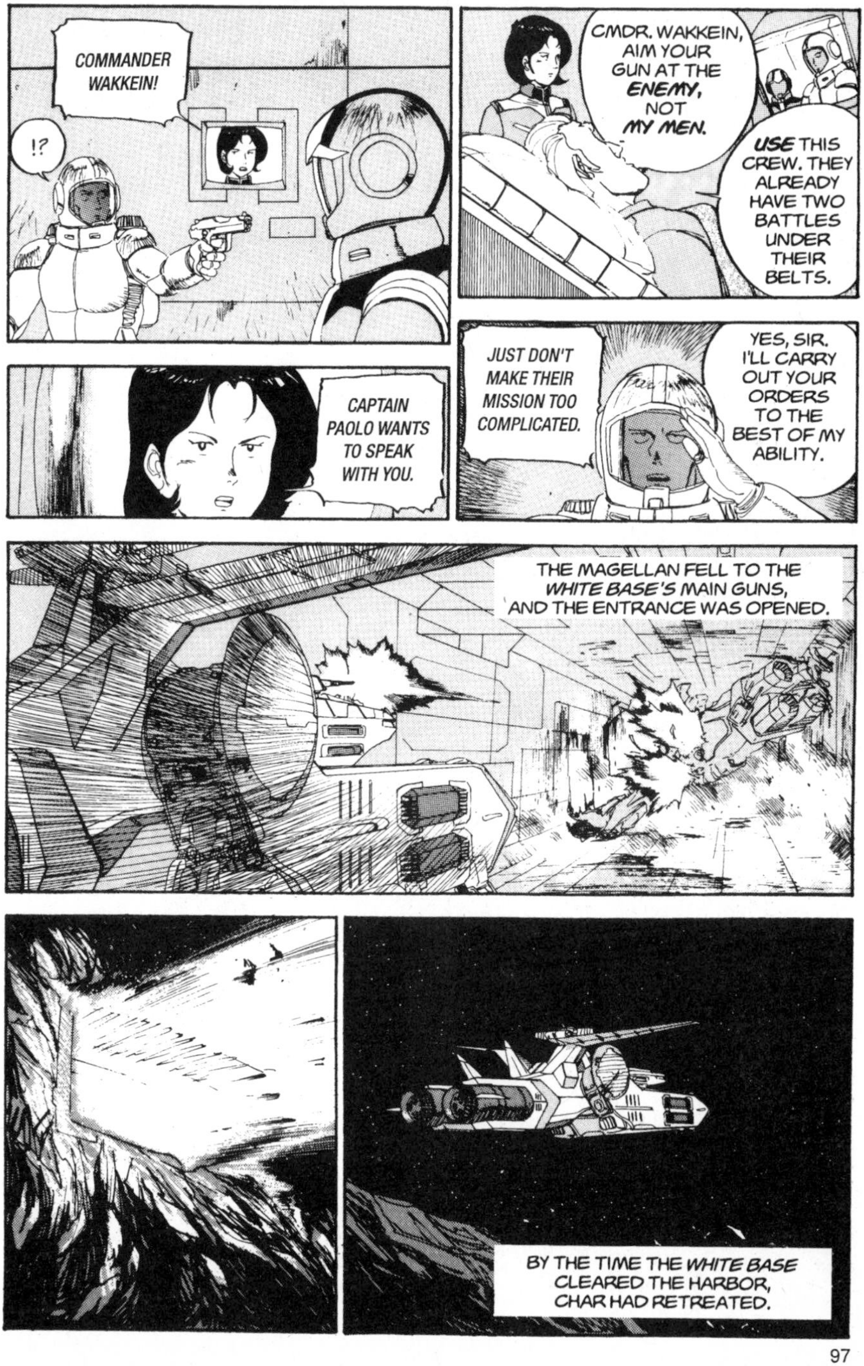
COMMANDER WAKKEIN!
!?
CMDR. WAKKEIN, AIM YOUR GUN AT THE ENEMY, NOT MY MEN.
USE THIS CREW. THEY ALREADY HAVE TWO BATTLES UNDER THEIR BELTS.
CAPTAIN PAOLO WANTS TO SPEAK WITH YOU.
JUST DON'T MAKE THEIR MISSION TOO COMPLICATED.
YES, SIR. I'LL CARRY OUT YOUR ORDERS TO THE BEST OF MY ABILITY.
THE MAGELLAN FELL TO THE WHITE BASE'S MAIN GUNS, AND THE ENTRANCE WAS OPENED.
BY THE TIME THE WHITE BASE CLEARED THE HARBOR, CHAR HAD RETREATED.

IN THE MIDST OF THE BATTLE, WE DIDN'T EVEN NOTICE WHEN THE CAPTAIN BREATHED HIS LAST. HE'D IGNORED HIS WOUNDS, GIVING ORDERS RIGHT TO THE END.

OUR WAR WITH ZEON IS ONLY GETTING MORE DESPERATE.

WE'RE LOSING THOSE WITH THE MOST TO TEACH US ONE BY ONE. IT'S BECOME A COLD AGE.

FINAL SALUTE FOR CAPTAIN PAOLO! ATTENTION!

AND THEN, WE HEADED TOWARD EARTH WITH A MISSION TO MAKE OUR WAY TO THE PLANET'S SURFACE.

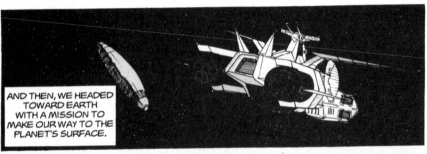

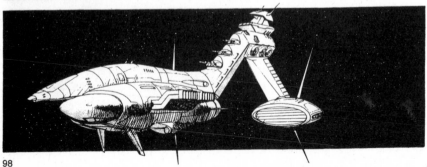

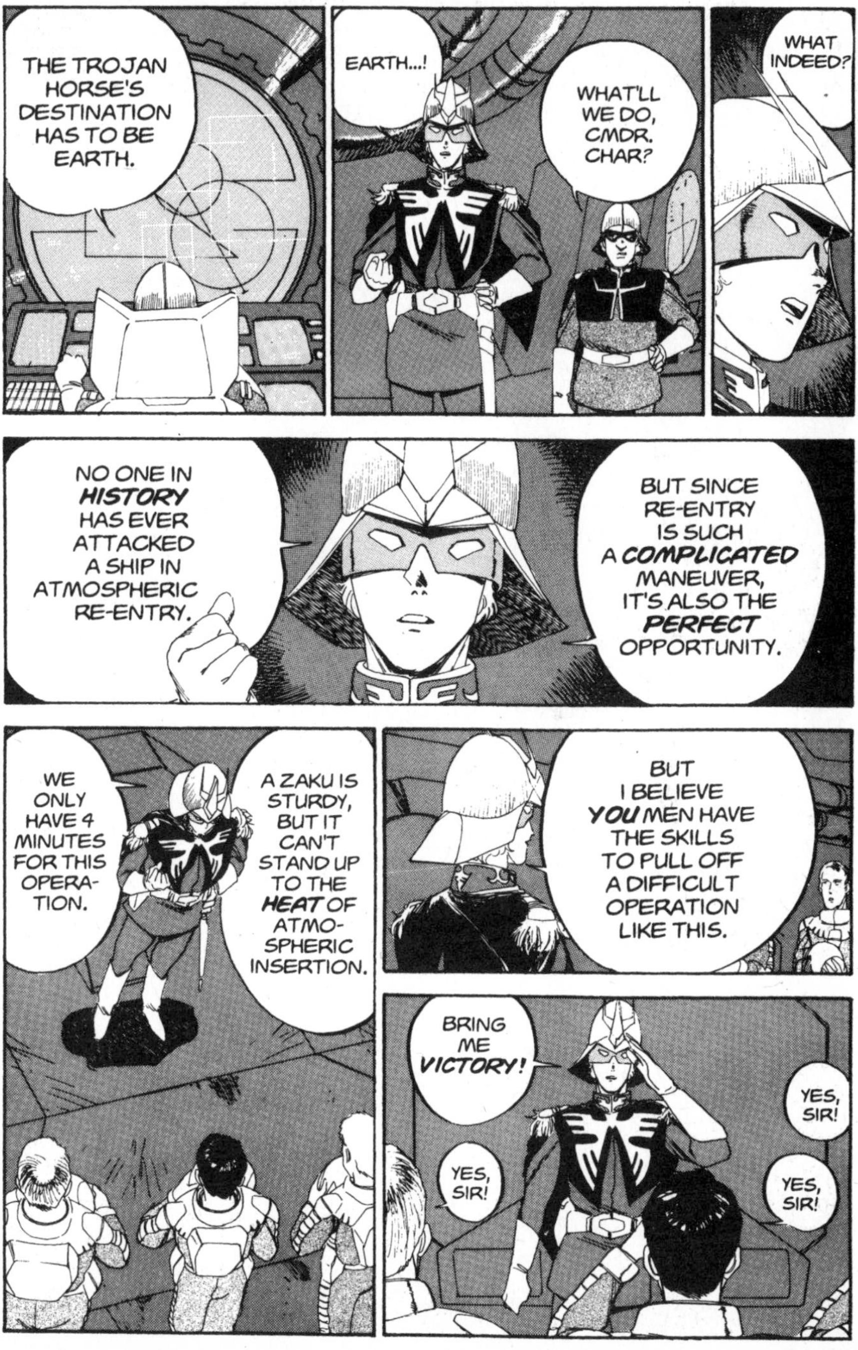
THE TROJAN HORSE'S DESTINATION HAS TO BE EARTH.
EARTH...!
WHAT'LL WE DO, CMDR. CHAR?
WHAT INDEED?
NO ONE IN HISTORY HAS EVER ATTACKED A SHIP IN ATMOSPHERIC RE-ENTRY.
BUT SINCE RE-ENTRY IS SUCH A COMPLICATED MANEUVER, IT'S ALSO THE PERFECT OPPORTUNITY.
WE ONLY HAVE 4 MINUTES FOR THIS OPERA-TION.
A ZAKU IS STURDY, BUT IT CAN'T STAND UP TO THE HEAT OF ATMO-SPHERIC INSERTION.
BUT I BELIEVE YOU MEN HAVE THE SKILLS TO PULL OFF A DIFFICULT OPERATION LIKE THIS.
BRING ME VICTORY!
YES, SIR!
YES, SIR!
YES, SIR!

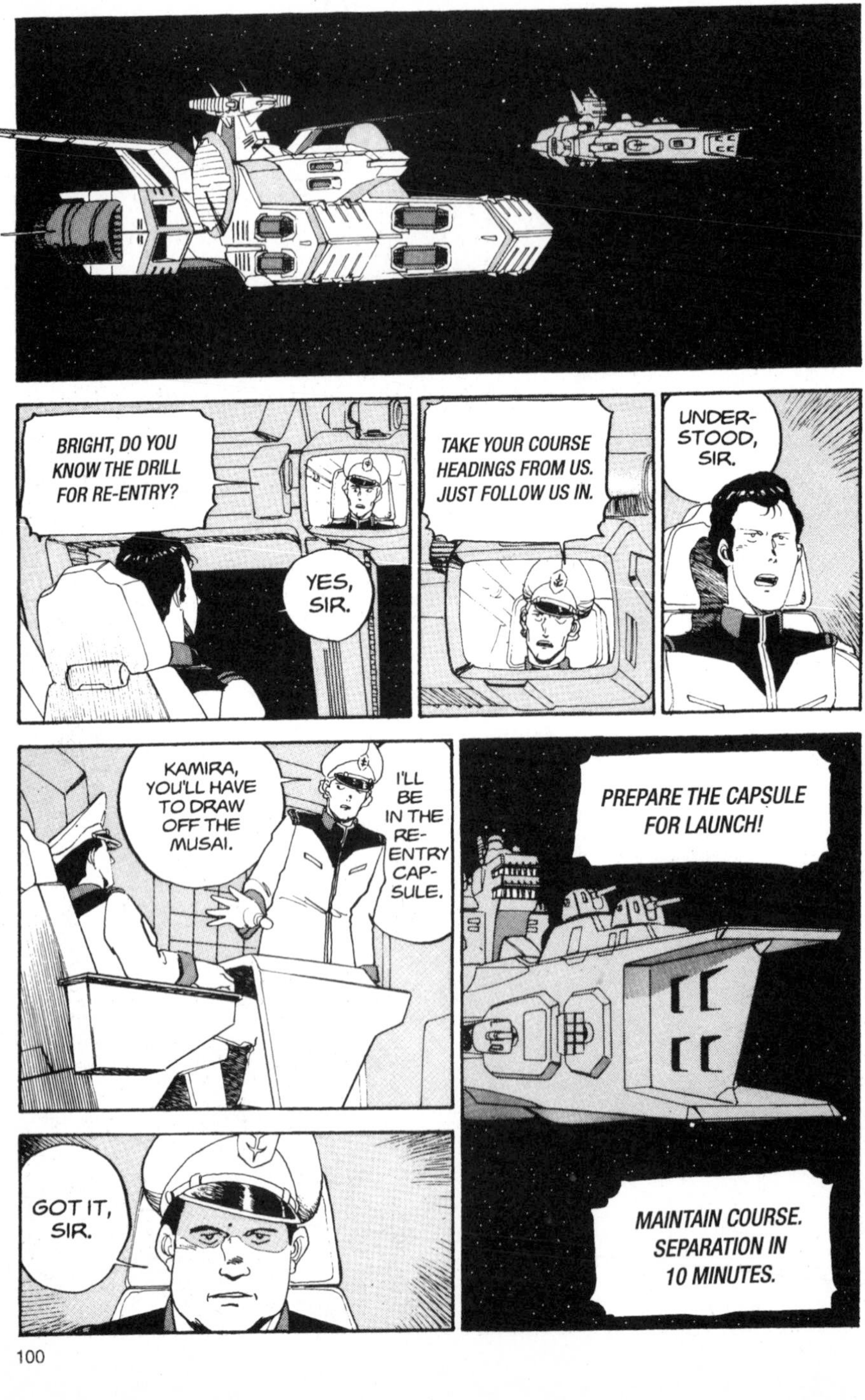

BRIGHT, DO YOU KNOW THE DRILL FOR RE-ENTRY?
YES, SIR.
TAKE YOUR COURSE HEADINGS FROM US. JUST FOLLOW US IN.
UNDER-STOOD, SIR.
KAMIRA, YOU'LL HAVE TO DRAW OFF THE MUSAI.
I'LL BE IN THE RE-ENTRY CAP-SULE.
GOT IT, SIR.
PREPARE THE CAPSULE FOR LAUNCH!
MAINTAIN COURSE. SEPARATION IN 10 MINUTES.

EXTEND SEPARATION ARM.

LAUNCH IN 5 SECONDS.

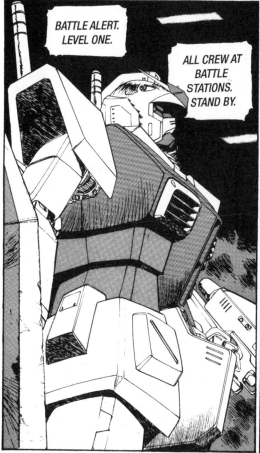

BATTLE ALERT. LEVEL ONE.

ALL CREW AT BATTLE STATIONS. STAND BY.

BI BI

ENEMY SIGHTED!

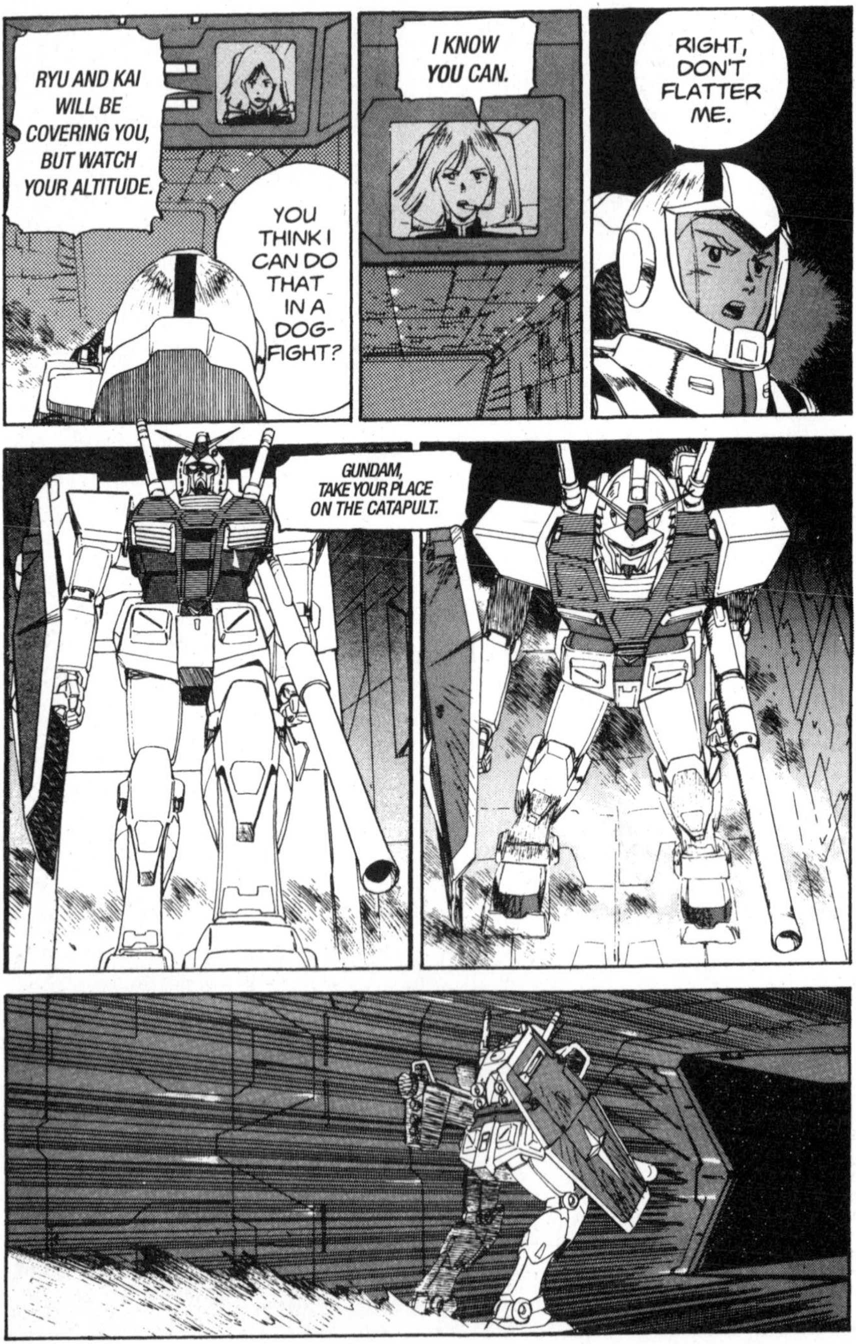
RYU AND KAI WILL BE COVERING YOU, BUT WATCH YOUR ALTITUDE.
YOU THINK I CAN DO THAT IN A DOG-FIGHT?
I KNOW YOU CAN.
RIGHT, DON'T FLATTER ME.
GUNDAM, TAKE YOUR PLACE ON THE CATAPULT.

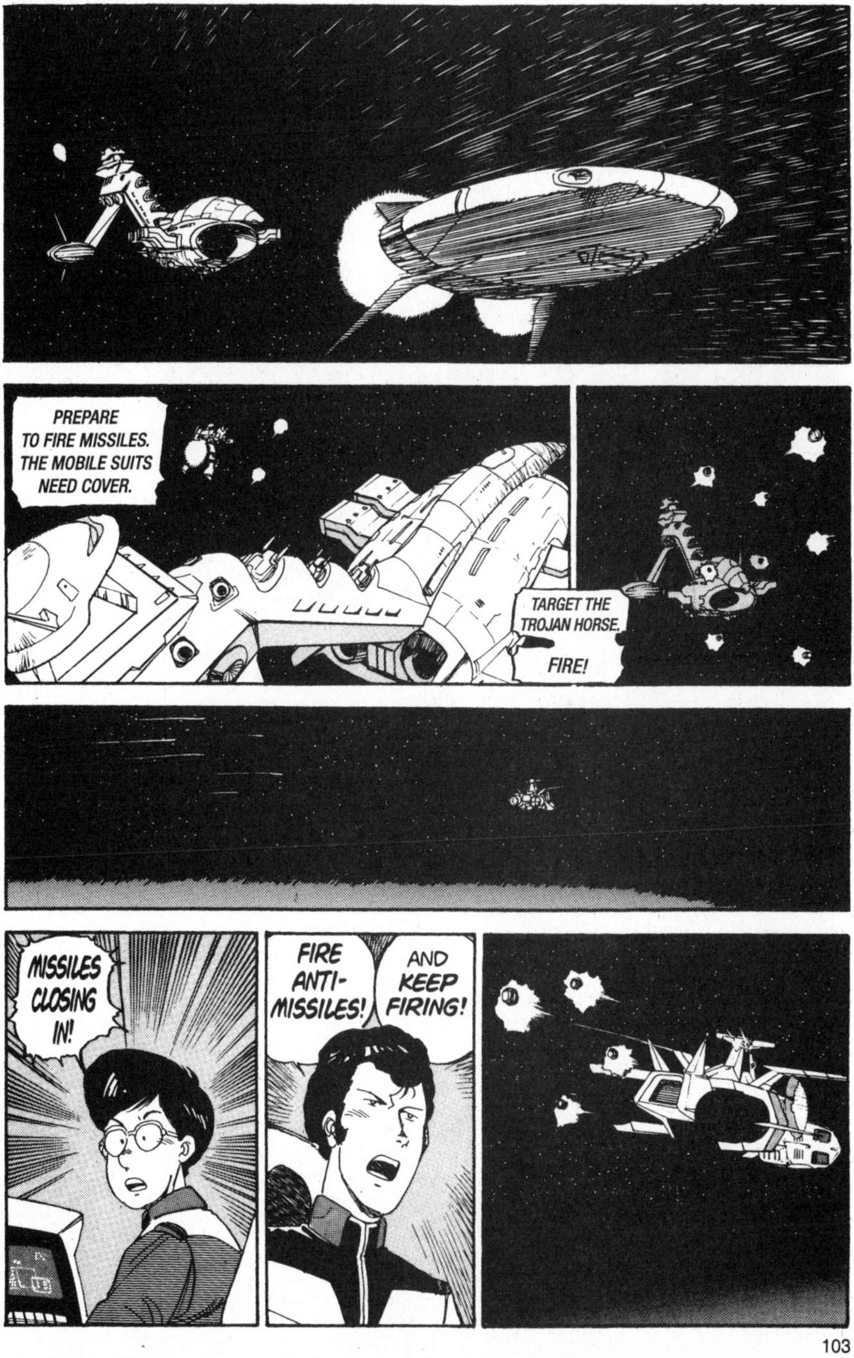
PREPARE TO FIRE MISSILES. THE MOBILE SUITS NEED COVER.
TARGET THE TROJAN HORSE.
FIRE!
MISSILES CLOSING IN!
FIRE ANTI-MISSILES!
AND KEEP FIRING!

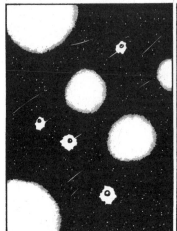

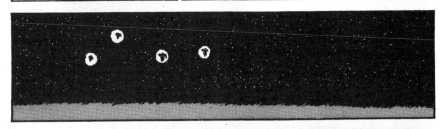

THIS TIME CHAR WON'T GET PAST ME.

I SHOULD HAVE GOT HIM BY NOW.

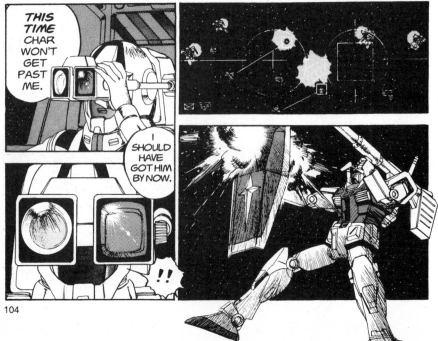

DAMMIT!

GOTCHA!

!

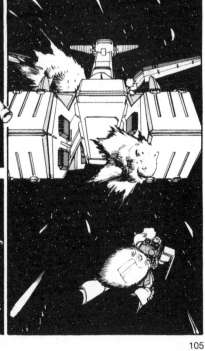

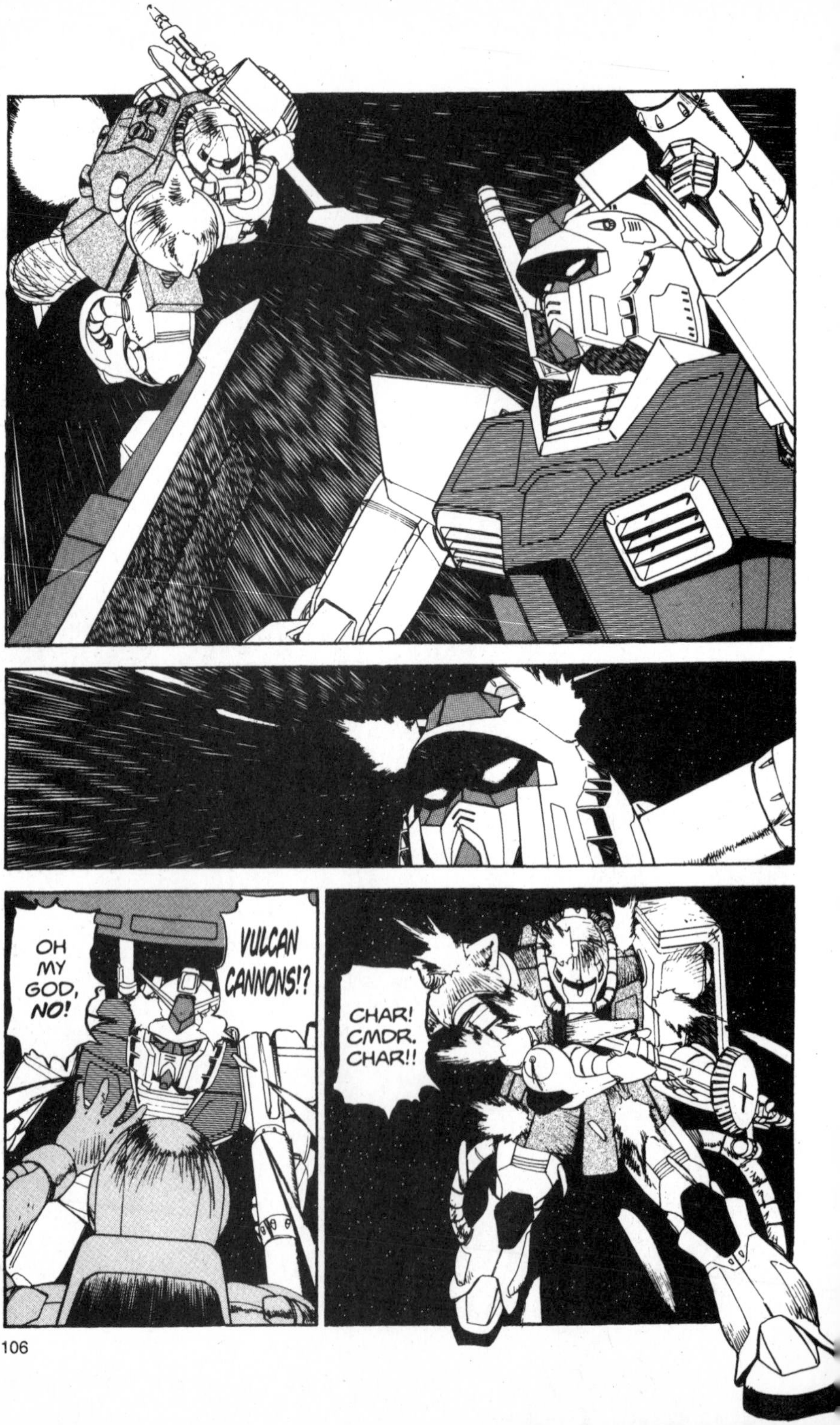
OH MY GOD, NO!
VULCAN CANNONS!?
CHAR! CMDR. CHAR!!

!!

J.Q.!!

DAMN THAT WHITE BASTARD!

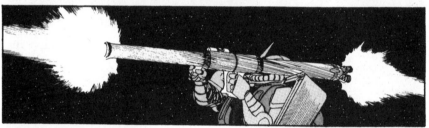

THE PILOT'S GOTTEN BETTER! LET'S SEE **HOW** GOOD...

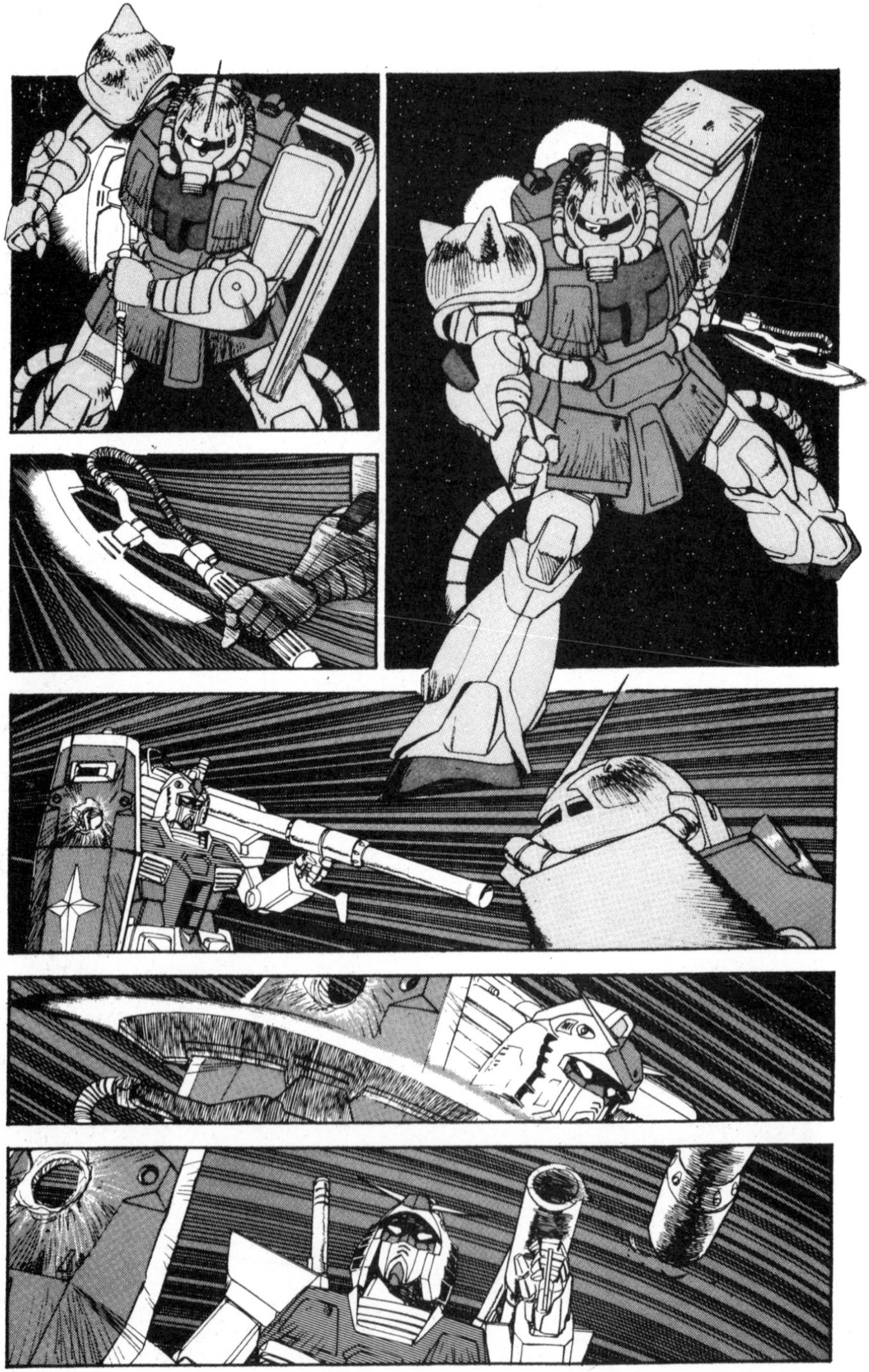

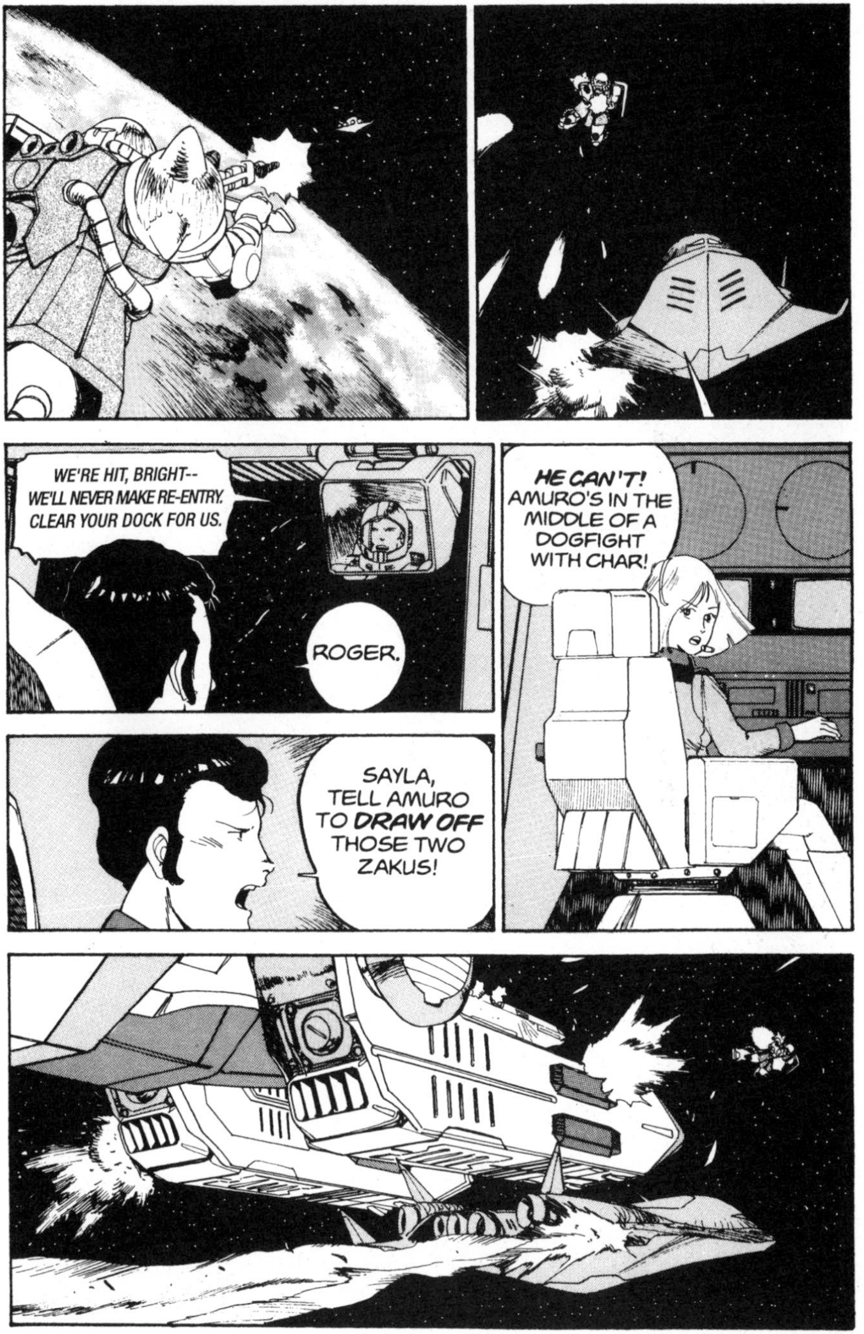

WE'RE HIT, BRIGHT-- WE'LL NEVER MAKE RE-ENTRY. CLEAR YOUR DOCK FOR US.
ROGER.
HE CAN'T! AMURO'S IN THE MIDDLE OF A DOGFIGHT WITH CHAR!
SAYLA, TELL AMURO TO **DRAW OFF** THOSE TWO ZAKUS!

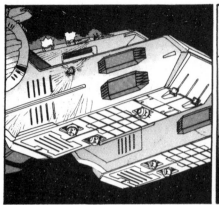

C'MON! HIT HIM!!

THE CAPSULE HAS DOCKED.

GOOD.

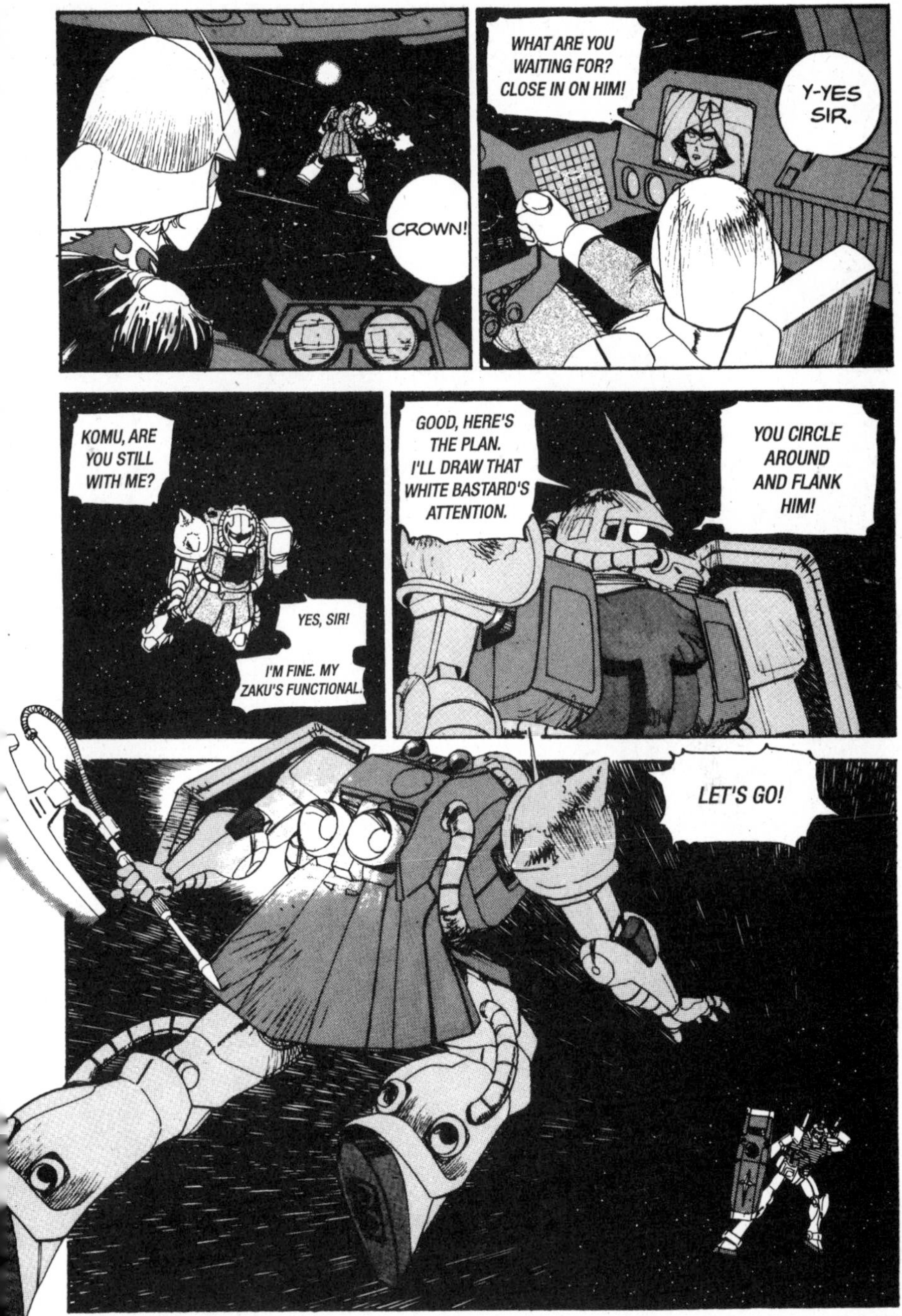
CROWN!
WHAT ARE YOU WAITING FOR? CLOSE IN ON HIM!
Y-YES SIR.
KOMU, ARE YOU STILL WITH ME?
YES, SIR!
I'M FINE. MY ZAKU'S FUNCTIONAL.
GOOD, HERE'S THE PLAN. I'LL DRAW THAT WHITE BASTARD'S ATTENTION.
YOU CIRCLE AROUND AND FLANK HIM!
LET'S GO!

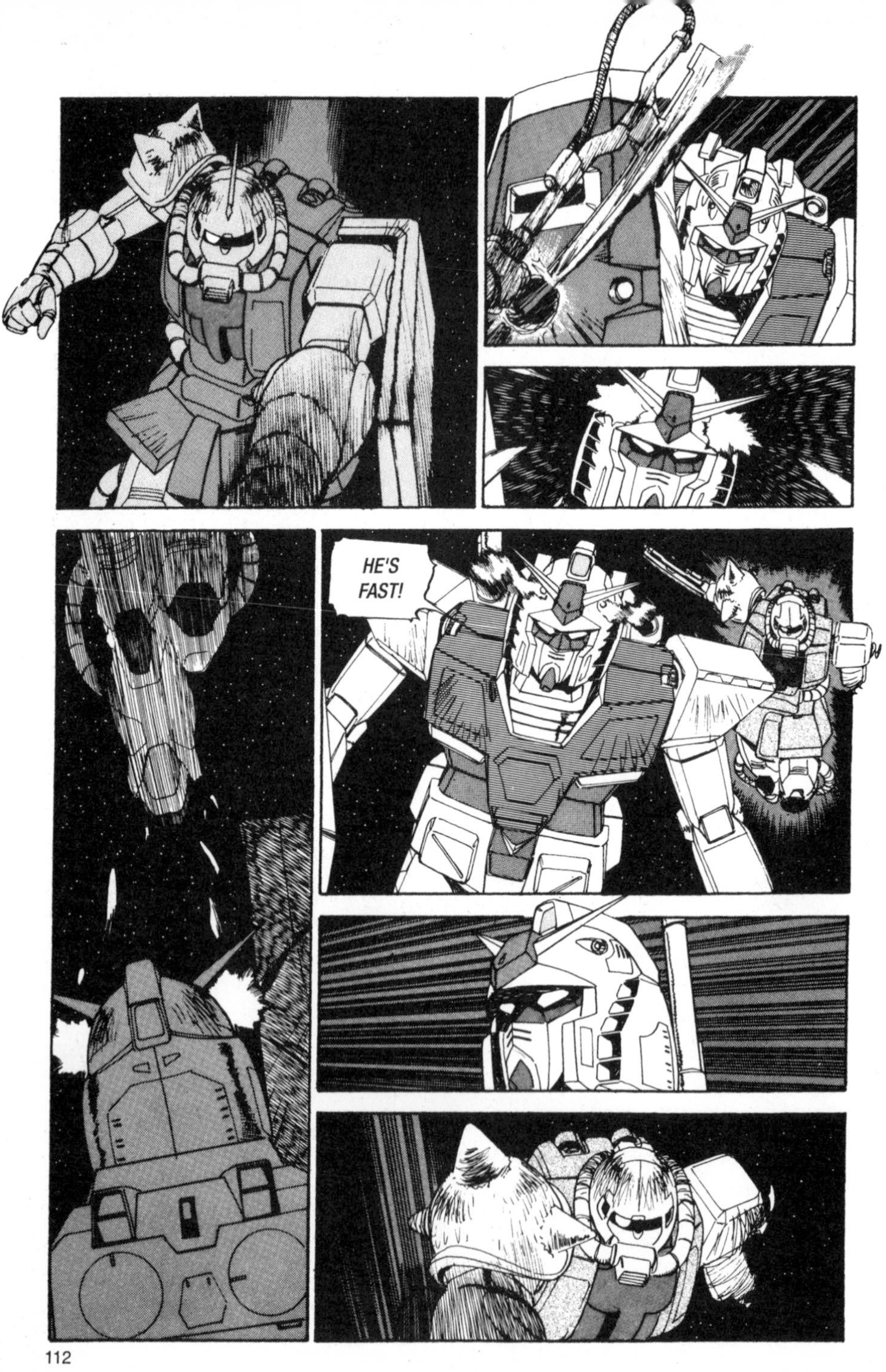
HE'S FAST!

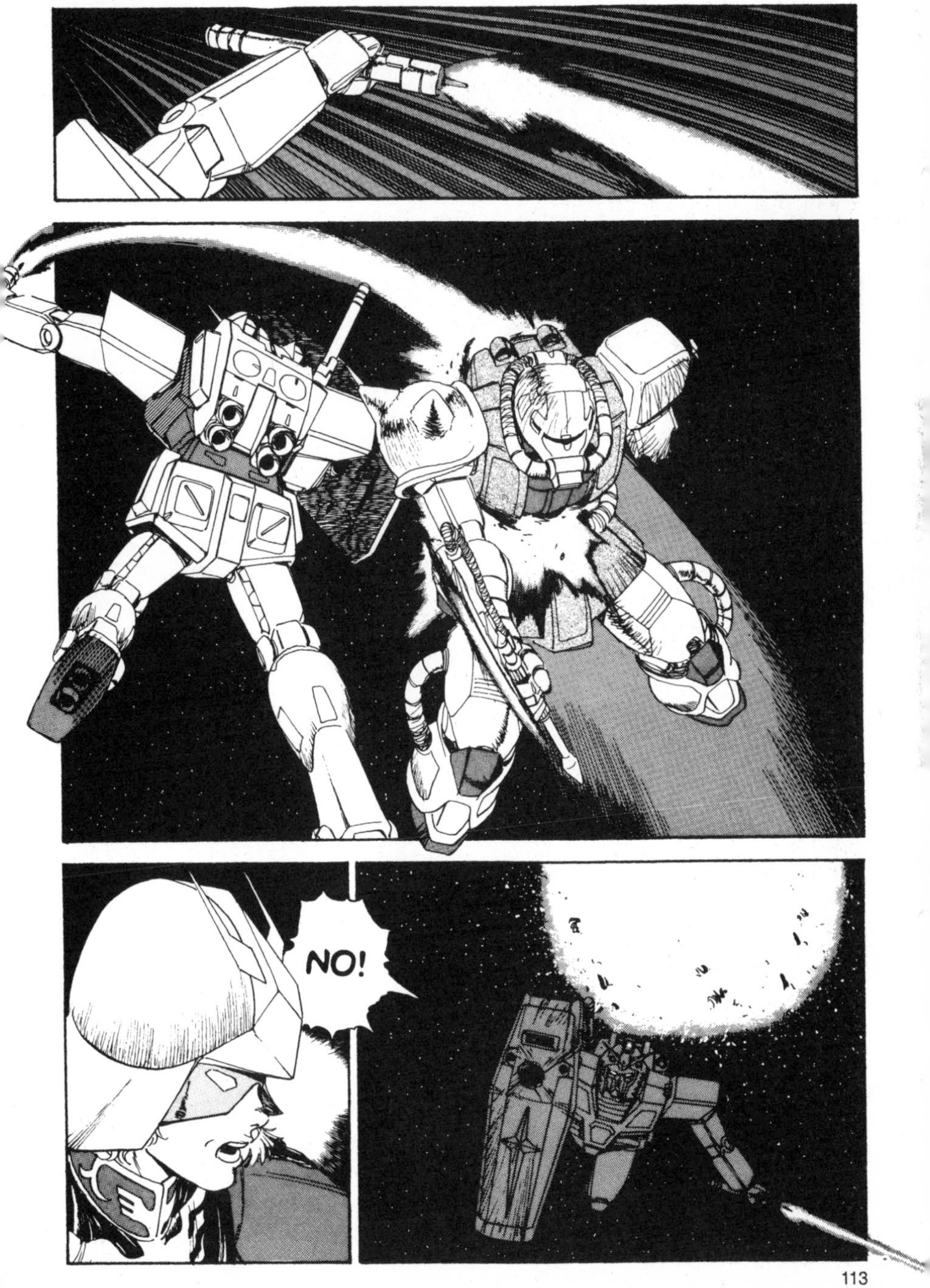
NO!

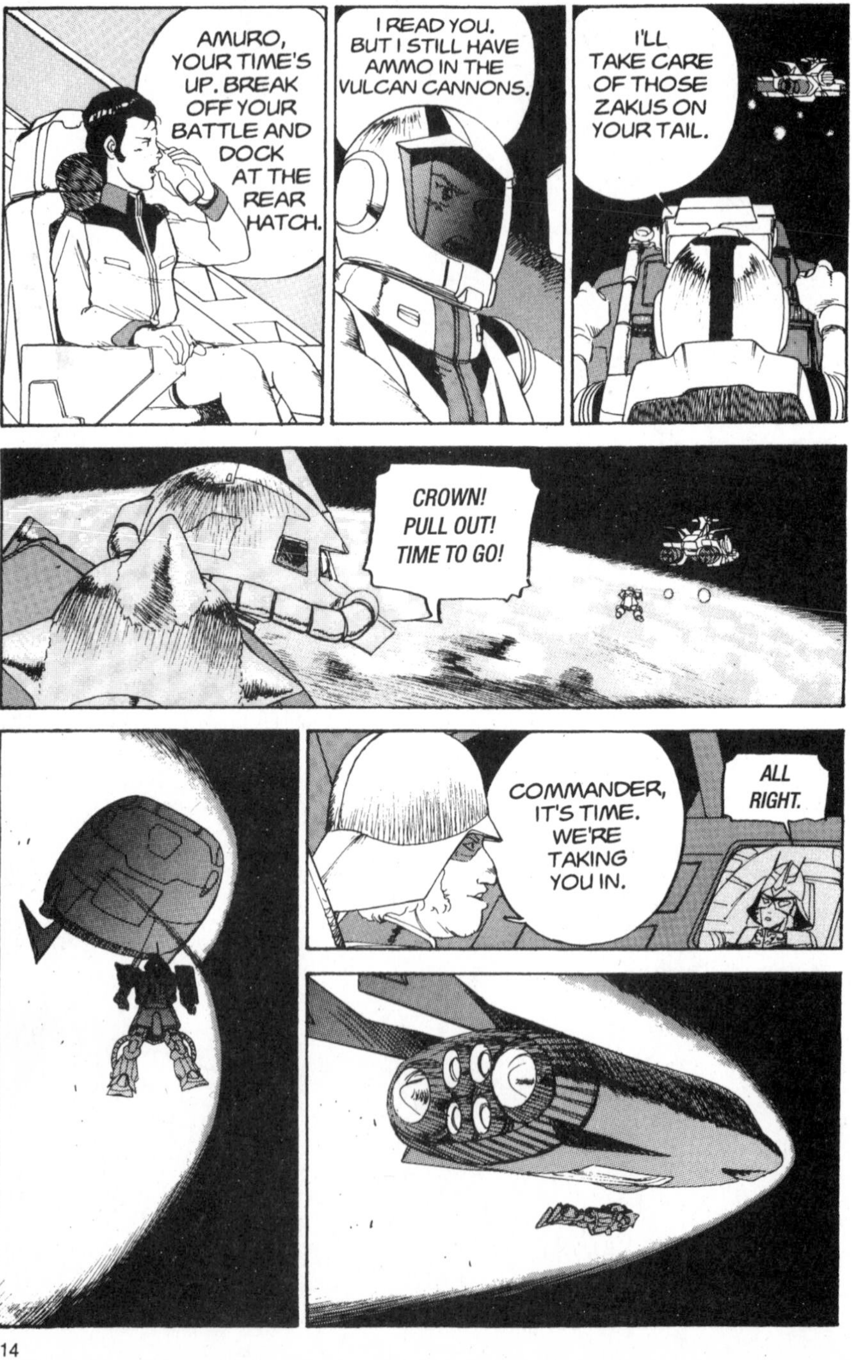
AMURO, YOUR TIME'S UP. BREAK OFF YOUR BATTLE AND DOCK AT THE REAR HATCH.
I READ YOU. BUT I STILL HAVE AMMO IN THE VULCAN CANNONS.
I'LL TAKE CARE OF THOSE ZAKUS ON YOUR TAIL.
CROWN! PULL OUT! TIME TO GO!
COMMANDER, IT'S TIME. WE'RE TAKING YOU IN.
ALL RIGHT.

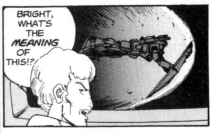

BRIGHT, WHAT'S THE *MEANING* OF THIS!?

GET THE GUNDAM BACK ABOARD!

WHY DON'T YOU GIVE AMURO THAT ORDER?

WATCH YOUR MOUTH! I'M YOUR *SUPERIOR OFFICER!*

I NEVER THOUGHT RE-ENTRY WOULD BE SO *FAST.*

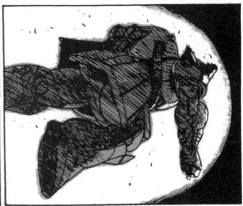

THERE'S *GOT* TO BE A WAY TO SURVIVE THIS.

CMDR... CHAR! MAYDAY! I NEED *HELP!*

DOREN, CAN WE...

NO. IT'S IMPOSS- IBLE TO GET HIM ABOARD NOW.

CROWN. YOUR SACRIFICE WON'T BE IN VAIN.

THAT WHITE BASTARD'S DOOMED, TOO.

115

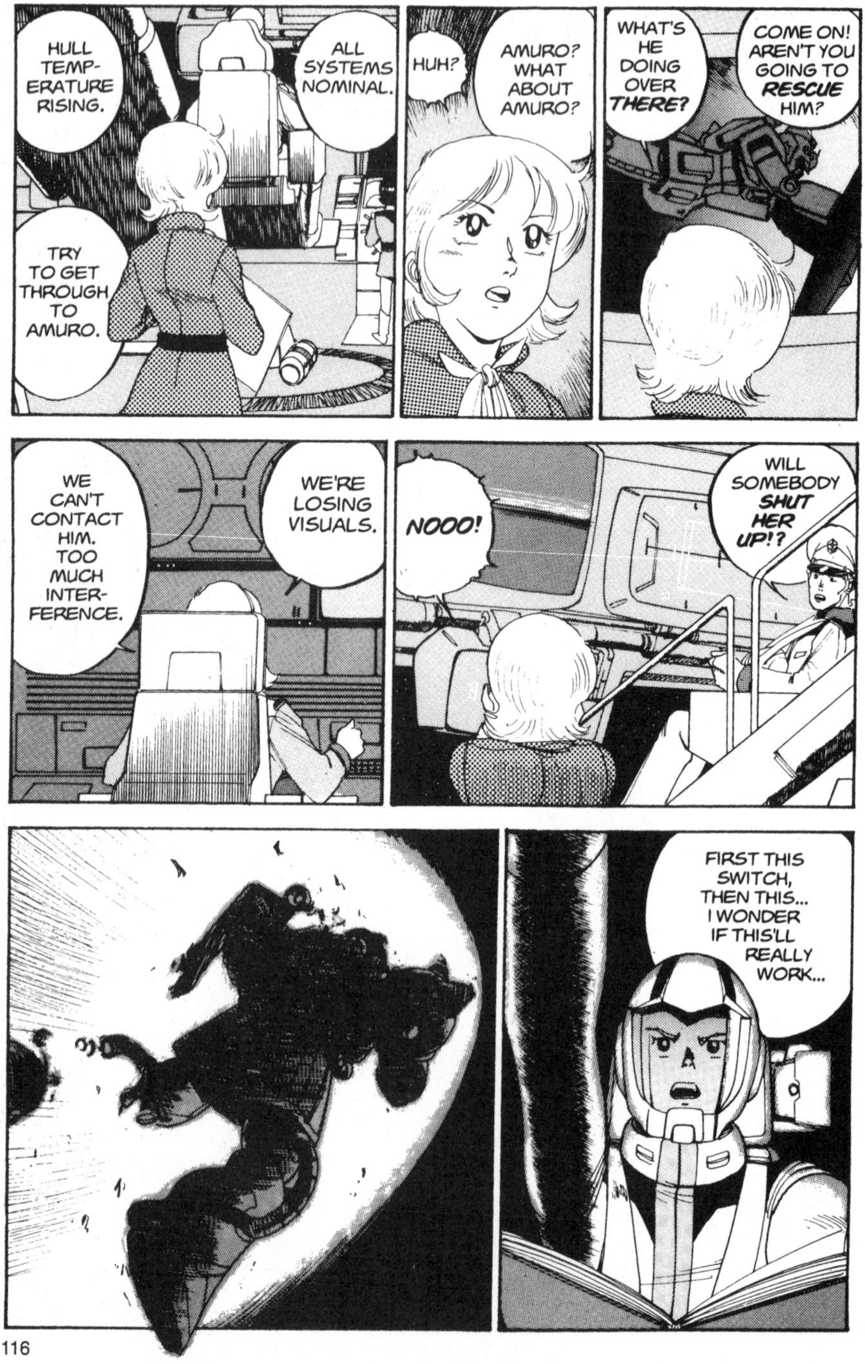
HULL TEMP-ERATURE RISING.
ALL SYSTEMS NOMINAL.
TRY TO GET THROUGH TO AMURO.
HUH?
AMURO? WHAT ABOUT AMURO?
WHAT'S HE DOING OVER *THERE?*
COME ON! AREN'T YOU GOING TO *RESCUE* HIM?
WE CAN'T CONTACT HIM. TOO MUCH INTER-FERENCE.
WE'RE LOSING VISUALS.
NOOO!
WILL SOMEBODY *SHUT HER UP!?*
FIRST THIS SWITCH, THEN THIS... I WONDER IF THIS'LL REALLY WORK...

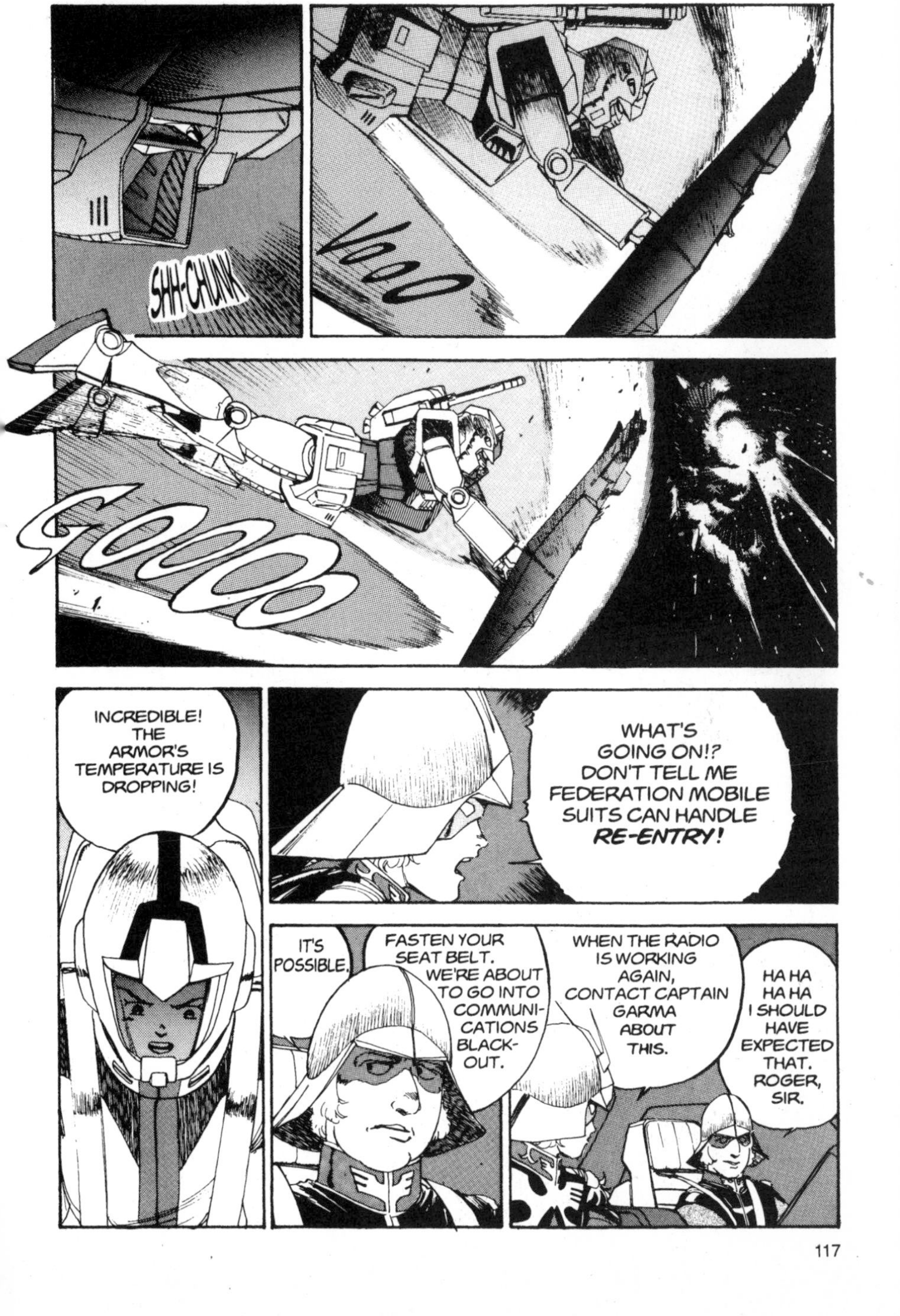
SHH-CHUNK
VOOO
GOOOO
INCREDIBLE! THE ARMOR'S TEMPERATURE IS DROPPING!
WHAT'S GOING ON!? DON'T TELL ME FEDERATION MOBILE SUITS CAN HANDLE RE-ENTRY!
IT'S POSSIBLE.
FASTEN YOUR SEAT BELT. WE'RE ABOUT TO GO INTO COMMUNICATIONS BLACKOUT.
WHEN THE RADIO IS WORKING AGAIN, CONTACT CAPTAIN GARMA ABOUT THIS.
HA HA HA HA I SHOULD HAVE EXPECTED THAT. ROGER, SIR.

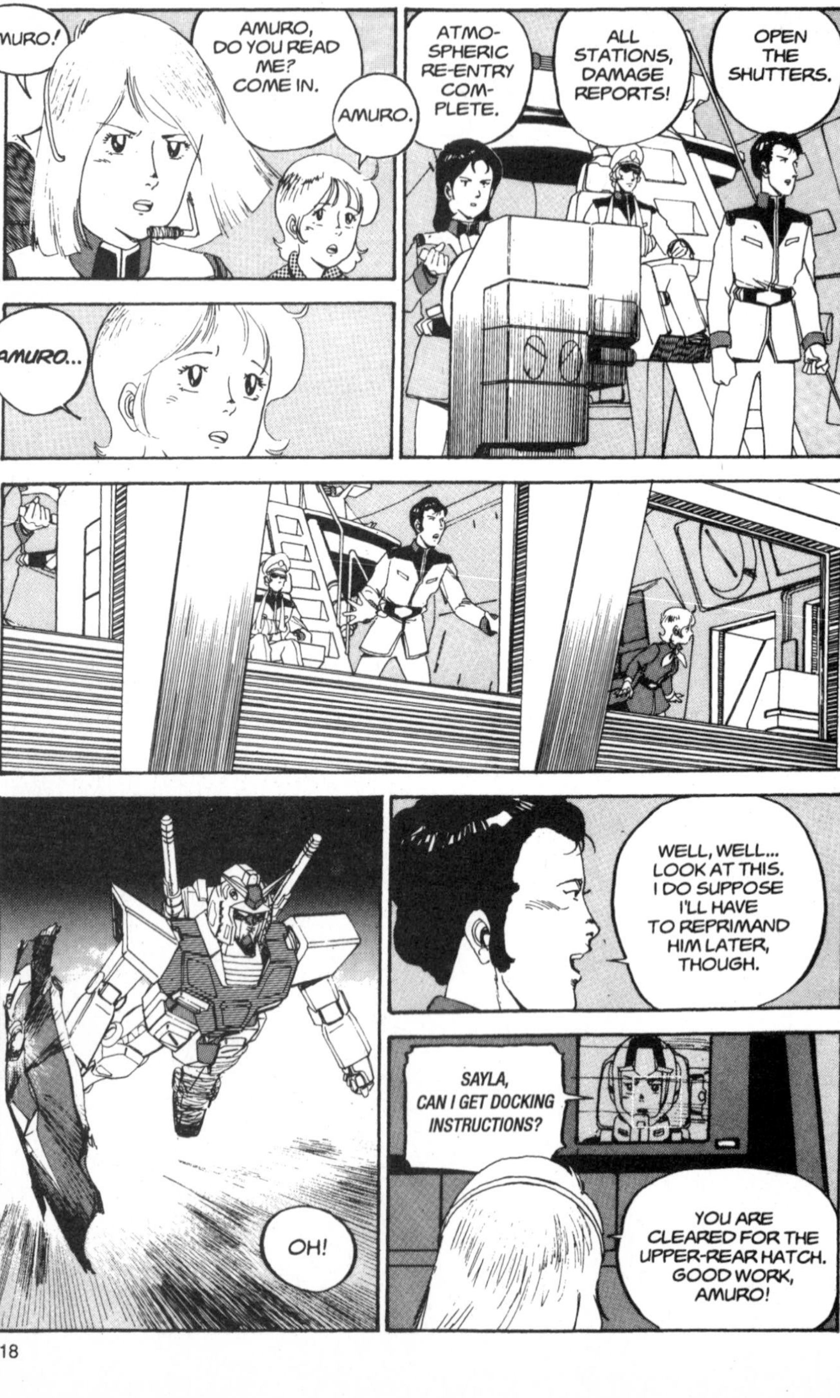
AMURO!
AMURO, DO YOU READ ME? COME IN.
AMURO.
AMURO...
ATMO-SPHERIC RE-ENTRY COM-PLETE.
ALL STATIONS, DAMAGE REPORTS!
OPEN THE SHUTTERS.
OH!
WELL, WELL... LOOK AT THIS. I DO SUPPOSE I'LL HAVE TO REPRIMAND HIM LATER, THOUGH.
SAYLA, CAN I GET DOCKING INSTRUCTIONS?
YOU ARE CLEARED FOR THE UPPER-REAR HATCH. GOOD WORK, AMURO!

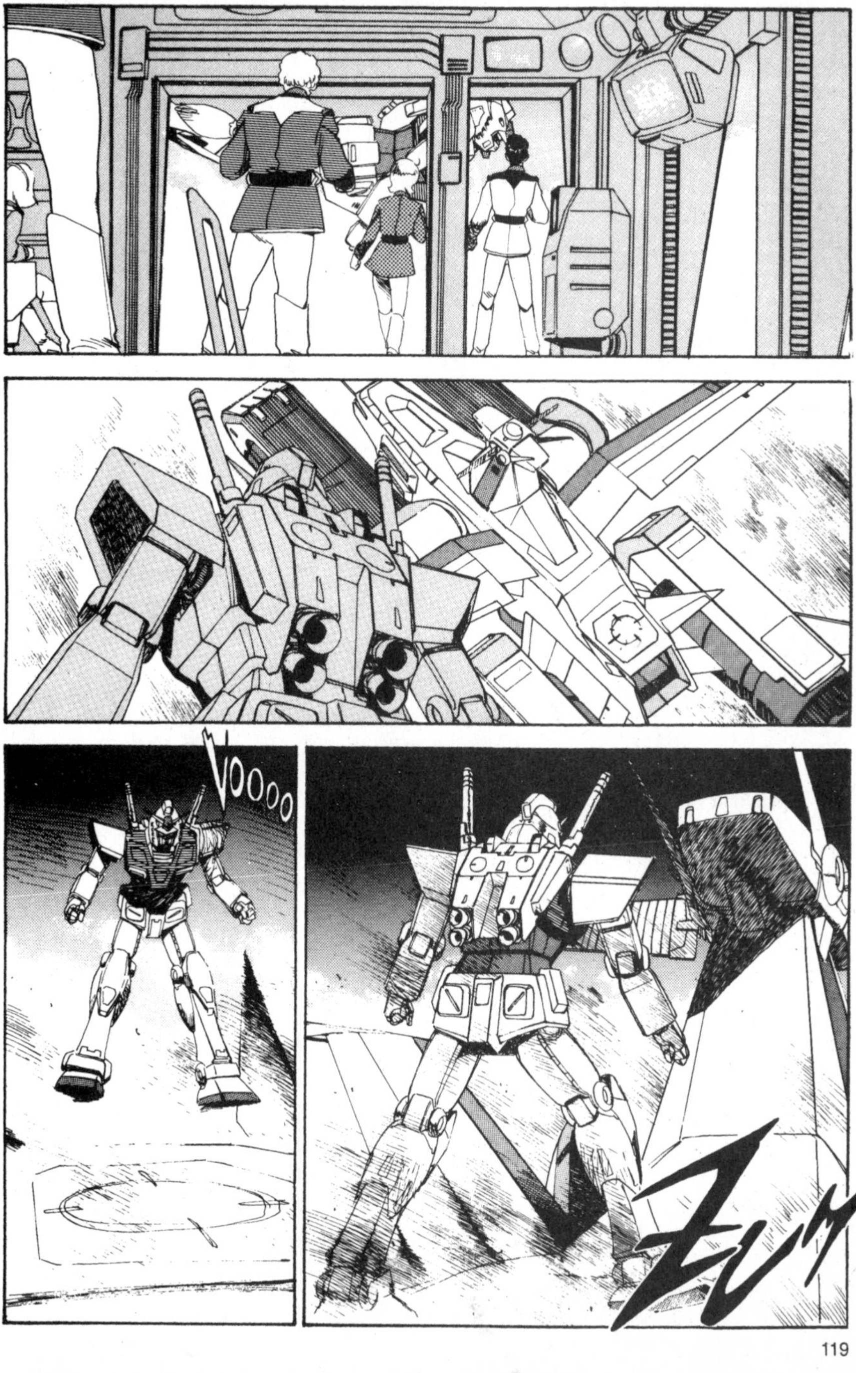
VOOOO

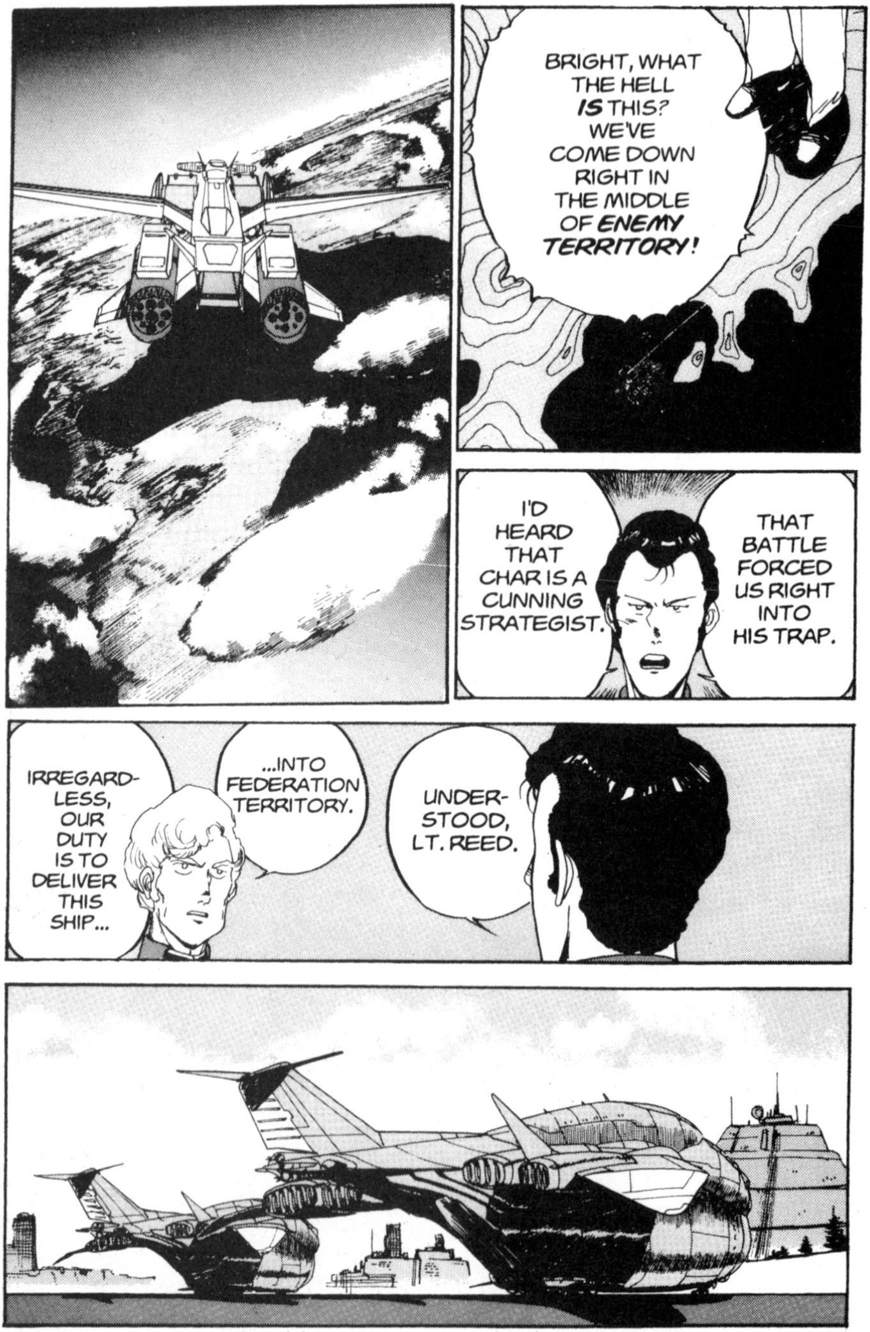
BRIGHT, WHAT THE HELL **IS** THIS? WE'VE COME DOWN RIGHT IN THE MIDDLE OF ***ENEMY TERRITORY!***
I'D HEARD THAT CHAR IS A CUNNING STRATEGIST.
THAT BATTLE FORCED US RIGHT INTO HIS TRAP.
IRREGARD-LESS, OUR DUTY IS TO DELIVER THIS SHIP...
...INTO FEDERATION TERRITORY.
UNDER-STOOD, LT. REED.

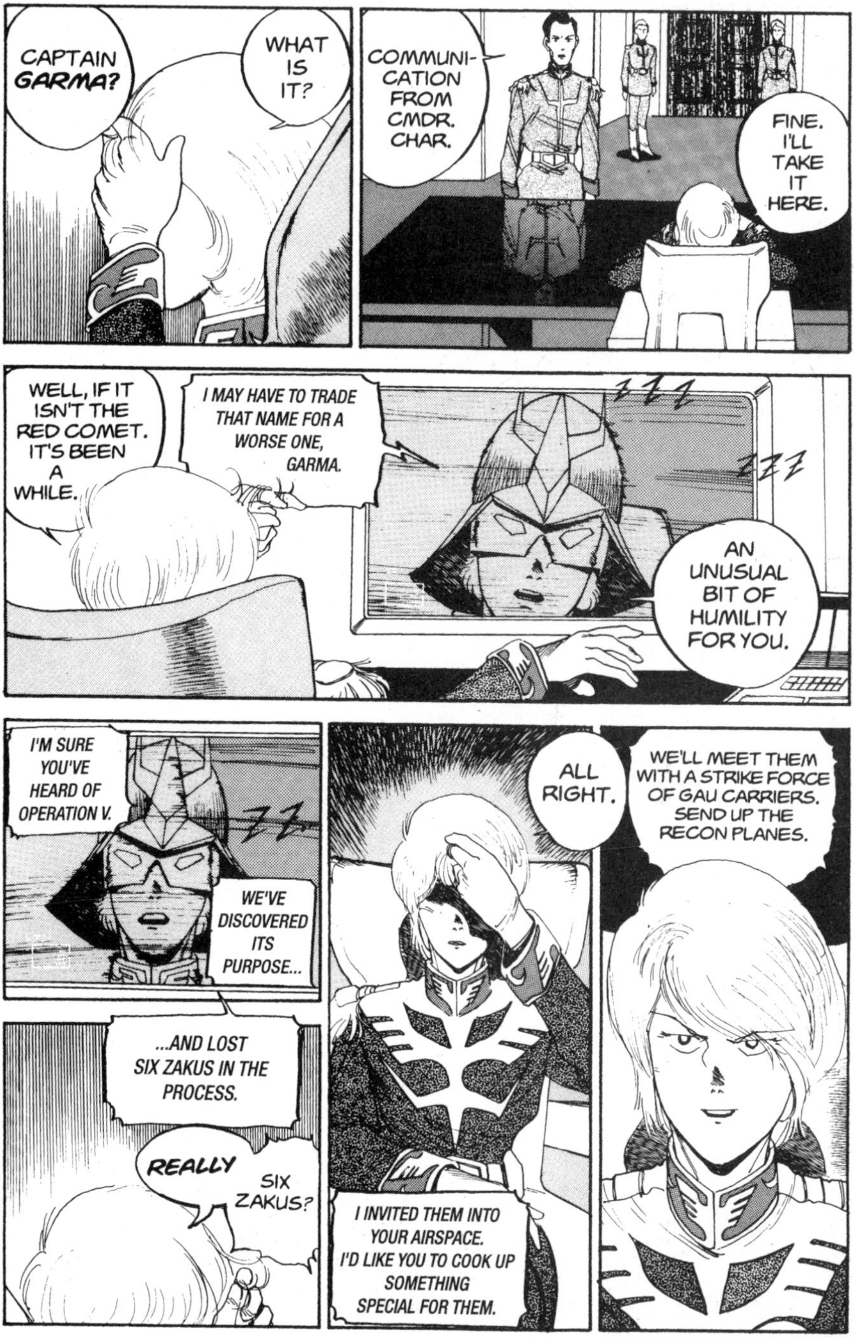
CAPTAIN GARMA?
WHAT IS IT?
COMMUNICATION FROM CMDR. CHAR.
FINE. I'LL TAKE IT HERE.
WELL, IF IT ISN'T THE RED COMET. IT'S BEEN A WHILE.
I MAY HAVE TO TRADE THAT NAME FOR A WORSE ONE, GARMA.
AN UNUSUAL BIT OF HUMILITY FOR YOU.
I'M SURE YOU'VE HEARD OF OPERATION V.
WE'VE DISCOVERED ITS PURPOSE...
...AND LOST SIX ZAKUS IN THE PROCESS.
REALLY SIX ZAKUS?
I INVITED THEM INTO YOUR AIRSPACE. I'D LIKE YOU TO COOK UP SOMETHING SPECIAL FOR THEM.
ALL RIGHT.
WE'LL MEET THEM WITH A STRIKE FORCE OF GAU CARRIERS. SEND UP THE RECON PLANES.

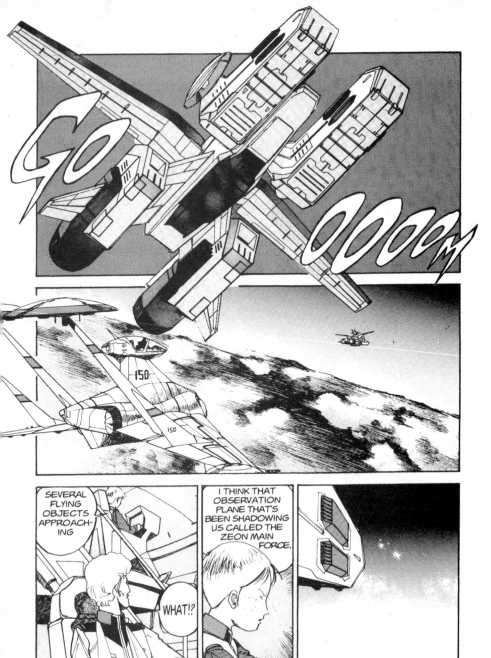

GO

OOOM

150

150

SEVERAL FLYING OBJECTS APPROACHING

WHAT!?

I THINK THAT OBSERVATION PLANE THAT'S BEEN SHADOWING US CALLED THE ZEON MAIN FORCE.

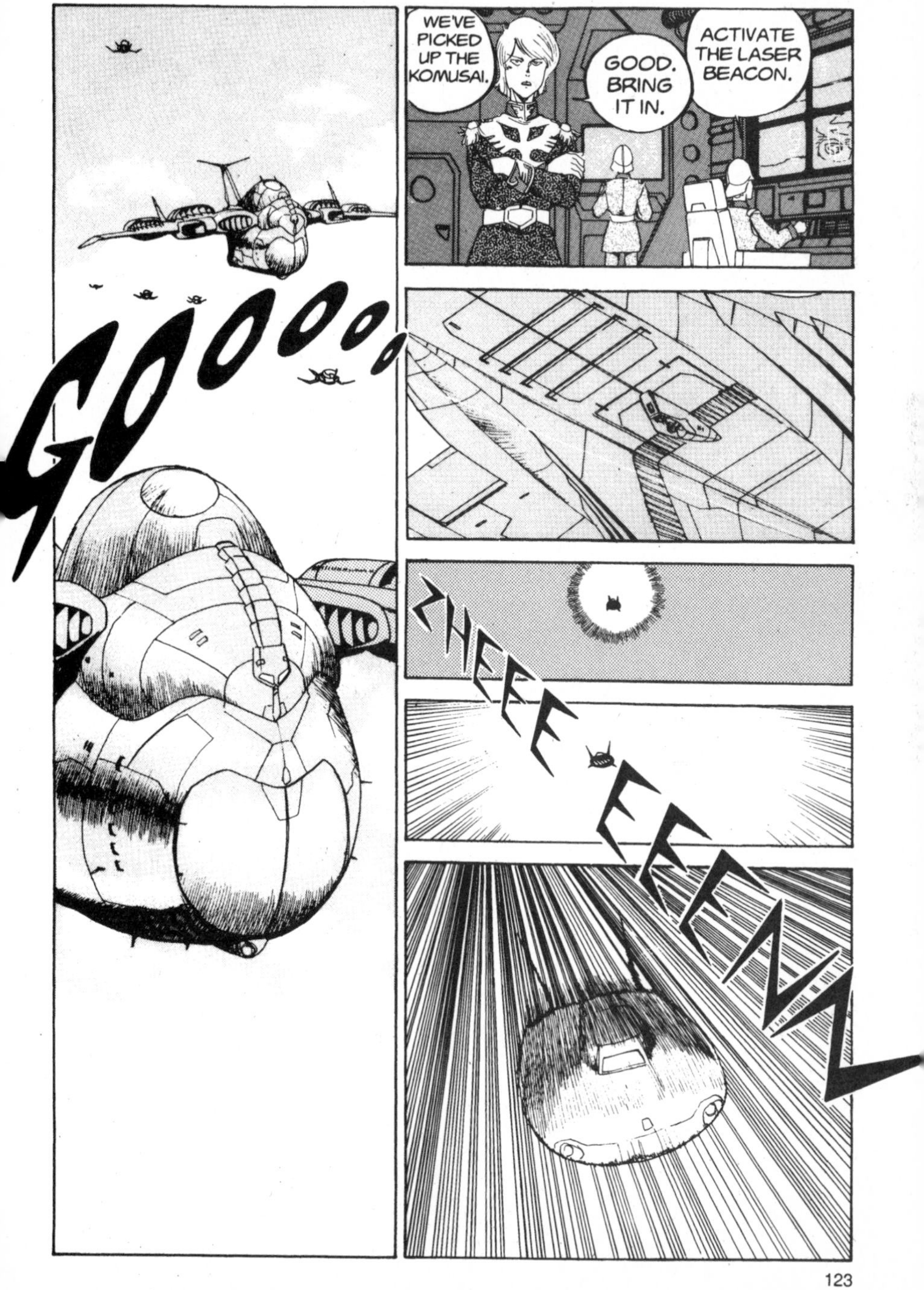
GOOOOO
WE'VE PICKED UP THE KOMUSAI.
GOOD. BRING IT IN.
ACTIVATE THE LASER BEACON.
ZHEEEEEEENN

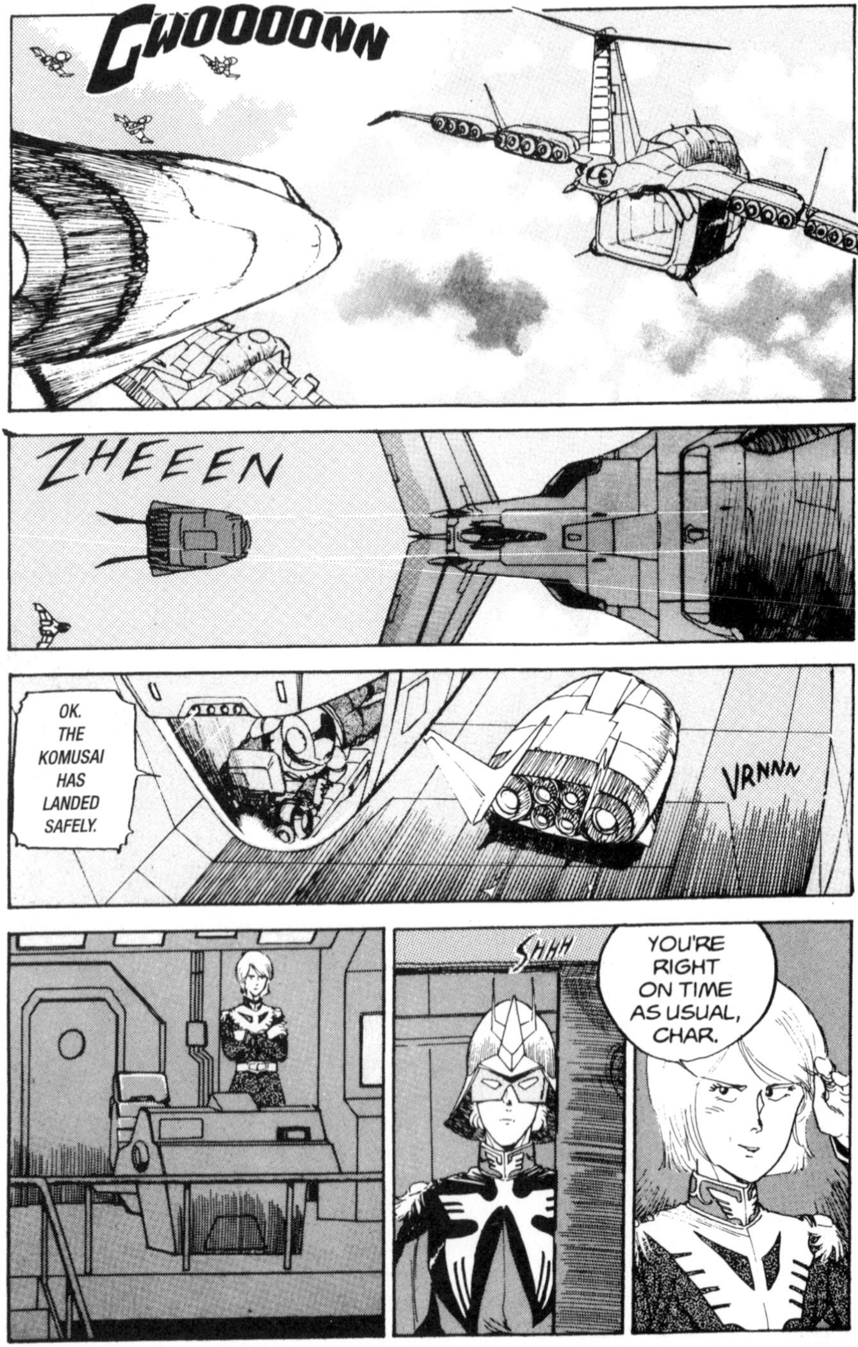
GWOOOONN
ZHEEEN
OK. THE KOMUSAI HAS LANDED SAFELY.
VRNNN
SHHH
YOU'RE RIGHT ON TIME AS USUAL, CHAR.

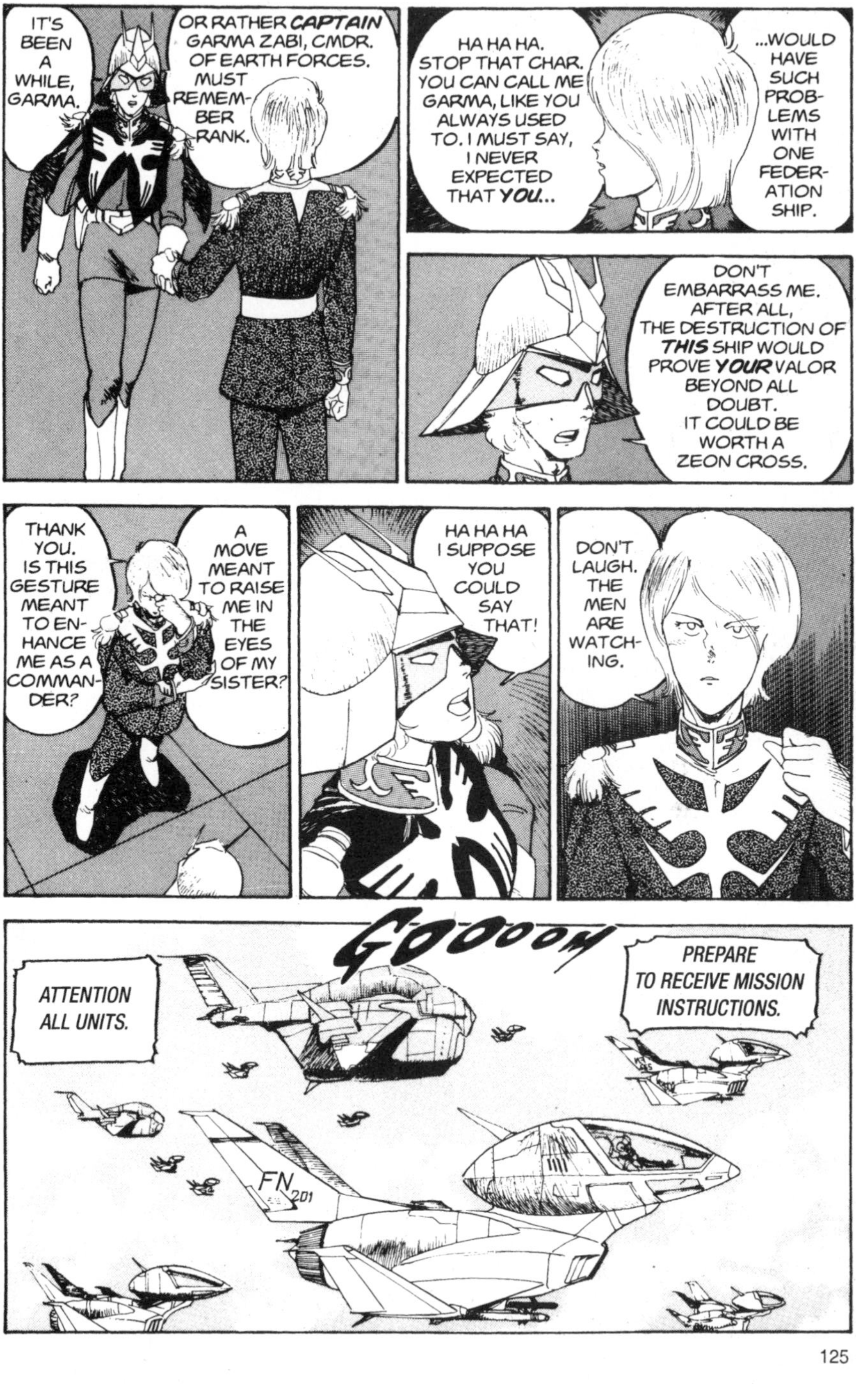
IT'S BEEN A WHILE, GARMA.
OR RATHER **CAPTAIN** GARMA ZABI, CMDR. OF EARTH FORCES. MUST REMEMBER RANK.
HA HA HA. STOP THAT CHAR. YOU CAN CALL ME GARMA, LIKE YOU ALWAYS USED TO. I MUST SAY, I NEVER EXPECTED THAT **YOU**...
...WOULD HAVE SUCH PROBLEMS WITH ONE FEDERATION SHIP.
DON'T EMBARRASS ME. AFTER ALL, THE DESTRUCTION OF **THIS** SHIP WOULD PROVE **YOUR** VALOR BEYOND ALL DOUBT. IT COULD BE WORTH A ZEON CROSS.
THANK YOU. IS THIS GESTURE MEANT TO ENHANCE ME AS A COMMANDER?
A MOVE MEANT TO RAISE ME IN THE EYES OF MY SISTER?
HA HA HA I SUPPOSE YOU COULD SAY THAT!
DON'T LAUGH. THE MEN ARE WATCHING.
GOOOOM
ATTENTION ALL UNITS.
PREPARE TO RECEIVE MISSION INSTRUCTIONS.
FN 201

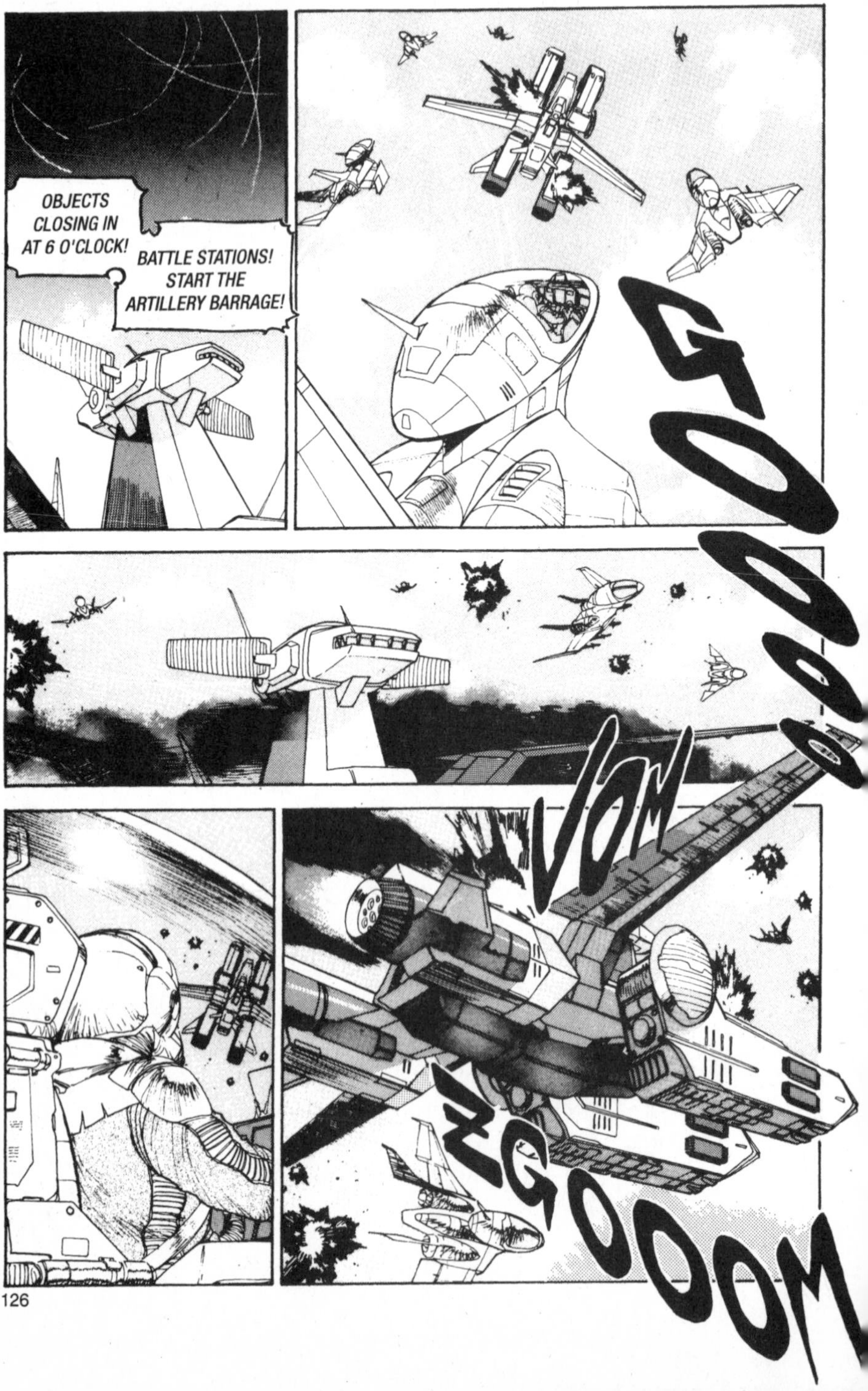
OBJECTS CLOSING IN AT 6 O'CLOCK!
BATTLE STATIONS! START THE ARTILLERY BARRAGE!
GOOOOO
VOM
ZGOOOOM

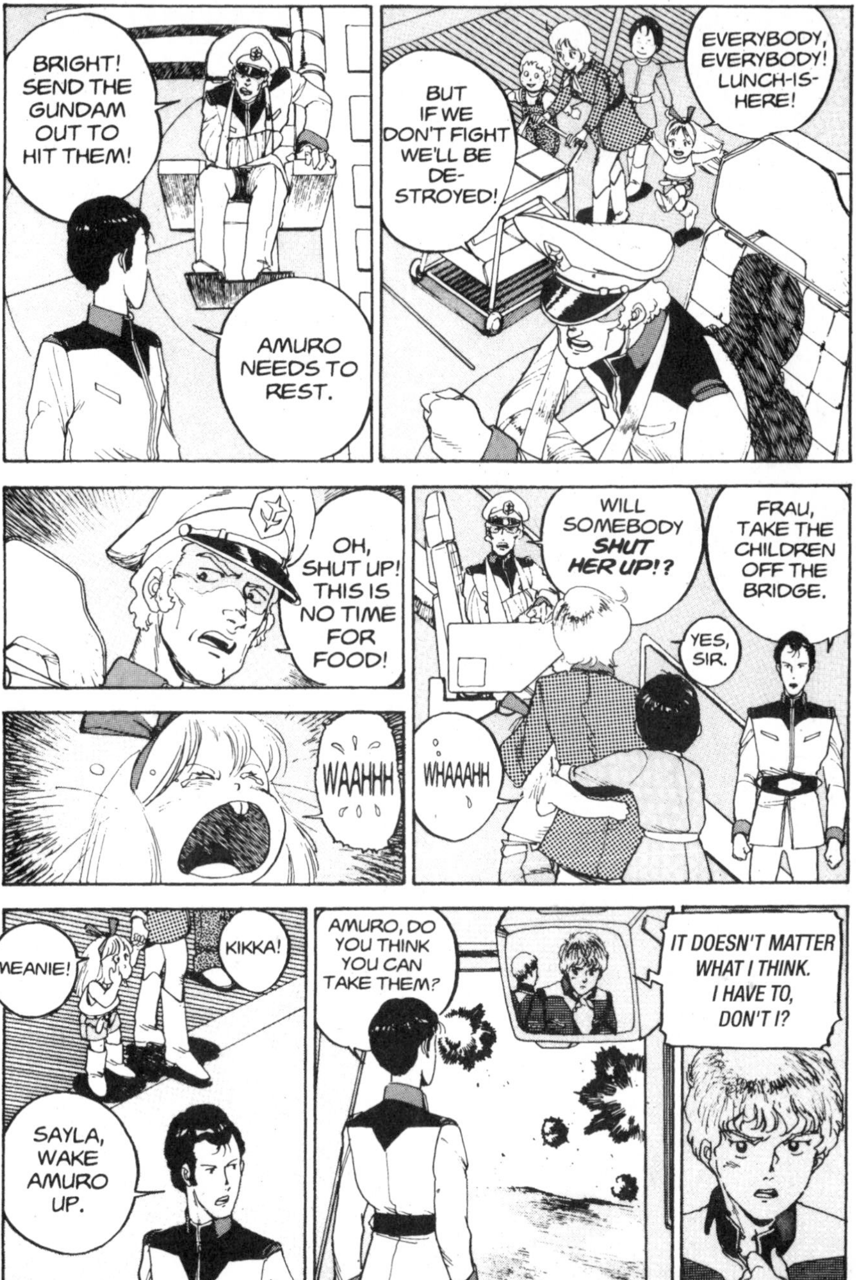
BRIGHT! SEND THE GUNDAM OUT TO HIT THEM!
AMURO NEEDS TO REST.
BUT IF WE DON'T FIGHT WE'LL BE DE-STROYED!
EVERYBODY, EVERYBODY! LUNCH-IS-HERE!
OH, SHUT UP! THIS IS NO TIME FOR FOOD!
WAAHHH
WILL SOMEBODY SHUT HER UP!?
FRAU, TAKE THE CHILDREN OFF THE BRIDGE.
YES, SIR.
WHAAAHH
MEANIE!
KIKKA!
SAYLA, WAKE AMURO UP.
AMURO, DO YOU THINK YOU CAN TAKE THEM?
IT DOESN'T MATTER WHAT I THINK. I HAVE TO, DON'T I?

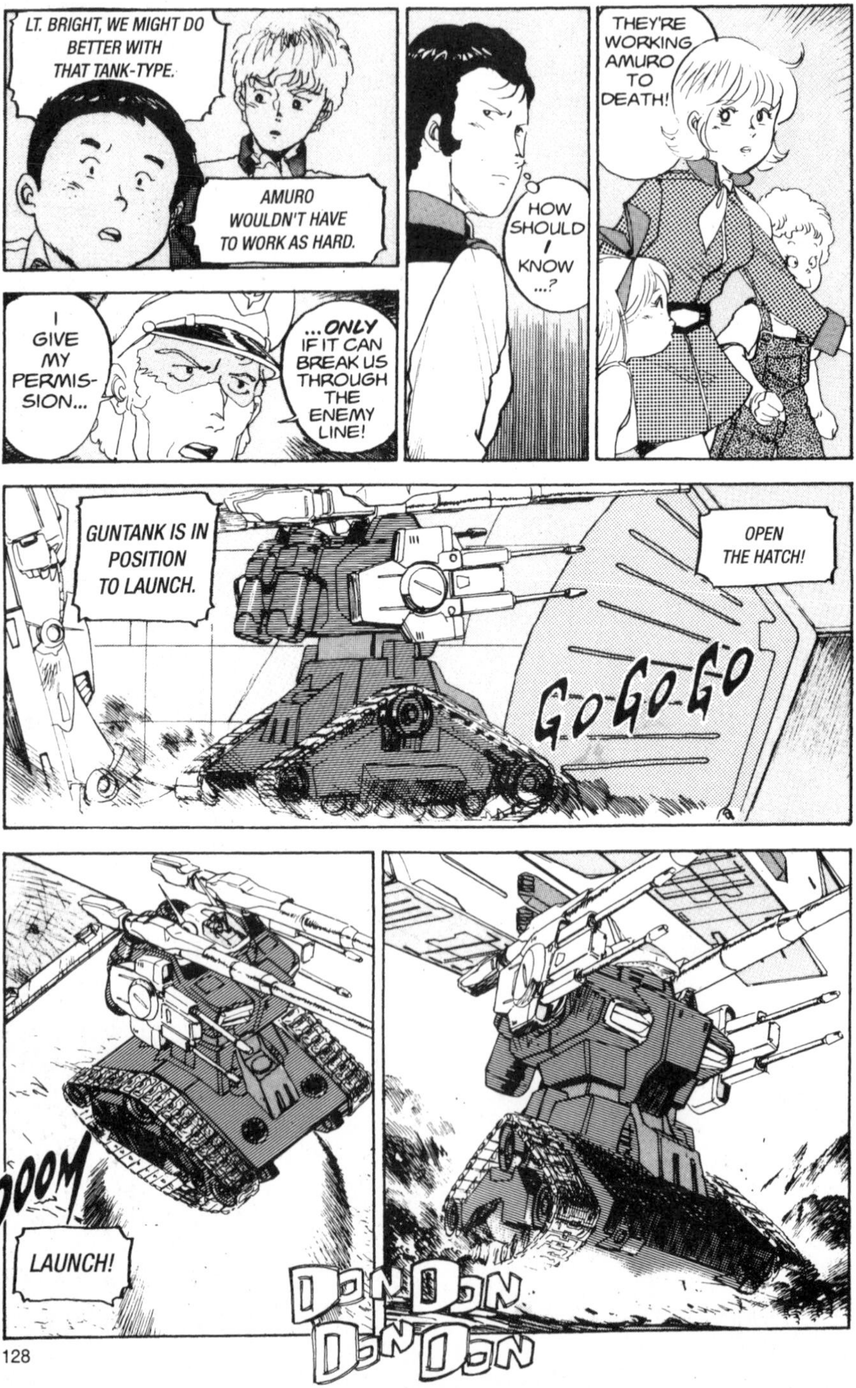
LT. BRIGHT, WE MIGHT DO BETTER WITH THAT TANK-TYPE.
AMURO WOULDN'T HAVE TO WORK AS HARD.
HOW SHOULD I KNOW ...?
THEY'RE WORKING AMURO TO DEATH!
I GIVE MY PERMISSION...
...ONLY IF IT CAN BREAK US THROUGH THE ENEMY LINE!
GUNTANK IS IN POSITION TO LAUNCH.
OPEN THE HATCH!
GO-GO-GO
GOOOM
LAUNCH!
DON DON DON DON

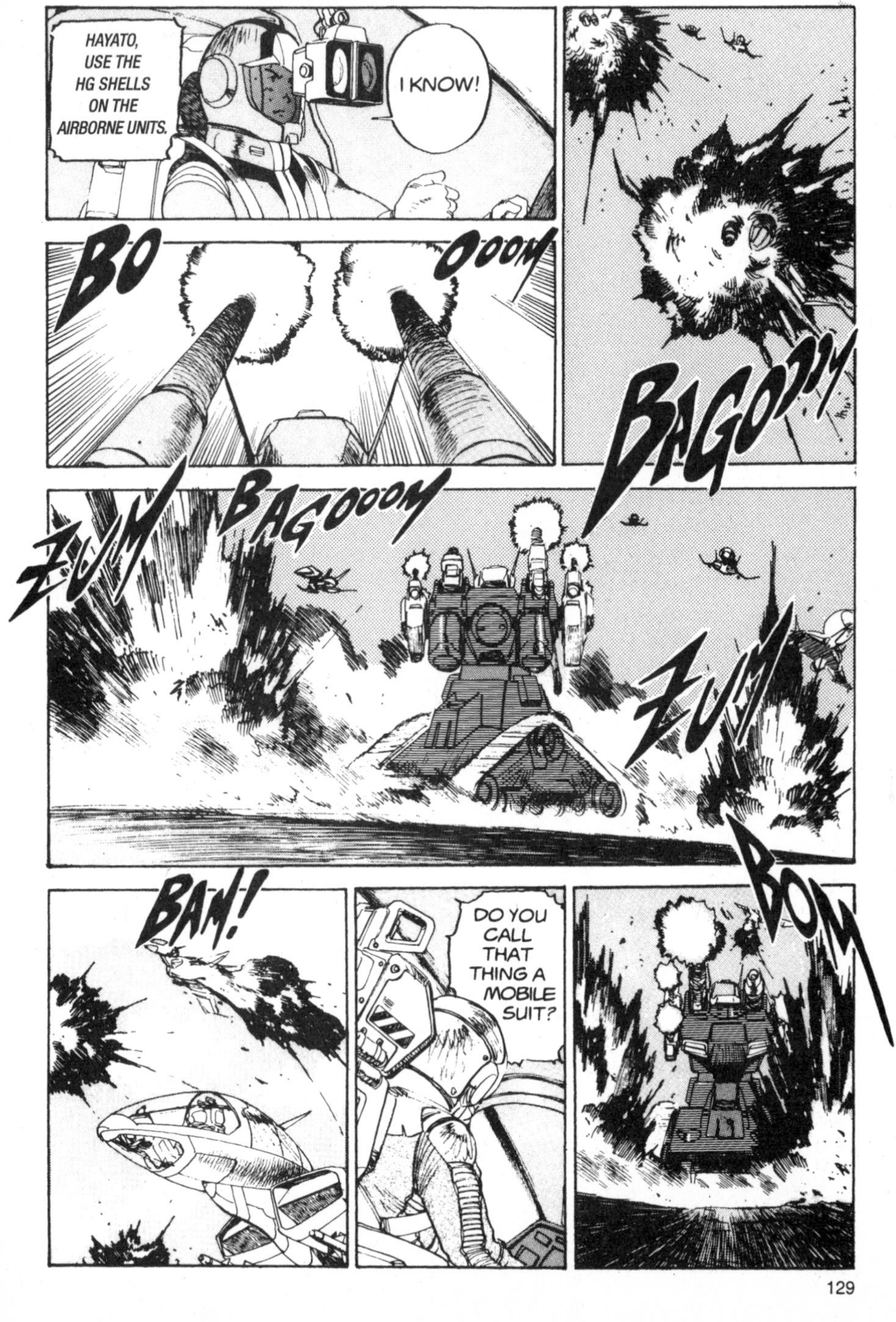
HAYATO, USE THE HG SHELLS ON THE AIRBORNE UNITS.
I KNOW!
BOOOOM
BAGOOM
ZUM
BAGOOOM
ZUM
BOM
BAM!
DO YOU CALL THAT THING A MOBILE SUIT?

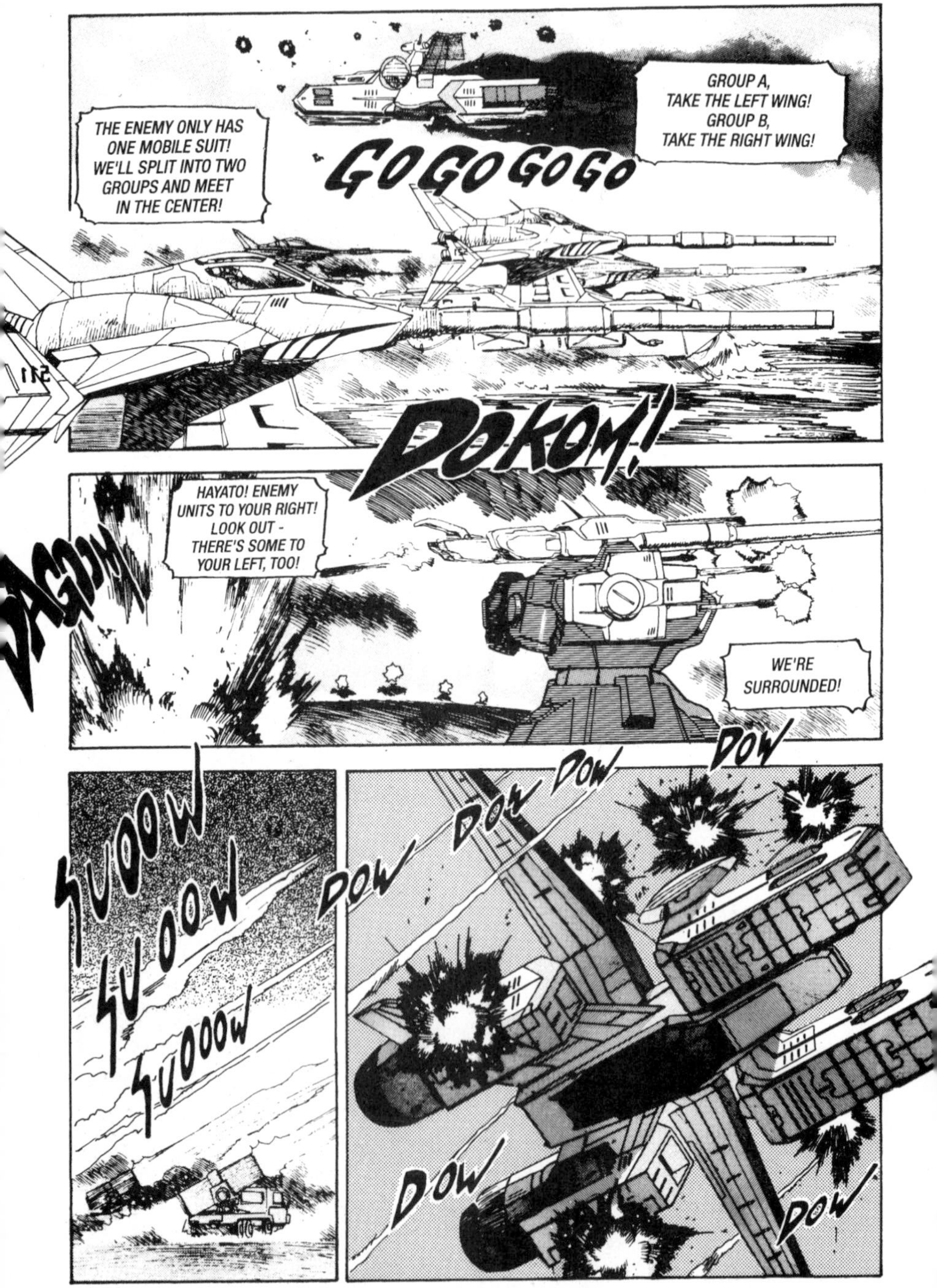
THE ENEMY ONLY HAS ONE MOBILE SUIT! WE'LL SPLIT INTO TWO GROUPS AND MEET IN THE CENTER!
GROUP A, TAKE THE LEFT WING! GROUP B, TAKE THE RIGHT WING!
GOGOGOGO
DOKOM!
HAYATO! ENEMY UNITS TO YOUR RIGHT! LOOK OUT - THERE'S SOME TO YOUR LEFT, TOO!
WE'RE SURROUNDED!
SUOOW
SUOOW
SUOOOW
DOW
DOW
DOW
DOW
DOW
DOW

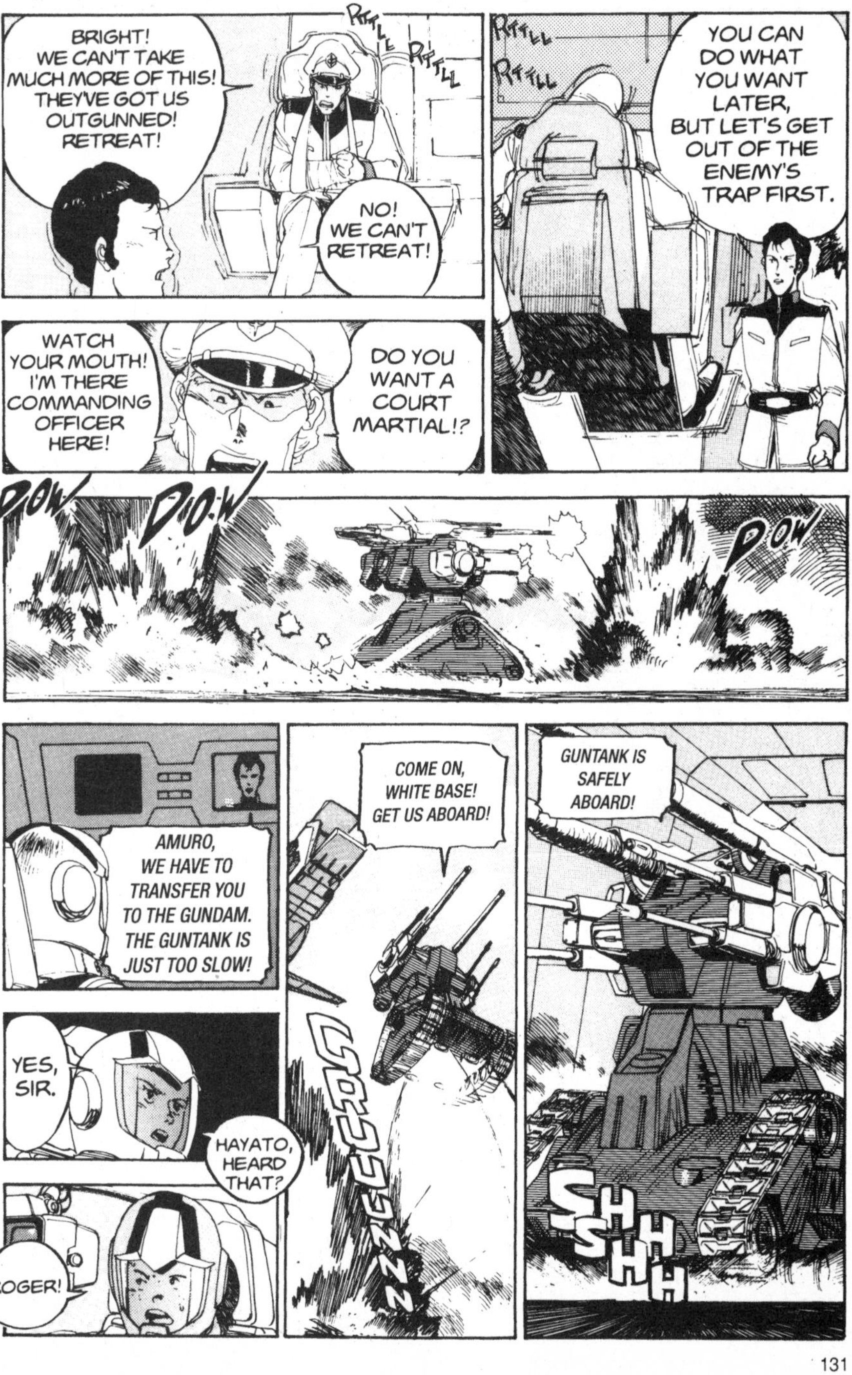
RTTLL RTTLL
BRIGHT! WE CAN'T TAKE MUCH MORE OF THIS! THEY'VE GOT US OUTGUNNED! RETREAT!
NO! WE CAN'T RETREAT!
WATCH YOUR MOUTH! I'M THERE COMMANDING OFFICER HERE!
DO YOU WANT A COURT MARTIAL!?
RTTLL RTTLL
YOU CAN DO WHAT YOU WANT LATER, BUT LET'S GET OUT OF THE ENEMY'S TRAP FIRST.
DOW DOW DOW
AMURO, WE HAVE TO TRANSFER YOU TO THE GUNDAM. THE GUNTANK IS JUST TOO SLOW!
YES, SIR.
HAYATO, HEARD THAT?
ROGER!
COME ON, WHITE BASE! GET US ABOARD!
GRUUUNNN
GUNTANK IS SAFELY ABOARD!
SHHH SHHH

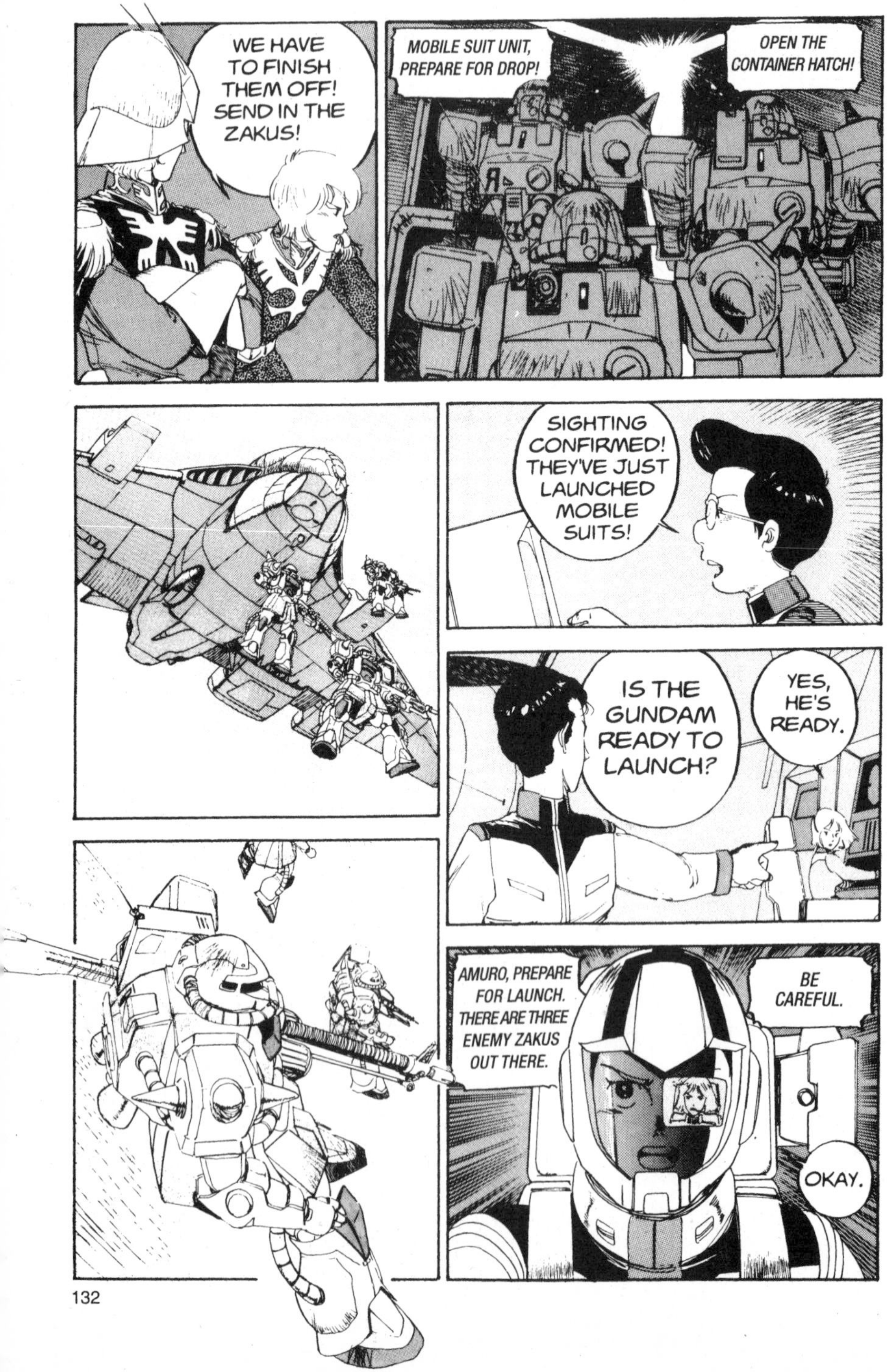
WE HAVE TO FINISH THEM OFF! SEND IN THE ZAKUS!
MOBILE SUIT UNIT, PREPARE FOR DROP!
OPEN THE CONTAINER HATCH!
SIGHTING CONFIRMED! THEY'VE JUST LAUNCHED MOBILE SUITS!
IS THE GUNDAM READY TO LAUNCH?
YES, HE'S READY.
AMURO, PREPARE FOR LAUNCH. THERE ARE THREE ENEMY ZAKUS OUT THERE.
BE CAREFUL.
OKAY.

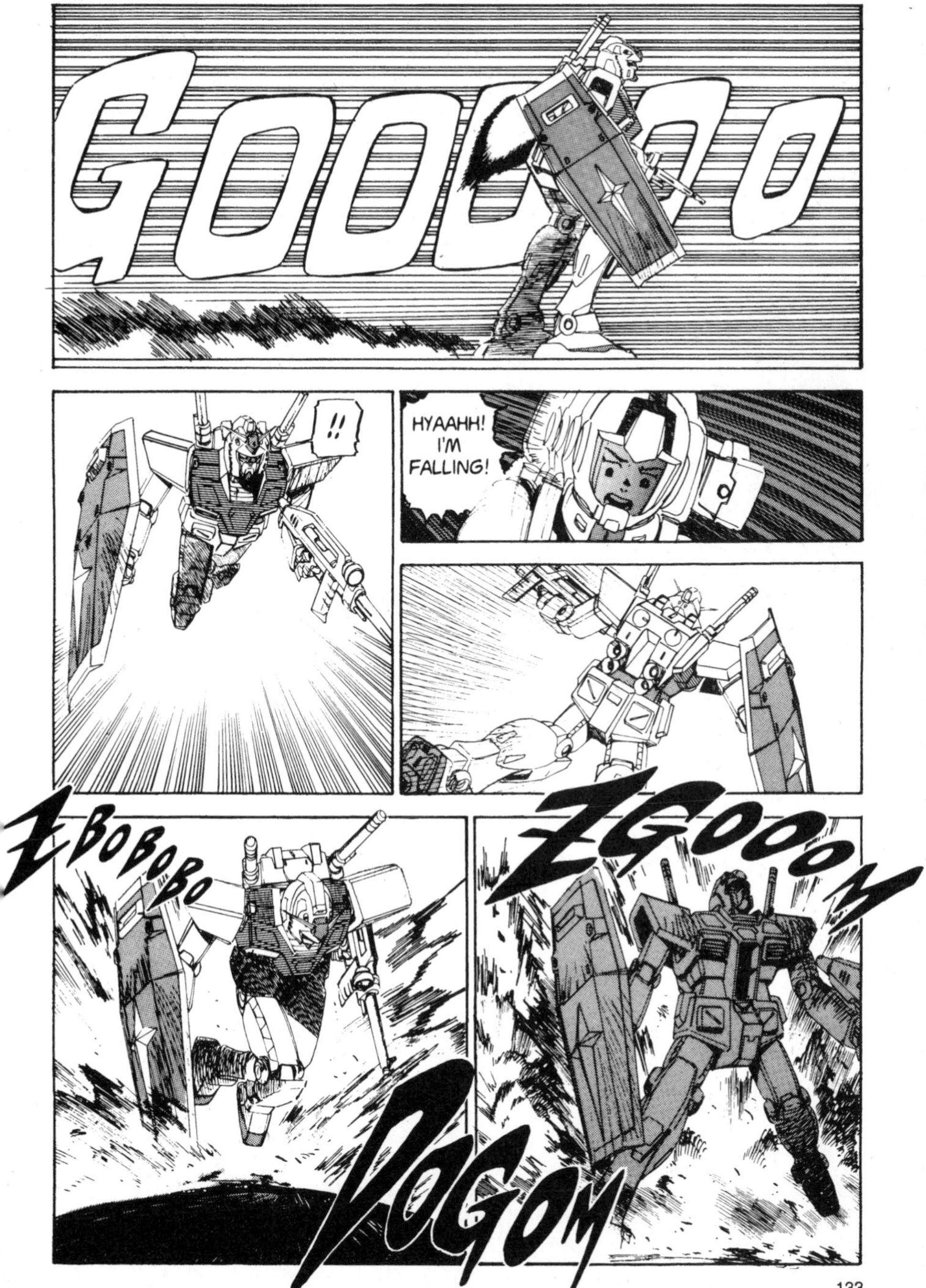
GOOOOO
!!
HYAAHH! I'M FALLING!
ZBOBOBO
DOGOM
ZGOOOOM

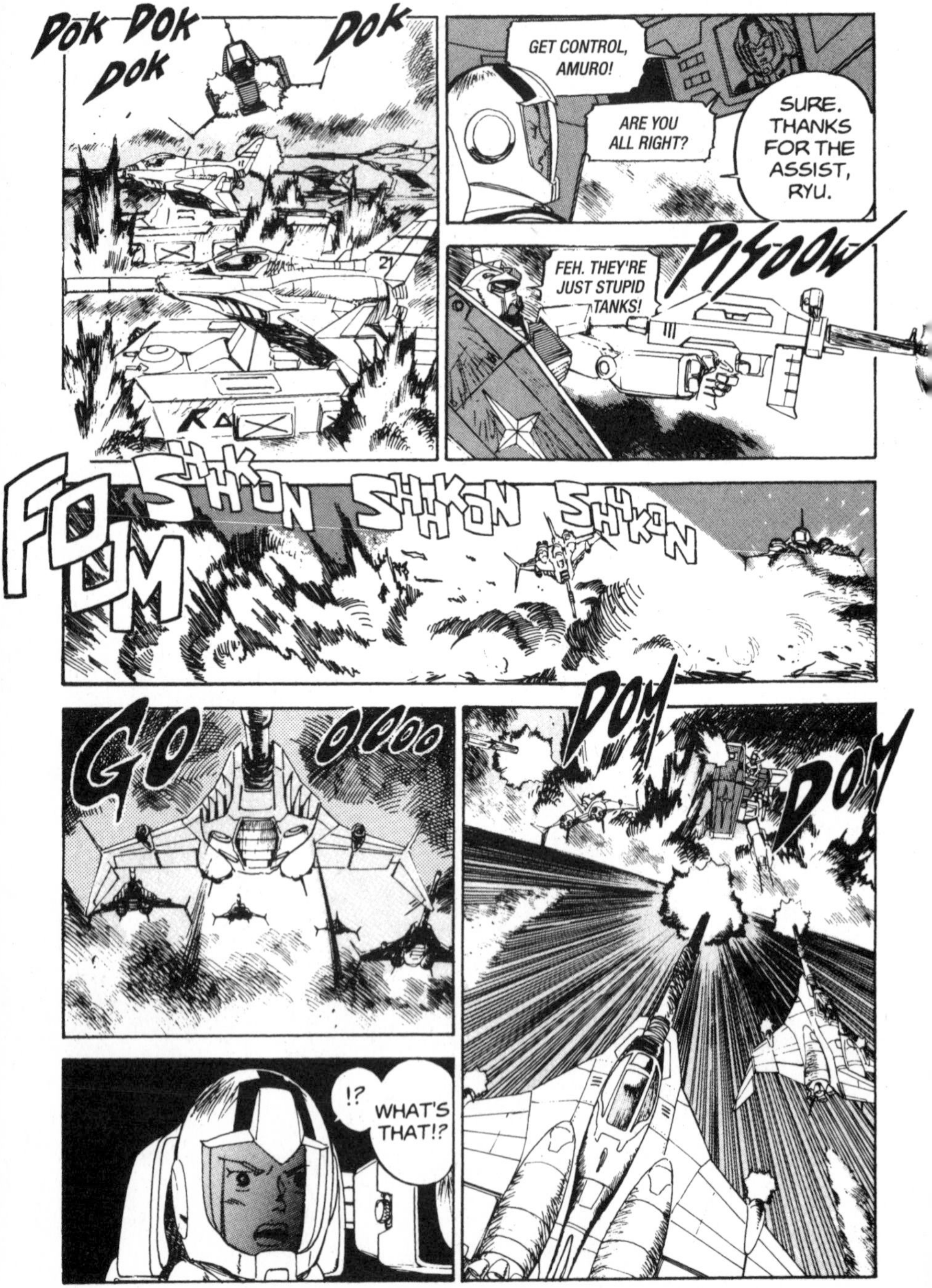
DOK DOK DOK DOK
GET CONTROL, AMURO!
ARE YOU ALL RIGHT?
SURE. THANKS FOR THE ASSIST, RYU.
FEH. THEY'RE JUST STUPID TANKS!
PISOOW
FOOM
SHKON SHKON SHKON
GOOOOO
DOM DOM
!?
WHAT'S THAT!?

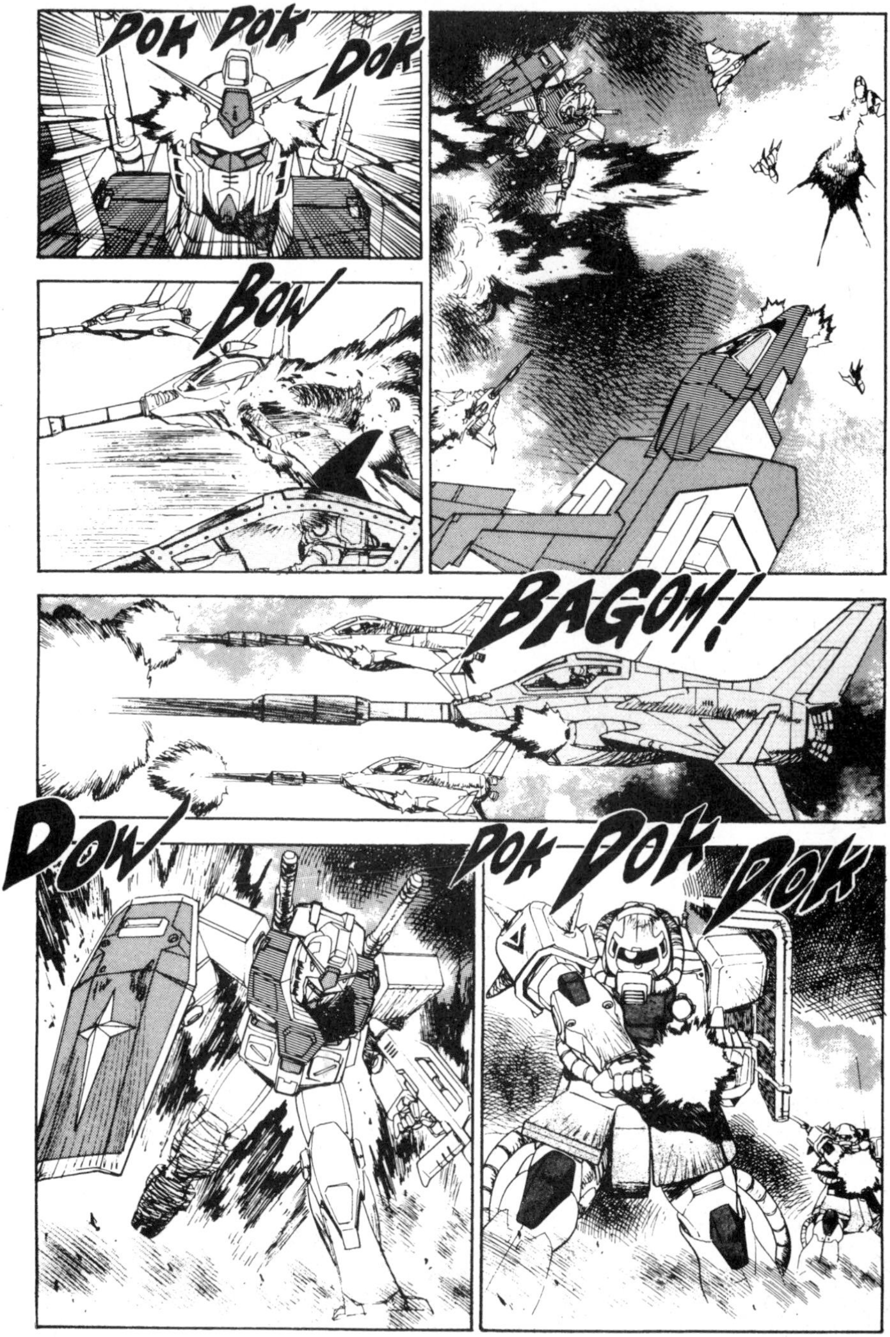
DOK DOK DOK
BOW
BAGOM!
DOW
DOK DOK DOK

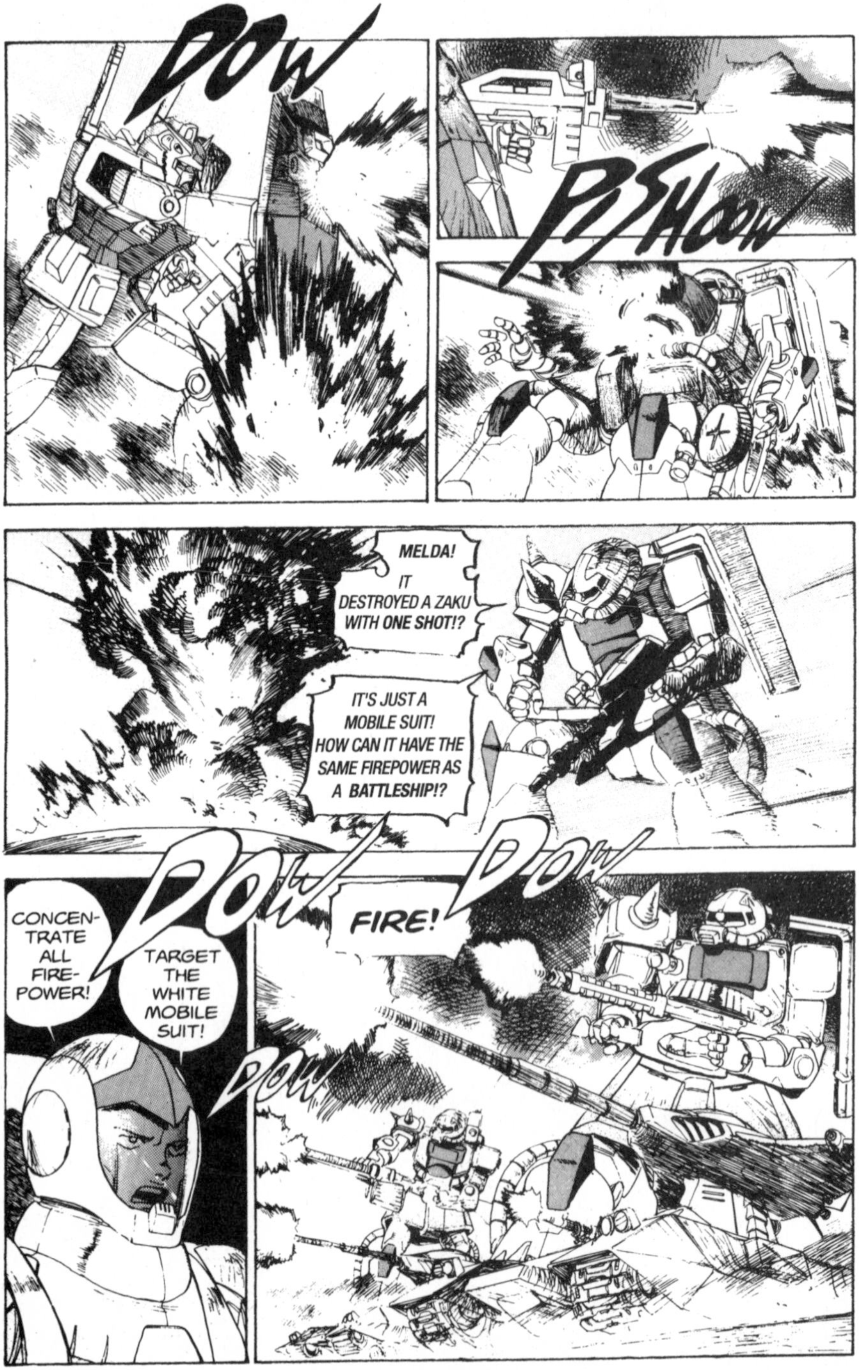
DOW
PISHOOW
MELDA!
IT DESTROYED A ZAKU WITH ONE SHOT!?
IT'S JUST A MOBILE SUIT! HOW CAN IT HAVE THE SAME FIREPOWER AS A BATTLESHIP!?
DOW DOW
CONCEN-TRATE ALL FIRE-POWER!
TARGET THE WHITE MOBILE SUIT!
FIRE!
DOW

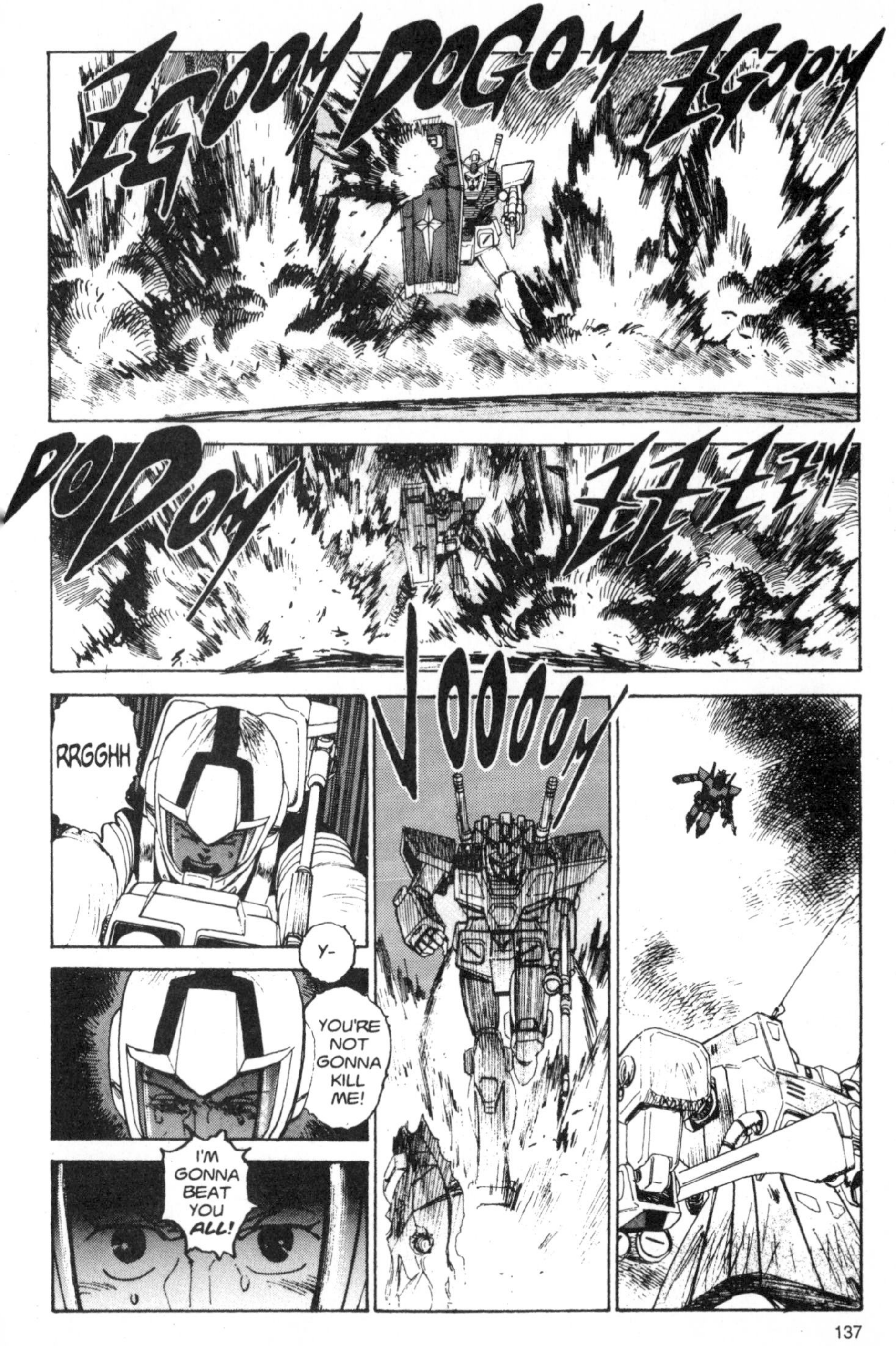
ZGOOM DOGOM ZGOOM
DODOM
RRGGHH
Y-
YOU'RE NOT GONNA KILL ME!
I'M GONNA BEAT YOU ALL!
JOOOOM

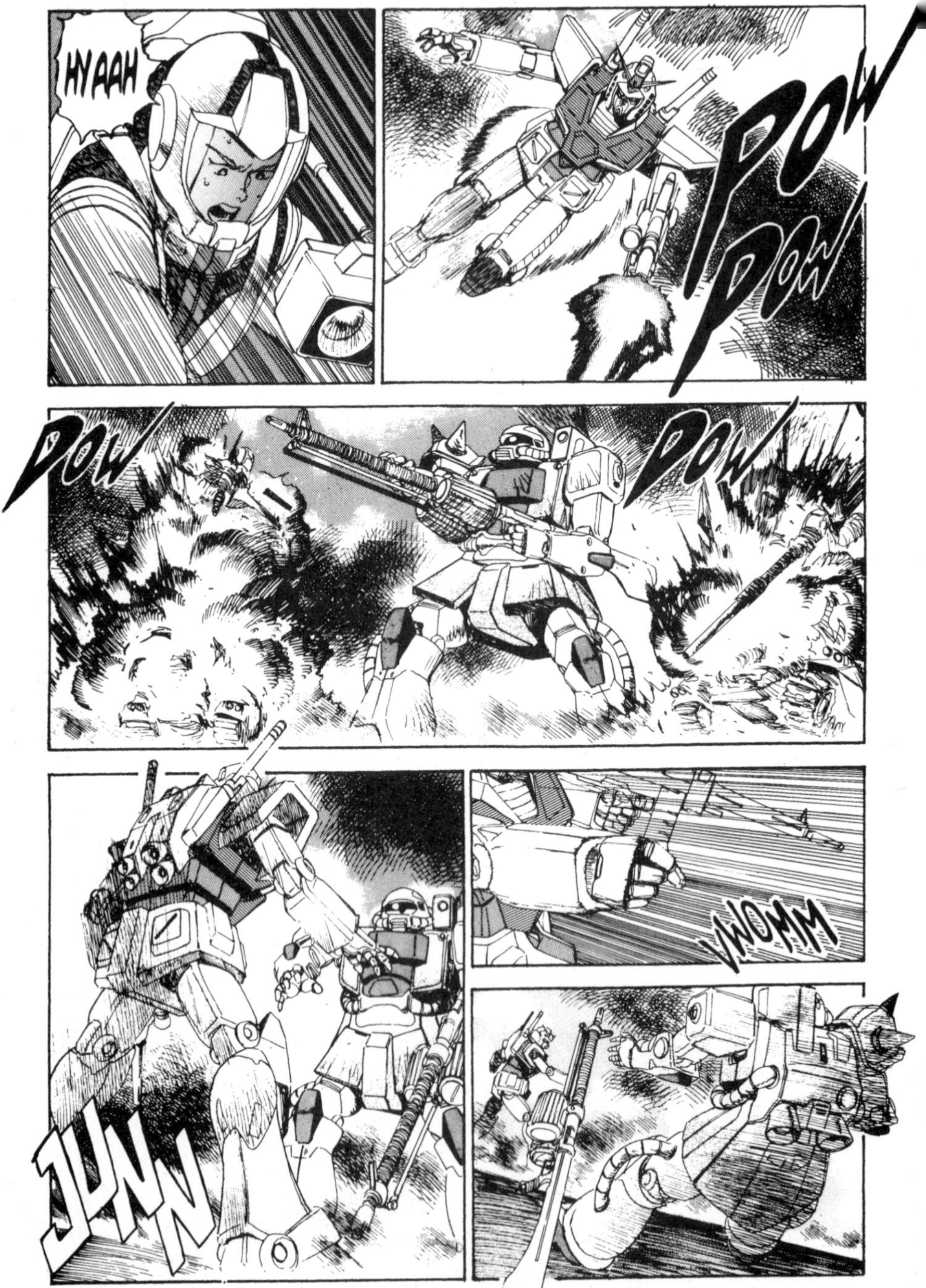
HYAAH
POW
DOW
DOW
DOW
JUNN
VWOMM

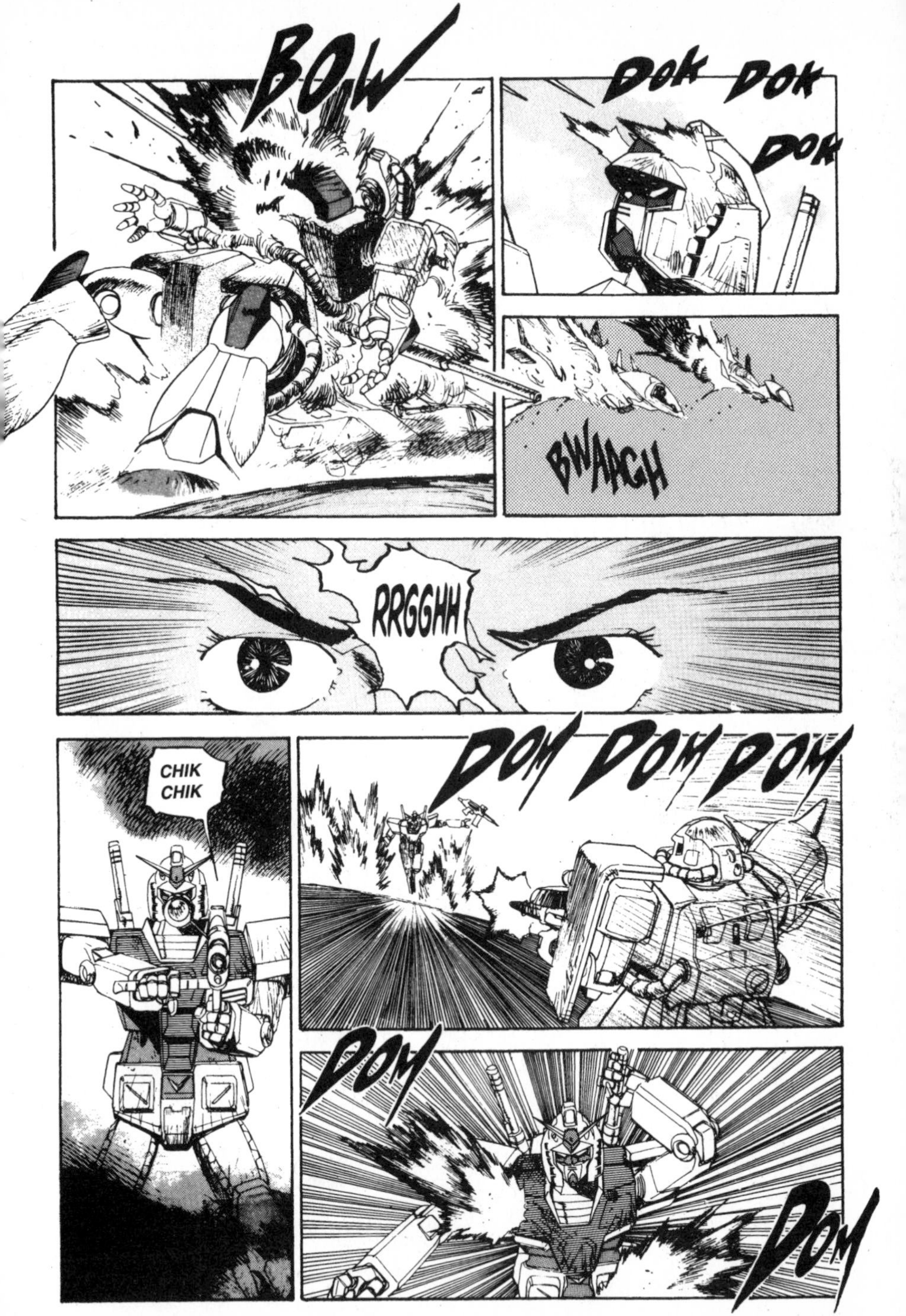
BOW
DOK DOK
DOK
BWARGH
RRGGHH
CHIK CHIK
DOM DOM DOM
DOM
DOM

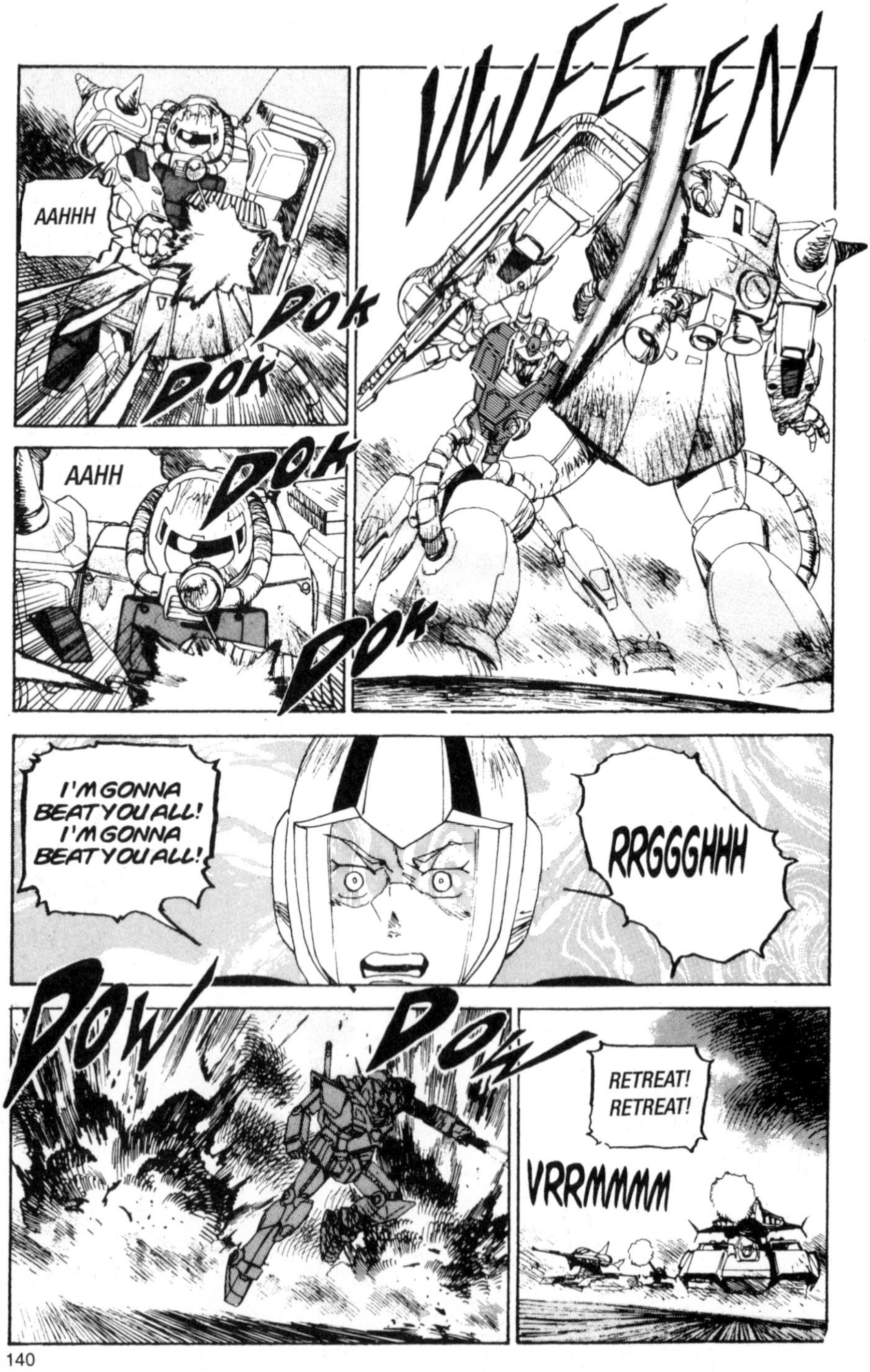
AAHHH
DOK
DOK
AAHH
DOK
DOK
VWEEEN
I'M GONNA BEAT YOU ALL! I'M GONNA BEAT YOU ALL!
RRGGGHHH
DOW
DOW
RETREAT! RETREAT!
VRRMMMM

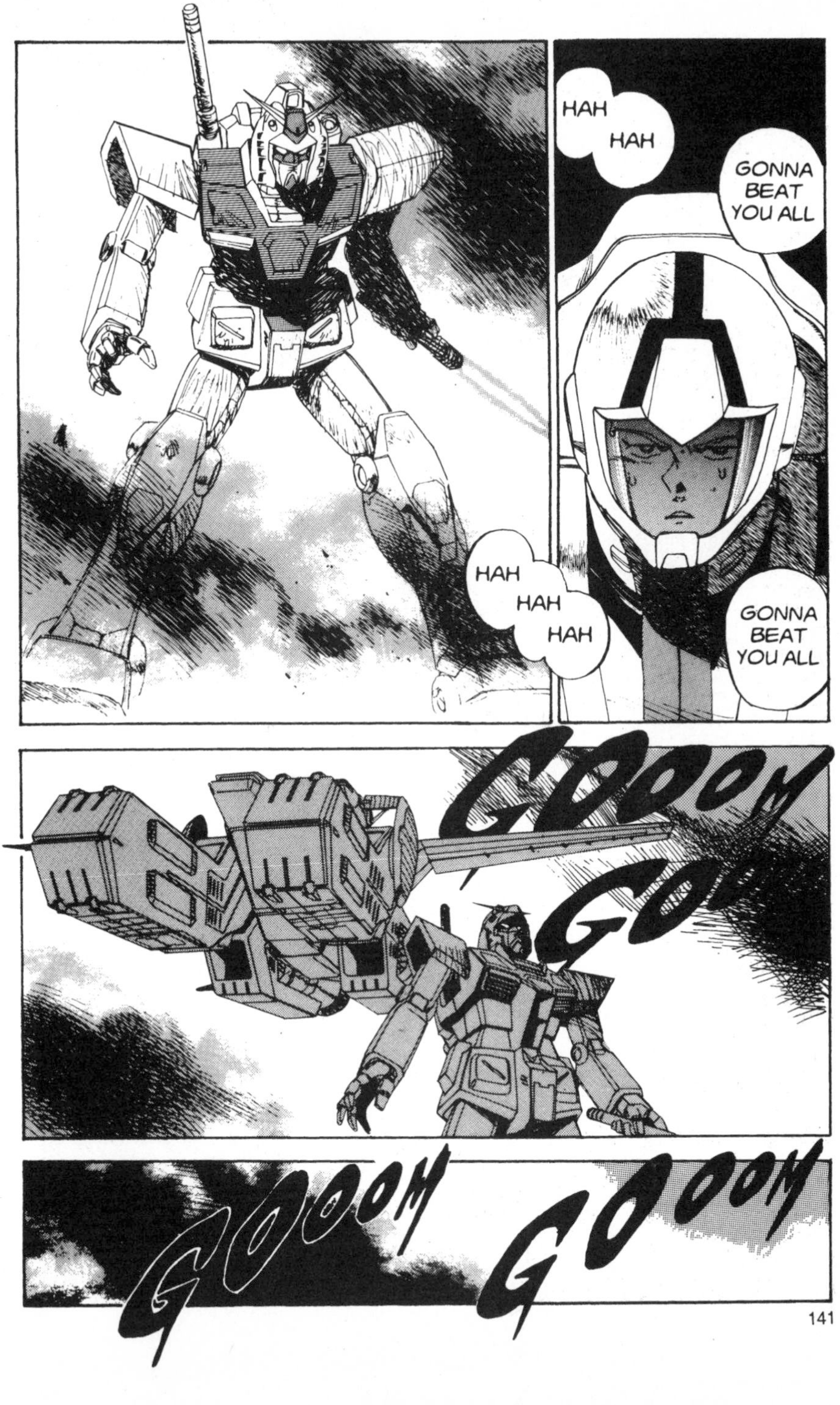
HAH
HAH
GONNA BEAT YOU ALL
HAH
HAH
HAH
GONNA BEAT YOU ALL
GOOOM
GOOOM
GOOOM

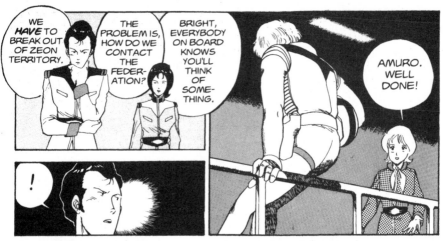

WE **HAVE** TO BREAK OUT OF ZEON TERRITORY.

THE PROBLEM IS, HOW DO WE CONTACT THE FEDER-ATION?

BRIGHT, EVERYBODY ON BOARD KNOWS YOU'LL THINK OF SOME-THING.

AMURO. WELL DONE!

!

SIGH

THANKS, FRAU.

A-AMURO!

GOOD WORK, AMURO.

MUST THINK HE'S SOMETHING **SPECIAL** NOW.

AMURO!! AMURO!!

YAY YAY

AMURO! WE BROUGHT YOU SOME PIE, 'CAUSE YOU WON!

YAY

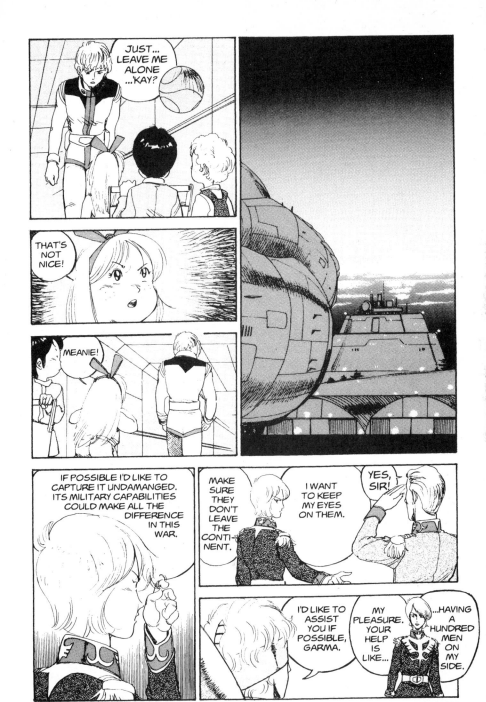

JUST... LEAVE ME ALONE ...'KAY?

THAT'S NOT NICE!

MEANIE!

IF POSSIBLE I'D LIKE TO CAPTURE IT UNDAMANGED. ITS MILITARY CAPABILITIES COULD MAKE ALL THE DIFFERENCE IN THIS WAR.

MAKE SURE THEY DON'T LEAVE THE CONTINENT.

I WANT TO KEEP MY EYES ON THEM.

YES, SIR!

I'D LIKE TO ASSIST YOU IF POSSIBLE, GARMA.

MY PLEASURE. YOUR HELP IS LIKE...

...HAVING A HUNDRED MEN ON MY SIDE.

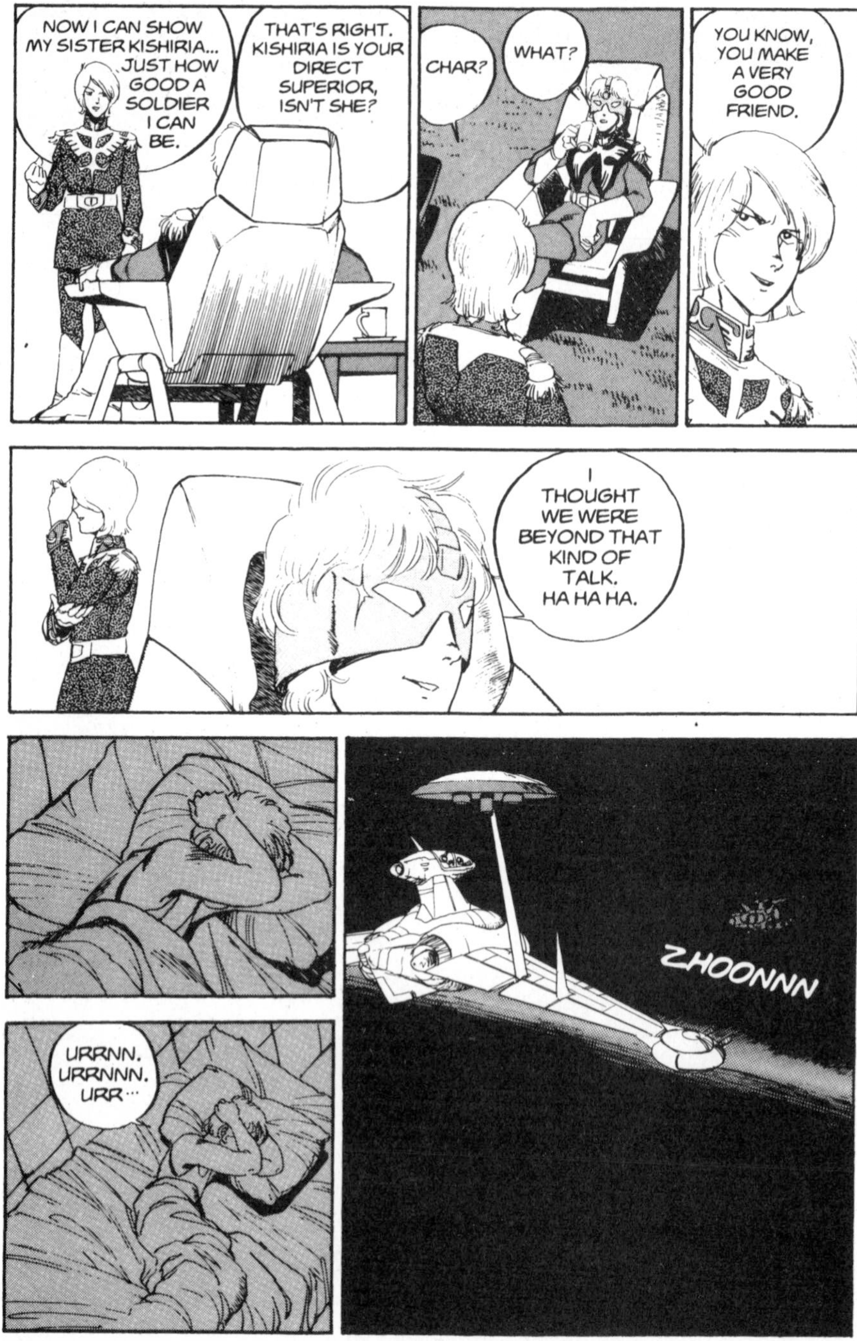
NOW I CAN SHOW MY SISTER KISHIRIA... JUST HOW GOOD A SOLDIER I CAN BE.
THAT'S RIGHT. KISHIRIA IS YOUR DIRECT SUPERIOR, ISN'T SHE?
CHAR?
WHAT?
YOU KNOW, YOU MAKE A VERY GOOD FRIEND.
I THOUGHT WE WERE BEYOND THAT KIND OF TALK. HA HA HA.
URRNN. URRNNN. URR...
ZHOONNN

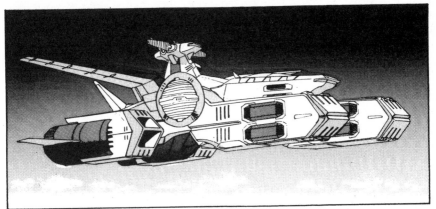

....

I HAVE A QUES- TION.

!!

YOU'RE BLOOD PRESSURE'S NORMAL. THERE REALLY ISN'T ANYTHING WRONG WITH YOU.

HOW FAR ARE YOU PLANNING TO *DRAG* US?

EVER SINCE WE LEFT SIDE 7...

...WITH ALL THE BATTLES, I HAVEN'T HAD A **WINK** OF SLEEP.

JUST HOW LONG ARE YOU PLANNING TO KEEP THIS UP?

WE'RE TRYING TO LAND SOME- PLACE SAFE.

BUT UNTIL THEN, YOU *MUST* BE PATIENT.

145

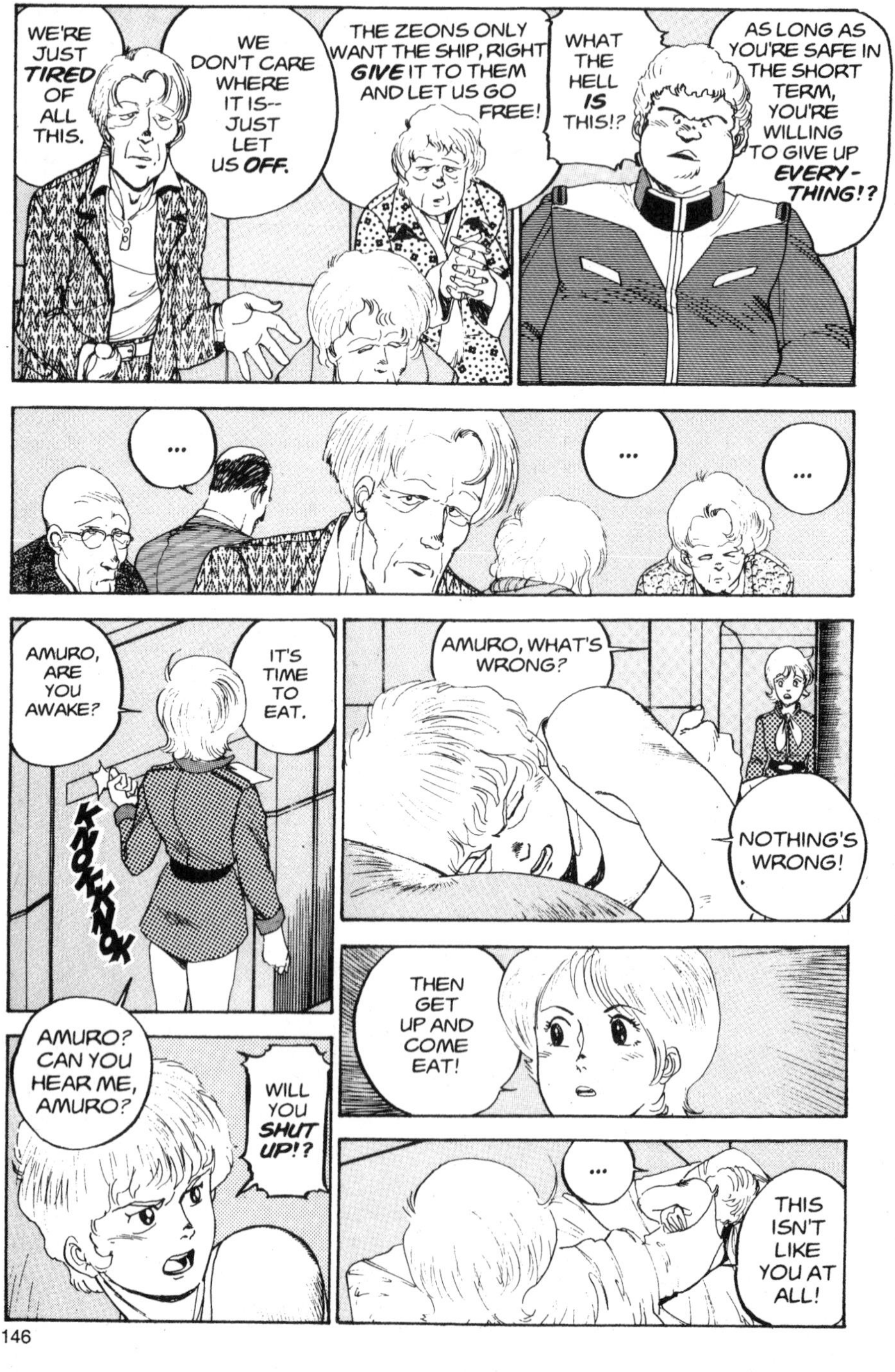
WE'RE JUST **TIRED** OF ALL THIS.
WE DON'T CARE WHERE IT IS-- JUST LET US **OFF**.
THE ZEONS ONLY WANT THE SHIP, RIGHT **GIVE** IT TO THEM AND LET US GO FREE!
WHAT THE HELL **IS** THIS!?
AS LONG AS YOU'RE SAFE IN THE SHORT TERM, YOU'RE WILLING TO GIVE UP **EVERY-THING**!?
...
...
...
AMURO, ARE YOU AWAKE?
IT'S TIME TO EAT.
KNOCK KNOCK
AMURO, WHAT'S WRONG?
NOTHING'S WRONG!
THEN GET UP AND COME EAT!
AMURO? CAN YOU HEAR ME, AMURO?
WILL YOU **SHUT UP**!?
...
THIS ISN'T LIKE YOU AT ALL!

AND GETTING IN A MOBILE SUIT TO KILL PEOPLE *IS* LIKE ME!?

WHAT ARE YOU *TALKING* ABOUT?

OH, STOP WHINING! BOTH THE FEDERATION AND THE ZEON ARE PUTTING OLD FOLKS AND CHILDREN INTO BATTLE.

THE FEDER-ATION IS JUST USING US AS BAIT.

STOP BITING YOUR NAILS!

THEY'RE THROWING US OUT HERE HOPING WE'LL JUST *DIE.*

YOU 'RE READING TOO MUCH INTO THIS.

LOOK, I'LL GET YOUR FOOD FOR YOU AND BRING IT HERE YOU NEED SOME *SLEEP.*

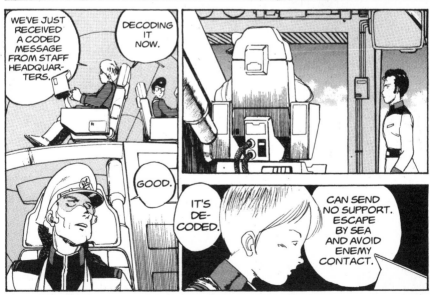

WE'VE JUST RECEIVED A CODED MESSAGE FROM STAFF HEADQUAR-TERS.

DECODING IT NOW.

GOOD.

IT'S DE-CODED.

CAN SEND NO SUPPORT. ESCAPE BY SEA AND AVOID ENEMY CONTACT.

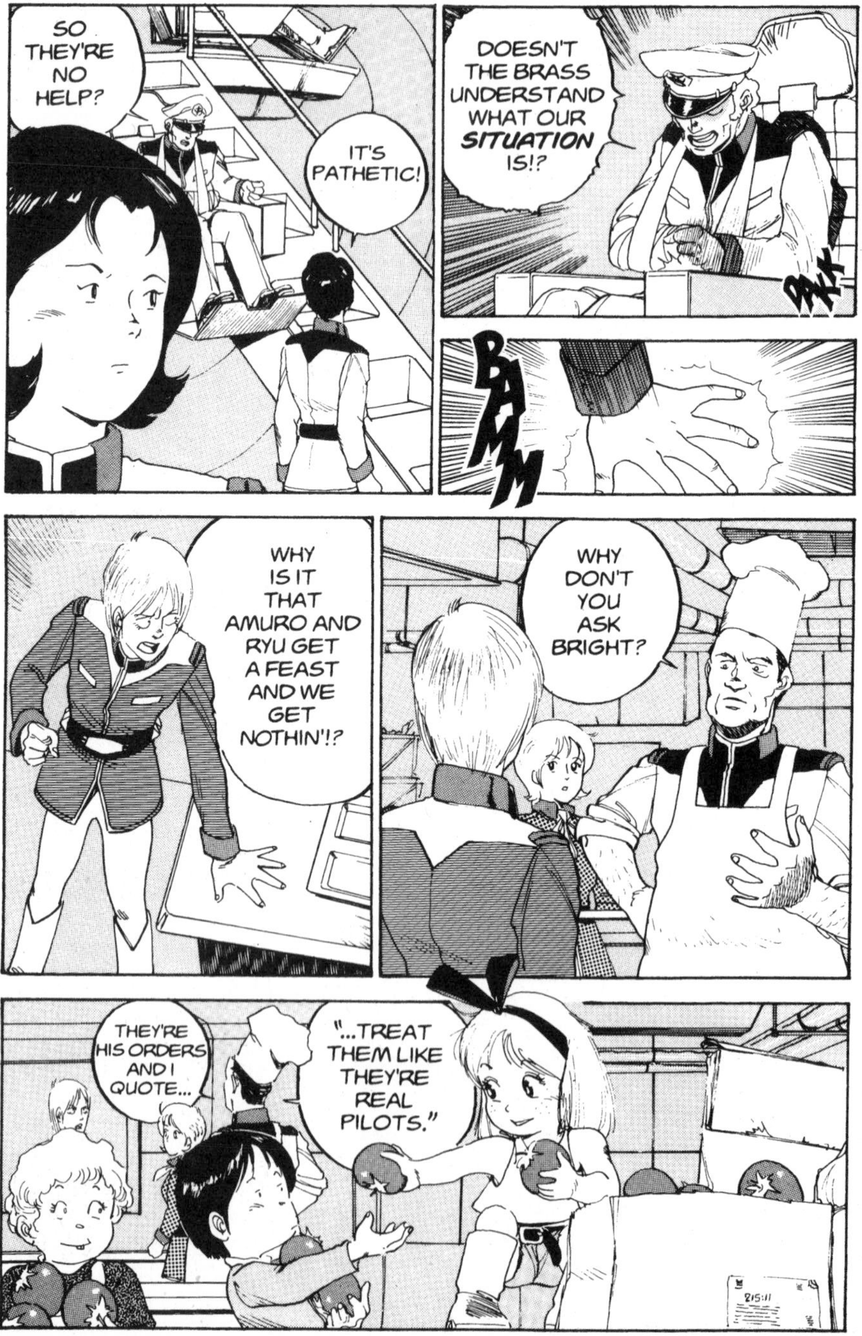
SO THEY'RE NO HELP?
IT'S PATHETIC!
DOESN'T THE BRASS UNDERSTAND WHAT OUR *SITUATION* IS!?
DAKK
BAMM
WHY IS IT THAT AMURO AND RYU GET A FEAST AND WE GET NOTHIN'!?
WHY DON'T YOU ASK BRIGHT?
THEY'RE HIS ORDERS AND I QUOTE...
"...TREAT THEM LIKE THEY'RE REAL PILOTS."

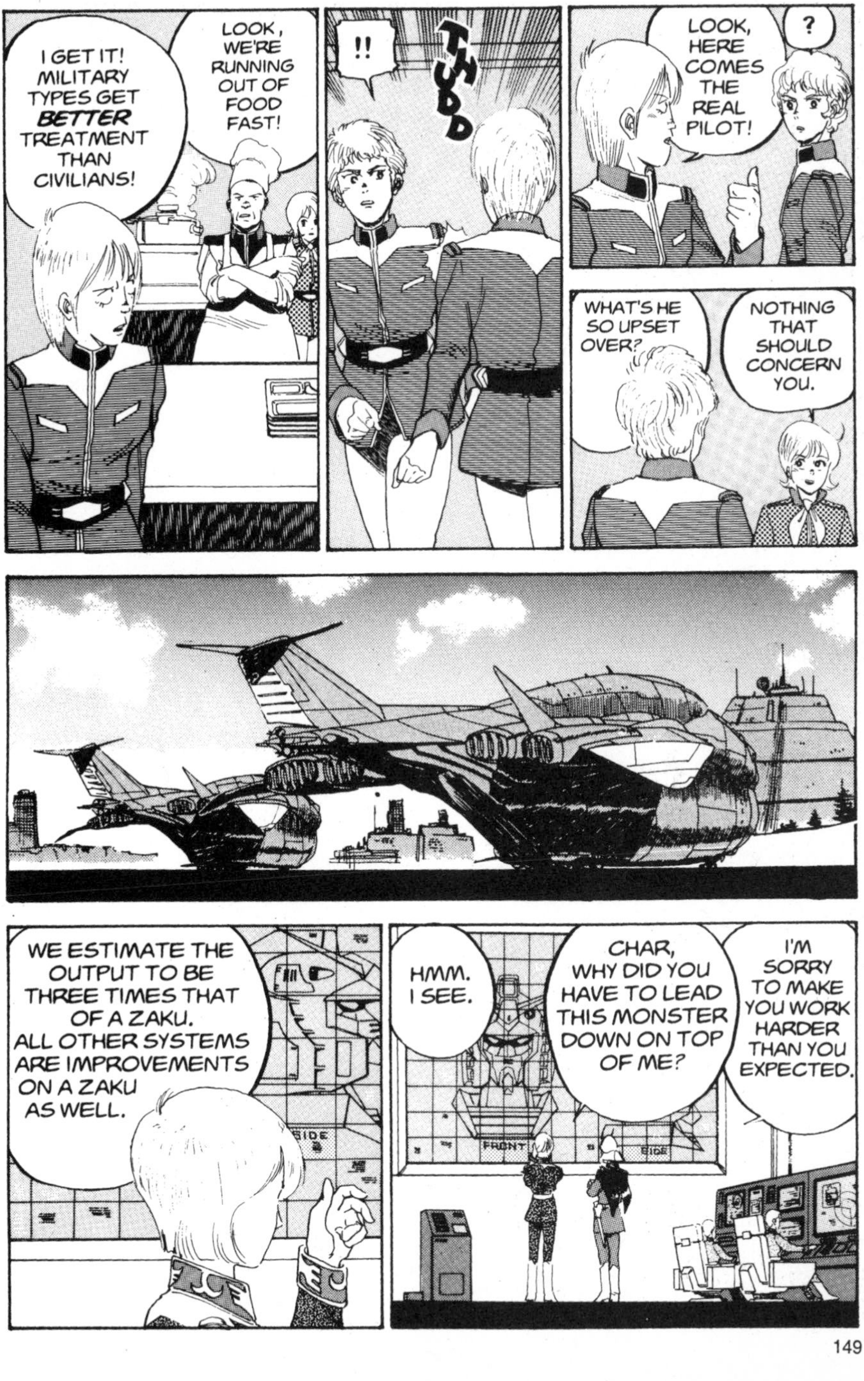
I GET IT! MILITARY TYPES GET **BETTER** TREATMENT THAN CIVILIANS!
LOOK, WE'RE RUNNING OUT OF FOOD FAST!
!!
THUDD
LOOK, HERE COMES THE REAL PILOT!
?
WHAT'S HE SO UPSET OVER?
NOTHING THAT SHOULD CONCERN YOU.
WE ESTIMATE THE OUTPUT TO BE THREE TIMES THAT OF A ZAKU. ALL OTHER SYSTEMS ARE IMPROVEMENTS ON A ZAKU AS WELL.
HMM. I SEE.
CHAR, WHY DID YOU HAVE TO LEAD THIS MONSTER DOWN ON TOP OF ME?
I'M SORRY TO MAKE YOU WORK HARDER THAN YOU EXPECTED.

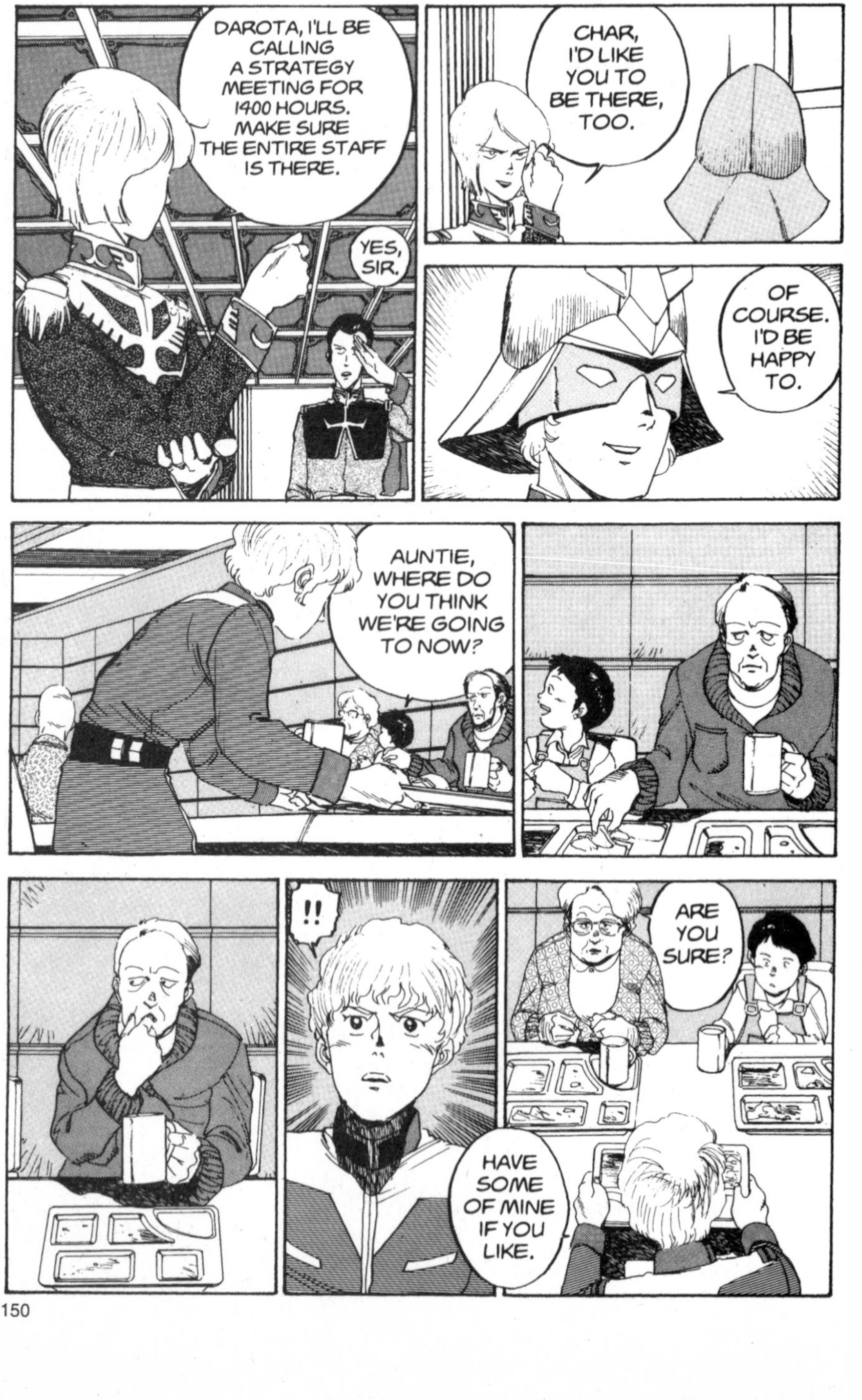
DAROTA, I'LL BE CALLING A STRATEGY MEETING FOR 1400 HOURS. MAKE SURE THE ENTIRE STAFF IS THERE.
YES, SIR.
CHAR, I'D LIKE YOU TO BE THERE, TOO.
OF COURSE. I'D BE HAPPY TO.
AUNTIE, WHERE DO YOU THINK WE'RE GOING TO NOW?
!!
ARE YOU SURE?
HAVE SOME OF MINE IF YOU LIKE.

GO AHEAD.

THANK YOU SO MUCH.

AMURO!

YOU'RE UNDER ORDERS TO EAT!

THEN DON'T MAKE ME EAT *HERE*!

VOOOM

GRRM

ALL RIGHT. SLOWLY. SLOWLY.

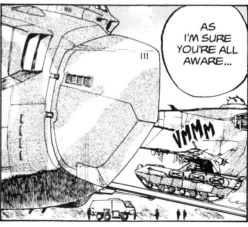

AS I'M SURE YOU'RE ALL AWARE...

VMMM

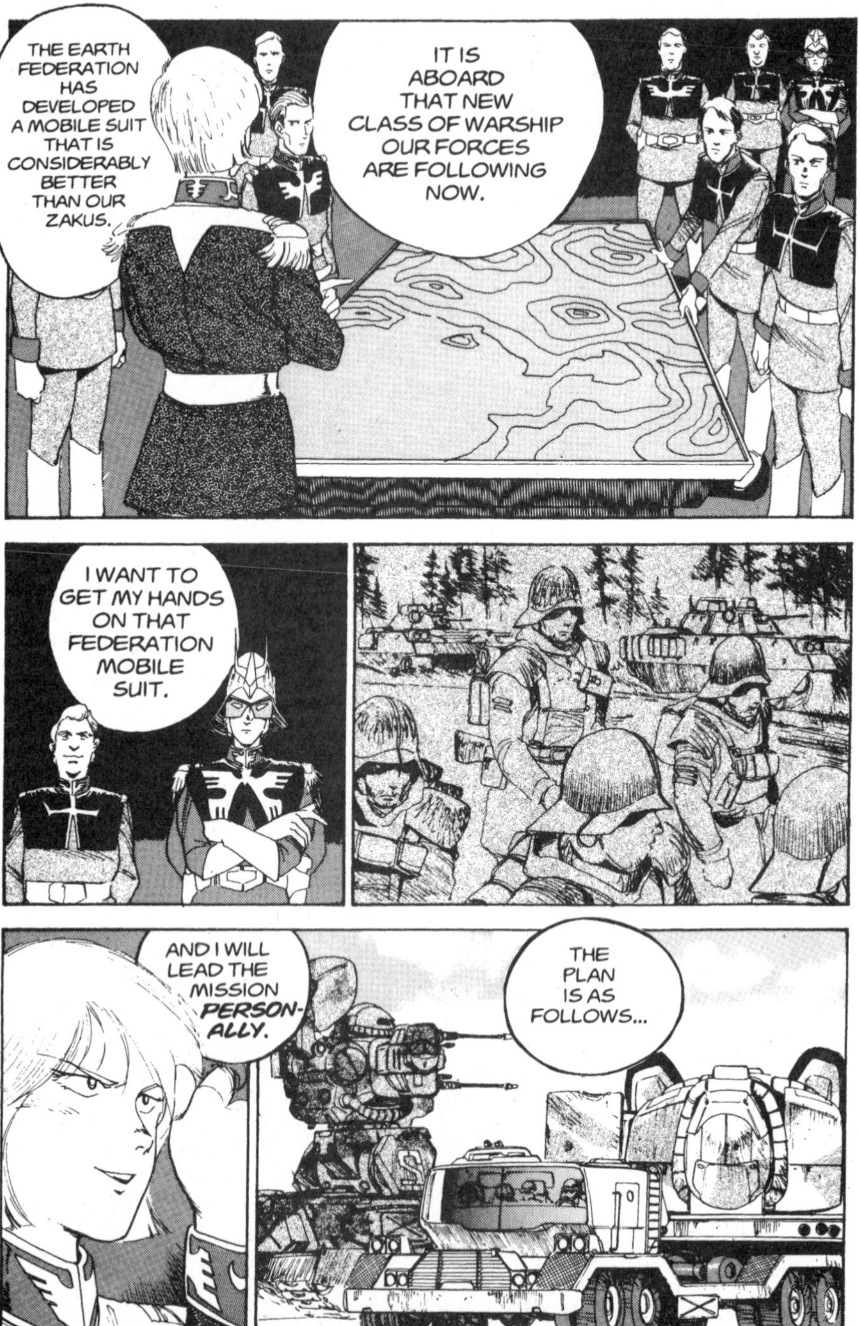
THE EARTH FEDERATION HAS DEVELOPED A MOBILE SUIT THAT IS CONSIDERABLY BETTER THAN OUR ZAKUS.
IT IS ABOARD THAT NEW CLASS OF WARSHIP OUR FORCES ARE FOLLOWING NOW.
I WANT TO GET MY HANDS ON THAT FEDERATION MOBILE SUIT.
AND I WILL LEAD THE MISSION ***PERSON-ALLY***.
THE PLAN IS AS FOLLOWS...

THE TROJAN HORSE IS TRYING TO ESCAPE INTO FEDERATION AIRSPACE.

WE'LL LEAD THE ENEMY TOWARD THEM.

WE'LL SEND TWO MOBILE DIVISIONS TO POINT S-4, SUPPORTED BY A THOUSAND UNITS OF CANNON AND ANTI-AIRCRAFT MISSILES.

AND IN ONE SHOT *CRUSH* THEM!

BAM

BUT CAPTAIN GARMA, IF YOU'LL ALLOW ME A WORD...

...WE HAVE BARELY THE MILITARY STRENGTH TO MAINTAIN THE BATTLE LINES AS IS!

OUR TROOPS ARE EXHAUSTED.

I CAN'T SEE ANY POSSIBLE WAY TO PRODUCE A FULL TWO DIVISIONS FROM THEM!

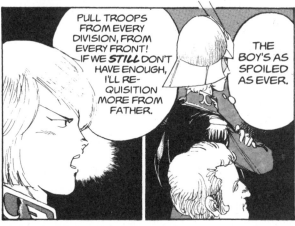

PULL TROOPS FROM EVERY DIVISION, FROM EVERY FRONT! IF WE *STILL* DON'T HAVE ENOUGH, I'LL REQUISITION MORE FROM FATHER.

THE BOY'S AS SPOILED AS EVER.

KATCH

ASSEMBLE OUR FORCES AT POINT S-4!

UNDERSTAND!?

153

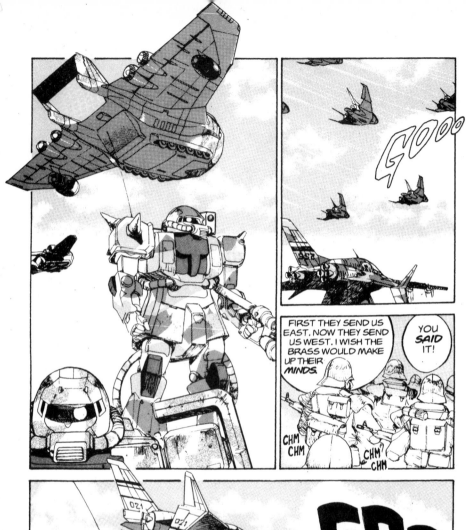

GOoo

FIRST THEY SEND US EAST. NOW THEY SEND US WEST. I WISH THE BRASS WOULD MAKE UP THEIR *MINDS.*

YOU *SAID* IT!

CHM CHM

CHM CHM

GRRR

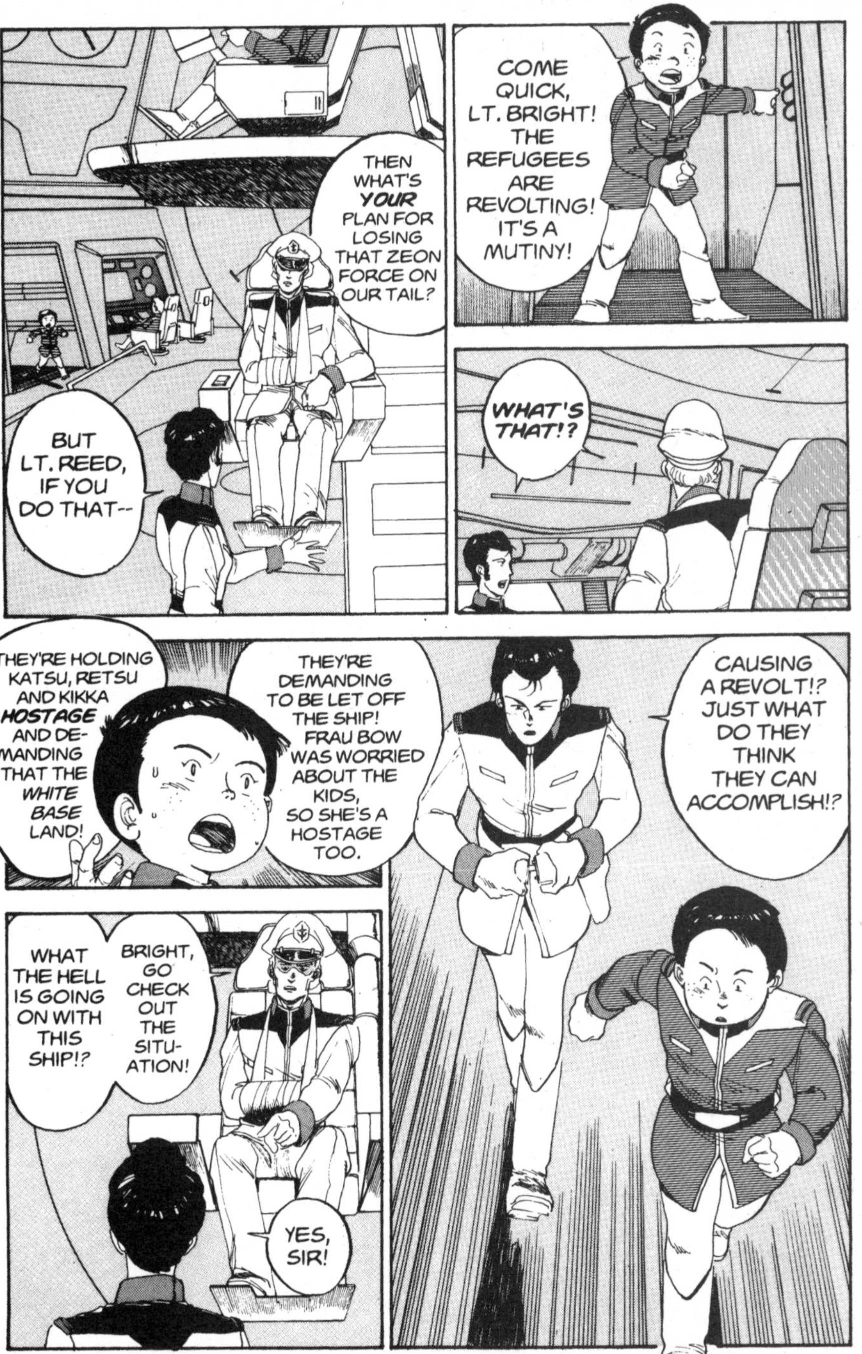
THEN WHAT'S **YOUR** PLAN FOR LOSING THAT ZEON FORCE ON OUR TAIL?
BUT LT. REED, IF YOU DO THAT--
COME QUICK, LT. BRIGHT! THE REFUGEES ARE REVOLTING! IT'S A MUTINY!
WHAT'S THAT!?
THEY'RE HOLDING KATSU, RETSU AND KIKKA **HOSTAGE** AND DE-MANDING THAT THE *WHITE BASE* LAND!
THEY'RE DEMANDING TO BE LET OFF THE SHIP! FRAU BOW WAS WORRIED ABOUT THE KIDS, SO SHE'S A HOSTAGE TOO.
WHAT THE HELL IS GOING ON WITH THIS SHIP!?
BRIGHT, GO CHECK OUT THE SITU-ATION!
YES, SIR!
CAUSING A REVOLT!? JUST WHAT DO THEY THINK THEY CAN ACCOMPLISH!?

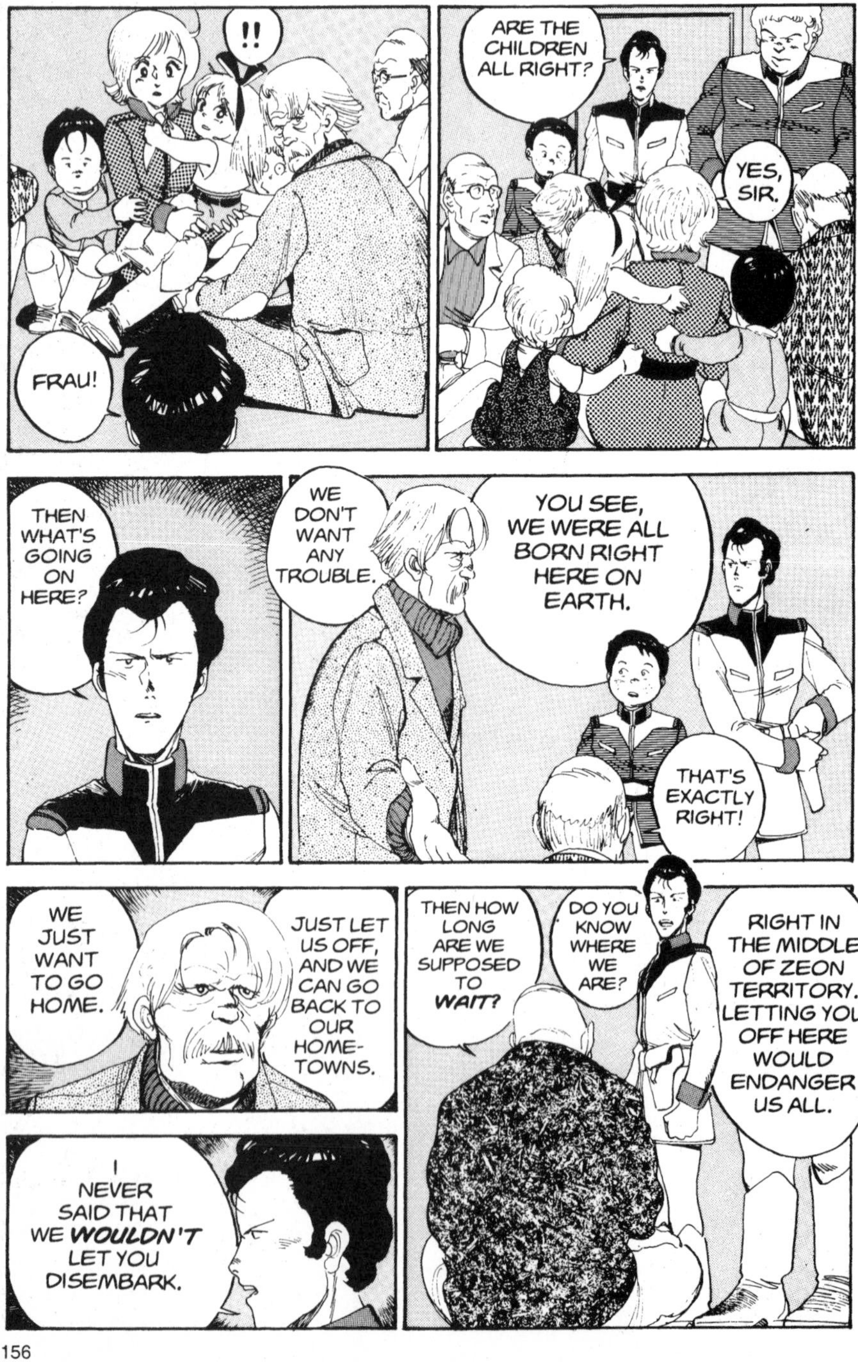
!!
FRAU!
ARE THE CHILDREN ALL RIGHT?
YES, SIR.
THEN WHAT'S GOING ON HERE?
WE DON'T WANT ANY TROUBLE.
YOU SEE, WE WERE ALL BORN RIGHT HERE ON EARTH.
THAT'S EXACTLY RIGHT!
WE JUST WANT TO GO HOME.
JUST LET US OFF, AND WE CAN GO BACK TO OUR HOME-TOWNS.
I NEVER SAID THAT WE ***WOULDN'T*** LET YOU DISEMBARK.
THEN HOW LONG ARE WE SUPPOSED TO ***WAIT?***
DO YOU KNOW WHERE WE ARE?
RIGHT IN THE MIDDLE OF ZEON TERRITORY. LETTING YOU OFF HERE WOULD ENDANGER US ALL.

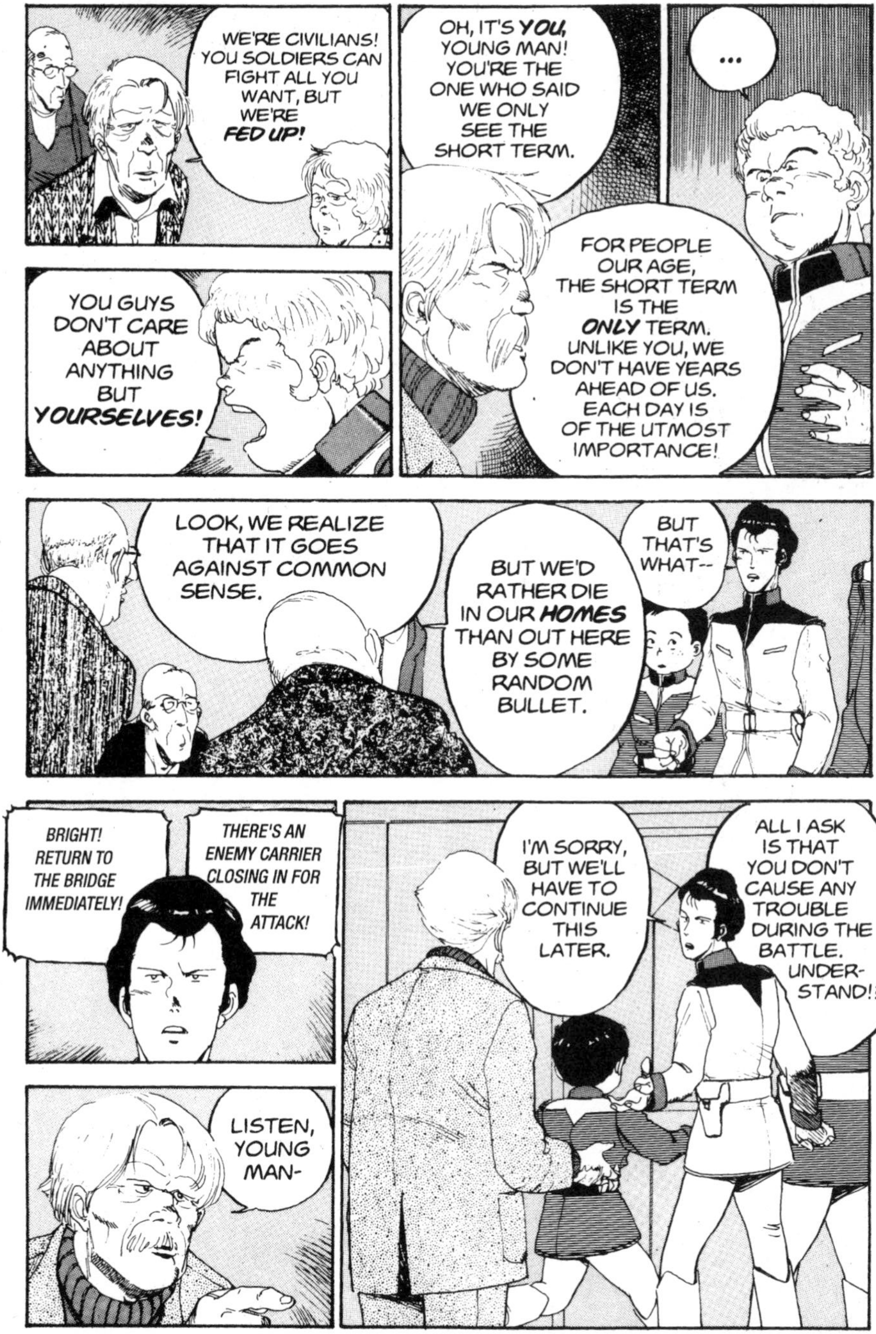
WE'RE CIVILIANS! YOU SOLDIERS CAN FIGHT ALL YOU WANT, BUT WE'RE FED UP!
OH, IT'S YOU, YOUNG MAN! YOU'RE THE ONE WHO SAID WE ONLY SEE THE SHORT TERM.
...
YOU GUYS DON'T CARE ABOUT ANYTHING BUT YOURSELVES!
FOR PEOPLE OUR AGE, THE SHORT TERM IS THE ONLY TERM. UNLIKE YOU, WE DON'T HAVE YEARS AHEAD OF US. EACH DAY IS OF THE UTMOST IMPORTANCE!
LOOK, WE REALIZE THAT IT GOES AGAINST COMMON SENSE.
BUT WE'D RATHER DIE IN OUR HOMES THAN OUT HERE BY SOME RANDOM BULLET.
BUT THAT'S WHAT--
BRIGHT! RETURN TO THE BRIDGE IMMEDIATELY!
THERE'S AN ENEMY CARRIER CLOSING IN FOR THE ATTACK!
LISTEN, YOUNG MAN-
I'M SORRY, BUT WE'LL HAVE TO CONTINUE THIS LATER.
ALL I ASK IS THAT YOU DON'T CAUSE ANY TROUBLE DURING THE BATTLE. UNDER-STAND!?

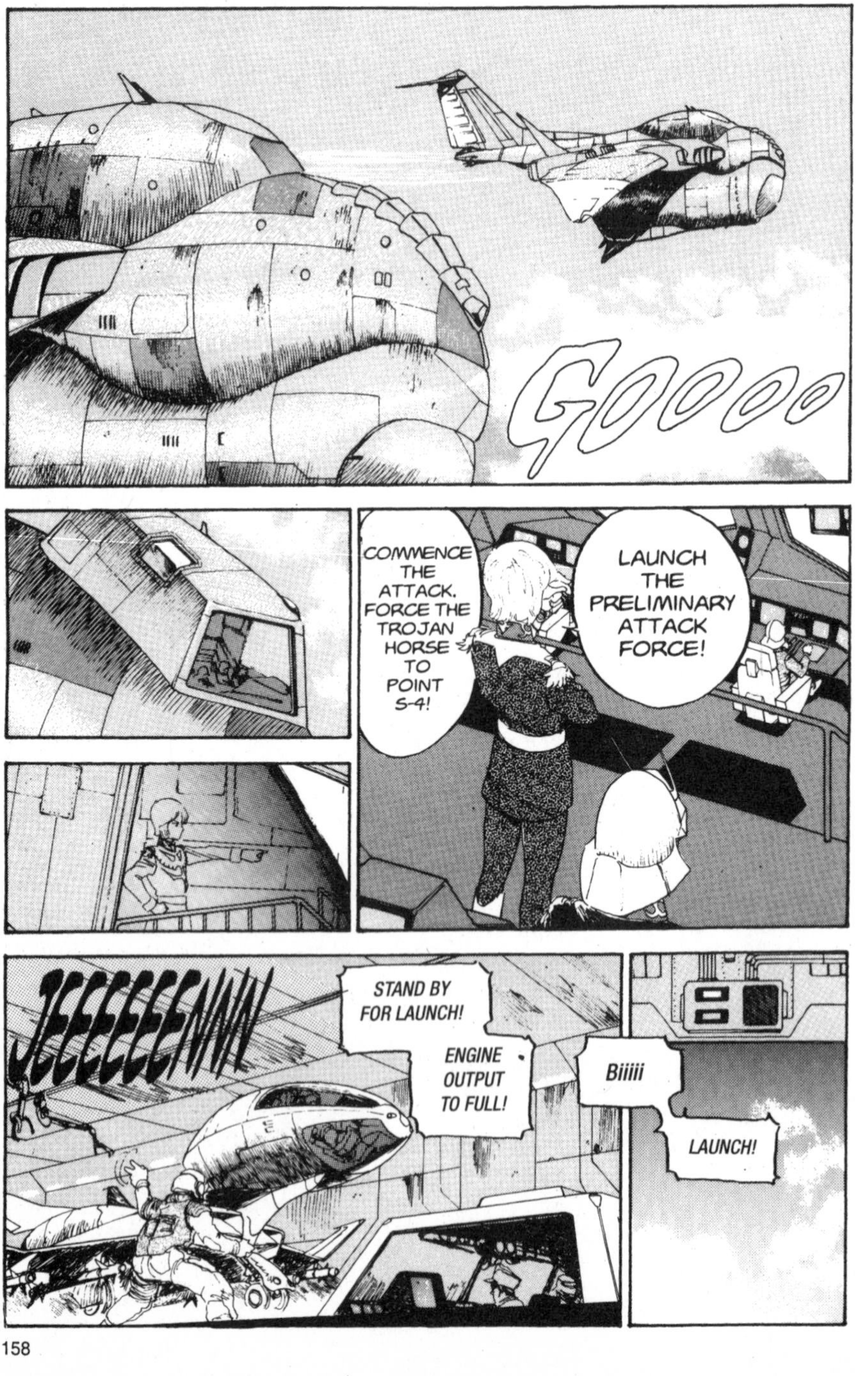
GOOOO
COMMENCE THE ATTACK. FORCE THE TROJAN HORSE TO POINT S-4!
LAUNCH THE PRELIMINARY ATTACK FORCE!
JEEEEENNN
STAND BY FOR LAUNCH!
ENGINE OUTPUT TO FULL!
Biiiii
LAUNCH!

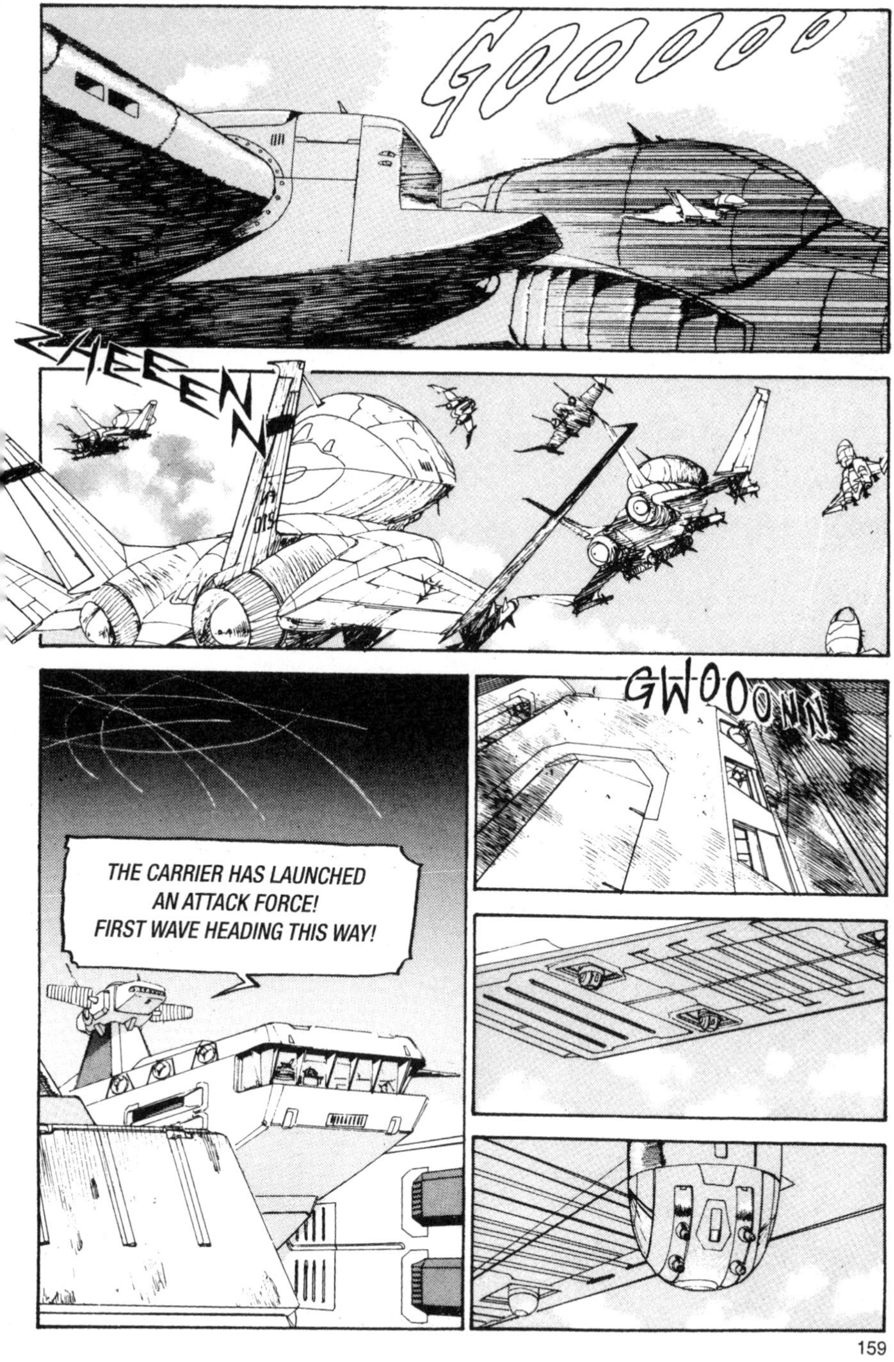
GOOOOOO
ZHEEENN
THE CARRIER HAS LAUNCHED AN ATTACK FORCE! FIRST WAVE HEADING THIS WAY!
GWOOOONN

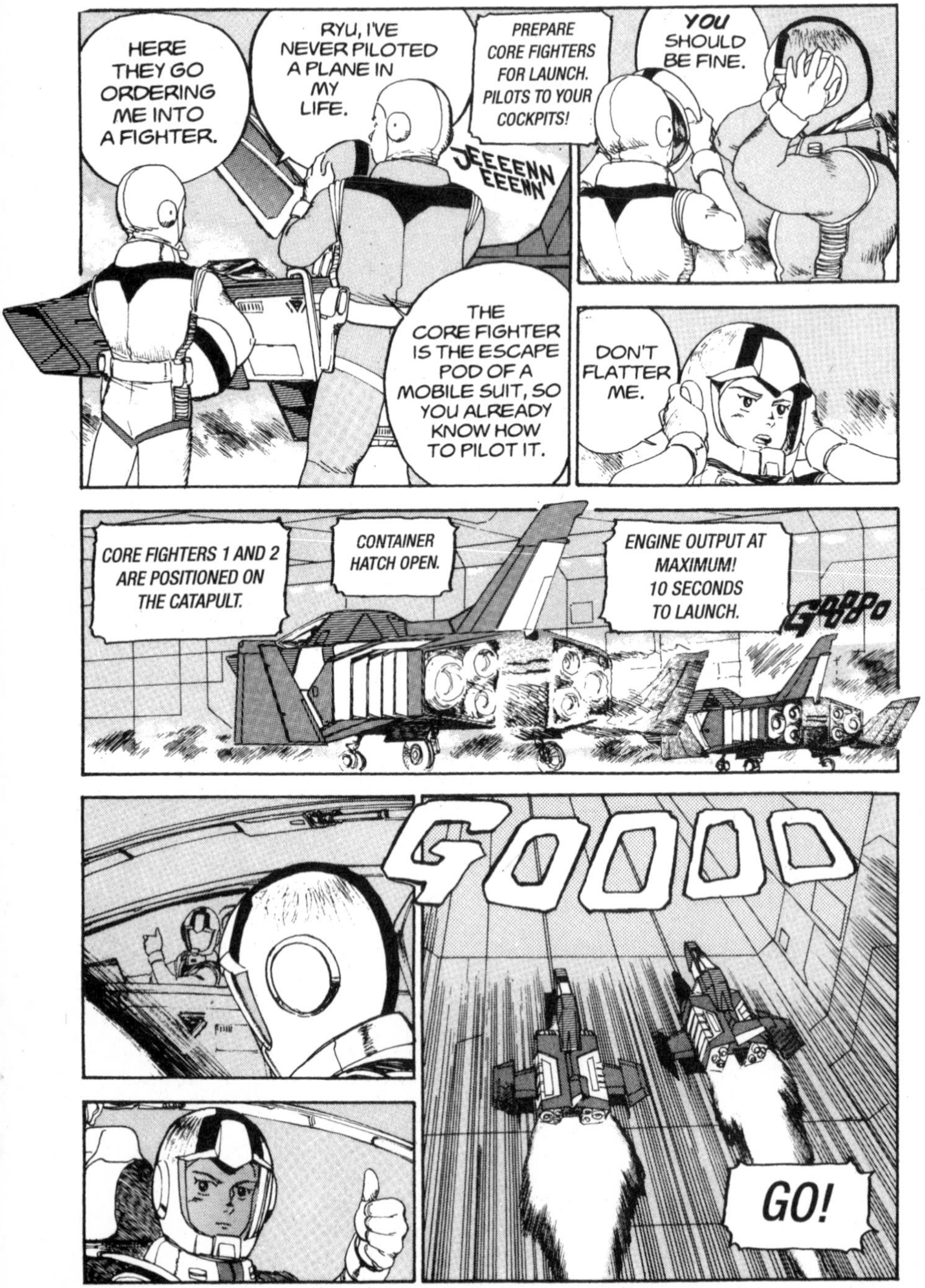
HERE THEY GO ORDERING ME INTO A FIGHTER.
RYU, I'VE NEVER PILOTED A PLANE IN MY LIFE.
PREPARE CORE FIGHTERS FOR LAUNCH. PILOTS TO YOUR COCKPITS!
JEEEENN EEEENN
THE CORE FIGHTER IS THE ESCAPE POD OF A MOBILE SUIT, SO YOU ALREADY KNOW HOW TO PILOT IT.
YOU SHOULD BE FINE.
DON'T FLATTER ME.
CORE FIGHTERS 1 AND 2 ARE POSITIONED ON THE CATAPULT.
CONTAINER HATCH OPEN.
ENGINE OUTPUT AT MAXIMUM! 10 SECONDS TO LAUNCH.
GOOOO
GO!

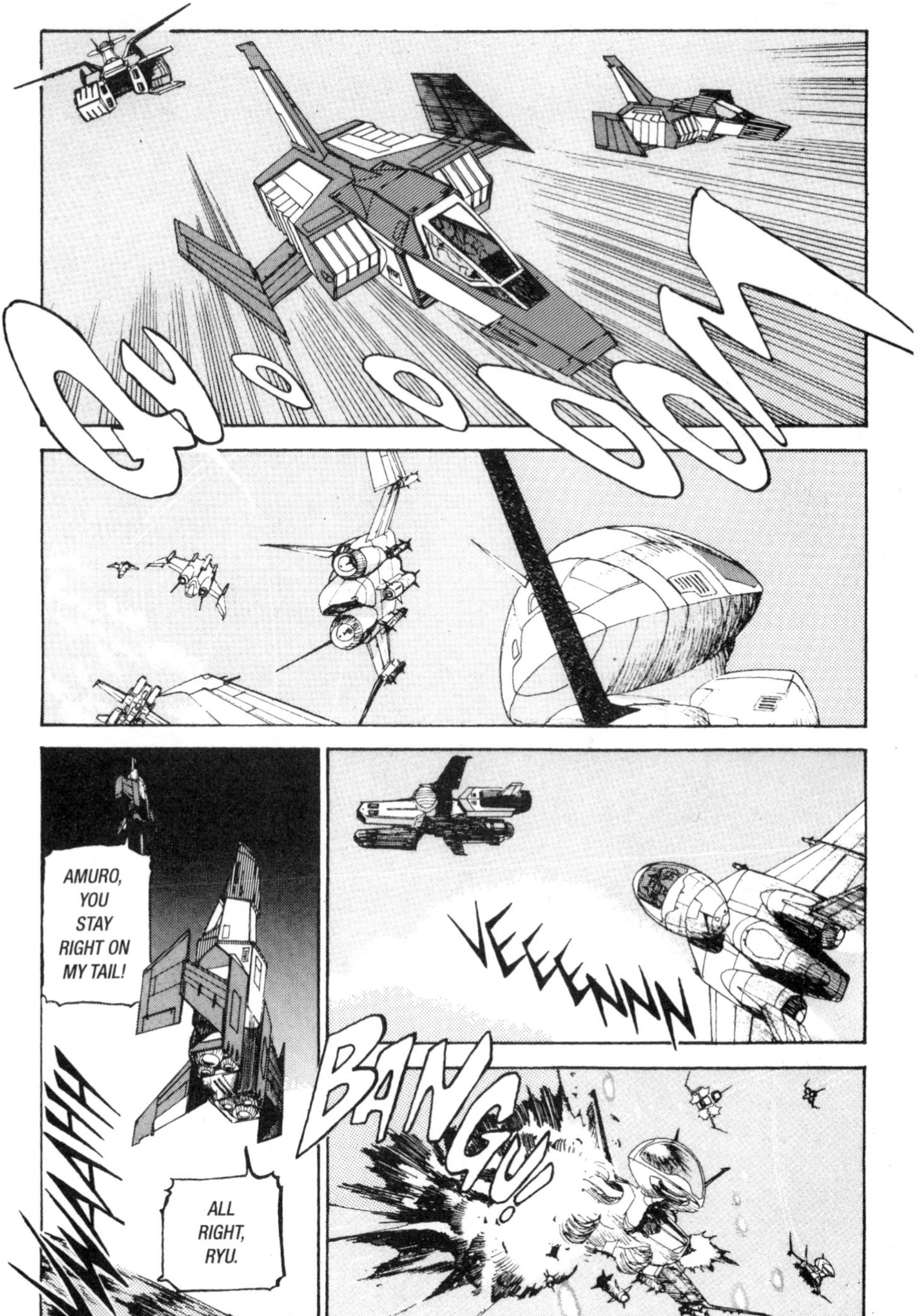

WOOOOM
AMURO, YOU STAY RIGHT ON MY TAIL!
WHAAHH
ALL RIGHT, RYU.
VEEEENNNN
BANG!!

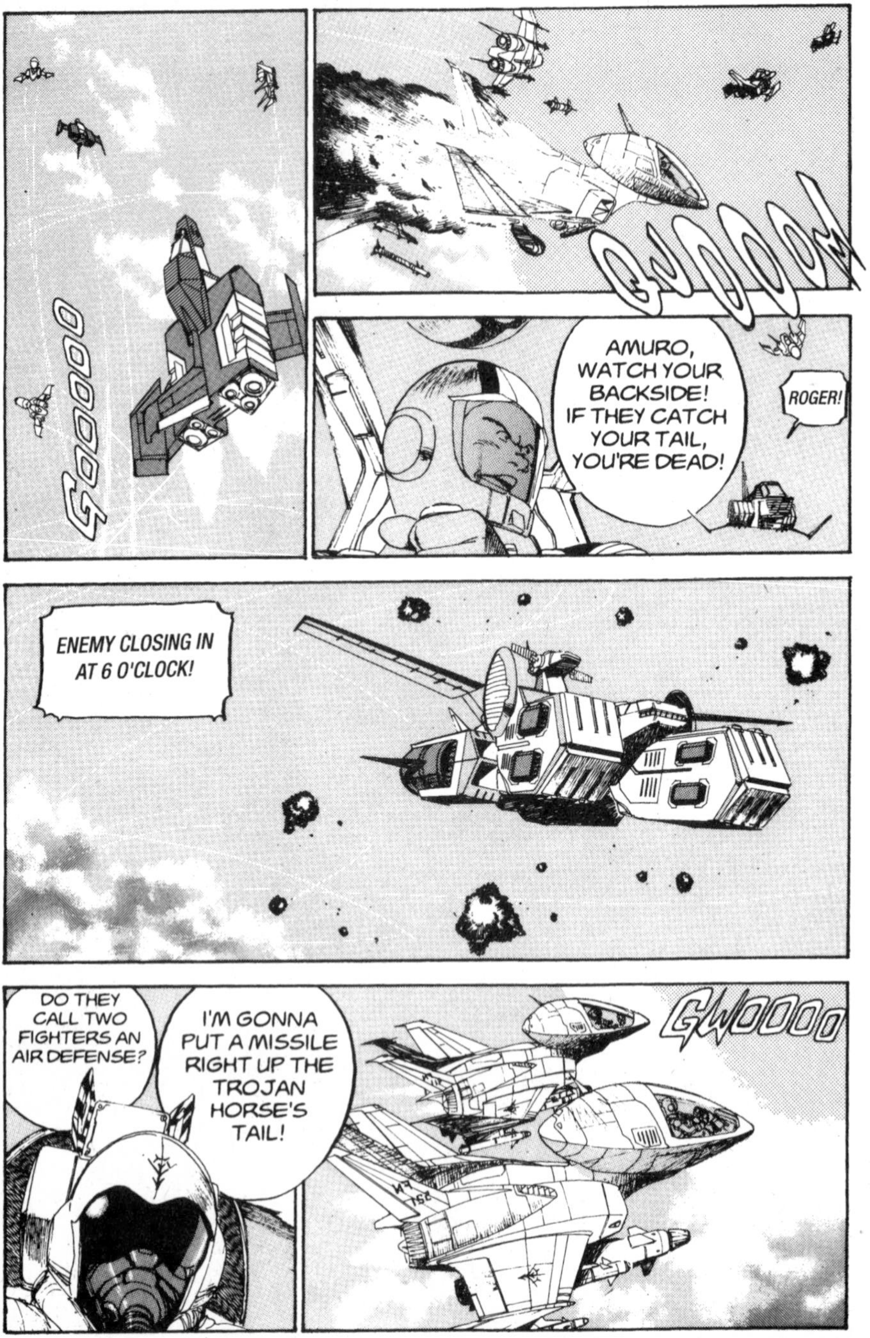
GOOOOO
AMURO, WATCH YOUR BACKSIDE! IF THEY CATCH YOUR TAIL, YOU'RE DEAD!
ROGER!
ENEMY CLOSING IN AT 6 O'CLOCK!
DO THEY CALL TWO FIGHTERS AN AIR DEFENSE?
I'M GONNA PUT A MISSILE RIGHT UP THE TROJAN HORSE'S TAIL!
GWOOOO

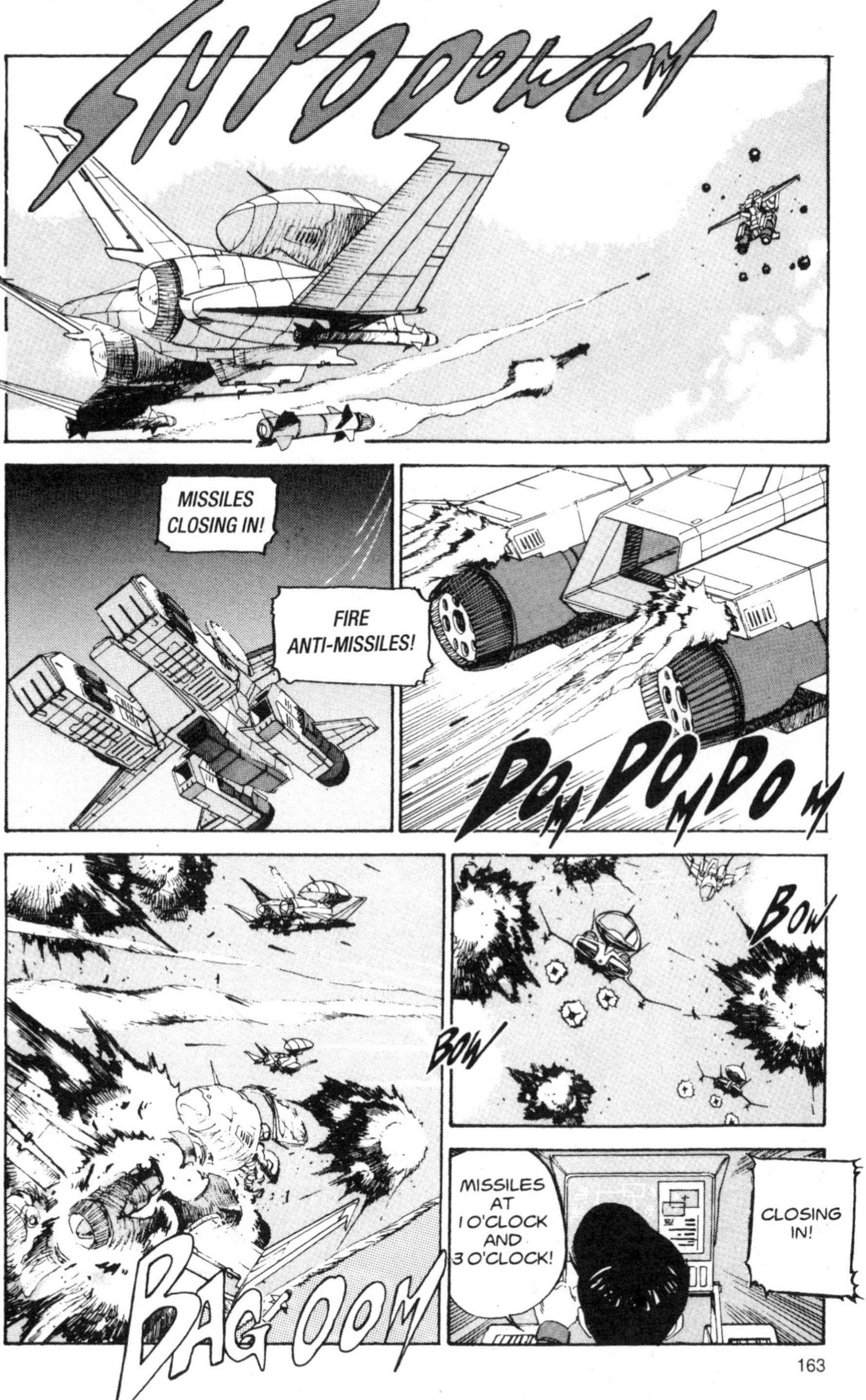
SHPOOOWOW
MISSILES CLOSING IN!
FIRE ANTI-MISSILES!
DOMPOMDOM
BOW
BOW
BAG'OOM
MISSILES AT 1 O'CLOCK AND 3 O'CLOCK!
CLOSING IN!

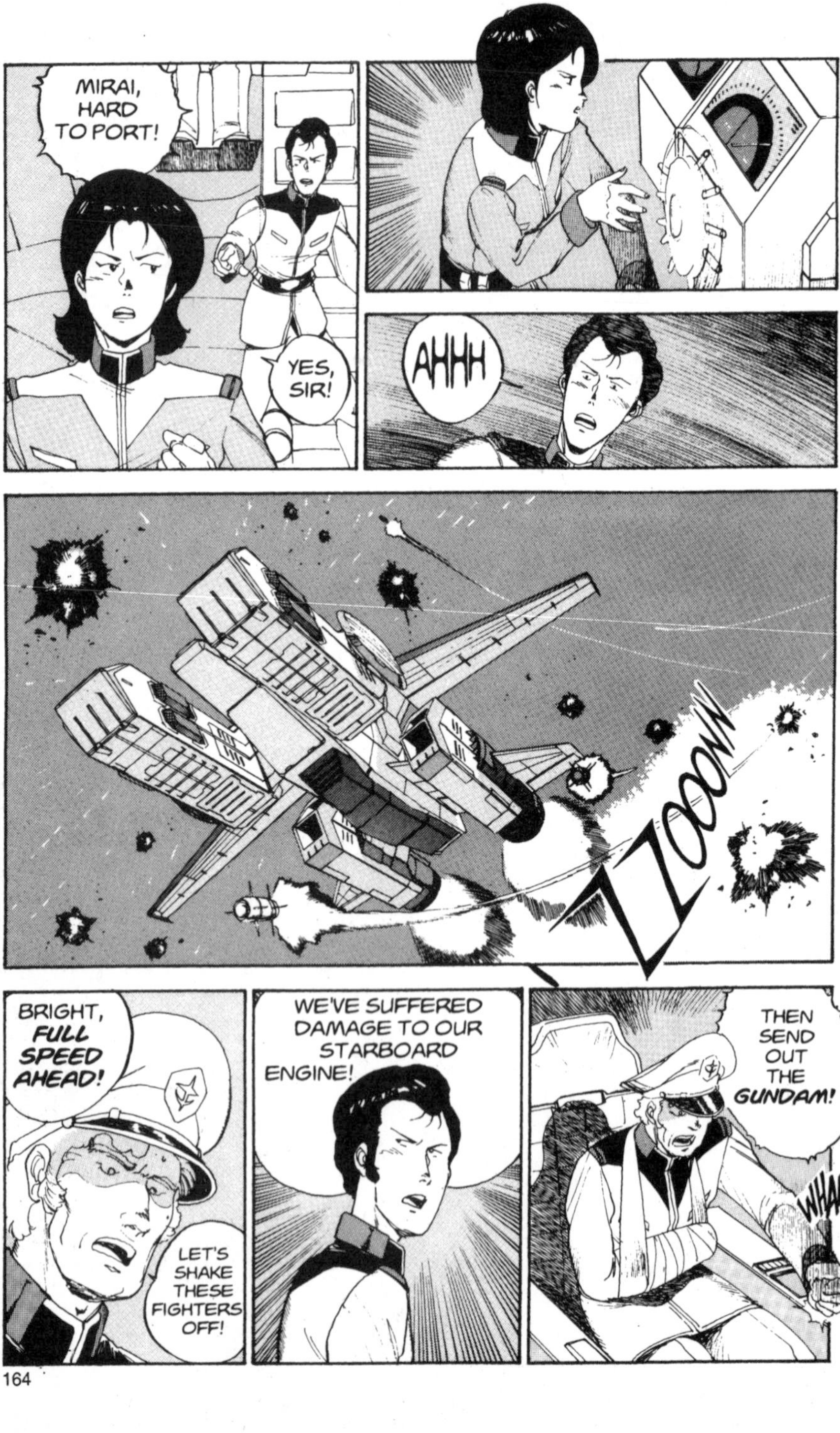
MIRAI, HARD TO PORT!
YES, SIR!
AHHH
ZZOOOWN
BRIGHT, FULL SPEED AHEAD!
LET'S SHAKE THESE FIGHTERS OFF!
WE'VE SUFFERED DAMAGE TO OUR STARBOARD ENGINE!
THEN SEND OUT THE GUNDAM!
WHAM

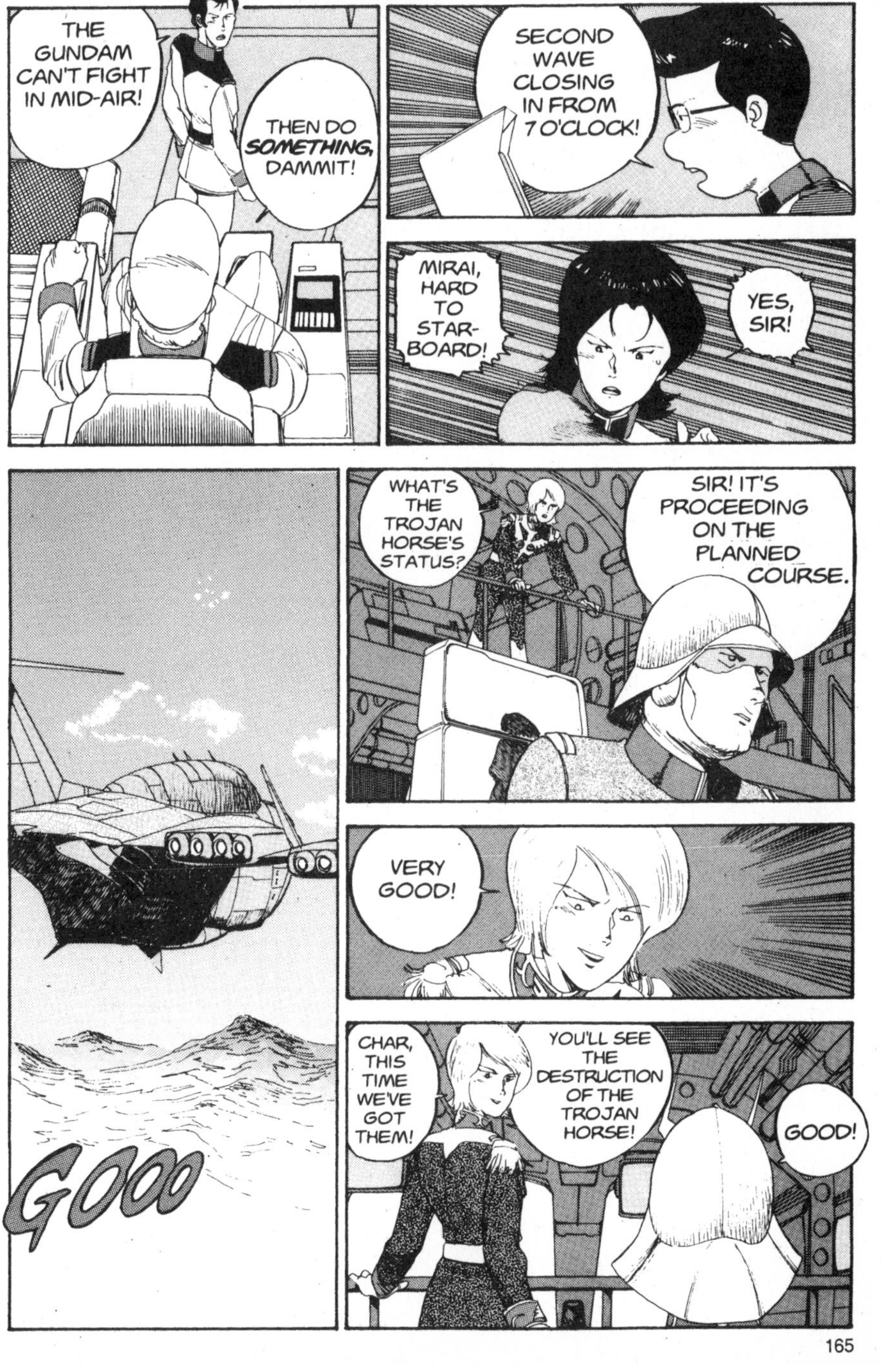
THE GUNDAM CAN'T FIGHT IN MID-AIR!
THEN DO **SOMETHING,** DAMMIT!
SECOND WAVE CLOSING IN FROM 7 O'CLOCK!
MIRAI, HARD TO STAR-BOARD!
YES, SIR!
GOOO
WHAT'S THE TROJAN HORSE'S STATUS?
SIR! IT'S PROCEEDING ON THE PLANNED COURSE.
VERY GOOD!
CHAR, THIS TIME WE'VE GOT THEM!
YOU'LL SEE THE DESTRUCTION OF THE TROJAN HORSE!
GOOD!

LOWER OUR ALTITUDE! WE'RE TOO MUCH OF A TARGET UP HERE.

YES, SIR.

THE TROJAN HORSE IS HEADING DIRECTLY TOWARD POINT S-4.

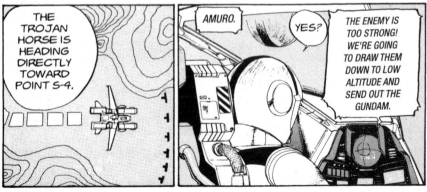

AMURO.

YES?

THE ENEMY IS TOO STRONG! WE'RE GOING TO DRAW THEM DOWN TO LOW ALTITUDE AND SEND OUT THE GUNDAM.

THERE ISN'T TIME FOR YOU TO CHANGE MODULES. YOU'LL HAVE TO LINK UP IN THE CORE FIGHTER. LAND ON THE LOWER DECK!

WHAT!? I CAN"T DO THAT!

JUST CATCH THE BRAKING CABLE. WE'LL TAKE CARE OF THE REST.

I'VE NEVER DONE ANYTHING LIKE THIS BEFORE! YOU DON'T KNOW WHAT YOU'RE ASKING!

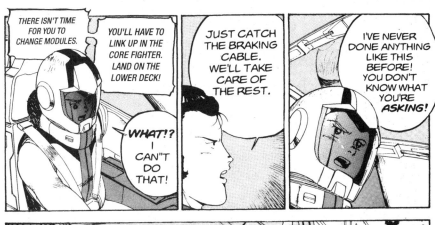

ZOOONN

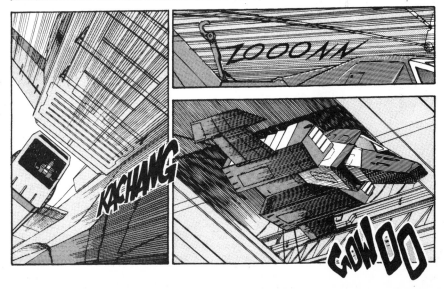

KACHANG

GOWOO

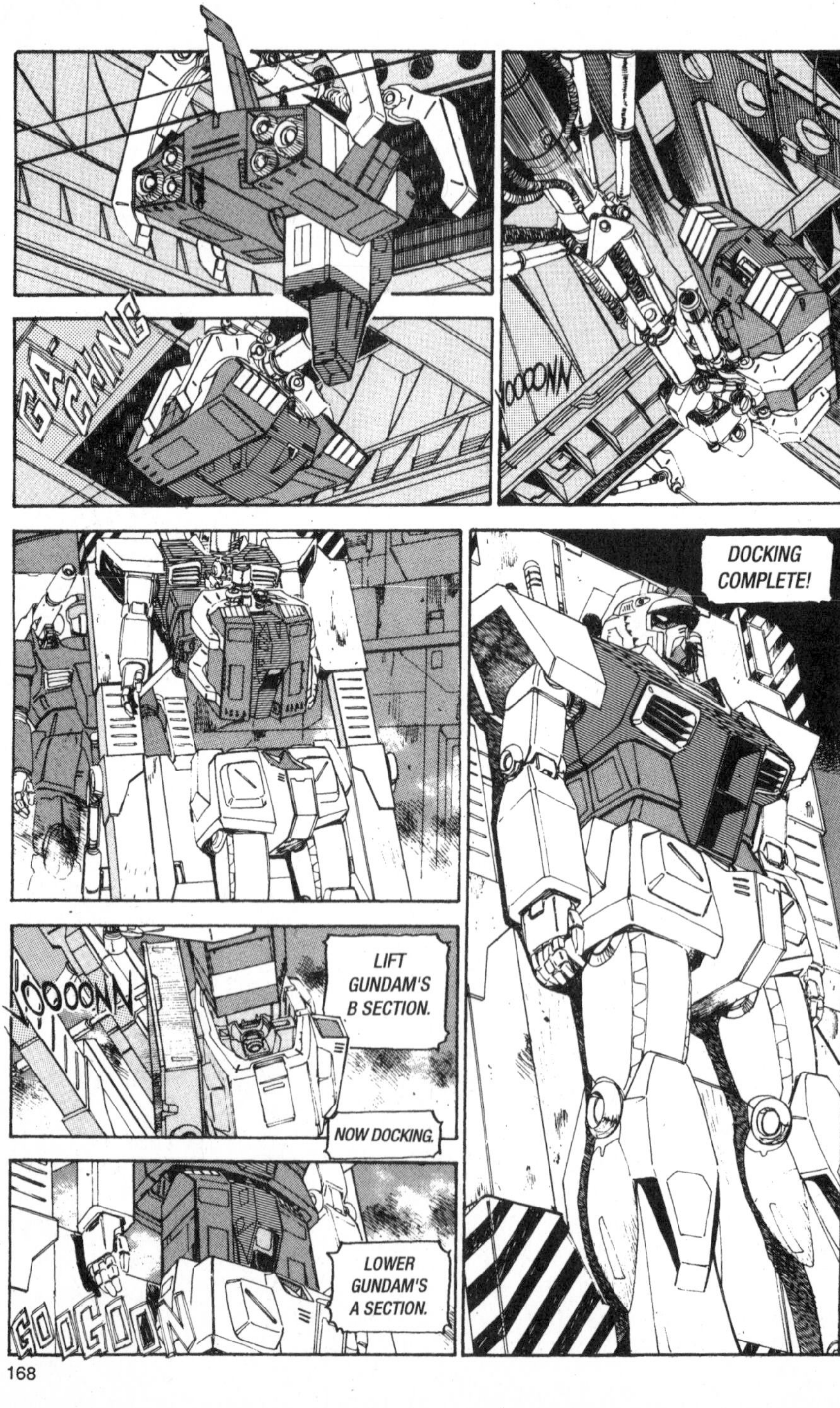
GA-CHING
VOOOONN
VOOOONN
LIFT GUNDAM'S B SECTION.
NOW DOCKING.
LOWER GUNDAM'S A SECTION.
GOGOON
DOCKING COMPLETE!

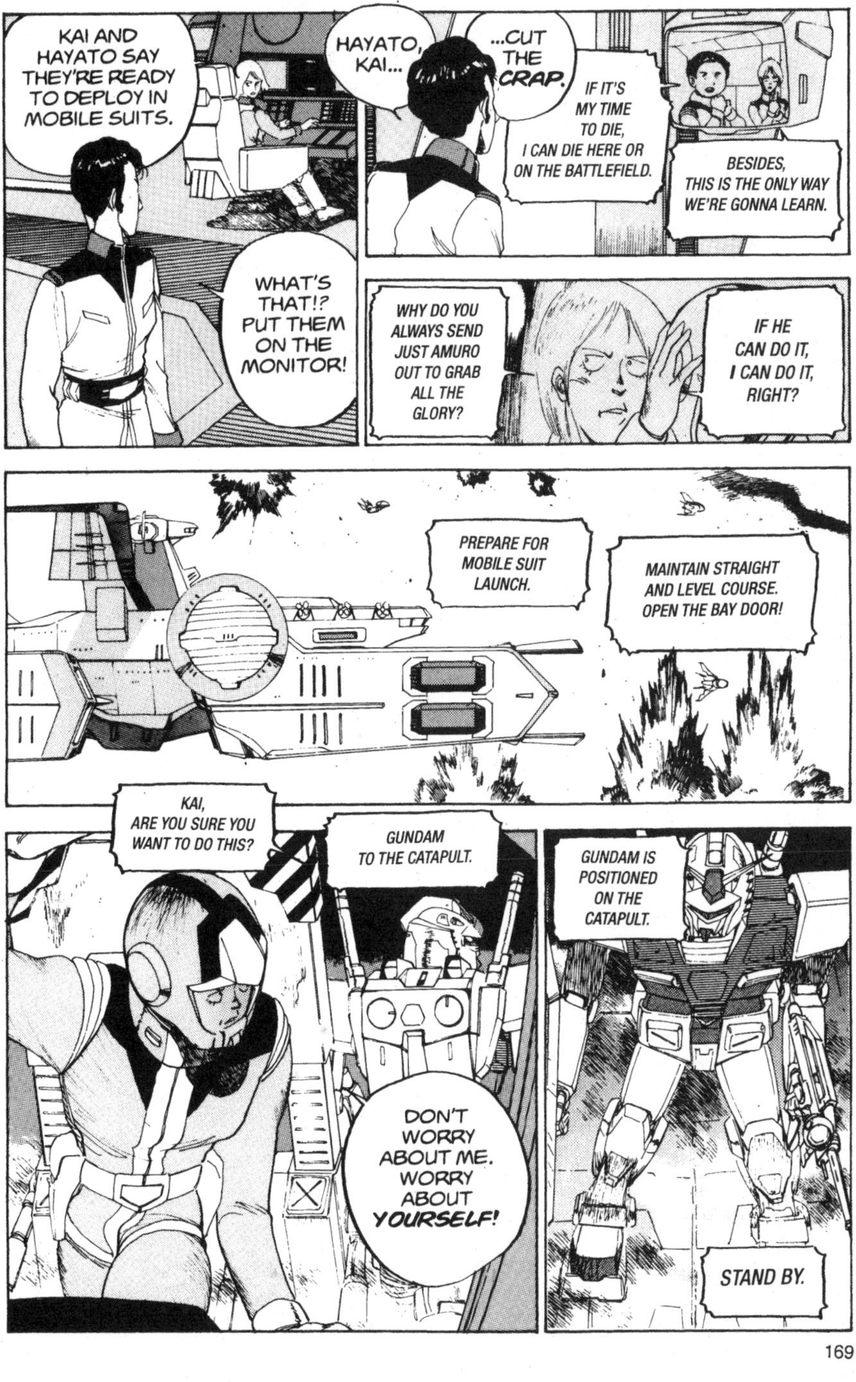
KAI AND HAYATO SAY THEY'RE READY TO DEPLOY IN MOBILE SUITS.
WHAT'S THAT!? PUT THEM ON THE MONITOR!
HAYATO, KAI...
...CUT THE CRAP.
IF IT'S MY TIME TO DIE, I CAN DIE HERE OR ON THE BATTLEFIELD.
BESIDES, THIS IS THE ONLY WAY WE'RE GONNA LEARN.
WHY DO YOU ALWAYS SEND JUST AMURO OUT TO GRAB ALL THE GLORY?
IF HE CAN DO IT, I CAN DO IT, RIGHT?
PREPARE FOR MOBILE SUIT LAUNCH.
MAINTAIN STRAIGHT AND LEVEL COURSE. OPEN THE BAY DOOR!
KAI, ARE YOU SURE YOU WANT TO DO THIS?
GUNDAM TO THE CATAPULT.
DON'T WORRY ABOUT ME. WORRY ABOUT YOURSELF!
GUNDAM IS POSITIONED ON THE CATAPULT.
STAND BY.

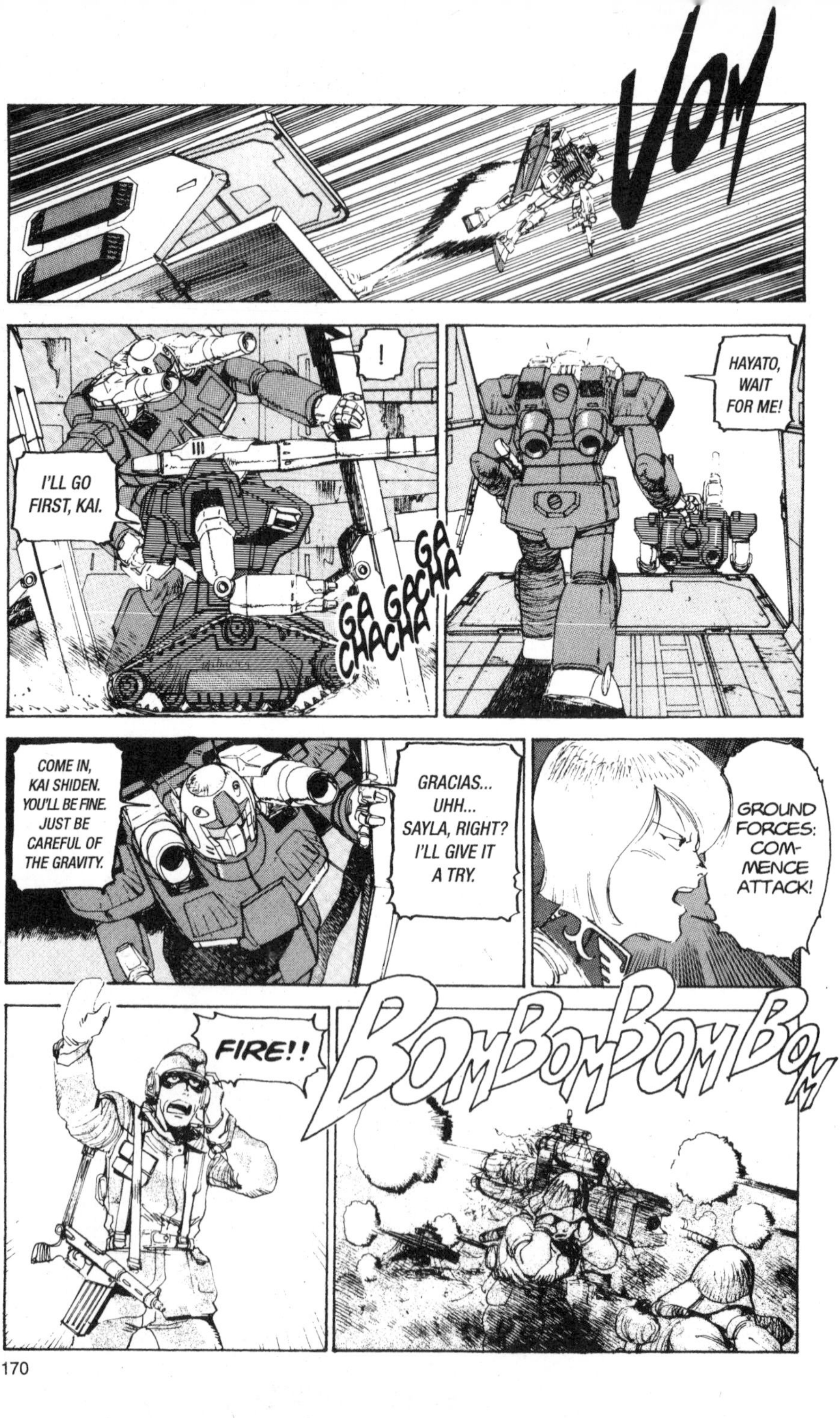
VOM
!
I'LL GO FIRST, KAI.
GA GACHA GA CHACHA
HAYATO, WAIT FOR ME!
COME IN, KAI SHIDEN. YOU'LL BE FINE. JUST BE CAREFUL OF THE GRAVITY.
GRACIAS... UHH... SAYLA, RIGHT? I'LL GIVE IT A TRY.
GROUND FORCES: COM-MENCE ATTACK!
FIRE!!
BOMBOMBOMBOM

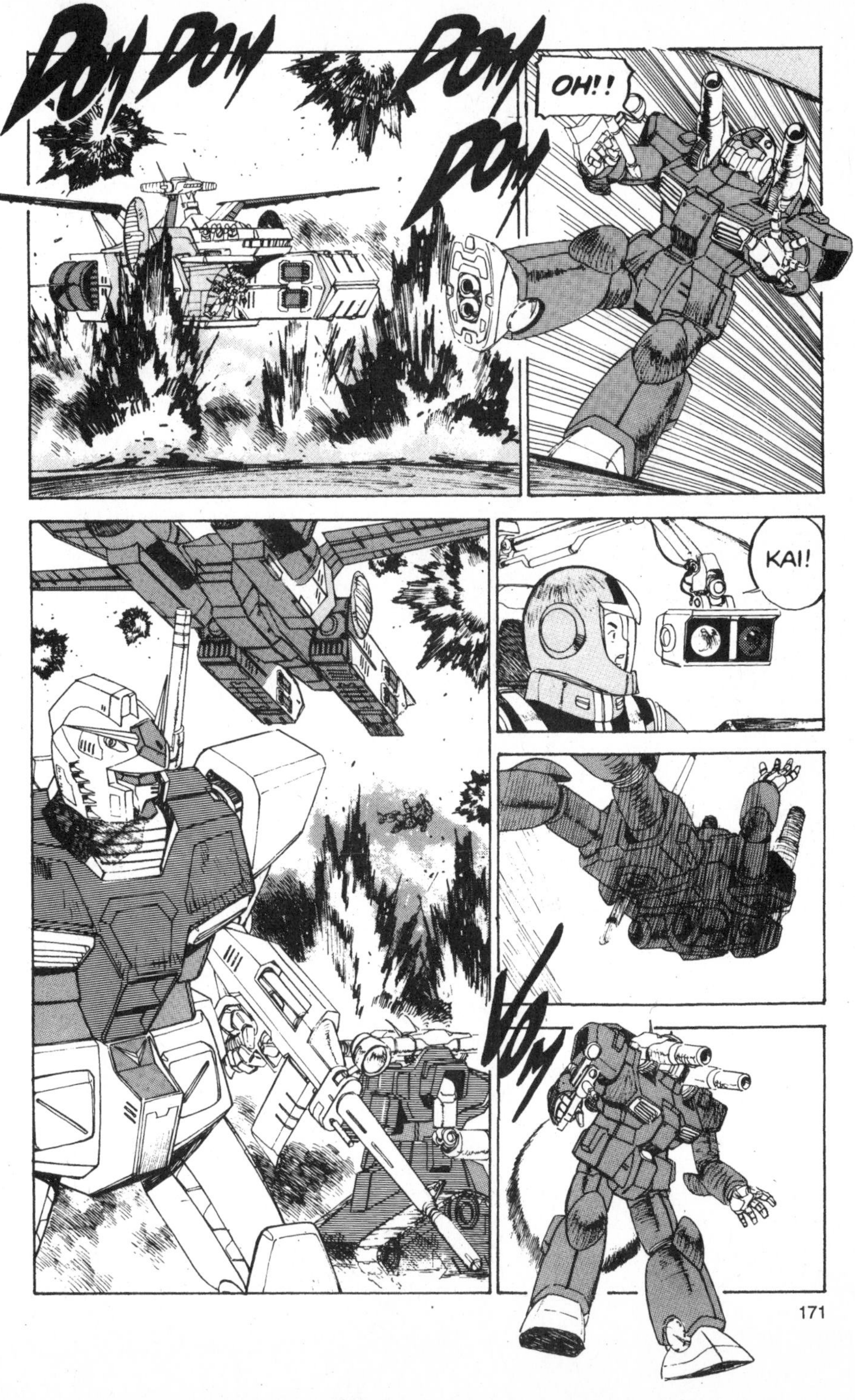
DOM DOM
DOM
DOM
OH!!
KAI!
VOM

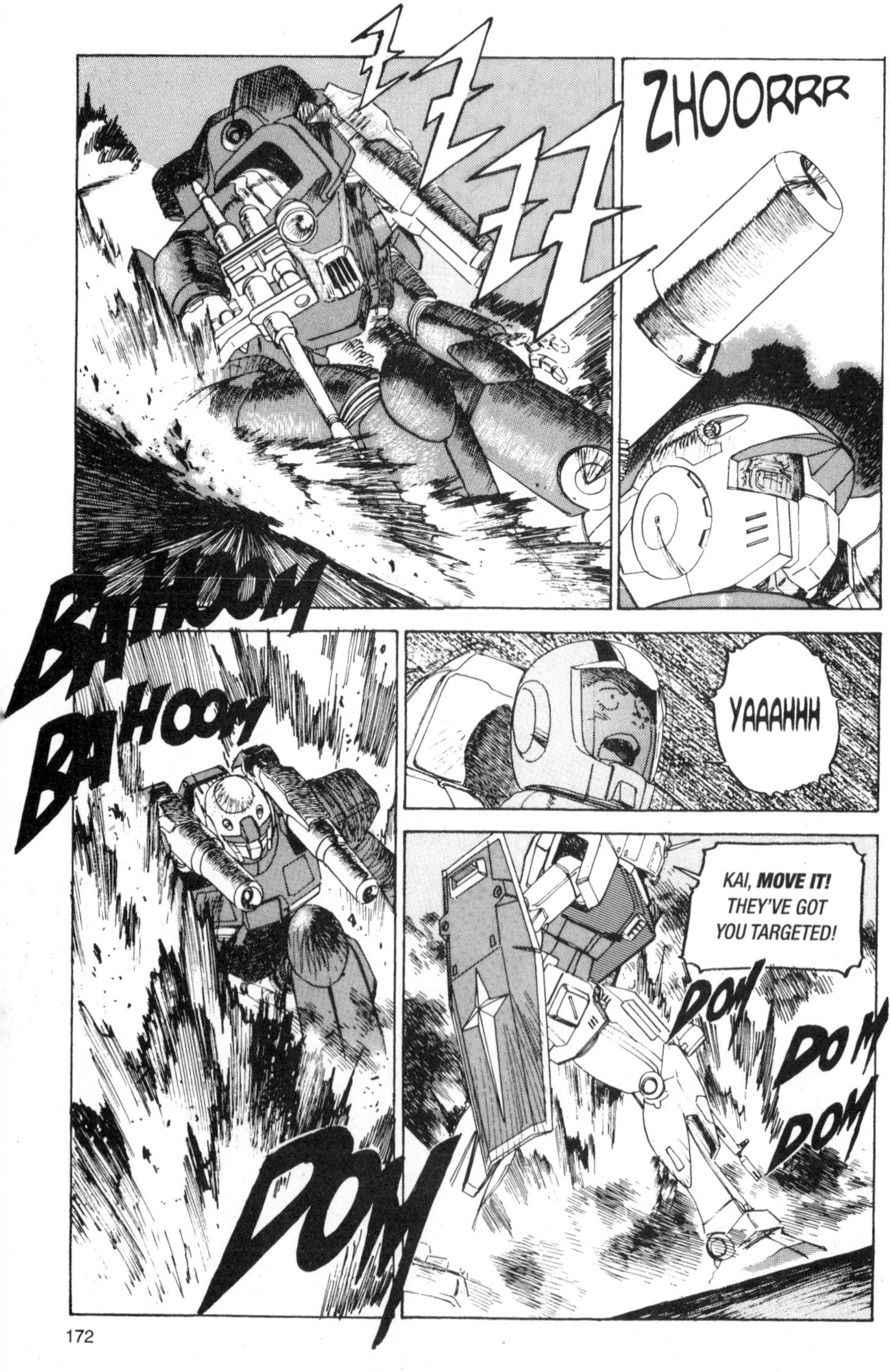
ZHOORRR
BAHOOM
BAHOOM
DOM
YAAAHHH
KAI, **MOVE IT!** THEY'VE GOT YOU TARGETED!
DOM
DOM
DOM

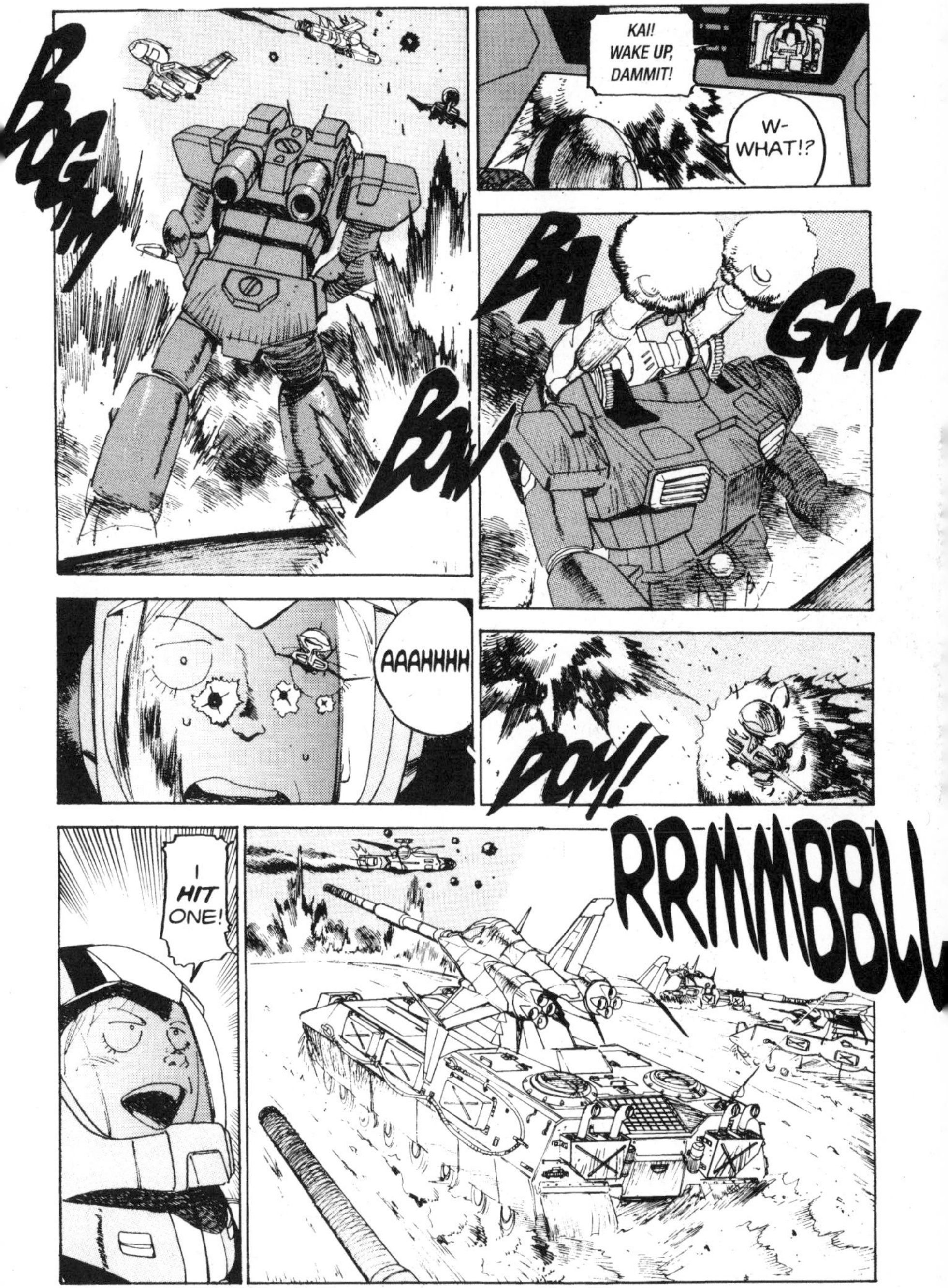
BOOM
KAI! WAKE UP, DAMMIT!
W-WHAT!?
BA
GOM
BOM
AAAHHHH
DOM!
I HIT ONE!
RRMMBBLL

DOGOM BGOOM ZGOOM BAGOM

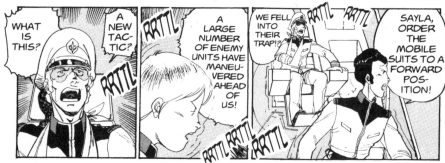

WHAT IS THIS?

A NEW TAC-TIC?

RRTTL

A LARGE NUMBER OF ENEMY UNITS HAVE MANEU-VERED AHEAD OF US!

RRTTL RRTTL

WE FELL INTO THEIR TRAP!?

RRTTL RRTTL

SAYLA, ORDER THE MOBILE SUITS TO A FORWARD POS-ITION!

AMURO, KAI, HAYATO, CLOSE BACK IN!

WHITE BASE IS UNDER ATTACK!

CONCENTRATE FIRE ON THE ENEMY DIRECTLY TO OUR FORWARD POSITION!

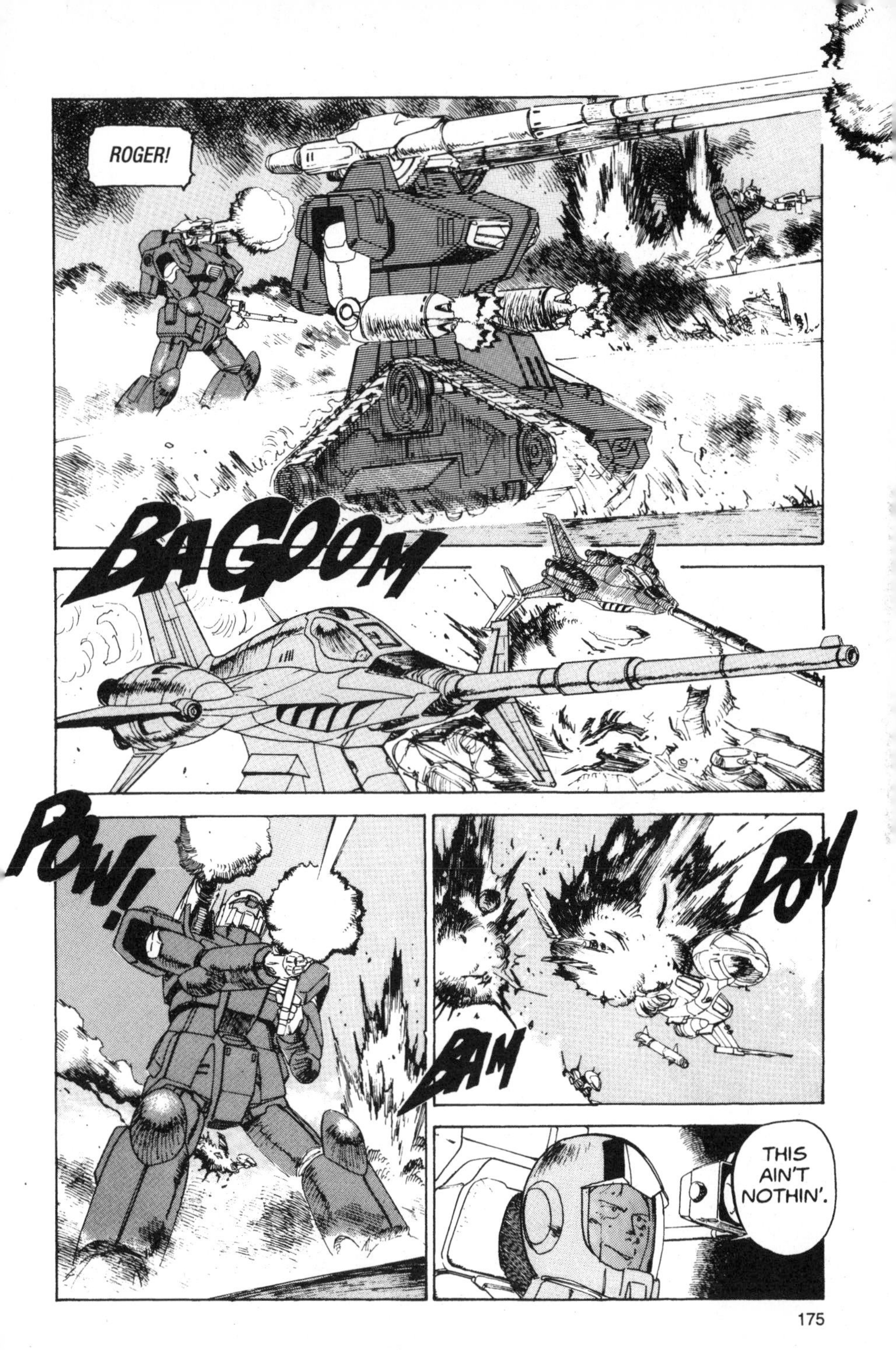
ROGER!
BAGOOM
POW!
DOM
BAM
THIS AIN'T NOTHIN'.

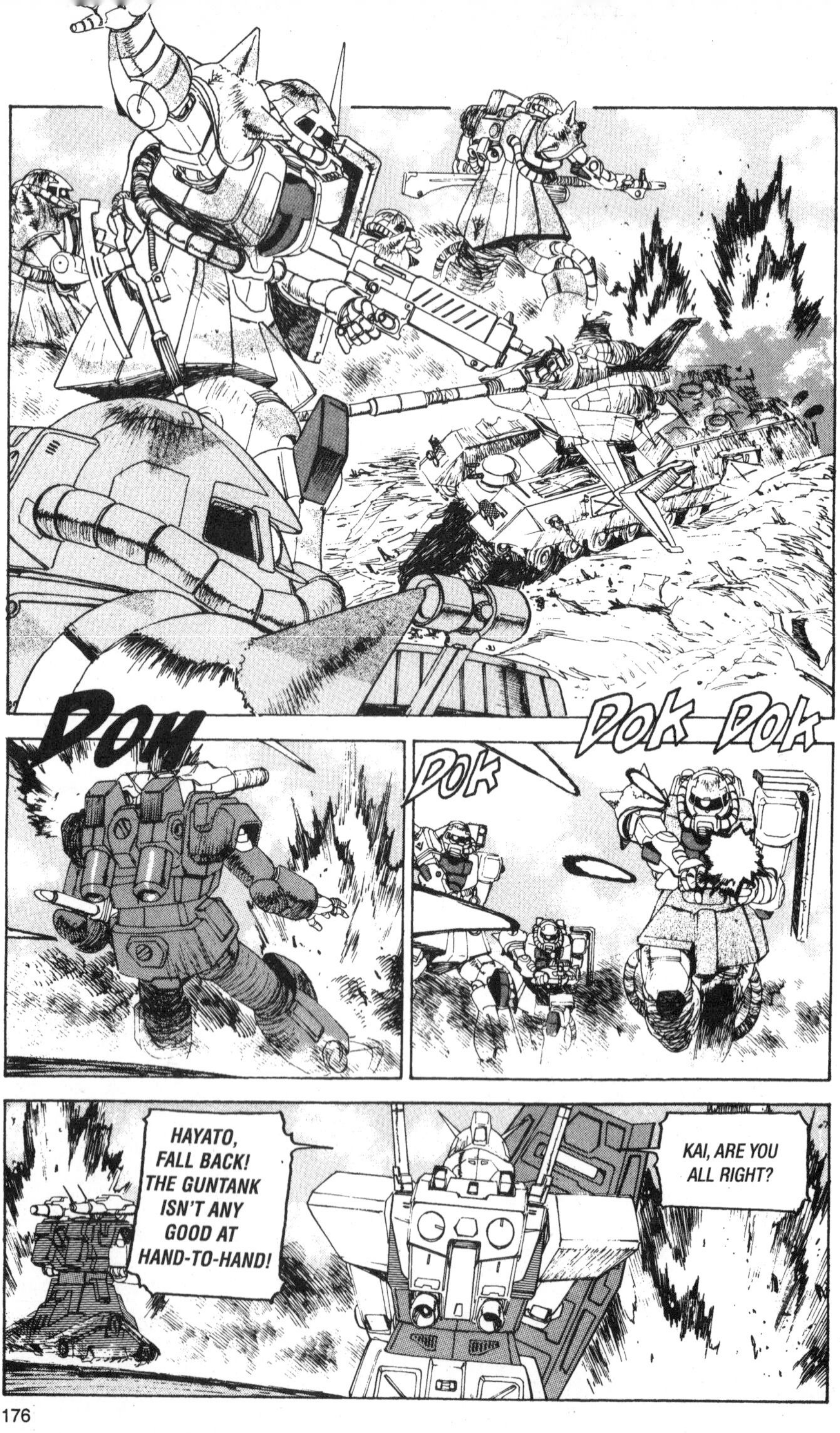
DOM
DOK DOK
DOK
HAYATO, FALL BACK! THE GUNTANK ISN'T ANY GOOD AT HAND-TO-HAND!
KAI, ARE YOU ALL RIGHT?

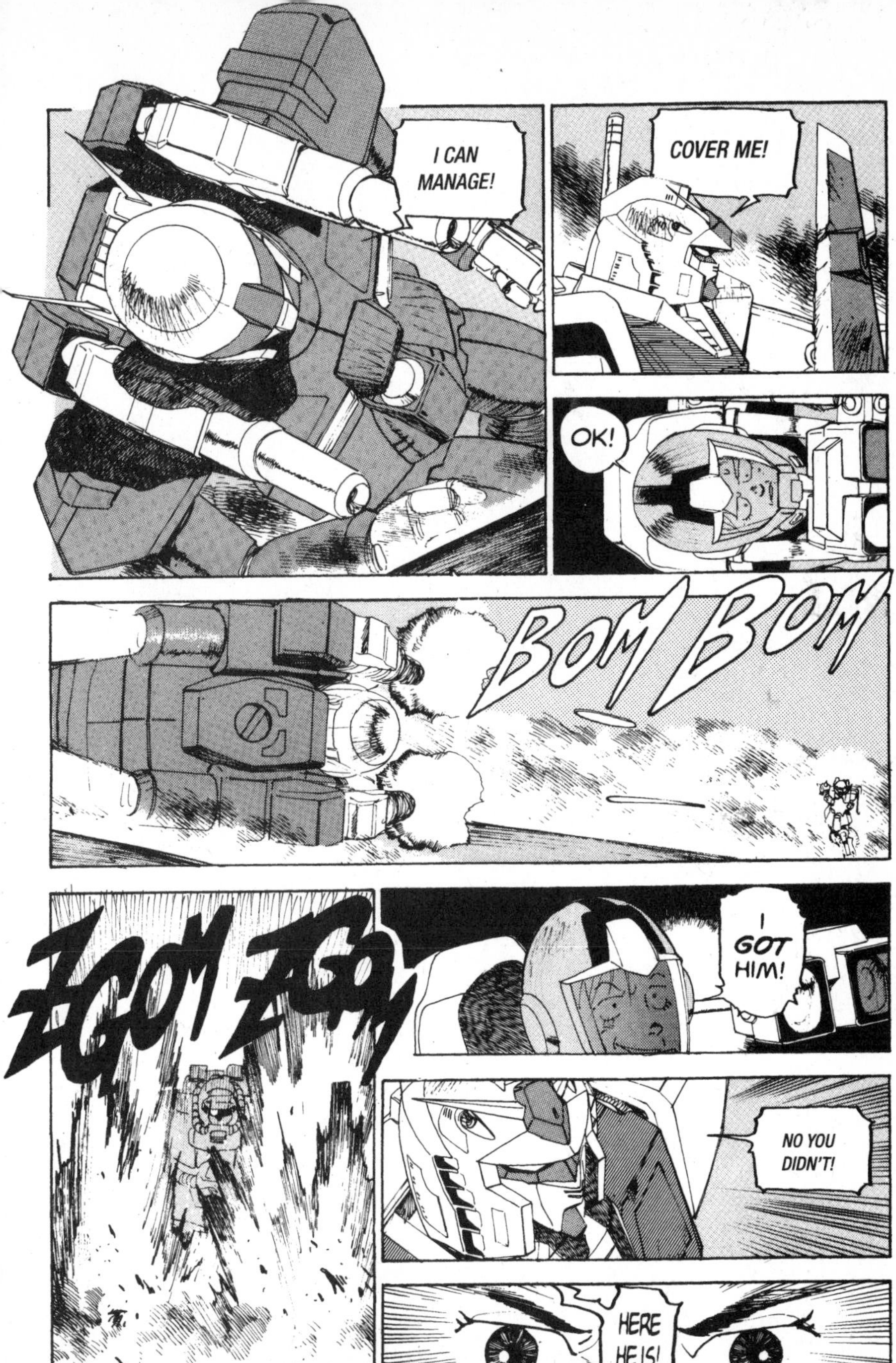
I CAN MANAGE!
COVER ME!
OK!
BOM BOM
ZGOM ZGOM
I GOT HIM!
NO YOU DIDN'T!
HERE HE IS!

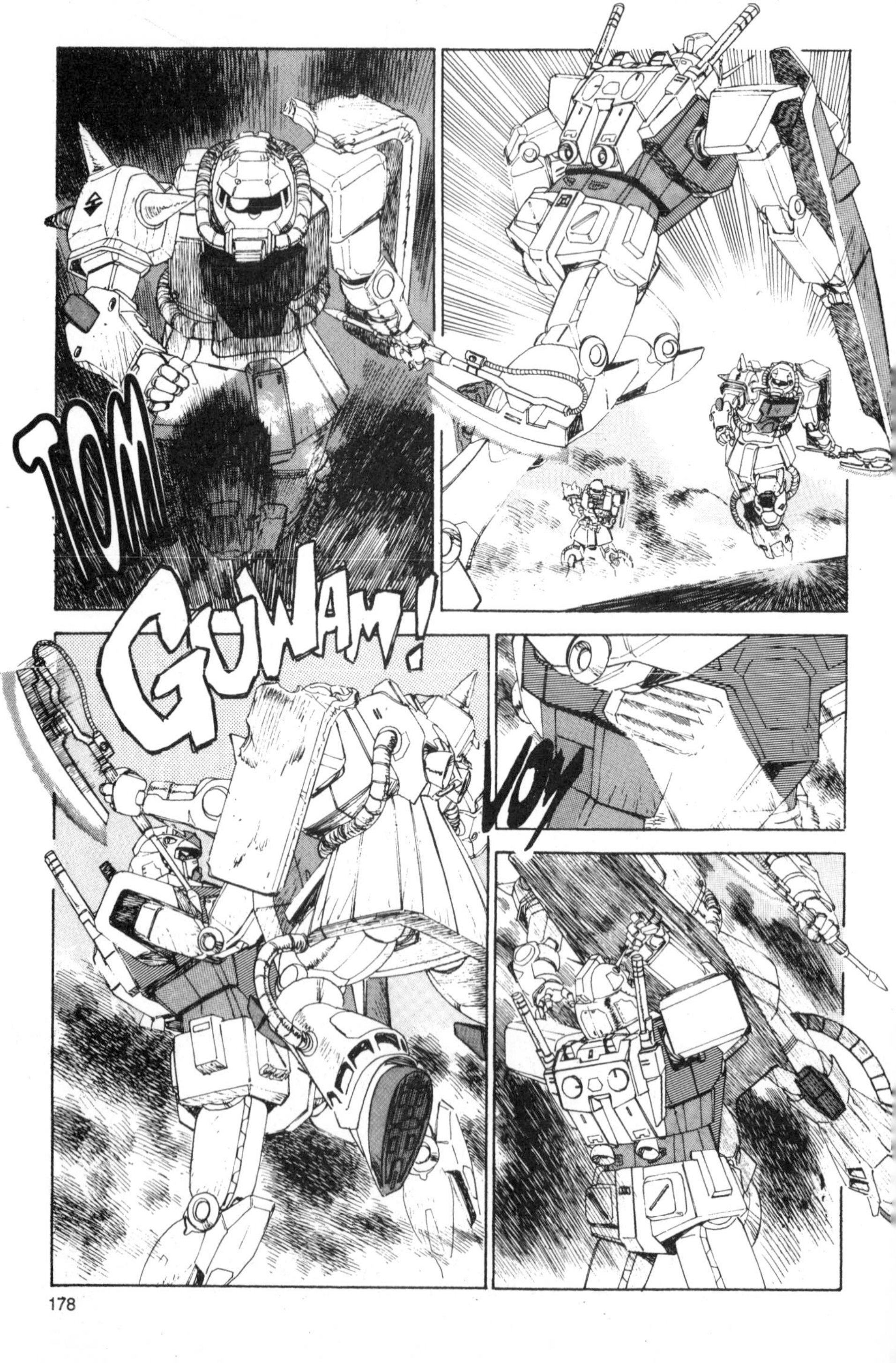

TOOM
GUWAM!
VOM

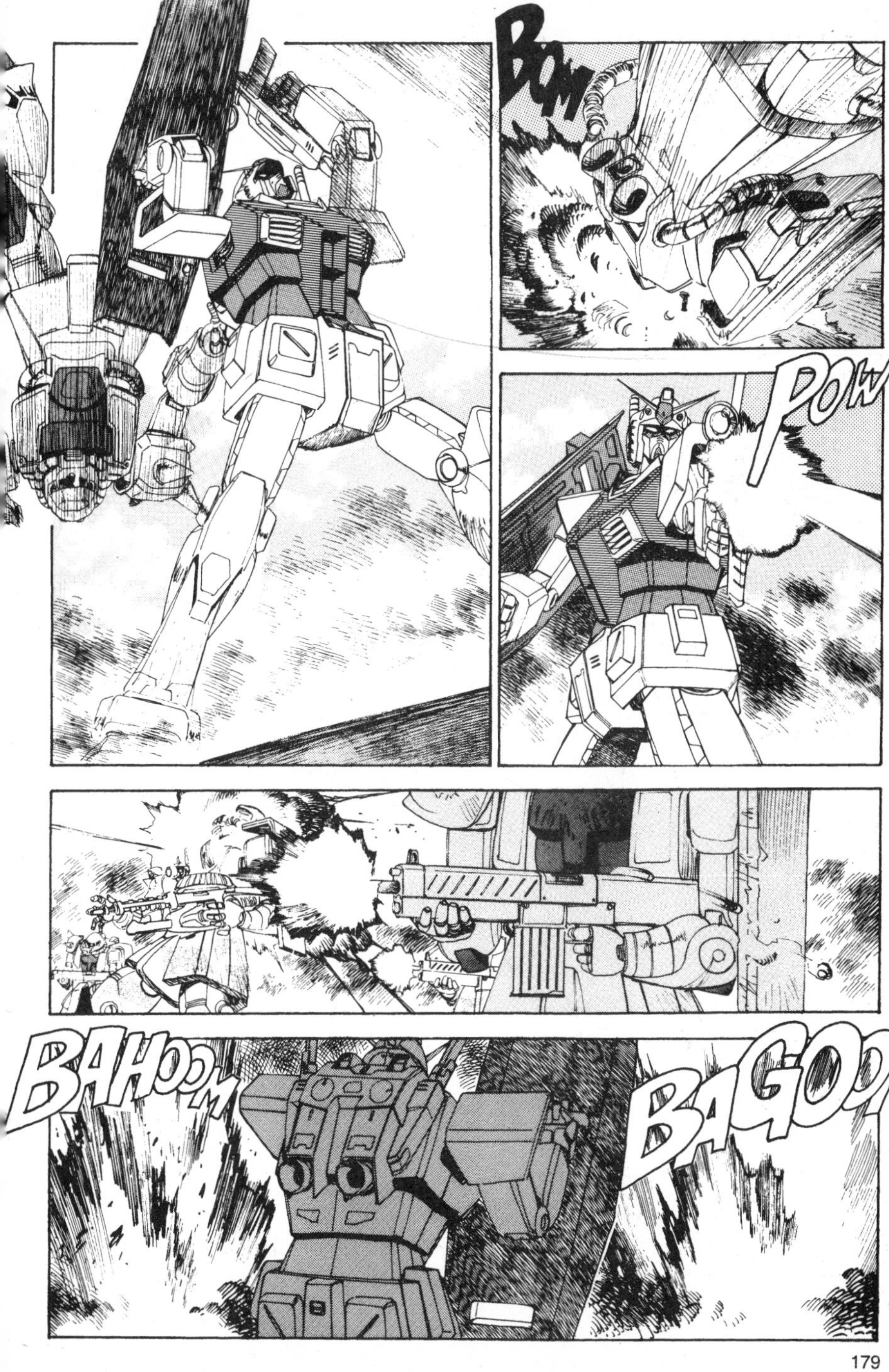
BOM
POW
BAHOOM
BAGOOM

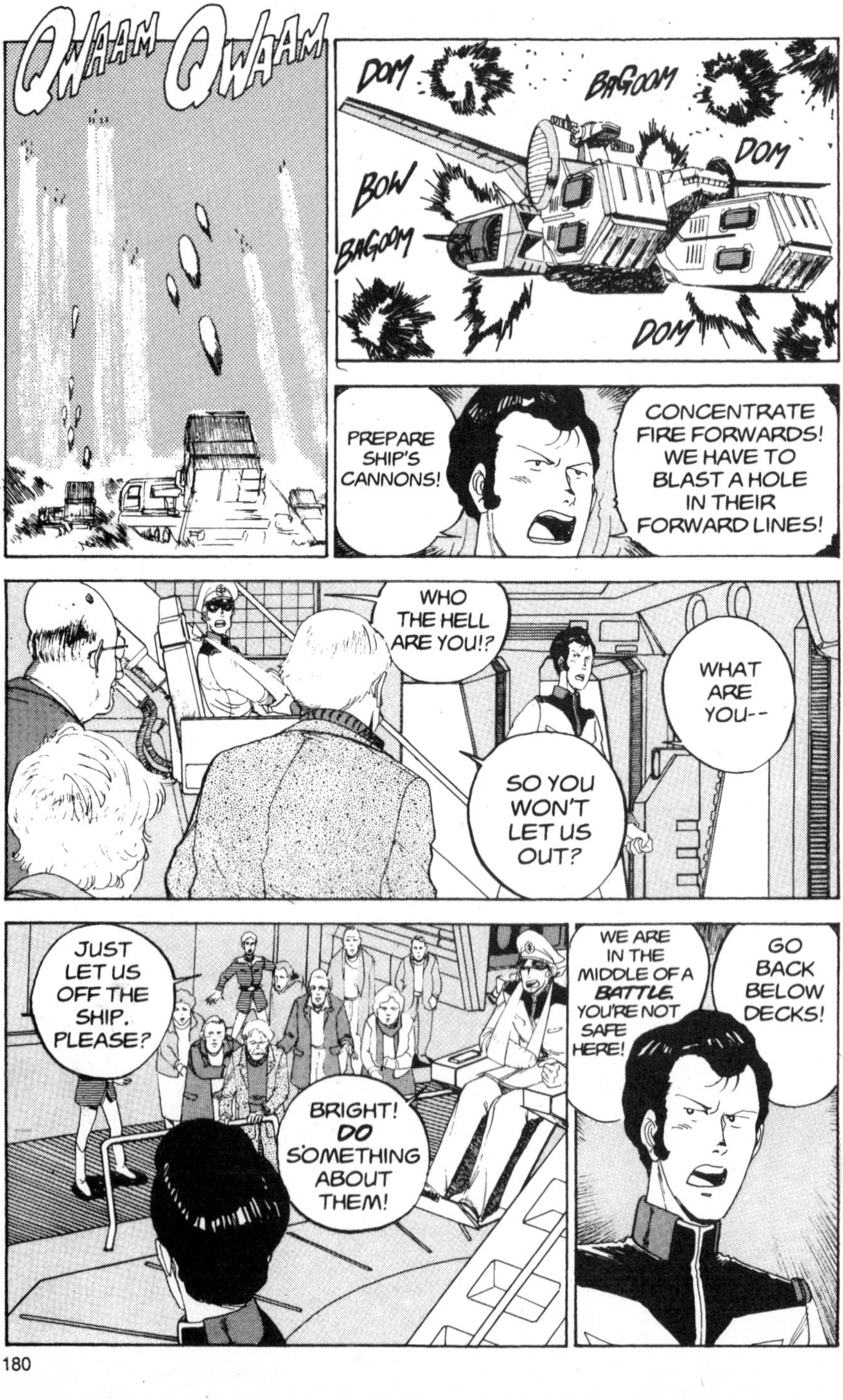
QWAAM QWAAM
DOM
BAGOOM
DOM
BOW
BAGOOM
DOM
PREPARE SHIP'S CANNONS!
CONCENTRATE FIRE FORWARDS! WE HAVE TO BLAST A HOLE IN THEIR FORWARD LINES!
WHO THE HELL ARE YOU!?
WHAT ARE YOU--
SO YOU WON'T LET US OUT?
JUST LET US OFF THE SHIP. PLEASE?
BRIGHT! DO SOMETHING ABOUT THEM!
WE ARE IN THE MIDDLE OF A BATTLE. YOU'RE NOT SAFE HERE!
GO BACK BELOW DECKS!

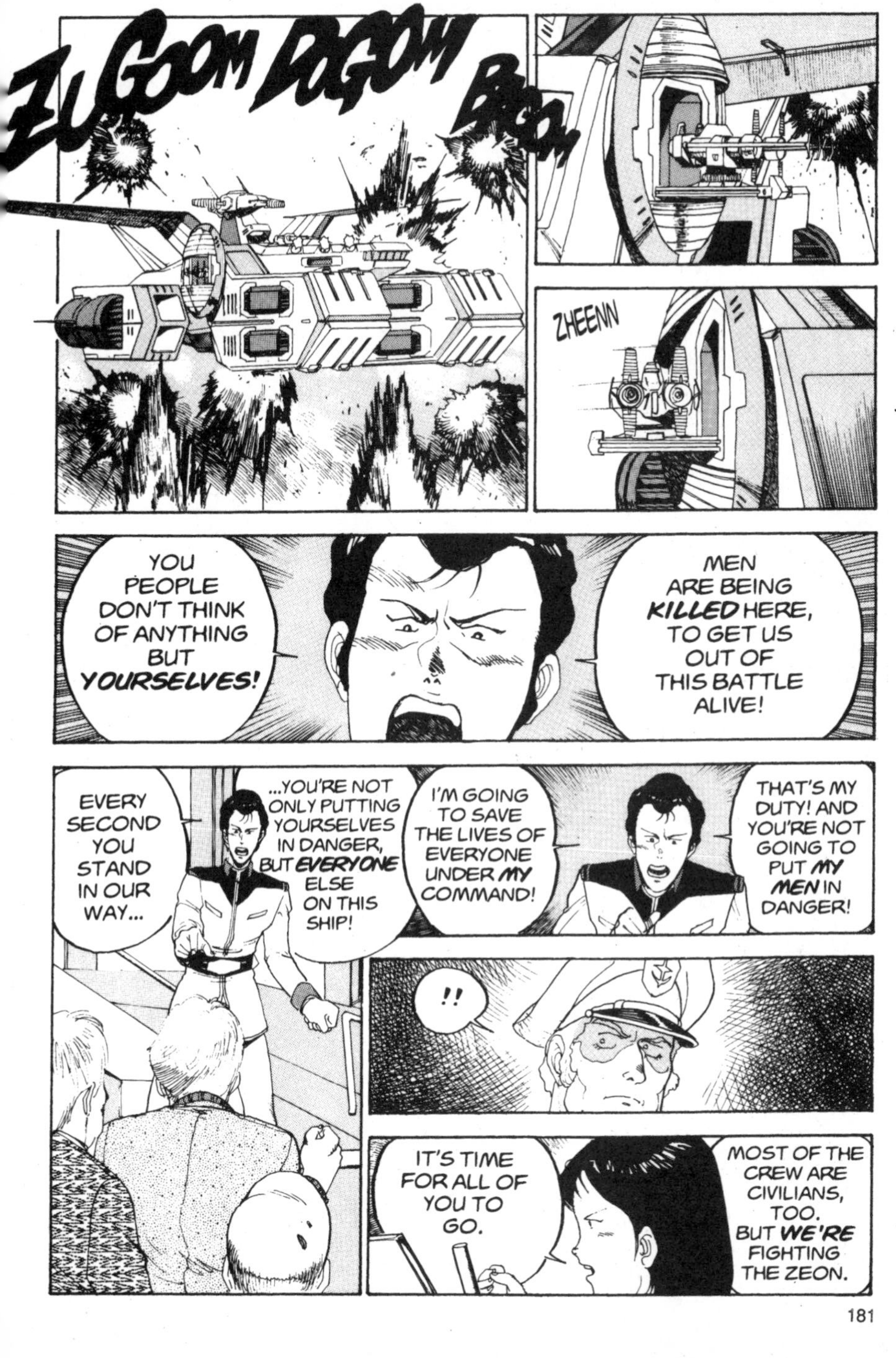
ZUGOOM DOGOM BAGOM
ZHEENN
YOU PEOPLE DON'T THINK OF ANYTHING BUT YOURSELVES!
MEN ARE BEING KILLED HERE, TO GET US OUT OF THIS BATTLE ALIVE!
EVERY SECOND YOU STAND IN OUR WAY...
...YOU'RE NOT ONLY PUTTING YOURSELVES IN DANGER, BUT EVERYONE ELSE ON THIS SHIP!
I'M GOING TO SAVE THE LIVES OF EVERYONE UNDER MY COMMAND!
THAT'S MY DUTY! AND YOU'RE NOT GOING TO PUT MY MEN IN DANGER!
!!
IT'S TIME FOR ALL OF YOU TO GO.
MOST OF THE CREW ARE CIVILIANS, TOO. BUT WE'RE FIGHTING THE ZEON.

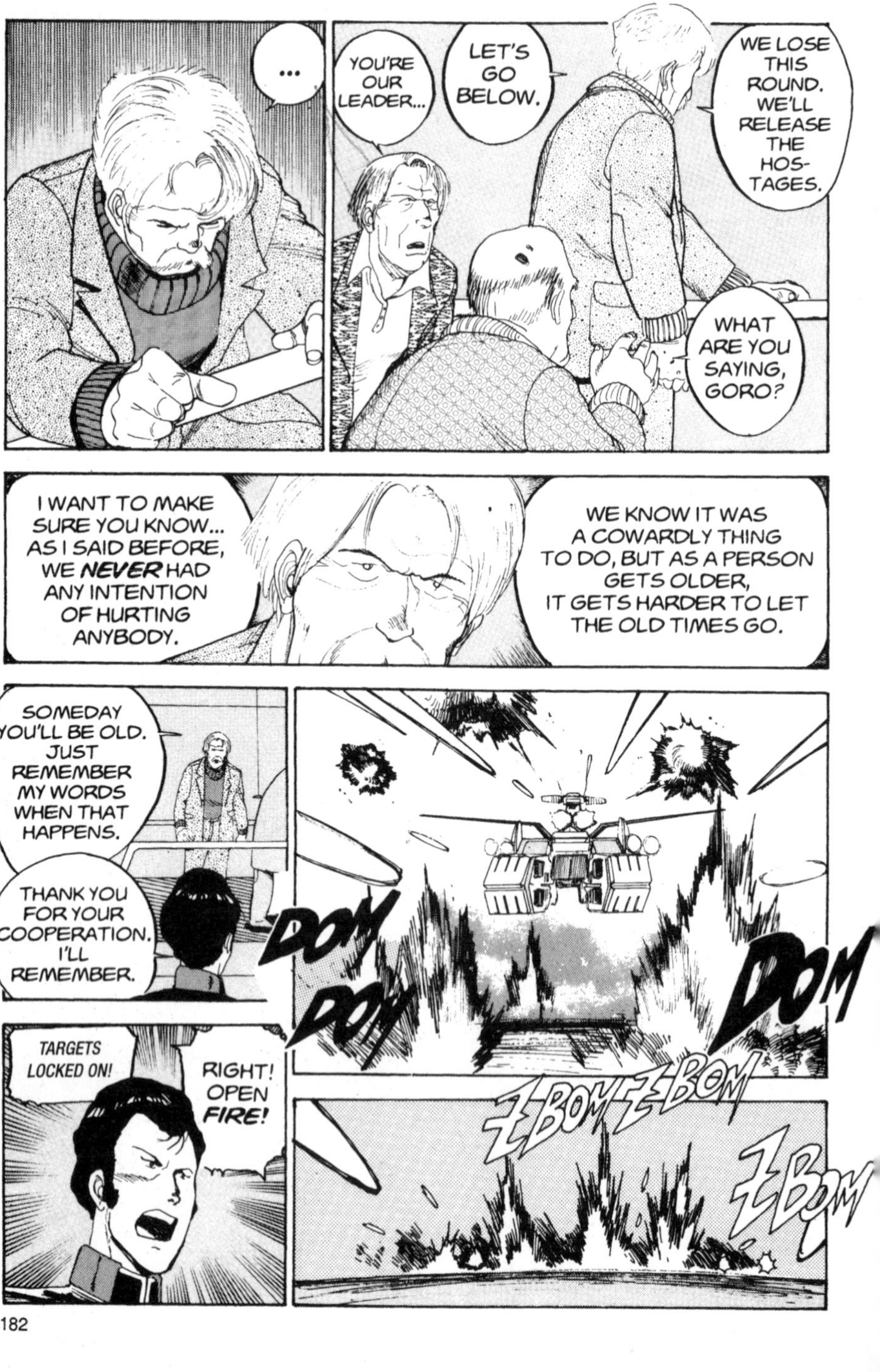
...
YOU'RE OUR LEADER...
LET'S GO BELOW.
WE LOSE THIS ROUND. WE'LL RELEASE THE HOS-TAGES.
WHAT ARE YOU SAYING, GORO?
I WANT TO MAKE SURE YOU KNOW... AS I SAID BEFORE, WE NEVER HAD ANY INTENTION OF HURTING ANYBODY.
WE KNOW IT WAS A COWARDLY THING TO DO, BUT AS A PERSON GETS OLDER, IT GETS HARDER TO LET THE OLD TIMES GO.
SOMEDAY YOU'LL BE OLD. JUST REMEMBER MY WORDS WHEN THAT HAPPENS.
THANK YOU FOR YOUR COOPERATION. I'LL REMEMBER.
DOM
DOM
DOM
TARGETS LOCKED ON!
RIGHT! OPEN FIRE!
ZBOM ZBOM
ZBOM

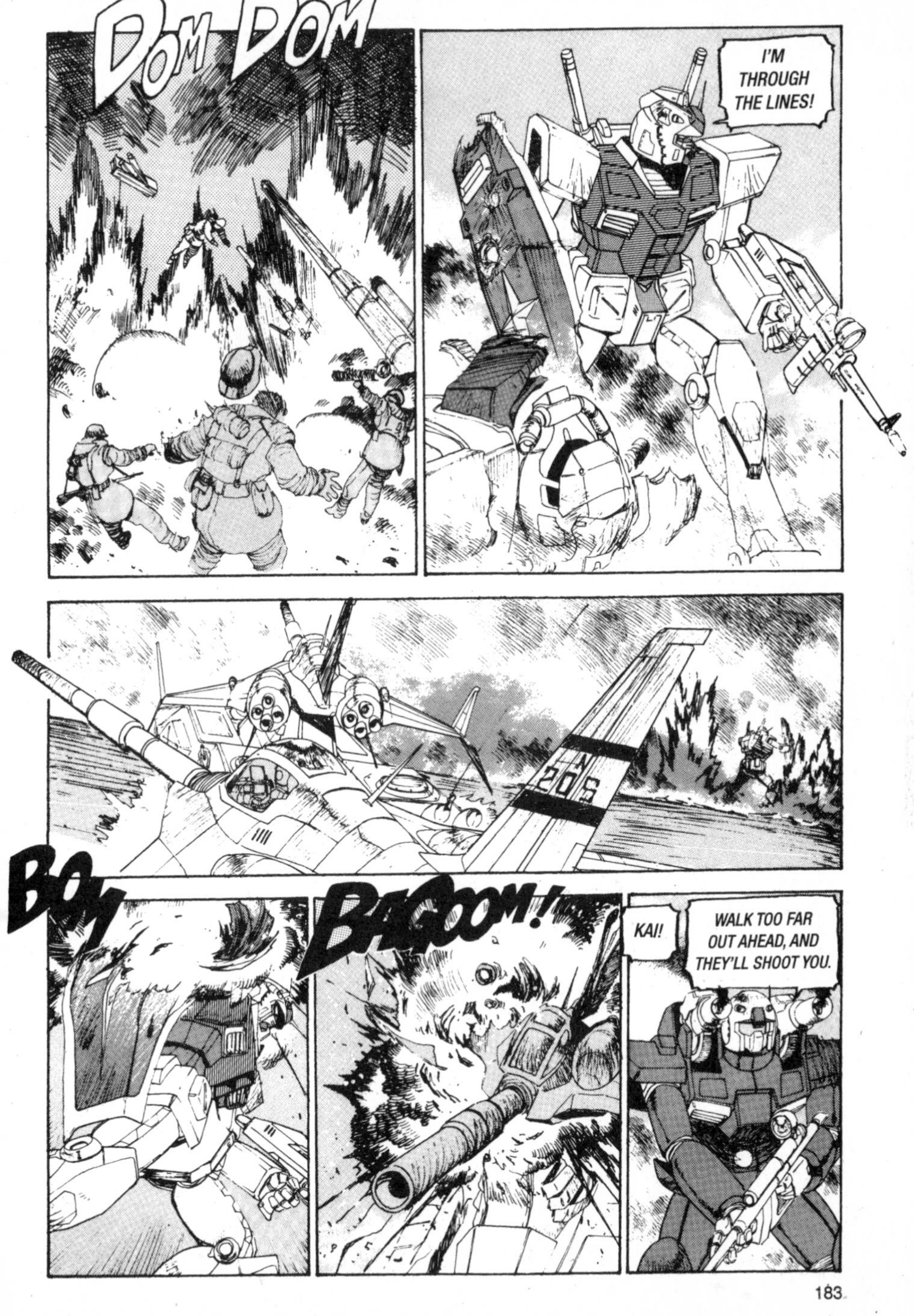
DOM DOM
I'M THROUGH THE LINES!
BOM
BAGOOM!
KAI!
WALK TOO FAR OUT AHEAD, AND THEY'LL SHOOT YOU.

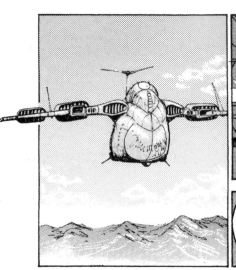

WHAT'S OUR SITUATION?

YES, SIR!

IT SEEMS THAT THE WHITE MOBILE SUIT...

...HAS CUT A HOLE THROUGH OUR LINES!

I SUPPOSE YOU DIDN'T HAVE ENOUGH MEN ON THE LINES.

THAT'S NOT POSS-IBLE. I **DON'T** MAKE TACTICAL MIS-TAKES!

THEN I'LL ATTACK THEM MYSELF!

YOU DON'T HAVE TO GO OUT PERSON-ALLY!

I STILL HAVE TO PROVE MYSELF TO MY SISTER.

I DON'T EXPECT A MAN WITH NO FAMILY TO UNDER-STAND. JUST STAND BY IN THE GAU.

UNDERSTOOD. BUT IF YOU NEED ANY BACKUP, YOU CAN CALL ON ME ANYTIME.

THANKS, BUT I DON'T THINK YOU'LL NEED TO WORRY ABOUT THAT.

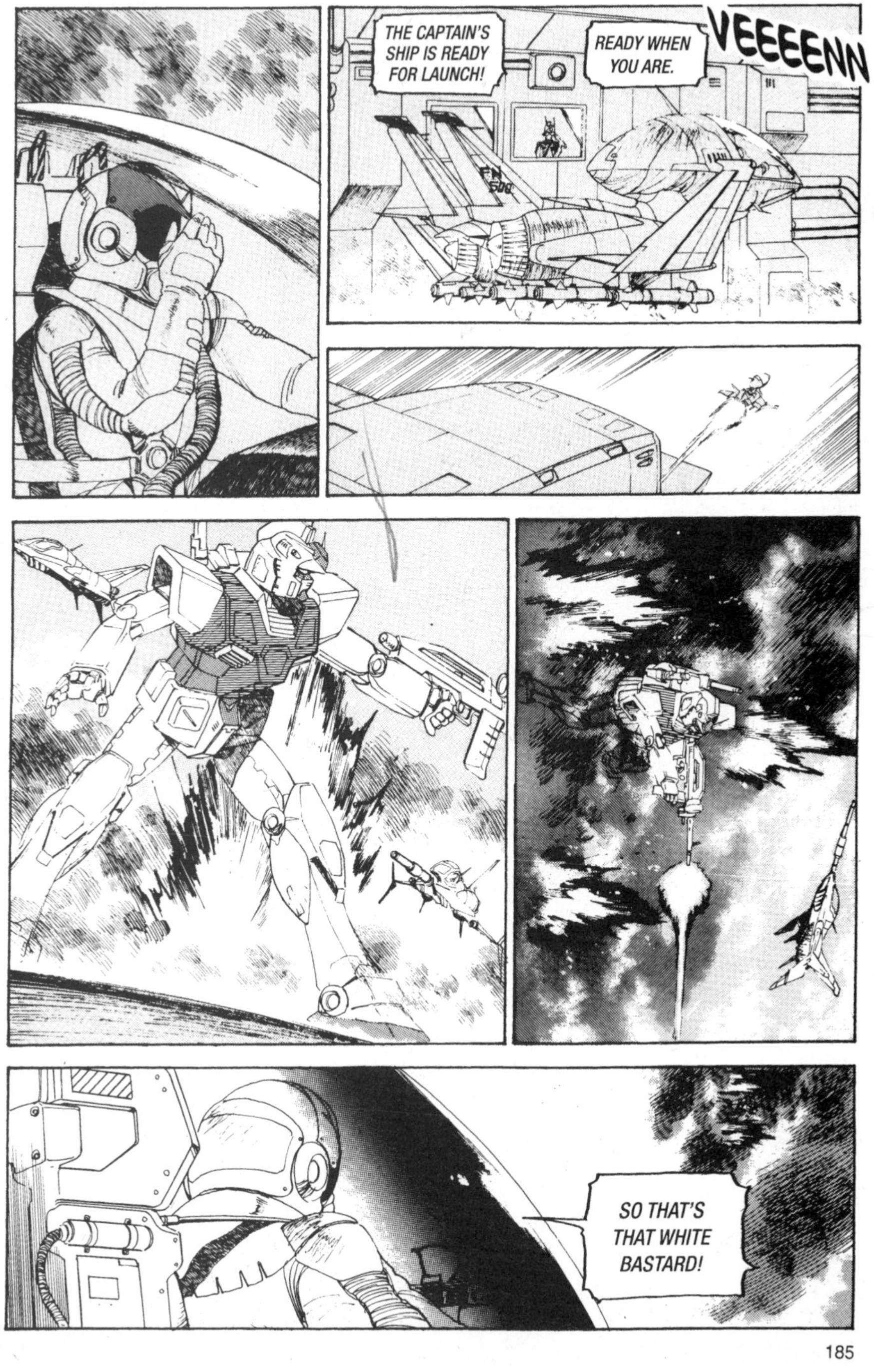
THE CAPTAIN'S SHIP IS READY FOR LAUNCH!
READY WHEN YOU ARE.
VEEEENN
SO THAT'S THAT WHITE BASTARD!

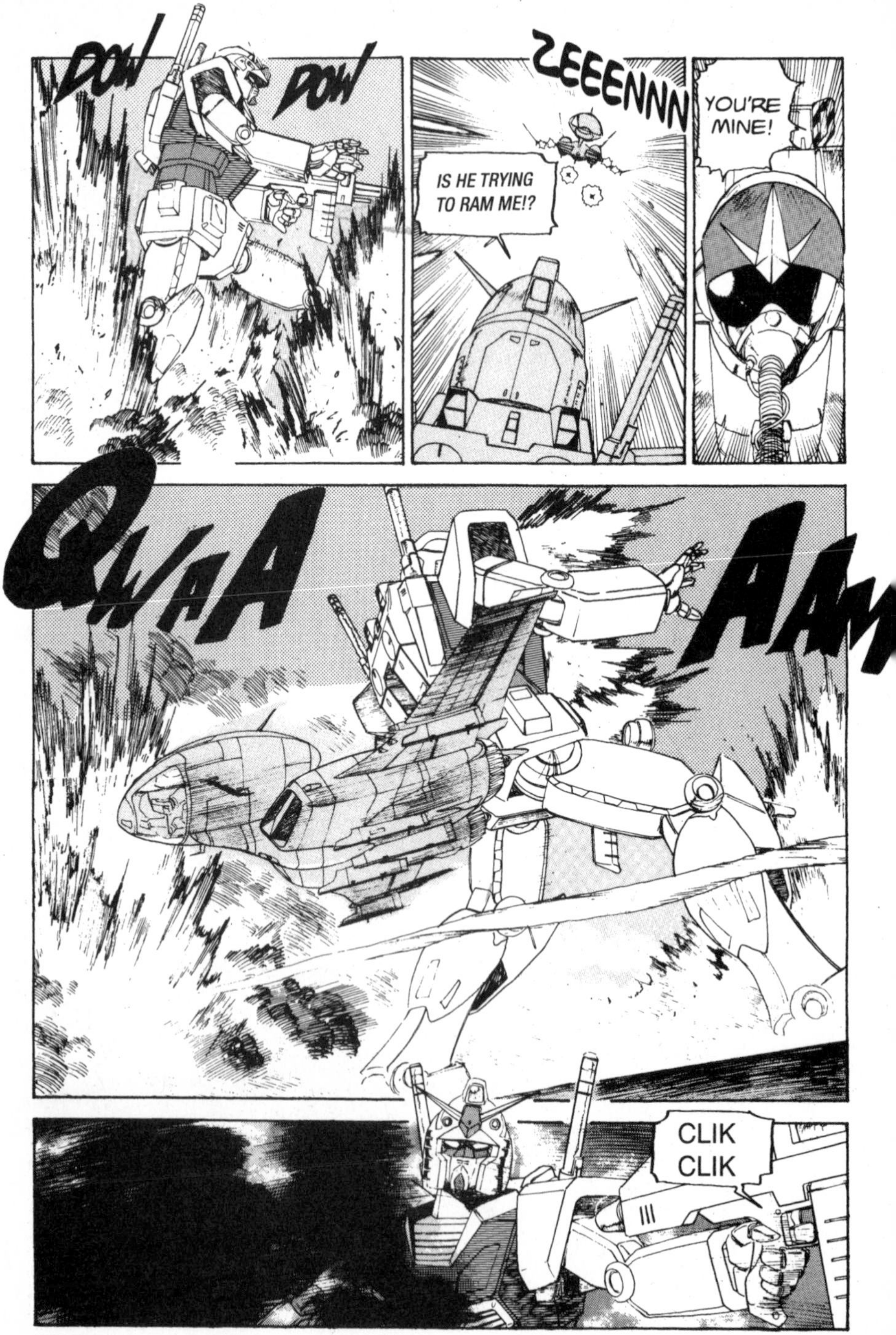
DOW DOW
ZEEENNN
IS HE TRYING TO RAM ME!?
YOU'RE MINE!
QWAA
AAM
CLIK CLIK

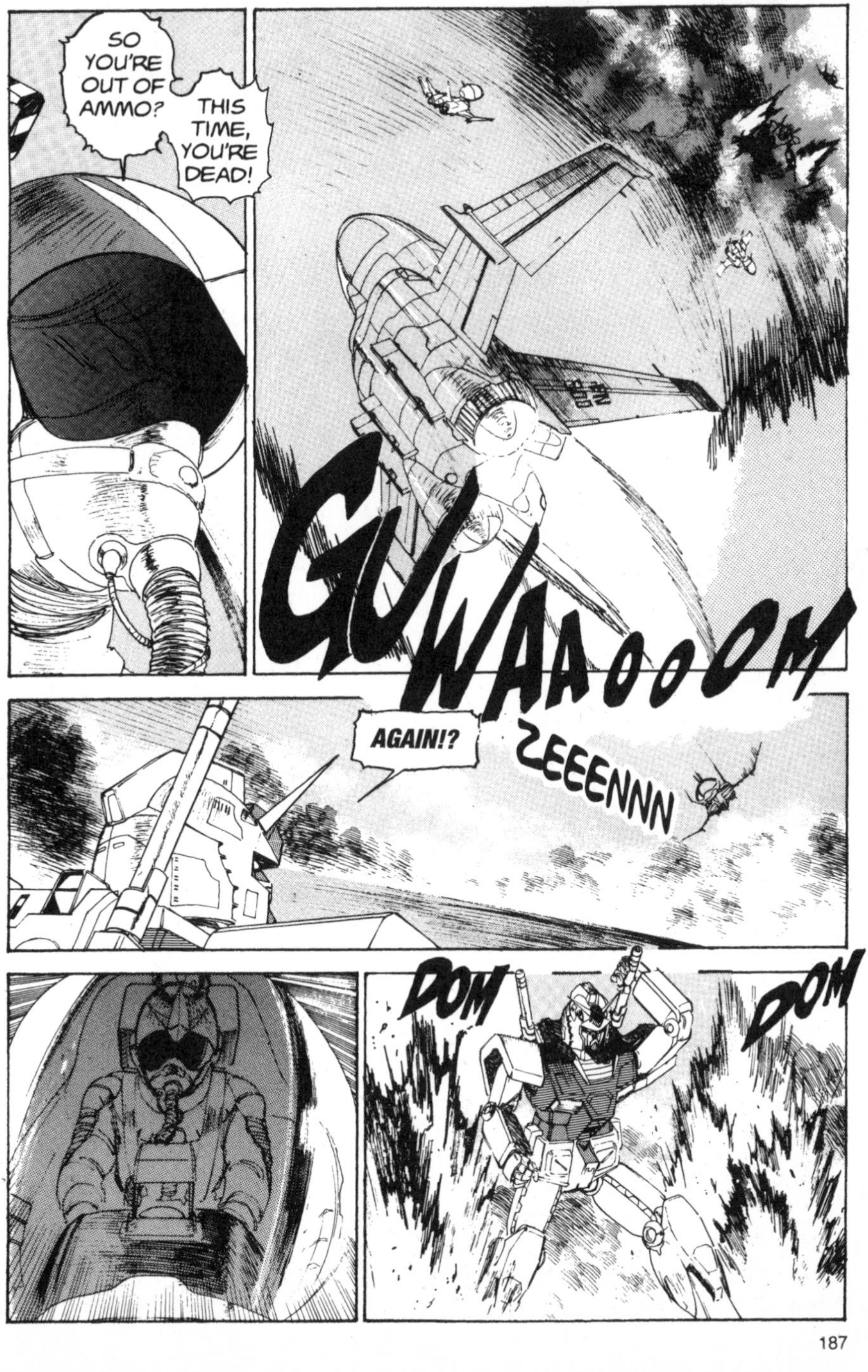
SO YOU'RE OUT OF AMMO?
THIS TIME, YOU'RE DEAD!
GUWAAOOOM
AGAIN!?
ZEEENNN
DOM
DOM

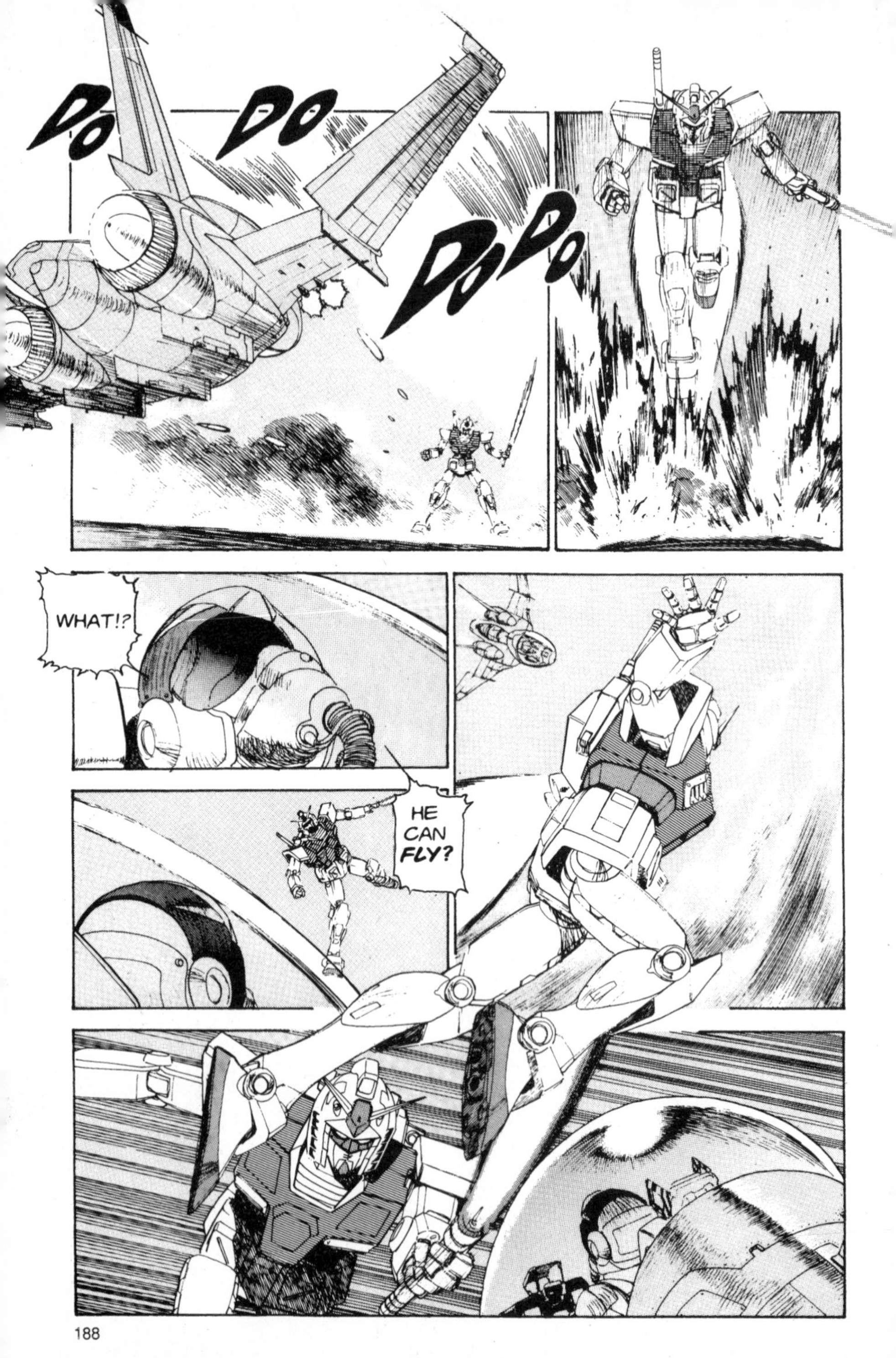
DO DO
DODO
WHAT!?
HE CAN FLY?

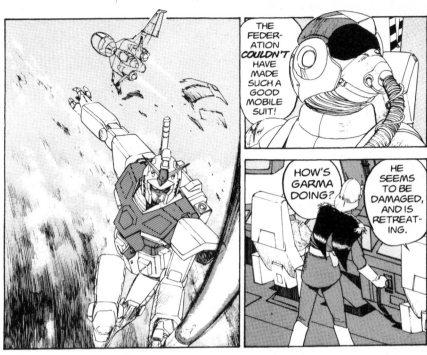

THE FEDERATION *COULDN'T* HAVE MADE SUCH A GOOD MOBILE SUIT!

HOW'S GARMA DOING?

HE SEEMS TO BE DAMAGED, AND IS RETREATING.

HAS HE BROADCAST AN S.O.S.?

NO SIR, NOT YET.

KACHK KACHK

THAT'S A SON OF THE ZABI FAMILY FOR YOU!

DOES HE THINK HE CAN CUT THROUGH BY HIMSELF!?

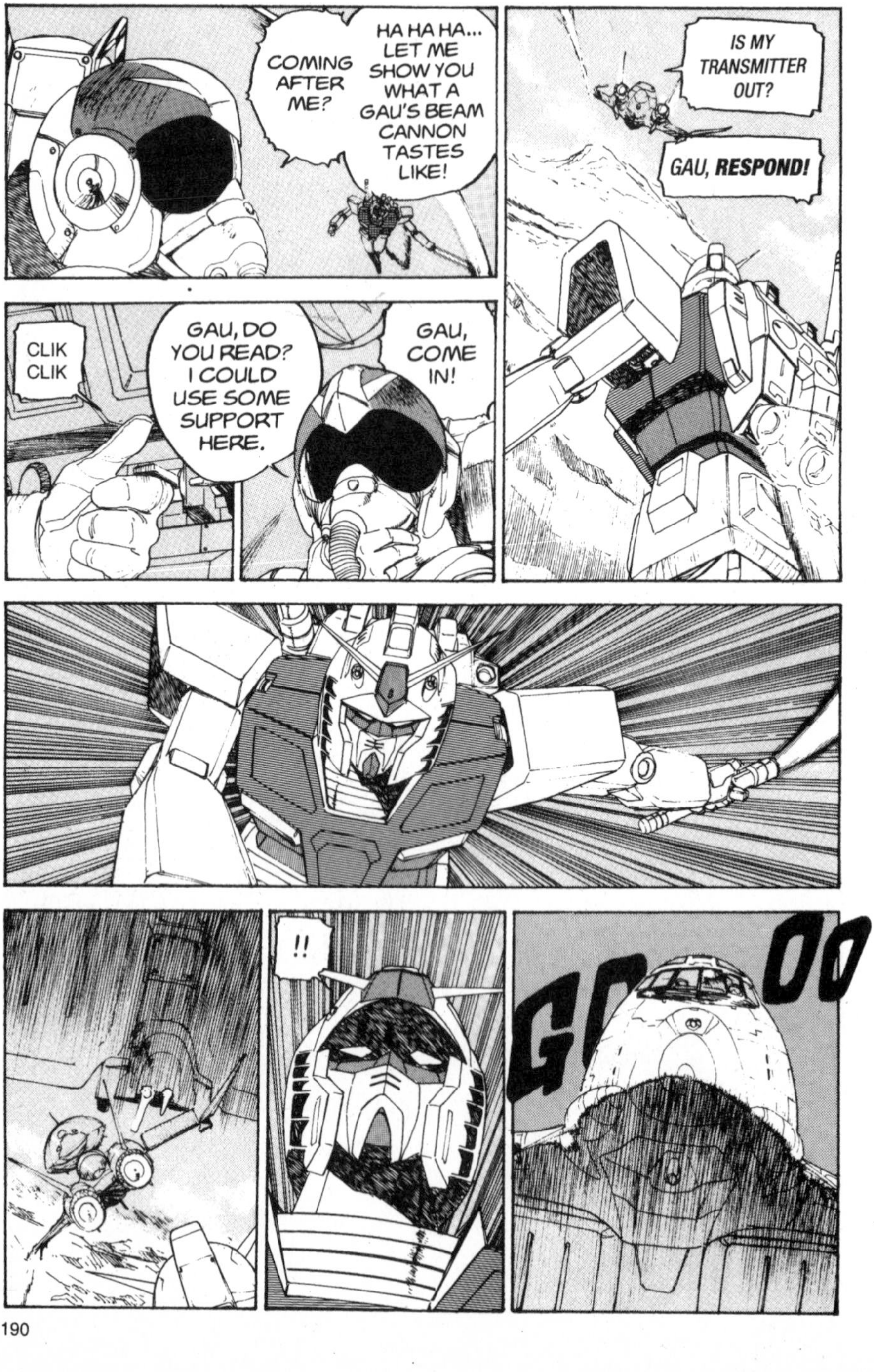
COMING AFTER ME?
HA HA HA... LET ME SHOW YOU WHAT A GAU'S BEAM CANNON TASTES LIKE!
IS MY TRANSMITTER OUT?
GAU, **RESPOND!**
CLIK CLIK
GAU, DO YOU READ? I COULD USE SOME SUPPORT HERE.
GAU, COME IN!
!!
GOOO

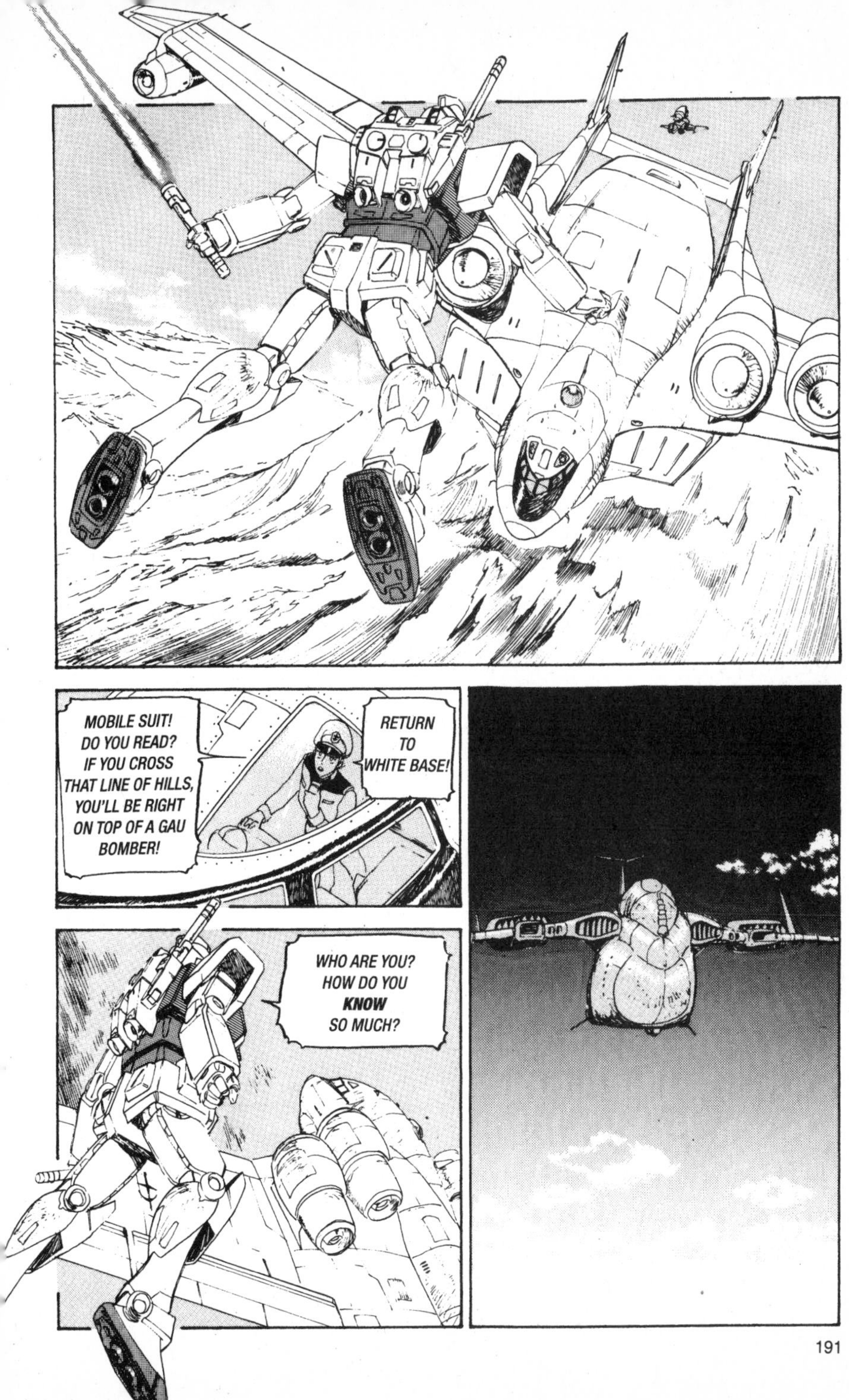
MOBILE SUIT! DO YOU READ? IF YOU CROSS THAT LINE OF HILLS, YOU'LL BE RIGHT ON TOP OF A GAU BOMBER!
RETURN TO WHITE BASE!
WHO ARE YOU? HOW DO YOU KNOW SO MUCH?

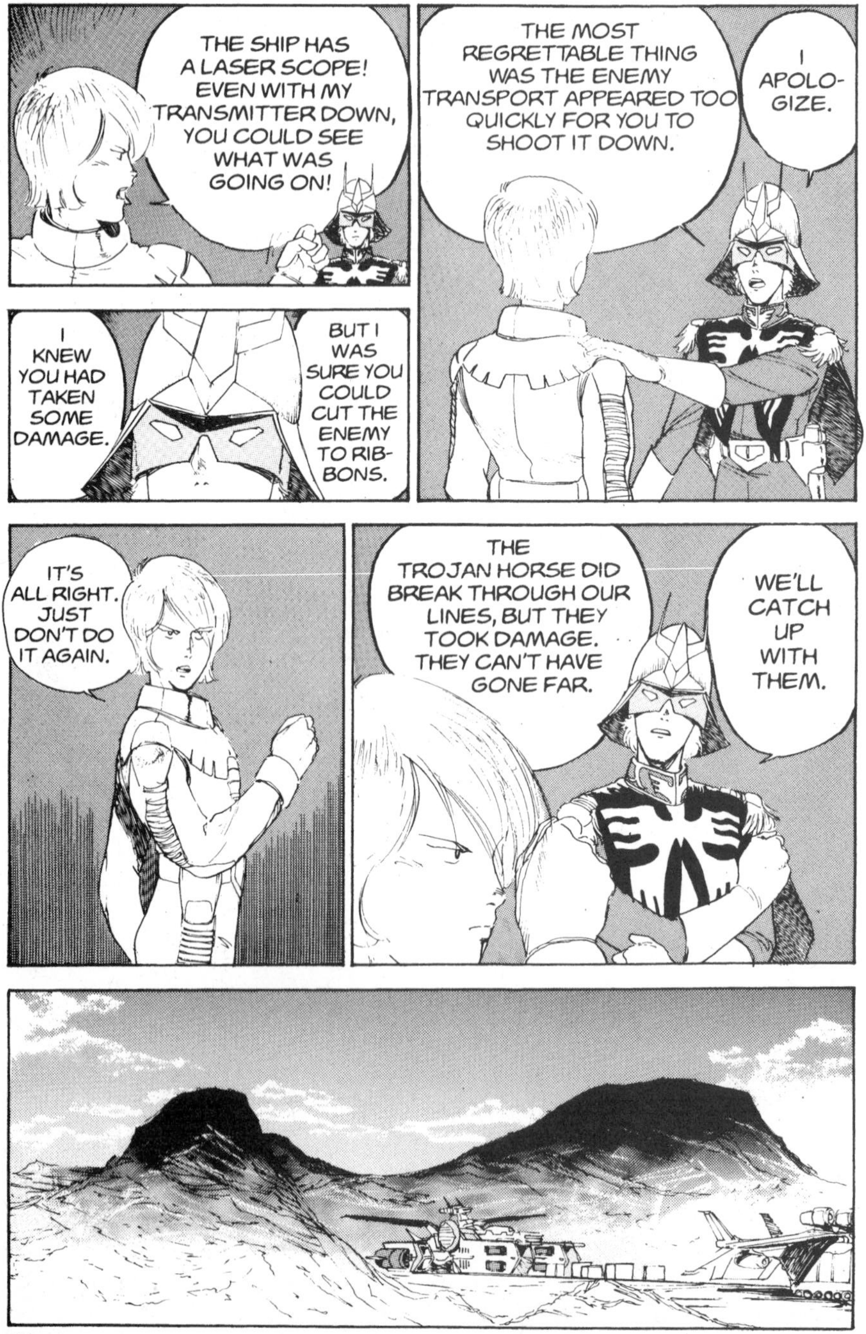
THE SHIP HAS A LASER SCOPE! EVEN WITH MY TRANSMITTER DOWN, YOU COULD SEE WHAT WAS GOING ON!
I KNEW YOU HAD TAKEN SOME DAMAGE.
BUT I WAS SURE YOU COULD CUT THE ENEMY TO RIB-BONS.
THE MOST REGRETTABLE THING WAS THE ENEMY TRANSPORT APPEARED TOO QUICKLY FOR YOU TO SHOOT IT DOWN.
I APOLO-GIZE.
IT'S ALL RIGHT. JUST DON'T DO IT AGAIN.
THE TROJAN HORSE DID BREAK THROUGH OUR LINES, BUT THEY TOOK DAMAGE. THEY CAN'T HAVE GONE FAR.
WE'LL CATCH UP WITH THEM.

VOLUME 1 — THE END

"The comic of the benchmark giant robot show to which every other that came after has been compared."

—*Manga Max*

"This graphic novel offers a good introduction to the whole phenomenon. For manga fans or fans of epic comics storytelling, this is definitely worth a look."

—*Comics Buyer's Guide*

"**Gundam** fans have probably already decided to grab this comic, but for newcomers by all means take a look at this classic series and see why **Gundam** is such a defining icon for anime in general."

—*EX: The Online World of Anime & Manga*

HISTORY OF THE

BY MARK SIMMONS

As the saga of **Mobile Suit Gundam** begins, humans have been living in space for more than fifty years. Billions of people live in artificial space colonies that orbit the earth, and whole generations have been born and raised without setting foot on the mother planet. When this great program of space colonization began, a new calendar was adopted to mark the start of a new era in human history, and our story is set in the year 0079 of this Universal Century. The following chronology reviews the events of the previous eight decades.

UC 0001-0050

UC 0001
With Earth's population at 9 billion,
an ambitious space colonization program begins.

UC 0027
Von Braun City, the first permanent lunar
settlement, is completed.

UC 0034
The Federation government creates the
Public Corporation of Space Transport (PCST),
an independent non-governmental organization, to
ferry colonists into space.

UC 0035
Construction of the space colony cluster
Side 3 begins.

UC 0040
At this point, 40% of the total population has migrated to space.

UC 0045
The asteroid Juno (later known as Luna 2)
is placed in lunar orbit.

The Minovsky Physics Society is founded at Side 3.

UC 0047
Development of the Minovsky-Ionesco
fusion reactor begins.

UC 0050
The total population reaches 11 billion,
of whom 9 billion have migrated to space.

EXPLANATION

In the first year of the Universal Century, Earth is overcrowded, polluted, and resource-starved. The Earth Federation government launches a grand space migration plan to address these crises, resettling the teeming billions in orbital colonies and allowing the ravaged Earth to regenerate.

In mere decades, hundreds of space colonies are constructed, using raw materials mined from the moon and relocated asteroids. As quickly as the colonies are built, they're filled by settlers, until some 80% of the human population has been transported to space. At this point the governing elites exempt themselves from the migration, and stay behind to enjoy the depopulated Earth.

Meanwhile, scientists tap new energy sources, from solar power satellites to fusion power. In the space colonies of Side 3, a researcher named Dr. Minovsky develops a new type of fusion reactor, fueled by a rare helium isotope. An energy transport fleet is created to collect precious helium-3 from the atmosphere of the gas giant Jupiter.

UNIVERSAL CENTURY

UC 0051-0070

UC 0051
The Federation government halts development of new colonies.

UC 0052
Zeon Zum Daikun moves to Side 3 and begins to propagate his philosophy of Contolism, agitating for the independence of the space colonies.

UC 0058
Under Daikun's leadership, Side 3 declares its independence, and the Republic of Zeon is established.

UC 0060
The Federal Forces launch an Armament Reinforcement Plan, organizing a space force and coverting Luna 2 into a military base.

UC 0062
The Zeon national guard becomes a full-fledged military.

UC 0065
The Minovsky Physics Society observes a unique electromagnetic wave effect within the Minovsky-Ionesco fusion reactor.

UC 0068
Zeon Zum Daikun dies, and Degin Sodo Zabi succeeds him as leader.

UC 0069.08.15
The Duchy of Zeon is established, with Degin Sodo Zabi as Duke. Zeon Zum Daikun's followers are purged.

UC 0070.03
The Zeon military successfully experiments with the radar-nullifying Minovsky effect.

UC 0070.05
Zeon completes the mega particle cannon.

UC 0070.12
Luna 2 is moved to a position in Earth orbit opposite that of the moon, in order to help construct a research colony at Side 7.

EXPLANATION

With the end of the migration program, the Federation stops constructing new space colonies, and the existing ones grow ever more crowded. The space colonists begin demanding political independence, a goal that is ultimately accomplished when the revolutionary Zeon Zum Daikun establishes an autonomous republic at Side 3.

Fearful that other colonies will follow Side 3's example, the Earth Federation responds with sanctions and a military buildup. Over the next decade, the Federal Forces assemble a huge space armada and establish military installations in Earth orbit. The Republic of Zeon responds in the same fashion, forming its own military and building its own space fleet.

Ten years after the Republic is founded, its leader dies of a mysterious illness. Daikun's right-hand man, Degin Sodo Zabi, takes over. Within a year, Zabi has turned the Republic into a militaristic monarchy, and ruthlessly purged Daikun's followers. The new regime is called the Duchy of Zeon—which, henceforth, we'll refer to simply as "Zeon."

Under Zabi, Zeon redoubles its military preparations. Using the latest fruits of Dr. Minovsky's research, the Zeon military develops jamming techniques that can render radar completely useless—a product of the so-called "Minovsky effect." These new discoveries also allow Zeon to create immensely powerful energy weapons and highly compact fusion reactors.

UC 0071-0078

UC 0071
Zeon begins development of new weapons for use under Minovsky effect conditions, and completes a compact Minovsky fusion reactor.

UC 0072
Zeon begins construction of the asteroid base Axis, in the asteroid belt, as a waystation for its Jupiter energy fleet.

UC 0073
Zeon completes the first version of a new type of weapon, dubbed the "mobile suit."

UC 0074.02
Zeon rolls out a prototype version of the MS-05, equipped with a Minovsky fusion reactor.

UC 0075.05
Zeon rolls out a combat-ready version of the MS-05 Zaku.

UC 0075.07
Zeon commissions the first Musai-class cruiser and decides to mass-produce the MS-05.

UC 0075.11
Zeon forms a mobile suit training battalion.

UC 0076.04
Zeon expands its mobile suit production facilities.

UC 0076.05
Zeon's training battalion begins practicing combat manuevers.

UC 0076.12
In anticipation of an Earth invasion, Zeon begins development of localized mobile suits.

UC 0078.01
Zeon begins mass production of the MS-06C Zaku II.

UC 0078.03
The Federal Forces secretly begin mobile suit development.

Several projects are begun simultaneously as part of the RX Plan.

UC 0078.05
Migration begins to Side 7's incomplete first colony.

UC 0078.10
The Duchy of Zeon announces a state of national mobilization. The military is divided into a Space Attack Force and a Mobile Assault Force.

EXPLANATION

The Duchy of Zeon continues its weapons research, setting out to develop a highly manueverable space fighter that can exploit the new battle-field conditions created by the Minovsky effect. This program ulti-mately produces the first combat-wor-thy mobile suit—the MS-05 Zaku, powered by a compact Minovsky fusion reactor.

At first, the Zeon military produces only a limited quantity of mobile suits, forming a training battalion to evaluate the Zaku's potential. After a few months, Zeon's leaders are satisfied that this new weapon has proved its worth. By the middle of UC 0076 the Zaku is in full production, and the training battalion has begun practicing mobile suit combat tactics.

As the outbreak of war draws ever closer, Zeon continues to refine the Zaku's design. Production of the improved Zaku II begins in UC 0078, while Zeon's researchers consider new mobile suit designs for a potential Earth invasion. The Federal Forces, meanwhile, launch their own belated mobile suit development program. They are aided by the famed Dr. Minovsky, who defected from Zeon in UC 0072 in protest against the Zabi family's ruthless militarism.

UC 0079

UC 0079.01.03

The Duchy of Zeon declares war against the Earth Federal Government, simultaneously launching surprise attacks on Sides 1, 2 and 4. Nuclear, biological and chemical weapons are used indiscriminately, and a colony drop operation drastically changes Earth's climate.

UC 0079.01.11

Side 6 declares itself neutral.

UC 0079.01.15

The Ruum Campaign takes place at Side 5. The Federal Forces space fleet is wiped out, and Zeon captures fleet commander General Revil.

UC 0079.01.31

The Antarctic Treaty is signed, outlawing the use of chemical and nuclear weapons and protecting the neutrality of Side 6 and the lunar cities.

UC 0079.02.01

Zeon announces the formation of the Earth Attack Force.

UC 0079.03.01

Zeon's Earth Attack Force stages its first drop operation.

UC 0079.03.13

Zeon captures the Federal Forces' California base.

UC 0079.04.01

The Federal Forces launch "Operation V" and the "Vinson Plan."

UC 0079.04.04

Zeon drops reserve forces. Using captured resources and facilities, Zeon begins building up its military power.

UC 0079.05

Zeon's space fortress Solomon is completed.

UC 0079.06

Zeon completes its last line of defense, consisting of Solomon, the space fortress A Bao A Qu, and the lunar base Granada.

UC 0079.07

The Federal Forces develop miniaturized beam weapons, using energy capacitor (E-cap) technology.

The *White Base* is launched.

The first prototype Gundam is completed.

UC 0079.08

The Federal Forces begin final testing of the Gundam at Side 7.

UC 0079.09.18

Zeon special forces assault the Side 7's research colony.

EXPLANATION

The war begins with a catastrophic assault on the space colonies of Sides 1, 2, and 4. Zeon forces use poison gas to massacre the inhabitants of these Federation-aligned colonies, and attack the Federation space fleets stationed there with nuclear weapons. Then, in an attempt to bring the war to a swift conclusion, the Zeons force a space colony out of orbit in order to drop it on the Federal Forces' underground headquarters. Though the colony drop fails, Earth's climate is drastically affected by the impact.

Zeon attempts this colony drop a second time, and the ensuing struggle turns Side 5 into debris. At this point, two weeks of all-out combat have killed half the human race. The warring parties, shocked by this carnage, negotiate a treaty that outlaws these destructive tactics and ensures that the war will be continued in a more human fashion.

Switching its tactics, Zeon launches an Earth invasion in order to capture the planet's precious resources. Throughout the month of March, Zeon's Earth Attack Force carries out drop operations over Central Asia, North America, Africa, and Oceania. Soon, the invaders have overrun half Earth's surface. Then a tense stalemate begins, as both sides concentrate on rebuilding their forces.

In April, the Federal Forces launch Operation V, a crash program to develop their own mobile suits. Three months later, the program has produced prototype mobile suits armed with devastating beam weapons; soon thereafter, testing of these desperately-needed new weapons begins at the research colony of Side 7. And this is where the story truly begins....